The Shape of Luke's Story

The Shape of Luke's Story

Essays on Luke–Acts

Robert C. Tannehill

Cascade Books
A division of *Wipf & Stock Publishers*
199 West 8th Avenue, Suite 3 • Eugene OR 97401

THE SHAPE OF LUKE'S STORY
Essays on Luke–Acts

Cascade Books
A Division of Wipf and Stock Publishers
199 West 8th Avenue, Suite 3
Eugene, Oregon 97401

ISBN: 1-59752-335-6

Cataloging-in-Publication Data

Tannehill, Robert C.
The shape of Luke's story : essays on Luke–Acts / Robert C. Tannehill.

   p. cm.

   ISBN 1-59752-335-6 (alk. paper)

   1. Bible. N.T. Luke—Criticism, narrative. 2. Bible. N.T. Acts—Criticism, narrative. 3. Bible. N.T. Luke—Criticism, interpretation, etc. 4. Bible. N.T. Acts—Criticism, interpretation, etc. 5. Bible. N.T. Gospels—Criticism, interpretation, etc. 6. Bible. N.T. Luke and Acts—Theology. 7. Narration in the Bible. I. Title.

BS2589 T36 2005

Manufactured in the U.S.A.

Contents

Part III: Acts as Narrative

Part IV: Hermeneutical Experiments

Abbreviations

AB	Anchor Bible
ABD	*Anchor Bible Dictionary,* edited by David Noel Freedman, 6 vols. (New York: Doubleday, 1992)
ACNT	Augsburg Commentary on the New Testament
AnBib	Analecta biblica
ANRW	*Aufstieg und Niedergang der römischen Welt*
ANTC	Abingdon New Testament Commentary
BETL	Bibliotheca Ephemeridum theologicarum Lovaniensium
Bib	*Biblica*
BVC	*Bible et Vie Chrétienne*
BZ	*Biblische Zeitschrift*
BZAW	Beihefte zur Zeitschrift für die alttestamentliche Wissenschaft
BZNW	Beihefte zur Zeitschrift für die neutestamentliche Wissenschaft
CBQ	*Catholic Biblical Quarterly*
ConNT	Coniectanea neotestamentica
CTM	*Currents in Theology and Mission*
ESEC	Emory Studies in Early Christianity
ETL	*Ephemeridum theologicarum Lovaniensium*
ExpT	*Expository Times*
FB	Forschung zur Bibel
FRLANT	Forschungen zur Religion und Literatur des Alten und Neuen Testaments
GBS	Guides to Biblical Scholarship
HNT	Handbuch zum Neuen Testament

HTKNT	Herder theologischer Kommentar zum Neuen Testament
ICC	International Critical Commentary
IDB	*Interpreter's Dictionary of the Bible,* edited by George F. Buttrick, 4 vols. (Nashville: Abingdon, 1962)
Int	*Interpretation*
ISBL	Indiana Studies in Biblical Literature
JBL	*Journal of Biblical Literature*
JR	*Journal of Religion*
JSNT	*Journal for the Study of the New Testament*
JSNTSS	Journal for the Study of the New Testament Supplements Series
JTS	*Journal of Theological Studies*
LCBI	Literary Currents in Biblical Interpretation
LCL	Loeb Classical Library
LD	Lectio divina
LXX	Septuagint
NIGTC	New International Greek Testament Commentary
NovT	*Novum Testamentum*
NRSV	New Revised Standard Version of the Bible
NT	New Testament
NTAbh	Neutestamentliche Abhandlungen
NTD	Das Neue Testament Deutsch
NTS	*New Testament Studies*
OBT	Overtures to Biblical Theology
OT	Old Testament
ÖTK	Ökumenischer Taschenbuchkommentar zum Neuen Testament
par.	parallel passages
PRS	*Perspectives in Religious Studies*
PTMS	Princeton Theological Monograph Series
RB	*Revue biblique*
RSV	Revised Standard Version of the Bible
SANT	Studien zum Alten und Neuen Testament
SB	Sources bibliques
SBLMS	Society of Biblical Literature Monograph Series
SBLSP	*Society of Biblical Literature Seminar Papers*

SBLTT	Society of Biblical Literature Texts and Translations
SBT	Studies in Biblical Theology
SNT	Studien zum Neuen Testament
SNTSMS	Society for New Testament Studies Monograph Series
TDNT	*Theological Dictionary of the New Testament,* edited by Gerhard Kittel and Gerhard Friedrich, translated by Geoffrey W. Bromiley, 10 vols. (Grand Rapids: Eerdmans, 1964–76)
THKNT	Theologischer Handkommentar zum Neuen Testament
TPINTC	Trinity Press International New Testament Commentaries
TWNT	*Theologisches Wörterbuch zum Neuen Testament,* edited by Gerhard Kittel and Gerhard Friedrich, 10 vols. (Stuttgart: Kohlhammer, 1957–64)
TZ	*Theologische Zeitschrift*
VT	*Vetus Testamentum*
VTSup	Vetus Testamentum Supplements
WMANT	Wissenschaftliche Monographien zum Alten und Neuen Testament
WUNT	Wissenschaftliche Untersuchungen zum Neuen Testament
ZNW	*Zeitschrift für die neutestamentliche Wissenschaft*

Preface

When I was a graduate student at Yale in the late 1950s and early 1960s, research on the theologies of the synoptic Evangelists, using redaction criticism, was still quite new to American biblical scholarship. I was interested in these new developments and did some specialized study of Luke and also of Acts. My dissertation was in Pauline studies, however, so it was only later that I returned to Luke-Acts and wrote the article, "The Mission of Jesus According to Luke 4:16-30," the earliest article in this volume.

By the time that this essay appeared in print, my interests were turning in a new direction. Stimulated by discussions of the parable as a special mode of communication, I began to think and write about the significance of poetic and rhetorical form in the short sayings attributed to Jesus. This eventually led to the publication of my book, *The Sword of His Mouth*.[1] I argued on the basis of formal analysis of some of the synoptic sayings that such language has powers beyond conveying information and establishing clear rules of behavior. My studies changed the way that I viewed the small units of material in the synoptic Gospels. I had learned to ask, what is the purpose or value of phrasing the saying or scene in just this way?— a literary-rhetorical question.

---

[1] Tannehill, *The Sword of His Mouth: Forceful and Imaginative Language in Synoptic Sayings,* Semeia Studies (Philadelphia: Fortress, 1975; reprint Eugene, Ore.: Wipf & Stock, 2003).

As my work on synoptic sayings was appearing in print, I joined the Society of Biblical Literature Seminar on Mark and began to think about literary form on a new level. Leading members of this group were discussing the Gospel of Mark as a unitary narrative that can be analyzed in literary terms like other narratives. They were discussing plot development, the narrator's point of view, depiction of characters, etc.

I wrote several essays on Mark from this perspective. Mark, however, had already attracted much interest from the early narrative critics. Instead of working further on Mark, I decided to return to my early interest in Luke-Acts. Literary questions about the shape of the Lukan story enabled me to view it with fresh eyes. I sought to understand major plot developments, the interactions of characters, and the narrator's interpretive role in shaping the narrative. These studies led to the publication of *The Narrative Unity of Luke-Acts*,[2] and also to the majority of the essays in this volume.

During this time I was involved in a debate about whether Luke-Acts is "anti-Jewish." My thoughts on this issue are found in the three essays in Part II of this volume, and also in the essay in Part IV entitled "Should We Love Simon the Pharisee?" My views are based on my literary studies, which lead me to emphasize the importance of the beginning and ending of Luke-Acts, along with narrative patterns that reveal rhetorical emphasis.

More recently I have come to recognize that there is more "indeterminacy" in biblical texts than past biblical scholarship was inclined to admit. This observation leads to issues concerning the ethics of interpretation. If the text by itself, or even in its historical context, so far as we can determine it, does not convey a single meaning and significance, how *should* we interpret it for society today? (I am assuming that biblical scholars, like other leaders and intellectuals, have social responsibilities.) These concerns are explicit or implicit in the three essays in Part IV of this volume (and, to some extent, in the earlier essay on "The Lukan Discourse on Invitations").

When I refer to a literary interpretation of Luke-Acts, I do not intend this to replace an interest in theology—or, more broadly, an interest in religious questions. On the contrary, I understand a literary approach to

---

[2] Tannehill, *The Narrative Unity of Luke-Acts: A Literary Interpretation,* 2 vols. (Philadelphia and Minneapolis: Fortress, 1986, 1990).

be a better way of exploring the religious significance of biblical texts. Some of us, at least, are interested in a literary-rhetorical approach to texts like Luke-Acts because we believe that such writings can exercise religious influence as stories. They can do so in complex and subtle ways that are not recognized if we only ask what they teach about points of doctrine.

In writing these essays, I have always aimed for clarity of argument based on the details of the text (although in recent years I am more inclined to recognize options in interpretation). Even though I argue from details, these essays are not just technical exercises. I relate the details to larger issues. I also try to remember that these words were very important to our religious ancestors and that they are still important to many who seek justice, love, and God.

Acknowledgments

All articles are reprinted by permission of the publishers.

1. "The Mission of Jesus according to Luke 4:16-30" was first published in *Jesus in Nazareth,* edited by Walther Eltester, Beihefte zur Zeitschrift für die neutestamentliche Wissenschaft 40 (Berlin: de Gruyter, 1972) 51–75.

2. "The Magnificat as Poem" was first published in *Journal of Biblical Literature* 93 (1974) 263–75; ©Society of Biblical Literature, 1974.

3. "What Kind of King? What Kind of Kingdom?" was first published in *Word & World* 12 (1992) 17–22; ©Luther Northwestern Theological Seminary, 1992.

4. "The Lukan Discourse on Invitations" was first published in *The Four Gospels 1992: Festschrift Frans Neirynck,* 3 vols., edited by F. Van Segbroeck et al., Bibliotheca Ephemeridum theologicarum Lovaniensium 100 (Leuven: Leuven University Press, 1992) 2.1603–16.

5. "The Story of Zacchaeus as Rhetoric" was first published in *Semeia* 64 (1993) 201–11; ©Society of Biblical Literature, 1994.

6. "Repentance in the Context of Lukan Soteriology" was first published in *God's Word for Our World,* vol. 2: *Theological and Cultural Studies in Honor of Simon J. De Vries,* edited by J. Harold Ellens, Journal for the Study of the Old Testament Supplement Series 389 (London: T. & T. Clark International, 2004) 199–215.

7. "Israel in Luke-Acts: A Tragic Story" was first published in *Journal of Biblical Literature* 104 (1985) 69–85; ©Society of Biblical Literature, 1985.

8. "The Story of Israel within the Lukan Narrative" was first published in *Jesus and the Heritage of Israel: Luke's Narrative Claim upon Israel's Legacy,* Luke the Interpreter of Israel 1, edited by David P. Moessner (Harrisburg, Pa.: Trinity, 1999) 325–39.

9. "Rejection by Jews and Turning to Gentiles: The Pattern of Paul's Mission in Acts" was first published in *Society of Biblical Literature 1986 Seminar Papers,* edited by Kent Harold Richards (Atlanta: Scholars, 1986) 130–41; ©Society of Biblical Literature, 1985. A revised version was published in *Luke-Acts and the Jewish People: Eight Critical Perspectives,* edited by Joseph B. Tyson (Minneapolis: Augsburg, 1988) 83–101, 150–52.

10. "The Functions of Peter's Mission Speeches in the Narrative of Acts" was first published in *New Testament Studies* 37 (1991) 400–414; ©Cambridge University Press 1991.

11. "The Composition of Acts 3–5: Narrative Development and Echo Effect" was first published in *Society of Biblical Literature 1984 Seminar Papers,* edited by Kent Harold Richards (Chico, Calif.: Scholars, 1984) 217–40; ©Society of Biblical Literature, 1984.

12. "Paul outside the Christian Ghetto: Intercultural Conflict and Cooperation in Acts" was first published in *Text and Logos: The Humanistic Interpretation of the New Testament,* edited by Theodore W. Jennings Jr., Scholars Press Homage Series 16 (Atlanta: Scholars, 1990) 247–63. This collection of essays was published in honor of Hendrikus W. Boers.

13. "The Narrator's Strategy in the Scenes of Paul's Defense" was originally published in *Foundations and Facets Forum* 8 (1992) 255–69; © Polebridge Press 1995. This issue was in honor of Robert W. Funk.

14. "Should We Love Simon the Pharisee? Reflections on the Pharisees in Luke" was first published in *Currents in Theology and Mission* 21 (1994) 424–33.

15. "Freedom and Responsibility in Scripture Interpretation" was first published in *Literary Studies in Luke–Acts: Essays in Honor of Joseph B. Tyson*, edited by Richard P. Thompson and Thomas E. Phillips (Macon, Ga.: Mercer University Press, 1998) 265–78.

16. "'Cornelius' and 'Tabitha' Encounter Luke's Jesus" was first published in *Interpretation* 48 (1994) 347–56; ©Union Theological Seminary in Virginia, 1994.

Part I

Theology, Poetry, Rhetoric

1

The Mission of Jesus according to Luke 4:16-30

This essay is the earliest in this collection. It is an example of redaction criticism, for it looks for evidence of the theological intentions of the Gospel writer in editorial modifications of prior traditions. My later move to narrative criticism does not involve a repudiation of redaction criticism, only a recognition of its limits. Even in this early essay I was interested in the function of a key passage within the larger writing, for I sought to show the connection between the Nazareth scene and theological themes in Luke–Acts and noted that the Nazareth scene fits literary patterns found elsewhere in Luke–Acts.

This article was important to me in clarifying how specific phrases in the Isaiah quotation (Luke 4:18-19) took on special meaning within Luke–Acts, an interest that I developed further in my later writings. This essay may still be useful because it contains details of argument not found in my later discussions of Luke 4:16-30 in The Narrative Unity of Luke–Acts, *2 vols. (Philadelphia & Minneapolis: Fortress, 1986, 1990) 1.60–73 and* Luke, *ANTC (Nashville: Abingdon, 1996) 90–95. There are some differences from my later work. I would no longer insist on the particular reading of the future verb in Luke 4:23 advocated here (there are other possibilities), and I would now argue that there is a theological necessity (for*

Luke as well as for us) that God's saving purpose embraces Jews as well as Gentiles. At the time I wrote this essay, I understood Luke's vision of God's saving work more narrowly.

By the scene at Nazareth with which he introduces his narrative of the ministry of Jesus, Luke intends to reveal to the reader certain fundamental aspects of the meaning of that ministry as a whole. This scene does not simply relate one event among others. These words and acts have typical and programmatic significance for the whole of Jesus' ministry as Luke understands it. In some respects they even point beyond the time of Jesus to the time of the church. Therefore we need to sharpen our understanding of what Luke is saying through this scene and of how he says it. This will require discussion of the historical origin of the materials used in this scene in order to detect Luke's contribution to the tradition. It will also require comparison of what we find in this scene with the theological themes and literary methods found elsewhere in Luke–Acts. In doing this, the importance of the Isaiah quotation for Luke's understanding of Jesus' mission will be brought out. Finally, the question of the relation of Luke's understanding of Jesus and his ministry to earlier tradition will be discussed.

The argument that this text is important for Luke's theology is not entirely dependent on evidence of Luke's editorial activity within the text itself. The placement of this scene, in contrast to the other synoptic gospels, at the beginning of Jesus' public ministry, and the appearance of themes which are important elsewhere in Luke's two volume work are sufficient indications of this importance. Even if Luke found the text in some source in nearly the same form in which he presents it to us, it is Luke who has interrupted Mark's order in order to place this scene at the beginning of Jesus' ministry, and it is within the context of Luke's work as a whole that themes from this scene are developed and interpreted. This warning is necessary because the literary and historical problems of this pericope are complex. Nevertheless, consideration of them is worthwhile, for this will help to explain why the text has its present form and will sharpen our insight into Luke's work and intentions.

The problem is posed sharply by the relation between Luke 4:16-30 and Mark 6:1-6. These texts can hardly refer to two different events, for, apart from the historical improbability that the events of Mark 6:1-6 could take place after the people of Nazareth had already attempted to stone

Jesus, the essential points of Mark 6:2-4 are all contained in Luke's narrative also, and Luke omits Mark 6:1-6 when he comes to it in the Markan sequence, indicating that he identified the two narratives. However, it might be possible to argue that Luke 4:16-30 represents a separate, pre-Lukan tradition of the event reported in Mark 6:1-6,[1] or, at least, that Luke 4:16-30 arose from combining the Markan account with another connected narrative which supplies the non-Markan material.[2] However, the most convincing view of the origin of this pericope is that Luke has rewritten the Markan account, supplementing it with fragments of tradition and with material of his own composition.[3] To be sure, evidence against this view has been found in individual verses, such as 4:23, which seem to show a pre-Lukan point of view, and in certain words and phrases which exhibit a Semitic coloration. However, the fact that an individual verse shows a pre-Lukan point of view is evidence that Luke possessed a non-Markan source for the story of the rejection of Jesus at Nazareth only if the verse fits together with other non-Markan material in a way to indicate the presence of a complete narrative. Otherwise we have only fragments of tradition that may well be of different origin. And the presence of words and phrases with Semitic coloration is evidence for pre-Lukan material only if they cannot be explained on the basis of Luke's frequent use of "Septuagintalisms."[4] These points must be kept in mind during the following argument.

---

[1] Cf., e. g., B. Violet, "Zum rechten Verständnis der Nazareth-Perikope Lc 4, 16-30," *ZNW* 37 (1938) 251–71, who argues for an Aramaic background; and Charles Masson, "Jésus à Nazareth," in *Vers les sources d'eau vive* (Lausanne: Payot, 1961) 38–69, who argues that both Mark 6:1-6 and Luke 4:16-30 go back to an older narrative in Ur-Markus, which, except for the setting and vv. 28-30, is more faithfully reproduced in Luke.

[2] Cf., e. g., A. R. C. Leaney, *A Commentary on the Gospel according to St. Luke* (New York: Harper, 1958) 50–64, who believes that Luke "used a separate tradition now represented by verses 16-22a, 23a, 25-30."

[3] Cf. J. M. Creed, *The Gospel According to St. Luke* (London: Macmillan, 1930) 65: "It is easier to suppose that Lk. has taken the narrative of Mk. vi. . . . as foundation for a representative and symbolic scene to open the public ministry of Jesus, and that he himself is mainly responsible for the section as it stands." Cf. also Erich Klostermann, *Das Lukas-Evangelium,* 2d ed. (Tübingen: Mohr/Siebeck, 1929) 62: "Jedenfalls zeigt die jetzige Perikope Risse im Zusammenhange, die daher rühren, dass ein paraphrasierender und novellistisch ausgestaltender Kommentar der Verwerfung in Nazareth, wie wir sie aus Mc 6 kennen, mit andersartigen Stücken verbunden ist."

[4] See the argument of H. F. D. Sparks that Luke is "an habitual, conscious, and deliberate 'Septuagintalizer'" in "The Semitisms of St. Luke's Gospel," *JTS* 44 (1943) 129–138. Luke 9:51 and 19:11 are good examples of such Septuagint influence in editorial verses.

Luke 4:22-30

Commentators have noted that the sequence of sentences in Luke 4:22-30 is rough. This roughness is explained when we realize that these verses are a patchwork of materials which have been put together by Luke not with a view to psychological plausibility but in order to bring out his own interpretation of the rejection of Jesus at Nazareth. The sequence in 4:22 has been the subject of considerable discussion. This verse seems to begin by reporting a favorable reaction to Jesus and his words. This is followed by the question "Is this not Joseph's son?" which is Luke's version of the questions in Mark that accompany the rejection of Jesus by the Nazarenes. So the verse seems to move very abruptly from acceptance to rejection. Because of this, some have argued that πάντες ἐμαρτύρουν αὐτῷ refers to bearing witness against Jesus.[5] This is doubtful and unnecessary. It is true that μαρτυρέω is occasionally used of witnessing against someone.[6] However, this must be made clear by the context, for in the overwhelming majority of its occurrences in the New Testament μαρτυρέω is used of a favorable or supporting witness, without any need being felt to clarify this by speaking of a "good" witness. In Luke 4:22 we are in no way prepared to understand πάντες ἐμαρτύρουν αὐτῷ in an unfavorable sense by what precedes it; nor is this required by the question which follows. In Luke there is no indication that the Nazarenes are hostile to Jesus at this point, for Mark's statement "They took offense at him" is significantly absent. In Luke's view the real reason for offense has not yet been brought out. The fact that Luke refers to Jesus as son of Joseph rather than son of Mary, as in Mark, is significant for Luke's understanding of the situation. Luke makes clear that in his view Jesus was not, properly speaking, the son of Joseph.[7] So the question of the Nazarenes indicates their failure to understand who Jesus is, perhaps also their blindness, but it is not an indication of hostility. With this in mind, the sequence of thought in 4:22 can be explained. In Mark 6:2-3 there is a strong contrast between the amazement caused by Jesus' wisdom and power and the offense caused by his local origin. Luke 4:22 is simply a compressed and weakened version

---

[5] Cf. B. Violet, "Zum rechten Verständnis," 256–58; Joachim Jeremias, *Jesus' Promise to the Nations*, trans. S. H. Hooke, SBT 1/24 (London: SCM, 1958) 44–45.

[6] Cf. Matt. 23:31; John 7:7; 18:23.

[7] Cf. 3:22-23.

of Mark 6:2-3. Luke retains a reference both to the amazed testimony of the Nazarenes to Jesus and to the question raised concerning his local origin. These two elements in Mark's narrative account for the two elements in Luke 4:22, which at first seem so difficult to relate. But whereas these two elements stand in sharp contrast in Mark, and the latter is seen as the reason for the Nazarenes' rejection of Jesus, this contrast is largely lost in Luke, and the rejection is given a different basis. Luke 4:22 simply indicates that the Nazarenes recognized Jesus' power and yet failed to understand his true role.[8]

Other aspects of 4:22 can be dealt with briefly. The reference to the witness and amazement of the Nazarenes may not only be Luke's rendering of Mark but also correspond to a positive Lukan interest. In this first account of Jesus' public ministry it must be made clear that Jesus makes an immediate impact, illustrating Luke's introductory summary in 4:15. The use of θαυμάζω with ἐπί is characteristic of Luke–Acts.[9] Τοῖς ἐκπορευομένοις ἐκ τοῦ στόματος αὐτοῦ is a "Septuagintalism."[10] It will be shown below that the reference to "words of grace" or "favor" reflects a central Lukan concern in this passage.

The interpretation of 4:22 above might be challenged on the basis of 4:23-24, for it may seem implausible that Jesus would speak of a request for miracles by the Nazarenes and of their failure to accept him unless they had already given some indication of skepticism and hostility. However, there is evidence that Luke understands 4:23-24 not as Jesus' response to present hostility but as a prophecy of what is to come. This is made clear by the reference to Capernaum. Although the rejection of Jesus at Nazareth in Mark is preceded by reference to events at Capernaum, Luke, by placing this scene at the beginning of Jesus' public ministry, makes such a reference to previous events at Capernaum impossible. To be sure, the scene at Nazareth is preceded by an introductory summary of Jesus' activity in 4:14-15. However, it is not clear that Luke intends to refer in 4:14-15 to activity prior to Jesus' coming to Nazareth. These verses can just as well be understood as a general summary of the events that

---

[8] Luke also makes the reason for amazement specific by relating this amazement to the words that Jesus has just spoken.

[9] Cf. John C. Hawkins, *Horae Synopticae* (Oxford: Clarendon, 1899) 16, 33.

[10] Cf. Num 32:24; Job 41:10 (11), 12 (13); Prov 3:16; Sir 28:12. Cf. also Luke 11:54; 19:22; 22:71; Acts 22:14; and the frequent use of διὰ τοῦ στόματος and τὸ στόμα ἀνοίγειν in Luke–Acts.

follow in Luke's narrative. In the light of the fact that there is no clear reference to events at Capernaum prior to Jesus' coming to Nazareth, it is doubtful that Luke understood 4:23 to refer to such prior events.

This conclusion is supported by the fact that there is a clear connection between 4:23 and the events which follow in Luke's narrative and that this connection has been emphasized by Lukan editorial activity. Immediately following the rejection at Nazareth Jesus descends to Capernaum, and 4:31-43 describes his activity there. This activity is introduced, following Mark, by reference to Jesus teaching on the Sabbath and the amazement of the people, just as in the scene at Nazareth. However, what follows stands in sharp contrast to the scene at Nazareth, for it reports Jesus' work of healing and ends by indicating that the crowds followed him and tried to prevent him from leaving. In 4:42 Luke clearly strengthens Mark's remark that "all are seeking you." This is part of a deliberate contrast between what took place at Capernaum and what took place at Nazareth, for the juxtaposition of these events is the result of Luke's own work. Luke is not only responsible for placing the Nazareth episode at the beginning of Jesus' ministry. He has also omitted Mark's account of the call of the first disciples so that the events at Capernaum immediately follow the scene at Nazareth. He does this in spite of the fact that it is important to Luke to refer to the presence of the twelve early in Jesus' ministry.[11] It is the desire to bring out the contrast between Nazareth and Capernaum which accounts for Luke's editorial activity, and it is in light of this contrast that we must explain 4:23. This means that 4:23 cannot be understood as an indirect reference to what the Nazarenes actually did say in the synagogue at Nazareth.[12] They could not have said this at that time, for the presupposition for this statement, the events at Capernaum, had not yet taken place. Therefore, we must take the future ἐρεῖτε seriously. This saying is only very indirectly a response to what the Nazarenes have

---

[11] For Luke it is important that the twelve apostles accompanied Jesus "during the whole time that the Lord Jesus went in and out among us, beginning from the baptism of John" (Acts 1:21-22), for they must be witnesses to the whole of the ministry of Jesus. Cf. Günter Klein, *Die Zwölf Apostel: Ursprung und Gehalt einer Idee,* FRLANT 77 (Göttingen: Vandenhoeck & Ruprecht, 1961) 203–10. It is true that Luke chooses to substitute non-Markan material for Mark's account of the call of the first disciples. But 5:1-11 is inserted into a section in which Luke is following Mark's order, and so we must explain why Luke chose to insert this material after the Capernaum events rather than before, as in Mark.

[12] Against Leaney, *Luke,* 119.

done and said to this point. Luke understands it as a prophecy of a later situation which will come about through the rest of the events narrated in chapter 4.[13]

We have not yet discussed the question of the origin of 4:23. This verse has certain points of contact with Mark 6:1-6, for Mark also refers to Jesus' πατρίς, to the Nazarenes talking about Jesus' miracles (using the verb γίνομαι), and to a lack of mighty acts in Nazareth (accompanied by use of the verb θεραπεύω). Furthermore, it can be argued that the contrast between Nazareth and Capernaum that Luke has constructed by bringing 4:16-30 into immediate conjunction with 4:31-43 is the basis of the prophecy of this contrast in 4:23.[14] On the other hand, there are some indications that this verse may be based upon pre-Lukan, non-Markan tradition. It speaks of a request by the Nazarenes, and there is no clear indication of such a request later in Luke's gospel.[15] Furthermore, it is strange that Jesus' prophecy should consist of a direct quotation of what the Nazarenes will say. The verse would be less awkward if Jesus simply indicated that the Nazarenes will later want him to perform in Nazareth the miracles that he had performed in Capernaum. The fact that Jesus' prophecy is a quotation is explained if it is a piece of tradition which was originally a challenge directed to Jesus but was transformed by Luke into a saying of Jesus. However, the tradition may consist only of the proverb "Physician, heal yourself," for the quotation of the proverb may be the reason for presenting the rest of the verse as a quotation. The proverb was in general circulation[16] and was not necessarily connected with Jesus in earlier tradition.

---

[13] The position taken here is similar to that of Hans Conzelmann, *Die Mitte der Zeit*, 4th ed. (Tübingen: Mohr/Siebeck, 1962) 28–29.

[14] The use here of εἰς instead of ἐν in a local sense is frequent in Luke–Acts. Cf. F. Blass and A. Debrunner, *Grammatik des neutestamentlichen Griechisch*, 10th ed. (Göttingen: Vandenhoeck & Ruprecht, 1959) sections 2 and 205.

[15] Conzelmann, *Mitte der Zeit*, 28–29, 41–42, argues that Luke understands 8:19-21 to be the fulfillment of this prophecy. The placement of this pericope is due to Luke's editorial work, but it is not clear that the request to "see" Jesus implies a desire for miracles, nor that such miracles would take place in Nazareth, nor that Luke equates Jesus' mother and brothers with the unbelieving Nazarenes. It is significant that Luke does not take over the reference to Jesus' relatives in the Markan parallel to Luke 4:24. On 8:19-21 see William C. Robinson, Jr., "On Preaching the Word of God (Luke 8:4-21)," in *Studies in Luke–Acts*, edited by Leander E. Keck and J. Louis Martyn (Nashville: Abingdon, 1966) 133.

[16] Cf. J. M. Creed, *Luke*, 68.

In spite of the objection just raised, the possibility that 4:23 reflects a challenge to Jesus which Luke found in his tradition deserves further consideration. This requires us to consider 4:24 also. If we assume that 4:23 is a challenge to Jesus which Luke found in his tradition, it can be argued that this challenge would hardly have circulated in Christian circles apart from a reply of Jesus to this challenge. Thus 4:24 seems to be necessary to complete the unit of pre-Lukan tradition. If 4:24 is pre-Lukan, non-Markan tradition, it is possible that 4:23 is also. If 4:24 is not, it seems less likely that ὅσα ἠκούσαμεν κτλ. in 4:23 is pre-Lukan tradition. The εἶπεν δέ at the beginning of 4:24 is superfluous in its Lukan setting. It can be explained in several ways. It would have a function if the quotation in 4:23 was not originally a word of Jesus but a challenge to Jesus, as suggested above. However, the fact that εἶπεν δέ is characteristic of Luke[17] casts doubt upon the view that it is part of an older tradition. It may simply be Luke's version of Mark's καὶ ἔλεγεν αὐτοῖς ὁ Ἰησοῦς or a reflection of the fact that 4:24 was originally independent of the preceding verse. The wording of Mark 6:4 and Luke 4:24 differs significantly. The fact that Luke, and only Luke, begins the saying with ἀμήν may be especially significant, for, in contrast to the frequency of this word in the other gospels, it occurs in Luke only six times. Luke sometimes substitutes ἀληθῶς for ἀμήν,[18] or simply omits the ἀμήν,[19] although his practice is not entirely consistent.[20] Thus there is evidence to suggest that Luke generally avoids the foreign word ἀμήν. It may seem easier to assert that its presence in this verse is an indication of non-Markan tradition than to assert that Luke added it on his own.[21]

---

[17] Cf. Hawkins, *Horae Synopticae*, 15, 31–32, and Henry J. Cadbury, *The Style and Literary Method of Luke* (Cambridge: Harvard University Press, 1920) 169.

[18] Luke 9:27; 12:44; 21:3. Cf. 11:5l.

[19] In the following passages Luke's λέγω ὑμῖν or σοι is probably a remnant of the ἀμὴν λέγω ὑμῖν or σοι which is found in the parallel passages: 7:9, 28; 10:12, 24; 12:59; 15:7; 22:18, 34.

[20] He retains the ἀμήν in 18:17, 29; 21:32. Ἀμήν occurs in passages without parallel at 12:37 and 23:43. Luke's practice with regard to this word is conveniently tabulated in Cadbury, *Style and Literary Method*, 157–58.

[21] It is doubtful that Papyrus Oxyrhynchus 1, 6 and Coptic *Gospel of Thomas* 31 contribute anything to our knowledge of the pre-Lukan history of these verses. They are probably dependent on Luke, for not only do they give Luke's version of the saying concerning the prophet but they follow it with a parallel saying concerning a physician, suggesting a knowledge of Luke 4:23 as well as 4:24. It is easier to explain the neat parallelism in Thomas as a change from Luke, suggested by the way in which the proverb "Physician, heal yourself" is used in the context of Luke, than to derive

In spite of the evidence above, it is doubtful that 4:24 represents tradition which is independent of Mark. The principal difference in wording between Luke and Mark is Luke's use of the word δεκτός instead of Mark's ἄτιμος. This difference may be the cause of the difference in the syntax of the two sayings, for the use of a positive rather than a negative concept requires some change in the structure of the sentence. There is reason for doubting that Luke's use of this key word rests on independent tradition. It is too easily explained as a play upon the final word of the quote from the LXX version of Isa 61:1-2 in the first part of this scene. The significance of the recurrence of this term is pointed up by the fact that, apart from two verses in Paul, this word occurs in the New Testament only at Luke 4:19 and 24, and in Acts 10:35, at the beginning of a sermon which contains clear reminiscences of Luke 4:16-30. Thus Luke's uses of this term are all connected with this scene at Nazareth and the Isaiah quotation. Although in 4:24 δεκτός is introduced into a saying of quite different character than the quotation of 4:19, the connection is meaningful for Luke. The use of the same word points up the relation between sharing in the time of salvation announced by Jesus and the acceptance of Jesus himself. People can only share in "the Lord's acceptable year" if they accept the one who announces and brings it. This observation causes me to question the view that 4:24 is based on non-Markan tradition. The argument based on Luke's avoidance of ἀμήν, while strong, is not decisive by itself, for another explanation than the presence of non-Markan tradition in 4:24 is possible. It is possible that the ἀμήν originally occurred at the beginning of 4:25. Luke then transferred it to the beginning of 4:24 and substituted ἐπ' ἀληθείας in 4:25, thereby providing the reader first with the word itself and then with its translation in the following verse. This would be especially appropriate since this is the first occurrence of ἀμήν in Luke's gospel.[22] These considerations not only suggest that 4:24 is based on Mark, but also cast further doubt on the view that 4:23 is part of a non-Markan tradition concerning Jesus.

Luke's version from the saying in Thomas. On this see Wolfgang Schrage, *Das Verhältnis des Thomas-Evangeliums zur synoptischen Tradition und zu den koptischen Evangelienübersetzungen*, BZNW 29 (Berlin: Töpelmann, 1964) 75–77.

[22] Cadbury sees this exchange of synonymous expressions as an example of a characteristic feature of Lukan style. Cf. "Four Features of Lukan Style," in *Studies in Luke–Acts*, edited by Keck and Martyn, 88–97.

In spite of some uncertainty as to the origin of 4:23-24, certain conclusions can be drawn about Luke's methods and concerns. 1) Even if 4:23-24 represents a unit of pre-Lukan tradition, the scene at Nazareth as a whole is a product of Lukan editorial activity. These verses do not fit together with what precedes or follows to make a more extensive unit of tradition. This has been supported by discussion of 4:22 and will be supported by discussion of 4:25-30 and 16-21. 2) Even if 4:23-24 represents a unit of pre-Lukan tradition, Luke's preference for this material rather than what he found in Mark reflects his particular concerns. Not only do these verses contribute to the rejection theme as this is reinterpreted by Luke, but the contrast between Nazareth and Capernaum and the use of δεκτός are given additional significance through the Lukan context (cf. 4:19, 31-43). These two points are even clearer if 4:23-24 is the result of Luke's own reworking of Mark.

In 4:25-27 we find a unit that was originally separate from the preceding verses. This is indicated by an important shift in perspective. Verse 24 concerns the prophet's relation to his πατρίς. As both Mark and Luke 4:23 make clear, this originally referred to Nazareth. But 4:25-27 speaks of the relation of the prophets to Israel. It may be that Luke is using 4:25-27 to hint at a broader interpretation of πατρίς in 4:24. The πατρίς in which Jesus is not acceptable is not only Nazareth but also Israel. However, this means that Luke is giving a definite twist to the original meaning of the word. Moreover, 4:24 and 25-27 also differ in that the former speaks of a failure to accept the prophet while the latter refers to instances in which the prophets were not sent to Israel, but to non-Israelites. The one speaks of human rejection, the other of God's sending. For Luke these two points of view are not incompatible, for in Luke–Acts God's plan of sending the gospel to the Gentiles is fulfilled through the rejection of the gospel by the Jews. However, the sharp change in point of view, with no attempt to relate the two aspects, is here a reflection of the separate origin of these sayings.

It has been suggested that 4:25-27 would connect well with 4:23.[23] However, the removal of 4:24 does not result in the restoration of an original sequence in a pre-Lukan source. Verse 23 is concerned with the contrast between Capernaum and Nazareth, while vv. 25-27 is concerned

---

[23] Karl Ludwig Schmidt, *Der Rahmen der Geschichte Jesu* (Berlin: Trowitzsch, 1919) 40.

with the contrast between Israel and the Gentiles.[24] Charles Masson recognizes this but argues that 4:25-27 is connected with 4:23 by suggesting that Jesus is arguing *a majori ad minus*.[25] If belonging to Israel does not entail a right to be healed by God, how much less does belonging to Jesus' own village. However, if this were the point of 4:25-27, it would be necessary to make the application clear and explicit, for it is not at all obvious from these verses themselves that they are concerned primarily with a situation in Nazareth. It might seem that this application is required in order to fit these verses into the historical setting of Jesus' rejection at Nazareth. But that is the question: whether these verses were originally meant to be understood in light of that limited historical situation. When we relate these verses to Luke–Acts as a whole, we discover a different explanation of the position and function of these verses: they were inserted here by Luke in order to suggest the connection between the rejection of Jesus and his turning to others which occurs at Nazareth and the rejection of the gospel by the Jews and turning of the missionaries to the Gentiles which Luke will trace in Acts. The connection of these verses with this dominant theme in Acts cannot be ignored when we seek to explain how these verses became part of this scene at Nazareth. They serve Luke's own purposes and so are probably Luke's own insertion, especially when we see that they have no connection with anything in the Markan story. Finally, Masson's argument falls apart when we note indications that 4:25-27 reflects a time and setting different from that of Jesus' ministry, while 4:23, unless it is Luke's own construction in preparation for 4:31ff., seems to reflect a situation within Jesus' ministry.

Joachim Jeremias describes 4:25-27 as "an early Aramaic tradition." In support of this he points to the following features of these verses:

Ἐπ᾽ ἀληθείας v. 25 (= ἀμήν); ἐν ταῖς ἡμέραις v. 25 . . .; here are three examples of the circumlocution for the divine name by the use of the passive, vv 25, 26, 27; the three and a half years' drought in the time of Elijah, v 25 (a Palestinian tradition, not found in the Biblical narrative

---

[24] Cf. Rudolf Bultmann, *Die Geschichte der synoptischen Tradition,* 4th ed. (Göttingen: Vandenhoeck & Ruprecht, 1958) 31.
[25] Masson, "Jésus à Nazareth," 57.

. . .); paratactic καί with adversative meaning in v 26 beginning and v 27b; οὐδεμία . . . εἰ μή v 26, οὐδεὶς . . . εἰ μή v 27 (אִם . . . לֹא).[26]

This indicates Semitic influence, but, of course, does not prove that these verses go back to the historical Jesus. In fact there is other evidence that these verses originated, not at the earliest stage of the tradition, but at a somewhat later time and in a milieu characterized by an overlap between Semitic and Greek language forms. This is shown by the use of the adjective Σιδωνίας, a clear instance of the influence of the LXX rather than the Hebrew text of the Elijah story. Furthermore, these verses provide an argument from the Old Testament for a mission to Gentiles and are most naturally explained as arising from the early church's argument over a mission to Gentiles. They do not focus on the possibility of the inclusion of Gentiles in the Kingdom at the final consummation, something that might take place apart from a Gentile mission, but rather, as the reference to the sending of Elijah makes clear, they indicate to whom God's messengers should address themselves. They argue that it is not the case that all Israel must receive salvation before it is offered to the Gentiles. Since the New Testament reflects a debate within the early church concerning a mission to the Gentiles,[27] it is unlikely that Jesus gave explicit directions concerning such a mission. Therefore, Luke 4:25-27 did not originate within the context of Jesus' ministry, but within the context of the early church's debate over the Gentile mission. These verses originally had nothing to do with the contrast between Nazareth and Capernaum that we find in 4:23.

Verses 28-30 are the construction of the Evangelist himself. This is shown by the language used. Πίμπλημι is found 22 times in Luke–Acts but only twice in the rest of the New Testament.[28] Ἀνίστημι is a favorite word in Luke–Acts.[29] This is particularly true of the participles ἀναστάς and ἀναστάντες.[30] Other words characteristic of Luke–Acts are διέρχομαι, ἄγω, πορεύομαι, and μέσος.[31] The nominative form αὐτός

---

[26] Jeremias, *Jesus' Promise,* 51. J. M. Creed denies that it is necessary to assume Aramaic idiom here to explain the use of εἰ μή. Cf. *Luke,* 68–69.

[27] Cf. Acts 10–11.

[28] With Luke 4:28 compare especially Acts 2:4 for the form and Acts 13:45 for the setting.

[29] Cf. Robert Morgenthaler, *Statistik des Neutestamentlichen Wortschatzes* (Zürich: Gotthelf, 1958) 182.

[30] Cf. Hawkins, *Horae Synopticae,* 14.

[31] Cf. Morgenthaler, *Statistik,* 181.

is also frequent in Luke's gospel.[32] The participles in these verses reflect Luke's preference for a participle rather than coordinate verbs.[33] The phrase ἐξέβαλον . . . ἔξω τῆς πόλεως is closely related to the way in which Luke describes a similar situation in Acts 7:58. Thus the language used gives no indication of pre-Lukan tradition and it is unlikely that Luke had any concrete knowledge on which to base these verses. Rather he has embellished the tradition of rejection at Nazareth by describing what he imagined would have taken place in this situation. The fact that it has been difficult for scholars to locate the cliff from which the crowd intended to cast Jesus down[34] and the fact that the very surprising escape of Jesus is described in the vaguest possible terms agree with these assertions.

We have seen that 4:22-27 is a patchwork of traditional materials. Luke has put these materials together in such a way as to build up to a climax in the violent rejection of Jesus in 4:28-30. In doing so, Luke has completely changed the reason for the rejection of Jesus by the Nazarenes. For Luke the fact that Jesus comes from their own town is not the cause of offense, as in Mark 6:3. This point is greatly weakened by Luke, and is separated from the first indication of anger in 4:28 by other material which indicates a different reason for this anger. Nor is the anger of the Nazarenes the result of a failure or refusal of Jesus to fulfill the Nazarenes' request for miracles.[35] Luke does not intend 4:23 to indicate that the Nazarenes requested miracles at that time, and the question of whether Jesus could perform miracles in Nazareth plays no role in Luke's account. The cause of the Nazarenes' anger, in Luke's view, is indicated by the contrasts in 4:23 and 25-27 which place Jesus' own people in an unfavorable position. Here Jesus announces that others are to benefit from his work rather than those to whom he is most closely related. These statements do not simply mean that Jesus will go elsewhere because he will be rejected at Nazareth. To be sure, human rejection has a role in the realization of God's purpose. Here as elsewhere Luke seems to see an

---

[32] Cf. ibid., 158, and Cadbury, *Style and Literary Method*, 193.

[33] Cf. Cadbury, ibid., 134–35.

[34] Cf. Schmidt, *Rahmen*, 42–43, and Walter Grundmann, *Das Evangelium nach Lukas*, THKNT 3 (Berlin: Evangelische Verlagsanstalt, 1964) 123.

[35] Masson, who supposes that in most respects Luke's narrative reflects a historical sequence of events, argues that Jesus' failure to perform miracles at Nazareth was the real cause of his rejection. Mark 6:5a originally referred to the time before the rejection and indicates the cause, not the result, of the rejection. Cf. "Jésus à Nazareth," 45–47, 53, 59, 65–66.

intersection between human rejection and the unexpected fulfillment of God's plan through that rejection. But 4:25-27 shows that Luke is not simply saying that Jesus will have to work elsewhere because of bad conditions in Nazareth; rather he is saying that it is God's plan that Jesus work elsewhere and that eventually the benefits of his work be given to the Gentiles. It is not so much that Jesus goes elsewhere because he is rejected as that he is rejected because he announces that it is God's will and his mission to go elsewhere. This means that Luke has reinterpreted the grounds for the rejection of Jesus at Nazareth in light of his own theological views.

Verses 23 and 25-27 formulate two quite different contrasts, as we have seen. Yet in Luke's mind these contrasts are related because both indicate that the benefits of Jesus' work will be given to others instead of Jesus' own people. Verse 23 points to Capernaum as the recipient of these benefits. This fits with Luke's understanding of the ministry of Jesus, for following 4:16-30 Jesus goes to Capernaum and in the rest of Luke's gospel there are no references to Jesus' presence in Nazareth. Jesus has moved beyond Nazareth once and for all, and it is the other cities of Israel that benefit from his work. Verses 25-27 do not fit so easily with Luke's presentation of the ministry of Jesus. In fact, these verses refer forward to the mission of the church, which will move beyond Israel to the Gentiles. However, such a reference is appropriate at this point because the Gentile mission is the climax of the movement beyond Jesus' own people that begins at Nazareth. Nazareth and the Gentile mission are the beginning and culmination of one movement. The rejection at Nazareth sets in motion the geographical development that is so important in Luke–Acts. This is a major reason why Luke places this scene at the beginning of his account of Jesus' ministry. It is the beginning of Jesus' "way,"[36] and the way beginning at Nazareth leads on to Jerusalem, and then to Antioch, Asia Minor, Greece, and Rome. Furthermore, the mission continues to encounter the rejection of Jesus' own people and the call of God to turn to others, a pattern which is first established at Nazareth.[37] And so, while the

---

[36] Cf. ἐπορεύετο 4:30 and William C. Robinson, Jr., *Der Weg des Herrn* (Hamburg: Reich, 1964) 30–43.

[37] Luke emphasizes in Acts 8:1-2, 4-5 (cf. 9:19-21) that the spread of the gospel beyond Jerusalem is the direct result of the death of Stephen and the related persecution of the church, which is the climax of the opposition by Jerusalem Jews that Luke begins to trace in Acts 4. Cf. also Acts 13:45-46; 28:24-28.

reference to the Gentiles in 4:25-27 may be historically out of place, it is appropriate in the light of Luke's total conception of the development which he wishes to trace.

The strange way in which this scene at Nazareth develops has been partly explained by indicating that it is a Lukan construction from diverse materials. However, it may still seem strange that Luke should have Jesus predict the rejection before it takes place. If we compare Luke's methods elsewhere, this also will not seem strange. Luke's presentation of Paul's preaching in Antioch of Pisidia is instructive. In Acts 13:40-41 Paul's sermon ends with a warning concerning a mysterious deed of God. For the men of Antioch this could only be a riddle, but for the reader the riddle is soon explained. Verses 44ff. relate that on the next Sabbath the Jews became jealous of the crowds of Gentiles who had gathered to hear the gospel and the Jews began to oppose Paul, to which Paul and Barnabas responded by announcing that they would turn to the Gentiles. It is clear that this turning to the Gentiles is the deed of God to which the mysterious words at the end of Paul's sermon referred. By means of these words Luke alludes to and interprets the rejection of the gospel by the Jews of Antioch and the turning of the mission to the Gentiles before they take place. Acts 3:22-26 has a similar function with regard to the Jewish opposition that follows. It is important to Luke that the major steps in the fulfillment of God's plan be announced ahead of time and that the relation between the prophecy and the fulfillment be clear. The way in which Luke's gospel points forward to the climactic events in Jerusalem shows this. Luke not only takes over Mark's passion predictions but adds an important reference to the Jerusalem events in 9:31, and then makes repeated reference to the journey to Jerusalem in the central section of his gospel. Furthermore, after the resurrection there is explicit reference to the fulfillment of these predictions (24:6-8). So the announcement of the rejection before it takes place conforms to Luke's literary methods and to his concern to trace the plan of God in history, a plan that is made plain through prophecy and its fulfillment.[38]

---

[38] Cf. Paul Schubert, "The Structure and Significance of Luke 24," in *Neutestamentliche Studien für Rudolf Bultmann zu seinem 70. Geburtstag am 20. August 1954,* BZNW 21 (Berlin: Töpelmann, 1954) 165–86.

Luke 4:16-21

Luke 4:16-21 is independent of Mark, being related only to Mark's statement that "when the Sabbath came, he began to teach in the synagogue." However, it seems to perform a function similar to Mark 1:14-15, Mark's introductory summary of the message of Jesus. Following the narrative of the temptation, both Mark and Luke report Jesus' return to Galilee and give a short summary of Jesus' activity. But Luke's summary in 4:14-15 contains no indication of the content of Jesus' message, as does Mark 1:14-15. This is supplied in Luke by the first part of the scene in Nazareth.

In considering the origin of Luke 4:16-21, it is important to observe that these verses could not have circulated apart from the Isaiah quotation. Apart from the quotation there would be no point in relating the events of 4:16b-17 and 20, for nothing noteworthy takes place. Rather these verses only indicate what is typical and customary in such a situation, and so provide the setting for the quotation itself. Even 4:21 gives no indication of a knowledge of events or words of Jesus independent of the Isaiah quotation. It may be doubted that we may properly speak of this as a "sermon" following the reading of the Scripture. All that is said is that this Scripture applies to Jesus and his ministry. The only historical knowledge that need stand behind this is the knowledge that Isa 61:1-2 was applied to Jesus in the tradition. There is no evidence here for tradition concerning the words of Jesus beyond the tradition of applying this Old Testament quotation to Jesus.

This conclusion is supported by the evidence of vocabulary and grammar. The only point at which there is evidence for the influence of pre-Lukan tradition is in the occurrence of the rare form Ναζαρά in 4:16. This form occurs only here and at Matt 4:13. It is likely that Luke 4:16a and Matt 4:13 rest upon a common tradition, for not only do they agree in using the rare form Ναζαρά, but both occur in the report of Jesus' movements following the temptation, and in Matt 4:13a reference to Jesus living in Capernaum follows the reference to Ναζαρά. This agrees with Luke's geographical sequence in 4:16 and 31, and may have seemed to Luke to provide justification for inserting a scene at Nazareth at the beginning of Jesus' ministry. However, Matt 4:13 reports no events at Nazareth and has no further connection with Luke 4:16-30. Thus it indicates that the reference to Nazareth in Luke 4:16a has a traditional base, but nothing more. At other points in 4:16-17, 20-21 there is clear evidence of Lukan vocabulary and style.[39] The phrase κατὰ τὸ εἰωθός and dative occurs in the New Testament only here and at Acts 17:2, which also speaks of preaching in a synagogue on the Sabbath. The phrase ἐν (or simple dative) τῇ ἡμέρᾳ τῶν σαββάτων (or τοῦ σαββάτου) is found only in Luke–Acts.[40] The use of πρός and accusative rather than the simple dative after λέγω, as in 4:21 and 23, is characteristic of Luke–Acts.[41] The same is true of the following words: οὗ with the meaning "where" 4:16, 17 (13 or 14 times Luke–Acts;[42] 11 times elsewhere in the New Testament), ἐπιδίδωμι 4:17 (7 times Luke–Acts; twice elsewhere), ἀτενίζω 4:20 (12 times Luke–Acts; twice elsewhere), and σήμερον 4:21 (20 times Luke–Acts; 21 times elsewhere).[43] The phrases ἤρξατο . . . λέγειν and ἐν τοῖς ὠσὶν ὑμῶν in 4:21 are not evidence of pre-Lukan tradition. The former is frequent in Luke,[44] and the latter is a "Septuagintalism."[45] The fact that 4:16-21 reveals a knowledge of the practice of the Jewish synagogue is no evidence of a pre-Lukan tradition concerning Nazareth.[46] The references to Jewish practice in this passage are evidence only for a general knowledge of such practice and not for an old tradition concerning a particular event at Nazareth.

---

[39] Of the 82 words and constructions listed by Friedrich Rehkopf, *Die lukanische Sonderquelle*, WUNT 5 (Tübingen: Mohr/Siebeck, 1959), as characteristic of pre-Lukan usage, only two (κατά 4:16; ἐρεῖν 4:23) occur in Luke 4:16-30, and the validity of these two is doubtful.

[40] Luke 13:14, 16; 14:5; Acts 13:14; 16:13. The closest non-Lukan parallel is John 19:31. The connection of Luke 4:16 with Acts 13:14 is especially close. The similarity to Acts 13:14 and 17:2 shows that Luke 4:16 is influenced by the way in which Luke is accustomed to describe synagogue scenes.

[41] Cf. Cadbury, *Style and Literary Method*, 203, and Hawkins, *Horae Synopticae*, 18, 36–37.

[42] Depending on the original text of Acts 20:6.

[43] Of these 21 occurrences outside of Luke–Acts, 8 are in Matthew and 8 in Hebrews. Nine of the 11 occurrences in Luke are without parallel, so the frequency of the word in Luke is not due to the material that it shares with Matthew.

[44] Ἄρχομαι λέγειν or λαλεῖν occurs ten times in Luke, twice in Acts. Note especially Luke 11:29 and 12:1, where the phrase occurs in what is probably Lukan editorial material. Luke also uses the construction ἄρχομαι + infinitive + λέγων.

[45] Cf., e.g., Deut 5:1, Judg 9:3, I Kingdoms 3:17. With Luke 4:21 compare 7:1, an editorial verse, and note the similar Septuagintalism which Luke introduces into a Markan passage at 9:44.

[46] Cf. Karl Heinrich Rengstorf, *Das Evangelium nach Lukas,* 9th ed. NTD (Göttingen: Vandenhoeck & Ruprecht, 1962), 67: "Der unbekannte Autor dieses Berichts . . . erweist sich wieder als sachkundiger Palästiner. Seine Schilderung des Verhaltens Jesu im Sabbatgottesdienst entspricht durchaus dem, was die rabbinischen Quellen berichten."

So far it has been argued that Luke 4:16-17 and 20-21 give indications of Lukan vocabulary and style and that these verses would not have been transmitted in the tradition apart from the Isaiah quotation, which is the center and point of this section. Now we must look at the quotation itself. The origin of 4:18-19 within the Greek-speaking church is indicated by the fact that it follows the LXX translation. With three exceptions, Luke 4:18-19 follows the LXX word for word, including its word order and its variations from the Hebrew text.[47] Only one of the exceptions is a variation in the choice of a word. In 4:19 Luke has κηρύξαι instead of the καλέσαι of the LXX. Since κηρύξαι is used to translate the same Hebrew word in the preceding verse, this might be some evidence of knowledge of the Hebrew text. However, since this is the only indication of this, it does not weigh very heavily. The use of κηρύξαι in 4:19 may simply be due to the occurrence of the same word in the preceding verse of the Greek text or to the importance of this word in the missionary language of the early church. The other two variations from the LXX are also variations from the Hebrew text. They are the omission of ἰάσασθαι τοὺς συντετριμμένους τῇ καρδίᾳ and the insertion of a phrase from Isa 58:6 ἀποστεῖλαι τεθραυσμένους ἐν ἀφέσει. This omission and insertion are very hard to explain if we assume that we have here an accurate account of what Jesus said while reading from the actual text of Isaiah. It is possible for the eye to skip a phrase, but it is hardly possible to explain the insertion of a whole phrase not present in the text. What we have in Luke 4:18-19 is an interpretive rendering designed to emphasize a particular point. Furthermore, the way in which the insertion is made is dependent on the LXX text. As Klostermann points out, the insertion is dependent on the catchword ἄφεσις, which occurs in the LXX of both Isa 58:6 and 61:1.[48] However, ἄφεσις is used in these two verses to translate two different Hebrew words,[49] and so the same connection is not suggested

---

[47] Variations in the LXX include translation of אֲדֹנָי יְהוָה by the simple κύριος, omission of the second יְהוָה, and substitution of "blind" for "imprisoned," thus giving a different meaning to וְלַאֲסוּרִים פְּקַח־קוֹחַ.

[48] *Lukas-Evangelium,* 63.

[49] Pointed out by A. George, "La prédication inaugurale de Jésus dans la synagogue de Nazareth," *BVC* 59 (1964) 27. George remarks, "Cette insertion s'explique mieux dans le texte grec où elle est appelée par le mot 'liberté' (ce mot correspond à deux termes distincts dans l'hébreu et assez différents dans l'araméen). Il faut donc ici un certain travail litttéraire de Luc ou de ses sources grecques sur la citation de Jésus."

by the Hebrew. Apart from this it might be possible to suppose that Luke had simply substituted the LXX translation for a different and older version of the Isaiah quotation in his source. However, what we encounter in Luke 4:18-19 is not simply the LXX translation of an earlier quotation but a text that could have been formed only on the basis of the LXX. Furthermore, as we shall see, the peculiar form of this text fits specifically Lukan emphases. Since this is the case, it is very likely that 4:16-21 is a Lukan composition. As pointed out above, these verses could hardly have circulated in the tradition without the Isaiah quotation. But this quotation presupposes the LXX translation and serves specifically Lukan interests. Therefore, 4:16-21 as a whole must be a Lukan composition. This is supported by the evidence of vocabulary and style.

Luke's methods and purpose in constructing this scene at Nazareth can be illumined by comparing it with some of the major scenes in Acts. In Acts 17 we find a major scene with an important sermon placed at Athens. This is striking because it is clear that Corinth, not Athens, was the center of Paul's work in Greece. However, Athens is a geographical symbol. It represents the height of Greek culture, and the scene placed there represents the encounter of the gospel with Greek culture. This means that the Athens scene is not primarily concerned with what happened on a particular day. It typifies a broad historical encounter, presenting this concretely in the form of an ideal scene. This purpose is furthered by placing the sermon of Paul in a setting that evokes what is typically Athenian. The scene at Nazareth has similar features. Nazareth also has a special significance for Luke. It is the place where Jesus grew up and so is the natural beginning point for the geographical development that Luke traces throughout his two volume work. This scene also is not primarily concerned with a particular event on a particular day but with the meaning of Jesus' mission as a whole and its consequences. And the references to the synagogue service show that here also the major pronouncement is given a fitting setting by sketching a scene typical of the place and time.

In Acts 13:13-52 we find another example of the way in which Luke constructs at key points in his narrative ideal scenes which have significance beyond the particular time and place in which they are set. The scene at Antioch of Pisidia is developed at length and is provided with a major speech. The particular location in Antioch is not important for understanding the significance of this speech, but the fact that it takes place in a synagogue of the diaspora is important, for it is clearly a sermon by a Jew to Jews concerning the Jewish hope. The sermon is meant to be typical of the proclamation of the gospel to Jews. Moreover, the event that follows also has typical significance. Following the warning at the end of the sermon (13:40-41), Luke reports that the Jews became jealous of the Gentiles and rejected the gospel. Paul and Barnabas replied with the solemn announcement that, in the light of Jewish rejection, they would turn to the Gentiles. The way in which this major scene builds up to a climax in this announcement would seem to indicate that this was a major turning point in the mission. However, in Acts 14:1 Paul is back in a Jewish synagogue again, and he continues to preach to Jews right to the end of Acts. Since Paul's missionary methods are just the same after Antioch as before, why does Luke place so much emphasis on what took place at Antioch of Pisidia? He does so because this event has typical significance for Paul's mission. This sequence of preaching to the Jews, rejection, and turning to the Gentiles is repeated in the chapters that follow, and Acts ends on this same note.[50] The scene at Antioch is not a turning point in Paul's work in the sense that what happens afterward is different than what happened before, and yet it does have a significance beyond Antioch of Pisidia, for what took place there is understood to be typical of what took place again and again in Paul's ministry, in fact, typical of what took place in Paul's ministry as a whole, for the significance of Paul's ministry for Luke is that in it God's plan of turning from the rebellious Jews to the Gentiles is concretely carried out in city after city. In Acts 13, near the beginning of the section of Acts which traces the missionary work of Paul, Luke places a major scene which interprets the work of Paul as a whole. It should not be surprising that the scene which Luke places at the beginning of the ministry of Jesus also serves to interpret the development that follows it. It does so by announcing that it is not those who are closest to Jesus but others who will benefit from his work, and by establishing the pattern of rejection by Jesus' own people and moving on to others that will be typical of the mission as a whole. It also does so by interpreting the whole mission of Jesus through the Isaiah quotation. The significance of this quotation is not limited to the particular situation in Nazareth. It is the title under which Luke places the whole ministry of Jesus and is to be understood as a summary of Jesus' work and message throughout Luke's

---

[50] Cf. 18:5-6; 28:17, 23-28.

gospel. It is characteristic of Luke that he has chosen to interpret these important aspects of the story that he is telling by constructing a major scene at a key point in his narrative.[51]

The significance of this quotation of Isa 61:1-2 for Luke becomes clear when we see that it expresses themes that are emphasized elsewhere in Luke–Acts. These themes must now be discussed in detail. The reference to the Spirit resting upon Jesus is to be understood in connection with the preceding narrative of Jesus' baptism. Although the descent of the Spirit at Jesus' baptism is related in Matthew and Mark also, it is Luke who brings out most clearly the significance of this event for the following ministry of Jesus. Apart from the genealogy, each of the major sections of material between the baptism of Jesus and the announcement in 4:18 is introduced by a reference to Jesus as the bearer of the Spirit. The first of these references, Luke 4:1, is related to a reference to the Spirit in Mark 1:12. However, Mark refers to the Spirit only in connection with Jesus' arrival in the desert. Luke's statement has broader significance, for the reference to Jesus being led in the desert "in the Spirit" is preceded by the statement that Jesus returned from the Jordan "full of the Holy Spirit." Luke is not content to speak of a manifestation of the Spirit in a particular event. He wishes to emphasize Jesus' continuing endowment with the Spirit. This is made quite clear by the fact that Luke, and Luke alone, refers to Jesus' endowment with the Spirit again after the temptation scene, this time in connection with a general summary of Jesus' work in Galilee (4:14). Thus Luke makes clear that the descent of the Spirit at Jesus' baptism was the basis of a continuing endowment with the Spirit and so prepares the way for the announcement in 4:18, which relates the Spirit to the whole of Jesus' mission. We can see, then, that the reference to the Spirit in 4:18 is emphasized by Luke's editorial activity in 4:1 and 14. The importance of this for Luke's understanding of the ministry of Jesus is confirmed by the fact that the sermon in Acts which deals most extensively with the ministry of Jesus accompanies its summary of Jesus' activity with the statement that "God anointed him with the Holy Spirit and power" (Acts 10:38), a clear echo of Luke 4:18.[52]

---

[51] On Luke's use of dramatic scenes and speeches see Martin Dibelius, *Studies in the Acts of the Apostles* (London: SCM, 1956) 109–22, 129–32, 150–65; and Ernst Haenchen, *Die Apostelgeschichte,* 13th ed. (Göttingen: Vandenhoeck & Ruprecht, 1961) 93–99.

[52] The missionary sermons in Acts are in large measure Luke's own composition and reflect his theology, though they make use of certain traditional themes. Cf. Ulrich Wilckens, *Die Missionsreden der Apostelgeschichte,* 2d ed. (Neukirchen-Vluyn: Neukirchener, 1963).

Apart from Heb 1:9 (an Old Testament quotation), Luke is the only New Testament writer who refers to the anointing of Jesus. He does so not only at Luke 4:18 and Acts 10:38, but also at Acts 4:27. Since Acts 4:27 follows a quotation in 4:25-26 and interprets elements of it, there is probably a connection between the reference to the anointing and the title Χριστός in 4:26. Luke's awareness of the connection between the title Christ and the act of anointing would influence his interpretation of the Isaiah quotation in Luke 4:18. That God had anointed Jesus would mean to Luke that Jesus was the Christ.[53]

The phrase εὐαγγελίσασθαι πτωχοῖς also has a significant place within Luke's editorial emphases. The verb εὐαγγελίζομαι occurs only once in Matthew and not at all in Mark, while it occurs ten times in Luke and is frequent in Acts.[54] Especially significant is the fact that Luke chooses to use this word in his editorial summaries of Jesus' activity. He introduces it at 4:43, rewriting the Markan statement. This summary of Jesus' mission is especially important, for it contains clear reminiscences of 4:18 (εὐαγγελίσασθαι, ἀπεστάλην). Εὐαγγελίζομαι is also used to describe the activity of Jesus in editorial summaries at 8:1 and 20:1, and it is applied to the work of the twelve sent out by Jesus at 9:6. In the latter two cases this is clearly due to Luke's changing of the Markan text. In the light of 4:43 and 8:1 the phrase ἡ βασιλεία τοῦ θεοῦ εὐαγγελίζεται in 16:16 probably also reflects Luke's own way of describing the work of Jesus. Thus it was to "announce good news" or to "announce the good news of the Kingdom" that Jesus was "sent," according to the editorial material of Luke's gospel. This same view is contained in the Isaiah quotation at Luke 4:18. Once again the importance of this for Luke's interpretation of Jesus is supported by the sermon before Cornelius, for Acts 10:36 speaks of the word which God sent to Israel, "announcing good news of peace through Jesus Christ."[55] The full significance of this announcing of good news

---

[53] It is possible, though not certain, that the absence of any reference to John as the one who baptized Jesus in Luke 3:21-22 is due to Luke's wish to avoid any confusion as to who it was who anointed Jesus. For Luke Jesus was anointed by God, in conformity with Isa 61:1. Cf. Wilckens, *Missionsreden*, 107–8.

[54] The noun occurs in Matthew and Mark, but not in Luke. The fact that Luke uses εὐαγγελίζομαι rather than adopting Mark's phrase τὸ εὐαγγέλιον κηρύσσειν may be due in part to the influence of Isa 61:1.

[55] I agree with Hans Conzelmann, *Die Apostelgeschichte* (Tübingen: Mohr/Siebeck, 1963) 64, that εὐαγγελιζόμενος refers here to the work of Jesus, not the apostles. Contrast Haenchen, *Apostelgeschichte*, 297.

becomes clear in the light of the full quotation in Luke 4:18-19, for this makes clear that it means announcing and bringing the time of salvation.

That it is the "poor" to whom the good news is announced also corresponds to a Lukan emphasis. The special concern of Jesus for the outcasts and poor is rooted in Luke's tradition, but Luke's gospel gives special emphasis to this and to the corresponding condemnation of the proud and rich.[56]

The most striking departure of Luke 4:18 from the Old Testament text is the insertion of the phrase from Isa 58:6 ἀποστεῖλαι τεθραυσμένους ἐν ἀφέσει. As pointed out above, this is dependent on the catchword connection between ἄφεσις in this phrase and in the phrase κηρύξαι αἰχμαλώτοις ἄφεσιν in Isa 61:1. Thus this insertion serves to emphasize the word ἄφεσις. This insertion can be explained from the special importance that this word had for Luke.[57] The significance of this word for Luke is shown by its important role in the Acts sermons, where it occurs in the phrase ἄφεσις ἁμαρτιῶν.[58] The same phrase occurs in the anticipatory summary of essential themes of Acts at the end of Luke's gospel (24:47). Although Luke is more cautious about introducing his own theological terminology within the body of the gospel itself, his concern with this theme is apparent in his handling of traditional material that relates to it. Luke introduces material not found in the other gospels that emphasizes Jesus' work of forgiveness (7:36-50, 19:1-10). His introduction to the parables of the lost sheep, lost coin, and prodigal son in 15:1-3 indicates that he understands these parables (probably rightly) as a justification of the mercy shown to sinners by Jesus, and his editorial introduction to Mark's story of the healing of the paralytic (Luke 5:17) turns it into a manifestation of Jesus' power of forgiveness before the leaders of all Israel. The Isaiah quotation in 4:18 speaks, of course, of release for "prisoners" and the "oppressed," and does not refer directly to release of sins. However, when these phrases are no longer applied to physical imprisonment, they leave considerable room for interpretation. Luke may

---

[56] Cf. Henry J. Cadbury, *The Making of Luke–Acts* (New York: Macmillan, 1927) 258–63.

[57] The explanation of Luke's omission from Isa 61:1 is not as certain. It is possible that there was no omission, for many texts contain the missing words, with a slight variation from the LXX. However, our best texts do not, and the insertion of the omitted words is easily explained. If the omission is original, it may be due to Luke's desire to move directly from the reference to the sending of Jesus to the phrase κηρύξαι αἰχμαλώτοις ἄφεσιν, and thereby emphasize this phrase.

[58] Cf. Acts 2:38; 5:31; 10:43; 13:38; 26:18.

well have included Jesus' work of healing in this release of the prisoners.[59] However, in the light of the importance to Luke of the "release of sins," this must be an important aspect of what he had in mind when he chose to emphasize the word ἄφεσις in Luke 4:18.[60]

The final phrase in 4:19 sums up the significance of what precedes. The announcement of good news to the poor, of release for captives and the oppressed, of sight for the blind, means the arrival of "the Lord's acceptable year." The context in the quotation makes quite clear that this refers to the time of salvation.[61] The importance of this idea to Luke is made clear by the fact that Luke chooses to end the quotation at this point, even though this is the middle of a sentence in the Old Testament text. Ending at this point makes this reference to the time of salvation the climax of the quotation and avoids the reference to the "day of recompense" that follows, which, since it would call up the negative idea of judgment, would disturb the emphasis that Luke wished to make. For Luke the ministry of Jesus means the coming of the time of salvation. Jesus in his ministry not only announces this time but brings this time through his work, for "release," the gift of sight to the blind, etc., take place through him. He is the one through whom God establishes this time of salvation.

It is in the light of this that we should interpret the reference to οἱ λόγοι τῆς χάριτος in 4:22. This verse refers back to the specific statements in 4:18-19 and 21. This connection suggests strongly that οἱ λόγοι τῆς χάριτος refers not simply to the form of Jesus' words or to the impression which they made, but to their content. Jesus, in citing the words of Isaiah, announces God's grace and favor, a point that Luke has emphasized by stopping the quotation before the reference to the "day of recompense." This is quite in keeping with Lukan use of the word χάρις, which is fairly frequent in Luke–Acts.[62] The word does not carry all of the meaning

---

[59] Cf. the reference to "healing all those oppressed (τοὺς καταδυναστευομένους) by the Devil" in Acts 10:38.

[60] Cf. R. Bultmann, *TWNT* 1.508: "Das Substantiv ἄφεσις heisst fast immer Vergebung . . . Auch wo ἄφεσις als Befreiung verstanden ist (zweimal Lk 4:18 . . .), ist diese als Vergebung wenigstens mitgemeint."

[61] Cf. 2 Cor 6:2, where, in a quotation from Isa 49:8, καιρὸς δεκτός is in parallelism with ἡμέρα σωτηρίας and then is interpreted by Paul as καιρὸς εὐπρόσδεκτος. On the background of ἐνιαυτὸν . . . δεκτόν see Grundmann, *TWNT* 2.57–59. Grundmann interprets this phrase as "die von Jahwe erwählte angenehme Zeit, die Heilszeit."

[62] Eight times in Luke, though it does not occur in Matthew and Mark; seventeen times in Acts.

that it has in Paul's letters and is often best translated simply as "favor." There is some variety in Luke's use of the term, and he can refer to the favor of humans as well as the favor of God. However, the great majority of the occurrences of this term refer to God's favor, and the closest parallel to Luke 4:22 is the description of the gospel as ὁ λόγος τῆς χάριτος αὐτοῦ (scil. τοῦ κυρίου) (Acts 14:3, 20:32; cf. 20:24). Not only the message of the apostles but also the message of Jesus in Luke 4:18-19 is quite appropriately described as "words of favor," for in it God's gift of the time of salvation is announced.

The preceding discussion makes clear that the quotation from Isaiah 61 in Luke 4:18-19 has great importance to Luke. One of the weaknesses of previous study of Luke 4:16-30, even among scholars interested in Luke's theological interpretation of his material, has been in failing to give sufficient attention to the Isaiah quotation. To be sure, this is clearly pre-Lukan material. However, it is Luke who chose to make this quotation the title under which the whole ministry of Jesus is placed. He did so because it expresses clearly certain important aspects of his own understanding of Jesus and his ministry. It presents Jesus as the one anointed with the Spirit and so commissioned by God to announce and establish the time of God's favor through the preaching of good news to the poor and the proclamation of the time of "release," which includes both Jesus' work of healing and his declaration of God's forgiveness. Even the fact that these ideas are expressed through the announcement of the fulfillment of the Old Testament promise is characteristically Lukan, as we see when we note the great importance that the scheme of promise and fulfillment has in Luke's thought.[63] When these themes are combined with the rejection of Jesus by his own people and his announcement that he has been sent to others, we receive a rather complete summary of Luke's understanding of the meaning of the event of Jesus Christ. At the beginning of Jesus' ministry Luke presents to the reader in one representative scene the meaning which he sees in this whole event, thereby giving the reader the key to understanding what follows.

---

[63] Cf. Paul Schubert, "The Structure and Significance of Luke 24," 165–86.

Luke and Early Gospel Tradition

In the light of Luke's intentions and methods, we cannot assess the value of Luke 4:16-30 simply by asking whether these verses accurately reproduce words and events that took place at a particular time at Nazareth. Luke did not intend to simply inform his reader about a particular event at Nazareth. He intended to present to the reader the meaning which he saw in the whole event of Jesus Christ. In fulfilling this intention Luke remains in an important sense a "historian," for he is interpreting the meaning of an event in history. But the validity of his work must be judged not by whether he accurately reports particular events but by whether the meaning of the event of the life, death, and resurrection of Jesus, and the beginning and spread of Christian faith, taken as a whole, is significantly interpreted by this scene at Nazareth. In exploring this issue it is legitimate to ask to what extent Luke has emphasized themes that were already present in the early gospel tradition. This question is not identical with the question of the validity of Luke's interpretation, for it is possible for an insight to be valid even if Luke was the first to discover it. However, it is relevant to the question of validity, for such agreement would indicate that Luke's interpretation was not something artificial or foreign imposed upon the early material, but an elucidation of what, in some form, was already there.

The fact that a cluster of Lukan themes can be found in an Old Testament quotation is an indication of the strong role that tradition played in the development of Luke's theology. We see here not only the influence of Old Testament tradition, but also Luke's dependence on the tradition of the early church, for there is evidence that Isaiah 61 already had a place in the tradition concerning Jesus prior to Luke. In Luke 7:18-23, which is Q material, the answer that Jesus gives to John the Baptist, although it is not an Old Testament quotation nor completely formed from Old Testament materials, gains its meaning through recalling the prophecies of the time of salvation in Isaiah. Isa 29:18-19 and 35:5-6 are among the relevant passages, but the reference to πτωχοὶ εὐαγγελίζονται shows that Isa 61:1 is also in mind. Furthermore, there is some likelihood that Isa 61:1-2 has influenced Matt 5:3-4.[64] This agreement between Luke and the older tradition in the application of Isa 61:1-2 to the work of

---

[64] Cf. πτωχοί, πενθοῦντες, παρακληθήσονται.

Jesus is a reflection of the fact that Luke has built his own theological interpretation upon elements in the tradition. This is not surprising in a writer whose interpretation of the apostles shows that he is concerned with the question of authoritative tradition.[65] This does not mean that there are no important differences between Luke's views and those of the earliest church, nor that Luke is content to repeat what has been handed on to him. What we encounter in Luke 4:16-30, and other points in Luke–Acts, is a Lukan theological construction. However, it is a Lukan construction in which Luke picks up and emphasizes certain important aspects of the early tradition concerning Jesus, both preserving and transforming this material. Jesus' answer to John the Baptist, as well as other early synoptic tradition,[66] indicates that the early tradition already saw the signs of the arrival of the time of salvation in the words and works of Jesus. Luke makes this view basic to understanding the whole ministry of Jesus.[67] Early gospel material is already concerned with the forgiveness that takes place through Jesus' call of the sinner to share in the Kingdom and with the defense of this offer of mercy to the sinner against critics.[68] Luke makes the forgiveness of sins basic to his understanding of the whole event of Jesus Christ.[69]

The significance that Luke attaches to Jesus' ministry through the scene at Nazareth helps to explain several other aspects of his thought. First, Luke 4:16-30 helps to make clear that Luke is aware of the priority of God's grace for human salvation. The way in which Luke connects forgiveness with repentance seems to indicate that repentance is the condition for forgiveness.[70] However, Luke sets both repentance and forgiveness in the context of the action of God, who through Jesus

---

[65] Cf. Klein, *Die Zwölf Apostel*, 202–16.
[66] Luke 10:23-24 par.; Mark 2:18-19a; Luke 11:15-22 par. The present stands over against the past as something new and greater: Luke 11:31-32 par.; 16:16 par.
[67] It is possible that Luke 7:18-23 has directly influenced the development of Luke's scene at Nazareth by suggesting the interpretation of Jesus' ministry given there. Note that this pericope not only implies that Jesus' words and works are fulfilling the prophecies of the time of salvation, including Isa 61:1, but also ends by referring to the possibility of taking "offense" at Jesus.
[68] This comes out most clearly in some of the parables. Cf. Joachim Jeremias, *The Parables of Jesus*, trans. S. H. Hooke, rev. ed. (New York: Scribner, 1963) 124–46.
[69] Ulrich Wilckens, "Interpreting Luke–Acts in a Period of Existentialist Theology," in *Studies in Luke–Acts*, edited by Keck and Martyn, 65–68, also emphasizes the importance of noting points of contact between Luke's theological reflection and the synoptic tradition that preceded him.
[70] Cf., e.g., Luke 24:47, Acts 2:38.

announces and brings the time of favor, the time of forgiveness. Forgiveness takes place through Jesus or through his name, and is understood as a special opportunity of the time of salvation that Jesus brings. It is in response to Jesus' announcement of the time of God's favor that people may repent and receive forgiveness. This is made clear by placing this announcement at the very beginning of Jesus' ministry. Second, the significance that Luke attaches to Jesus' ministry explains why Luke was content to refer to the death of Jesus without interpreting it as an atoning death or giving it any special connection to the forgiveness of sins.[71] Here also Luke's view is dependent on older tradition, for the interpretation of the death and resurrection in Acts is related to an early tradition that understands these events as the rejection of Jesus by the leaders of Israel and his vindication in the face of his enemies.[72] Luke chose to use this pattern of thought because it fit his concern with the rejection of Jesus, and then of the gospel, by the Jews, and the turning of the church's mission to the Gentiles. But Luke could be content with this negative view of the death of Jesus because the gospel material provided him with an alternate interpretation of the saving significance of Jesus. There was no need to attach the possibility of forgiveness through Jesus to his death because forgiveness through Jesus was already a reality during Jesus' ministry, a fact that emphasis on the connection between forgiveness and Jesus' death might tend to obscure. In interpreting the event of Jesus Christ, the church had to come to terms with the tradition concerning his words and deeds. Paul gave little help in this respect, but Luke made a contribution. Picking up an aspect of the early gospel tradition, he made clear that the death and resurrection of Jesus do not stand alone as the saving event, for the ministry of Jesus was already an encounter between humans and the saving God. It is important to keep this in mind in contemporary theological reflection on the question of "atonement." Luke reminds us of it clearly and forcefully through the scene at Nazareth by which he interprets the whole mission of Jesus that follows.

---

[71] A few verses in Luke–Acts might seem to be exceptions to this statement. However, Luke 22:19b-20 is doubtful textually and, in any case, comes from the tradition rather than reflecting Luke's own emphasis; Acts 8:32-33 contains a quotation from Isaiah 53, but there is no reference to the significance of the suffering for others; and the reference to "blood" in Acts 20:28 is probably part of a traditional phrase that Luke thought appropriate to Paul. These verses do not carry much weight in light of the consistently negative interpretation of the death of Jesus in the mission sermons to Jews in Acts.

[72] Cf. U. Wilckens, *Missionsreden,* 111ff.

2
The Magnificat as Poem

This article was written while I was finishing my book The Sword of His Mouth: Forceful and Imaginative Language in Synoptic Sayings *(Philadelphia: Fortress; Missoula, Mont.: Scholars, 1975). In that book I studied synoptic sayings in light of their poetic and rhetorical form. I chose to work on the Magnificat because I wanted to experiment with a poetic unit that was somewhat longer than the short sayings that were my primary subject in* The Sword of His Mouth. *In both my study of synoptic sayings and in this article I am arguing that formal literary features are clues to the power and purpose of the language. The goal of interpretation, then, is not just to tell us what is being said (in plainer language) but to explain what is gained by saying it* in this way.

*I have discussed the Magnificat in later writings (*The Narrative Unity of Luke–Acts, *2 vols. [Philadelphia & Minneapolis: Fortress, 1986, 1990] 1.26–32;* Luke, *ANTC [Nashville: Abingdon, 1996] 53–57), where I place it in the context of Luke's infancy narrative. This important section of Luke is a developing disclosure of God's saving purpose in which the Magnificat has a special role, along with the other poetic hymns and angelic annunciations. However, the following article is my most detailed discussion of the poetic characteristics of the Magnificat, especially formal repetitive patterns that reinforce and expand the patterns of thought in this hymn.*

The following essay is an offshoot of a larger project, dealing primarily with the synoptic sayings tradition, which attempts to demonstrate the importance of studying the poetic and rhetorical form of a text.[1] In this essay I shall analyze certain features of poetic form in the Magnificat and attempt to show their significance for our understanding of this text.

In approaching this text it is helpful to recall the New Criticism's emphasis on the organic unity of a poem.[2] Within the context of a poem the meaning of a word is modified and enriched by intense interaction with other words. Words carry meaning not through direct, atomistic reference to objects outside the poem but only as part of the complex system of cross reference which is the poem itself. Within the poem words are closed off from their ordinary reference to the outside world. If the poem can nevertheless be a "window to the world," as Murray Krieger maintains,[3] it allows us to see the world only through itself as a complex, organic whole. The complexity and uniqueness of this window permits a unique vision of the world, which attacks our tendency to interpret the world through stereotypes.

While it is doubtful that this view of poetry is sufficient in itself to distinguish the language of literary art from other language,[4] it does point to a feature of language that is highly developed in poetry and contributes greatly to its power. In the following discussion of the Magnificat we shall be especially concerned with characteristics that promote such interaction of the parts, giving this poem a complex unity that makes its vision

---

[1] When this essay originally appeared, only one small part of the larger project had been published. See Robert C. Tannehill, "The 'Focal Instance' as a Form of New Testament Speech: A Study of Matthew 5:39b-42," *JR* 50 (1970) 372–85.

[2] For appreciative and critical discussion of this aspect of the New Criticism, see Murray Krieger, *The New Apologists for Poetry* (Bloomington: Indiana University Press, 1956); and *idem*, *A Window to Criticism* (Princeton: Princeton University Press, 1964).

[3] *A Window to Criticism*, 3–5.

[4] Context is important in all discourse, for words apart from context tend to be equivocal. Indeed, Stephen Ullmann asserts that "polysemy is a fundamental feature of human speech" and "far from being a defect of language, polysemy is an essential condition of its efficiency" *(Semantics: An Introduction to the Science of Meaning* [Oxford: Blackwell, 1962] 159, 167–68). In both discursive language and literary art, context provides a filter that selects from these multiple meanings. However, literary art tends both to maximize the contextual interaction between words and to employ the context-filter to produce more complex and subtle meanings. In discursive prose the context-filter commonly produces univocal meaning without depth, while in literary art some of the multivocity of words may be preserved, or even emphasized through reinforcing several meanings, and the connotative fringe of words may be maintained. This line of thought was suggested to me by a lecture of Paul Ricoeur.

distinctive. We shall be concerned with various forms of repetitive pattern, such as parallelism, rhythm, and strophic pattern. We shall also note the recurrence of certain words or word roots and the presence of sound patterns in certain verses. These repetitive patterns have various functions. They bring out links or contrasts between particular parts. Roman Jakobson reminds us that the constituents of a poetic sequence, because of the presence of "parallelism" (i.e., repetitive pattern), prompt "one of the two correlative experiences which Hopkins neatly defines as 'comparison for likeness' sake' and 'comparison for unlikeness' sake.'"[5] Repetitive patterns also retard the forward movement of thought, the common tendency to pass on quickly from one thought to another. By doubling back on what has already been said and expressing it in a new way, the text gains in intensity and depth.[6] Repetitive pattern may also encourage a feelingful participation in meaning. It invites hearers to step into the text with their whole selves, just as the rhythm of music invites us to join the dance, or at least to tap a foot. Thus repetitive pattern not only makes possible deepening of thought but also savoring of mood, helping the text to address the hearer at those levels where thought and feeling are not separate. We will also discover that these patterns unite contrasting elements or hold together what might seem to be separate. Thus the unity of the text is complex, a unity in tension. This forces us beyond the obvious and commonplace to a deeper meditation on the event being celebrated and awakens a sense of wonder that does not dissolve in being stated.

Although the question of the origin of the Magnificat has received much attention from scholars, it will not concern us here. I shall neither argue for a pre-Lucan origin nor attempt to reconstruct a Hebrew or Aramaic version of the poem. Those who wish to do so should note that there are certain formal features of the Magnificat that are dependent on peculiarities of the Greek language.[7] The fact that parallels to most phrases of the Magnificat can be found in various parts of the OT does not prove

---

[5]"Closing Statement: Linguistics and Poetics," in *Style in Language,* edited by Thomas A. Sebeok (Boston: Technology Press of MIT, 1960) 368–69.

[6]Luis Alonso Schökel contrasts the sequential ordering of thoughts in discursive, rational knowledge and the tendency of poetic apprehension to pause "in a kind of pleasant leisure," unfolding itself in a circular motion and so requiring repetition when it comes to verbal expression. See *Das Alte Testament als literarisches Kunstwerk* (Köln: Bachem, 1971) 250–51.

[7]See the discussion of vv. 51-53 below.

a pre-Lucan origin, for there is good evidence elsewhere of the evangelist's intimate knowledge of the LXX.[8]

The use of the language of tradition is not necessarily a sign that creative ability is lacking. Traditional language is language already heavy with meaning. It carries the weight of its use in the past, and skilled poets can awaken this past meaning and use it for their own purposes. In the case of the Magnificat, there seems to be a deliberate attempt to speak so that one always hears the echoes of the biblical tradition in the background. This act of praise gains in power because in it reverberate Israel's many acts of praise in response to God's deeds. For the purpose of this psalm, this must be so, since it wishes to celebrate the deed that fulfills Israel's hope.[9]

Parallelism and Coupling

Viewed in its narrative context, the Magnificat is like an aria in opera. The artistic conventions of opera allow the composer to stop the action at any point so that, through a poetic and musical development exceeding the possibilities of ordinary life, a deeper awareness of what is happening may be achieved. A similar deep participation in the meaning of an event is made possible by the placement of this poem in Luke's narrative. We must now examine the poetic form that makes this possible.

46 μεγαλύνει / ἡ ψυχή μου / τὸν κύριον
47 καὶ ἠγαλλίασεν / τὸ πνεῦμά μου / ἐπὶ τῷ θεῷ /
τῷ σωτῆρί μου

---

[8]See H. F. D. Sparks, "The Semitisms of St. Luke's Gospel," *JTS* 44 (1943) 129–38.
[9]It is possible that the Magnificat not only uses traditional language but a traditional genre. Hermann Gunkel thought so, classifying it as an "eschatological hymn." See "Die Lieder in der Kindheitsgeschichte Jesu bei Lukas," in *Festgabe von Fachgenossen und Freunden A. von Harnack: Zum siebzigsten Geburtstag dargebracht* (Tübingen: Mohr/Siebeck, 1921) 43–60. See, however, the criticism of Gunkel by Douglas Jones, "The Background and Character of the Lukan Psalms," *JTS* 19 (1968) 44–45. According to Jones the Magnificat is a psalm of mixed type, reflecting the disintegration of psalm types in the post-exilic period. See also Heinz Schürmann (*Das Lukasevangelium,* HTKNT 3 [Freiburg: Herder, 1969] 1.71), who speaks of a mixed form of eschatological hymn and personal thanksgiving but suggests that this may actually constitute a normal type.

48 ὅτι ἐπέβλεψεν / ἐπὶ τὴν ταπείνωσιν / τῆς δούλης αὐτοῦ.
   ἰδοὺ γὰρ ἀπὸ τοῦ νῦν / μακαριοῦσίν με / πᾶσαι αἱ γενεαί,
49 ὅτι ἐποίησέν μοι / μεγάλα / ὁ δυνατός.
   καὶ ἅγιον / τὸ ὄνομα αὐτοῦ
50 καὶ τὸ ἔλεος αὐτοῦ / εἰς γενεὰς / καὶ γενεὰς /
   τοῖς φοβουμένοις αὐτόν.
51 ἐποίησεν / κράτος / ἐν βραχίονι αὐτοῦ
   διεσκόρπισεν / ὑπερηφάνους / διανοίᾳ / καρδίας αὐτῶν
52 καθεῖλεν / δυνάστας / ἀπὸ θρόνων
   καὶ ὕψωσεν / ταπεινούς,
53 πεινῶντας / ἐνέπλησεν / ἀγαθῶν
   καὶ πλουτοῦντας / ἐξαπέστειλεν / κενούς.
54 ἀντελάβετο / Ἰσραὴλ / παιδὸς αὐτοῦ
   μνησθῆναι / ἐλέους
55 καθὼς ἐλάλησεν / πρὸς τοὺς πατέρας ἡμῶν /
   τῷ Ἀβραὰμ / καὶ τῷ σπέρματι αὐτοῦ / εἰς τὸν
   αἰῶνα.

The first two lines are synonymous parallelism, a traditional repetitive pattern of OT poetry. These lines immediately establish the mood of celebration, the use of repetitive pattern to express this mood, and the close relation of this text to Israel's acts of praise in the OT. Once this has been established, the Magnificat uses parallelism in a more flexible way. Verses 48a and 49a are synonymous in that they describe the same event, but they also suggest a contrast between the humble and the great. In v. 51 we also find two descriptions of one event. Here the second line carries the thought beyond the first, an example of what is sometimes called "synthetic" parallelism. Verses 52 and 53 contain strong antithetic parallelism. Note that parallelism does not pervade the whole of the Magnificat.

In parallelism a process of "coupling" takes place between corresponding words in the parallel lines. We should no longer hear these words separately but in their interaction with each other. Such couplings suggest other couplings, so that even where words are not strictly synonyms or antonyms, similarities and contrasts are brought out.[10] This interaction

---

[10]For a more complex theory of the role of "coupling" in poetry, see Samuel R. Levin, *Linguistic Structures in Poetry* (The Hague: Mouton, 1962).

between words encourages us to turn a thought over in our minds. Generally words slip past us too quickly. We absorb their conventional meaning and then pass on to something else. Poetry must slow us down and make us listen more carefully, so that we recognize the deeper meanings. The simple device of saying things twice involves a retardation of the forward movement of thought which gives place to deeper meaning, including the felt meanings that are important to our total humanness. The coupling of elements in parallelism also causes words to blend and modify each other. Synonyms are not simply synonyms. They differ in subtle ways, and the parallel lines contain significant variations, thereby bringing out different aspects of a thought, helping it to grow in richness of meaning.[11] This may loosen words from their literal sense, especially when they are coupled with other words that are not literally equivalent.

A few examples will suggest the significance of this coupling process for the Magnificat. By itself the term "humiliation" in v. 48 is somewhat vague. However, in the poem we do not encounter it by itself. The complex similarity and difference between vv. 48a and 49a,[12] signaled by the similarity between the beginning of the two lines, invites us to compare the other elements of these lines. This brings into prominence the contrast between the "humiliation" of the Lord's "slave girl" and the "great things" which "the mighty one" has done for her. This emphasizes the insignificance of the girl in comparison with God, and so the wonder of what has happened. Later we discover, however, that this word "humiliation" has additional meaning. In v. 52 there is a second reference to the "humble," this time in antithetic parallelism with "rulers." Thus the position of the humble is understood in terms of a two-fold contrast, with God and with human rulers. Both aspects are brought to the fore by coupling, adding richness to the thought. This in turn suggests a contrast between "the mighty one" (ὁ δυνατός) in v. 49 and the "rulers" (δυνάστας) in v. 52, a contrast invited by the similar sound of the words and emphatically developed in vv. 51-53. In vv. 52-53 we find two antithetic parallelisms that form an inverted synonymous parallelism (chiasm) with each other.

---

[11]According to James Muilenburg, synonymous parallelism "is in reality very seldom precisely synonymous. The parallel line does not simply repeat what has been said, but enriches it, deepens it, transforms it by adding fresh nuances and bringing in new elements, renders it more concrete and vivid and telling" ("A Study in Hebrew Rhetoric: Repetition and Style," in *Congress Volume: Copenhagen, 1953*, VTSup 1 [Leiden: Brill, 1953] 98 [97–111]).

[12]Verse 48b, which is parenthetical, will be discussed below.

This sets up a complex interaction of words that has the following effects, among others: the doubling of the antithetic parallelism is one sign of very strong rhetorical emphasis. The antithesis between (and within) the lines prevents us from thinking of the acts described as minor and temporary adjustments. We are forced to compare extremes, and so to think of a radical overturn of society. The parallelism between vv. 52 and 53 suggests that the reference to food in v. 53 is not to be restricted to its literal sense. Being filled with good things is a vivid instance of the exaltation of the humble and stands for everything else that the rich have and the poor lack.

Parallelism brings about such couplings between words in parallel lines. However, there are also other repetitive patterns within the Magnificat, as I shall show below. These bind the whole poem together and encourage us to note couplings beyond adjacent lines. For instance, both the sense and position of "his slave girl" in v. 48 relate it to "the Lord" in v. 46, a coupling that suggests that "Lord" is here given a specific application, making it something more than a formality. Thus the couplings within the Magnificat are quite complex. This complex interaction of words will be clarified further by what follows. However, the couplings noted above already suggest that the Magnificat contains a basic triangular tension, with the humble, the mighty God, and the oppressive rulers of the world forming the three corners. Many of the couplings in the Magnificat can be aligned with these three poles, or with the event that determines their relationship. This also means that the contrast between great and humble (or closely related words) forms a central axis within the Magnificat.

Strophic Pattern and Rhythm

The synonymous parallelism of the first two lines gives added weight to the introductory statement of praise. The rest of the poem is attached to this by the conjunction ὅτι, found in both vv. 48a and 49a. This suggests that there are two correct ways of viewing the structure of the entire poem. On the one hand, the first two lines form the introductory statement of praise and the rest of the poem states the reason for the praise by reciting God's marvelous acts. This accurately states the general structure of thought but ignores important formal characteristics that transform thought into poetry. Attention to these formal characteristics suggests that the hymn can also be divided into two strophes, vv. 46-50 and 51-55.[13] The larger part of both strophes consists of clauses with a strong action verb in first position (except for conjunctions). This emphasizes the verbs, gives vigor to the whole text, and marks off the clauses clearly. When verbs recur in the same position, a kind of rhythm of clauses develops, even though the clauses may vary somewhat in length. Verses 48b and 53 are exceptions to this pattern. Verse 48b is also unique in other ways, for this statement has no parallel in the rest of the text, although the reference to the "generations" suggests a certain link with v. 50. If it is an original part of the text, it is parenthetical and is so marked by the change in form. Both form and thought connect v. 53 with its context, but there is a special reason for the change in word order, as we shall see below.

The other seeming exceptions are actually part of a larger pattern, for vv. 49b-50 and 54b-55 correspond and serve to mark the end of the two strophes. If the clauses beginning with a verb continued throughout, no division into strophes would be apparent. However, such a division serves a purpose here. It marks off two aspects of the expanding thought, for the first strophe speaks of the meaning of God's act for the child's mother and the second of its meaning for Israel as a whole. Note that vv. 49a and 54a, which are immediately before the verses we are considering and so in comparable position in their strophes, refer, on the one hand, to "me" and, on the other, to "Israel." This does not mean that one of these two aspects is a secondary addition.[14] Indeed, the juxtaposition of these two aspects through the strophic pattern is central to the text's poetic vision, as we shall see below. Furthermore, the vigorous stress on God's action through placing verbs first in their clauses can lose its impact if carried on too long. The verbs in vv. 51ff. gain new vigor because they pick up the verb of v. 49a after intervening material of a contrasting type. In vv. 49b-50 there are no finite verbs at all, and the thought shifts from the particular act being celebrated to the perspective of the ages. By making it part of a larger pattern, the author was able to evoke this perspective of the ages, thus placing the birth of the child within the context of the history of Israel, its merciful God, and his promise, without ruining the pattern of

---

[13]Schürmann has also proposed this division; see *Das Lukasevangelium,* 1.70–71.

[14]Gunkel regarded v. 48 as secondary ("Die Lieder," 57–58). If this verse and the "for me" in v. 49 are removed, the connection with Luke's narrative setting vanishes. Schürmann, on the other hand, suggests that the second part of the Magnificat could be a secondary addition (see *Das Lukasevangelium,* 1.78).

the poem with its emphasized verbs. He accomplished this by placing the contrasting material at the end of each strophe, so that each strophe begins with vigorous verbs and then broadens its perspective, stepping back to view the panorama of the generations and sinking almost to a stillness at the end.

That vv. 49b-50 and 54b-55 were meant to correspond and so mark off the sections of the poem is shown by similarities of form and content. Both passages refer to God's mercy (ἔλεος) and relate this to the generations of Israel's history. In both passages there is a shift from the preceding use of strong, initial, finite verbs and a marked variation from the length of the preceding lines, thus deliberately interrupting the pattern that had been established.[15] It is true that there is no completely consistent pattern of line length in the poem. The author seems to have relied as much on the return of a verb in initial position as on line length to mark the lines and establish a sense of rhythm. Nevertheless, rhythm is a significant feature of the text, and this includes a rhythmic contrast between vv. 46b-49a, 51-54a and 49b-50, 54b-55.

Just as much of the vocabulary of the Magnificat is borrowed from the OT, so this rhythm is modeled on that of OT poetry. It can best be analyzed in the way that Norman K. Gottwald suggests.

> Meter, insofar as it exists in Hebrew poetry, is actually the rhythmical counterpart of parallelism of thought. Rhythm is not due to syllabic quantities but to the less definable instinct of balancing parts whose exact accentual values are not measurable and probably never were. . . .
> In Hebrew poetry regularity of stress is subordinated to regularity of balanced ideas. Thus the tendency to fill out lines with incomplete parallelisms by means of compensation . . . is due to the desire to oppose word-masses of about the same weight while varying and emphasizing the thought.[16]

In rhythmical analysis of this type of poetry we should keep in mind that "the basic unit of poetic composition is the line, which constitutes normally one half . . . of the parallelism. It expresses a complete thought

---

[15]The καθώς in v. 55 subordinates this verse to v. 54. Hence the following verb is not comparable to those in the preceding verses.

[16]*IDB* 3.834.

and has grammatical and syntactic unity."[17] The analysis should be guided
by

> the caesura or stop, both in its sharper form at the end of lines and in its
> feebler form within lines. The groupings that result from these breaks
> are essentially thought-units and the word-masses balance. . . . Parallelism
> of thought, and corresponding word-mass, is the substance and mode
> of Hebrew poetic expression.[18]

Thus the parallel lines of biblical poetry engender a rhythm of small
sense units in which a major word and its adjuncts rhythmically balance
other such units. The line, which is normally a complete sentence,
subdivides into small sense units that rhythmically correspond to those in
parallel lines even when they do not correspond in meaning. These small
units may vary somewhat in length. They are determined by two factors:
by the pressure which parallelism exerts toward balancing the small units
within parallel lines and by natural grammatical groupings within the
sentence.

Not only in the OT but also in the synoptic gospels we find passages
with marked rhythm, based not on a pattern of syllables or accents but on
parallel lines and balancing sense units within them. Here also the line
consists of a major syntactic unit and the rhythmic foot of a minor syntactic
unit so that a noun, a verb, or a participle forms the core of a foot and the
conjunctions, articles, prepositions, and generally the personal pronouns
attach themselves to these more important words. This leaves some
uncertainties in determining how the words of a line should be grouped,
but we are dealing with rhythm that is an outgrowth of parallelism and
for which there probably were no detailed or strict rules. We are least
likely to go astray in analyzing rhythm if we look both at the natural
syntactic units, consisting of an important word or an important word
and its adjuncts, and at the way in which parts of parallel lines correspond
to one another, suggesting certain divisions within the lines. The text of

---

[17]Ibid., 831.
[18]Ibid., 835. Cf. also Martin J. Buss, *The Prophetic Word of Hosea: A Morphological Study,* BZAW
111 (Berlin: Töpelmann, 1969) 45–46; Hans Kosmala, "Form and Structure of Ancient Hebrew
Poetry," *VT* 14 (1964) 423–45; C. F. Burney, *The Poetry of Our Lord* (Oxford: Clarendon, 1925)
59–62.

the Magnificat printed above has been divided into rhythmic feet on this basis.

The recurrent short lines of the Magnificat and the parallelism, which is especially marked at the beginning and in the antithetic lines of vv. 52-53, clearly suggest a repetitive pattern. It is natural to bring this out by reading rhythmically. This is especially true because the small units within the lines are natural sense units, so that the rhythm reinforces the meaning. Such rhythm has the same effect as the rhythmic beat of music. It involves us more fully in the experience of hearing. We respond not only with the mind but also with the feelings and the body. The text suggests that a more than intellectual response is appropriate, for its rhythm invites the whole person to step into its meaning. Furthermore, rhythm is one of the ways in which a poem asserts its own unity and particularity. Through its rhythm the poem separates itself from all language which does not conform to its rhythm, which is one sign of its underlying claim to be a unique vision of the world rather than an example of what we all know and say. This is important to the work of art, for it must resist our tendency to reduce all expression to the commonplace. Rhythm's role in both inviting full participation in meaning and in asserting the poem's individuality helps to explain the traditional importance of this aspect of poetic form.

The text of the Magnificat printed above shows that most of vv. 46b-49 and 51-54a falls into a pattern of three rhythmic feet per line. However, the pattern is not a rigid one. Verses 47 and 51b contain four feet each. Note that these are the second lines of their respective strophes and so balance one another. These longer lines slow the poem's pace slightly after the initial statements of each strophe, giving them added weight. Verse 52b is a short line of two feet. This quickens the pace of the poem at this point. Since vv. 52-53, as we shall see below, are the climax of the poem and since vv. 51-52 are dominated by violent images, this irregularity and acceleration seem to fit the sense and contribute to the poetic force of these lines. Verse 48b is rhythmically troublesome. Perhaps we should regard "for behold" as anacrusis to a line of three feet, as indicated in the printed text above. However, the initial words of this line seem to be deliberately interruptive, and the clause does not parallel adjacent clauses in form or thought, which makes it rather unrhythmical and signals the parenthetical status of this line.

While the lines just discussed vary the rhythmic pattern slightly, only to have it reemphasized by the following line, vv. 49b-50 and 54b-55 clearly depart from the pattern. They interrupt the previous rhythm, and they do so in the same way, placing first a clause that is too short, followed by one that is unusually long. The lines of the poem in vv. 46-49a and 51-54a consist of complete clauses, each with a single finite verb. We must judge the length of the lines in vv. 49b-50 and 54b-55 on a similar basis, rather than dividing natural syntactic units in an attempt to maintain a pattern of line length. In both vv. 50 and 55 we find a single long clause. There is no excuse for dividing these clauses into two lines each. Indeed, it is the *change* in line length in vv. 49b-50 and 54b-55 that is significant.[19] This change corresponds to a change in the use of verbs, for the finite verbs disappear in vv. 49b-50 and 54b. Thus vv. 49b-50 and 54b-55 resemble each other in both content and form and contrast with the verses preceding them. This means that the Magnificat as a whole follows a repetitive pattern consisting of a series of lines dominated by finite verbs in initial position with contrasting lines at the end (vv. 49b-50), and another such series brought to an end by vv. 54b-55.[20] Just as vv. 49b-50 and 54b-55 are related in meaning, so vv. 48a, 49a and 51-53 are closely related in meaning, as we shall see below. Thus the Magnificat goes through the same pattern twice, and it is proper to represent this by dividing the text into two strophes, the first of seven lines (vv. 46-50) and the second of nine (vv. 51-55).

---

[19]To be sure, there is a syntactic ambiguity in vv. 54b-55. It would be possible to regard καθὼς . . . πατέρας ἡμῶν as a parenthesis and to understand τῷ Ἀβραὰμ καὶ τῷ σπέρματι as datives of advantage with μνησθῆναι ἐλέους, which yields the sense: "To remember mercy . . . for Abraham and his seed forever." It might be argued that this makes better sense than "he spoke . . . to Abraham and his seed forever," for God did not speak directly to all of Abraham's seed and did not speak "forever." However, this is not strong, for Abraham's "seed" may refer to the other "fathers," or, more likely, to the fact that all Israel was addressed in the persons of their representatives, the fathers. "Forever" can refer not to the length of the speaking but to the length of time for which the spoken promise is valid. Furthermore, Luke uses both πρός with accusative and the simple dative with λαλέω. Indeed, with λαλέω and εἶπον he tends to shift from one construction to the other in the same context for purposes of variation. Cf. Luke 1:18, 19, 22; 1:34, 35; 2:15, 17, 18, 20; 6:8-10; 7:40, 43; 7:48, 50; 9:12, 13; 9:57-60; 10:26, 28, 29; 11:1, 2; 11:5; 12:13-16; 13:23. So it is unlikely that the change from πρός and accusative to the simple dative indicates a difference in grammatical function. Since the successive terms "our fathers" and "Abraham" are so closely related in meaning, it is natural to relate them grammatically and to see them as standing in apposition. Therefore, v. 55 forms one syntactical unit.

[20]In discussing rhythm in Isaiah, Alonso Schökel notes that a broadening of the rhythm is sometimes used to achieve a pause. Cf. *Das Alte Testament als literarisches Kunstwerk,* 150–51. This is the case in Luke 1:50 and 55.

Enrichment through Interaction of the Parts

In light of what we have discussed so far, we can begin to appreciate how various repetitive patterns bind the whole of the Magnificat into a tight unity and cause a complex interaction of the parts. These forms of repetition go well beyond couplet parallelism. The whole text is embraced by a repetitive strophic pattern that invites us to compare its two parts. The rhythm both encourages deeper participation and supports certain contrasts within the text. A complex interaction of parts also takes place through repeated use of the same words or the same word roots at various points in the text.[21] Even more important, however, is the way in which successive clauses, even though they are neither completely synonymous nor completely antithetical, pick up in different words something of the preceding clauses and so gradually enforce, enrich, and expand the thought.

This must be clarified through examining the development of the text, beginning after the introductory statement of praise. Verses 48-49a set the theme for the rest of the hymn but do so in a particular, limited way, focusing on the significance of God's gift of the child for his mother. This gives a sharp focus to the words but would seem to make them so personal as to lack relevance for other people. Readers here are listening in on someone else's song, a song in which they cannot directly share. The personal aspect of the introductory verses ("my soul," "my spirit") begins to stand out strongly in light of this marked personal reference of the verses that follow. This limitation to the child's mother does not continue throughout the hymn, for an important expansion of thought takes place. The special way in which vv. 48-49a are formulated provides the basis for this expansion of thought. Verses 48a and 49a both begin with "because" (ὅτι) and the verb. This formal relation supports a relation in meaning, for both refer to God's act in the gift of the child and they do so in a way that tends toward antithesis. "Humiliation" contrasts with "great things," and "slave girl" with "the mighty one." This tension between the lowly and the great gives these verses their power and points forward to a related tension in vv. 51ff. Verse 48b is the first indication that the event celebrated is significant for "all generations," which provides some preparation for

---

[21] Μεγαλύνει—μεγάλα, γενεαί—γενεάς, ἔλεος—ἐλέους, ταπείνωσιν—ταπεινούς, δυνατός—δυνάστας, ἐποίησεν—ἐποίησεν.

vv. 50 and 55. However, v. 48b preserves the personal reference: it is the mother's place of honor before all generations that is the cause for joy. In vv. 49b-50 the form changes, as we have seen, and this reflects a change in the thought. The perspective shifts from the very particular to the all-encompassing, from praise for God's special act for a humble woman to God's eternal holiness and his mercy for generations and generations. How these two perspectives are related is unclear at this point. The poem makes us wait.

In vv. 51-52 the verbs in initial position reappear. The connection with vv. 48a, 49a is quite deliberate. Verse 51a rephrases v. 49a, repeating the same verb (ἐποίησεν) and reemphasizing God's power. Verses 52b-53a develop the reference to the woman's humble station in v. 48a, and again there is a verbal link (ταπείνωσιν, ταπεινούς). Verses 51-54a double back on the thought of vv. 48a, 49a, speaking of the same event, reverting to the same form of sentence, and, in part, using related words. Yet there are also important changes. First of all, vv. 51-54a speak with full rhetorical power. What has already been said must now be said more strongly. It must resonate so that its importance is fully felt. A number of features of the text indicate this concern. Conjunctions are eliminated, which makes the verbs even more prominent and their rhythmic return even clearer.[22] Articles are eliminated, which makes the text more concise and forceful.[23] In v. 51 the words become stronger and more graphic (cf. "arm," "scattered") than in v. 49a, and it may be no accident that guttural *k* and *kh (ch)* sounds appear in the words that describe God's action against the proud,[24] for the harsh sound seems appropriate. Verses 52-53 are very carefully constructed. They are forceful, first of all, because they are antithetic, and the antithesis is much sharper than the suggested contrast in vv. 48a, 49a. Furthermore, the antithetic pattern is repeated twice, resulting in synonymous parallelism between the two verses. The link in

---

[22]There is a special reason for the exceptions in vv. 52 and 53. The conjunctions serve to indicate the special link between antithetic clauses, distinguishing them from the larger series of clauses.

[23]This is only partially explained by the generality of the meaning. For instance, we would expect articles with ἐν βραχίονι αὐτοῦ and Ἰσραὴλ παιδὸς αὐτοῦ. According to Blass-Debrunner-Funk (*A Greek Grammar of the New Testament* §259), this is due to "strong Semitic coloring." If so, it would still have the effect described above. However, can one maintain that vv. 51-54a are more "Semitic" than the rest of the Magnificat? On the contrary, there are features of vv. 52-53 which are dependent on peculiarities of Greek.

[24]Κράτος, βραχίονι, διεσκόρπισεν. Cf. καθεῖλεν (v. 52) and καρδίας.

thought between the two verses is carefully reinforced by formal links. A chiastic pattern is used, and the juncture of the two verses is strengthened by words of similar sound (ταπεινούς, πεινῶντας).[25] On top of that, we find a rhyme pattern (θρόνων, ἀγαθῶν; ταπεινούς, κενούς). All of this tightly unifies vv. 52-53 and makes them very forceful. Once again, this agrees with the pattern of thought, for vv. 52-53 are also the climax of the central thought which begins in vv. 48a, 49a and is progressively expanded. We can also understand now why v. 53 does not follow the dominant pattern of placing the verbs in initial position. Here other interests conflicted with that pattern. In v. 53 it is not the verbs but the words "hungry" and "rich" which carry the antithesis. Therefore, they are placed in the position of emphasis at the beginning of their clauses. At the same time, this makes possible the play of sound between the words at the juncture of the verses.

All of this means that the thought which is first expressed in vv. 48a, 49a increases in power in vv. 51-54a. At the same time it expands in breadth and resonates with deeper significance, which brings us to the second major difference between the two passages. Verse 51a does not really go beyond v. 49a except that the personal reference is removed. However, in v. 51b something new is introduced: God's mighty act is not only for the humble (v. 48a) but against the proud. In vv. 52-53 this thought develops into a sharp antithesis between the meaning of God's act for the mighty and for the humble, for the hungry and for the rich. Furthermore, the text is no longer speaking of the meaning of God's mighty act for one woman only. This act now embraces societies and their rulers, taking on eschatological dimensions. What has happened to the simple thought that the mighty God has done great things for a humble woman? Through the repetitive patterns that we have discussed, it has expanded to encompass God's social revolution through eschatological reversal, and the words announcing this have assumed the force appropriate to such a topic. This does not mean that the latter thought has replaced the former. Patterned speech makes words interact with each other, with a result that no part by itself could produce. The poem presents God's choice of the lowly mother and God's overturning of society as *one* act. It suggests an underlying qualitative unity between what appear to be separate events; for in both, God's surprising concern for the lowly is manifest. Thus the mighty God's regard for a humble

---

[25]By chance this can be mimicked in English translation: "*hum*ble, *hun*gry."

woman becomes the sign of God's eschatological act for the world. In that small event this great event lies hidden. The humble mother, the gift of the child, become images which resonate with all of the meaning of that child for people in God's eternal purpose.[26]

Although vv. 52-53 may be called the climax of the poem, as is indicated by the rhetorical force of these verses, neither the strophic pattern nor the thought is complete there. Verse 54a serves as a bridge to the final lines, for, although Israel has not been mentioned before, the final lines wish to speak specifically of Israel's promise. Then the pattern of the preceding verses is broken by vv. 54b-55, but only to complete the pattern of the whole and return to the thought of v. 50. Again we find reference to God's mercy, and again this is placed in the perspective of the generations. But here also the thought expands. In vv. 49-50 the thought seems to shift from a specific situation to general praise of God, leaving unclear the relation between God's mighty act for a humble woman and his mercy to "generations and generations." However, this relation is clear and specific in vv. 54b-55: the gift of the child is the act of mercy that fulfills the promise given to Israel at the beginning of its history. Thus this gift is placed within the context of Israel's long history of hope and is celebrated as its fulfillment, which makes explicit the significance of the poem's extensive use of traditional biblical language. The gift of the child gains in significance not only because the poem finds hidden there God's mighty act in which societies are overturned but also because it is placed within this perspective of Israel's history and hope. The former gain takes place through the juxtaposition of the two strophes; the latter through the contrasting lines which conclude each strophe.

Conclusion

A text which contains such careful patterns of repetition and contrast is striving for the organic unity of literary art, a unity which causes the

---

[26]The remarkable use of the aorist tense in vv. 51-54a to describe actions which, even for the Christian, are still largely future can be explained by the need of the poem to present the events described in vv. 48-49a and in 51-54a as one. In this way the text achieves its unique poetic vision in which the mother's personal experience is already a fulfillment of the earth-shaking events still to come. A change in tense at v. 51 would break apart what the text must hold together. Recall that v. 51a simply repeats the verb of 49a in order to establish the link clearly.

various parts of the text to interact so that one phrase enforces another and deepens its meaning. By establishing formal patterns that link the various elements and by doubling back on the thought, much meaning can be concentrated in few words. Through these formal features of the text the thought gains in impact and expands in significance. However, this is true only if the reader submits to the text's way of speaking. Readers must honor the unity of the text. They must allow line to interact with line and word with word, sensing their mutual reinforcement or the tension between them. They must feel the rhythm of returning thought and returning form, and savor the mood thus evoked. Careful analysis of details can sometimes awaken us to relations that we would otherwise miss, but the final goal must be hearing the text as a dynamic unity, a unity in which form and meaning are inseparable.

In its dynamic unity this text holds together the small and the great, the birth of a baby to an unimportant woman and the fulfillment of Israel's promise through the overturn of human society. By means of the text what would otherwise appear ordinary and insignificant becomes great with significance. In other words, the text enables us to see the mother and her baby as *signs*. They remain signs only so long as we understand them through the tensive unity of the text. We shatter this unity not only when we regard the mother and baby as ordinary but also when we completely remove them from the ordinary, giving them a special, superhuman status. The poem speaks of God's choice of the humble. If we lose an honest sense of the lowliness of these people, we will not be able to appreciate the wonder that the text proclaims. Furthermore, even for us the great things announced by the text are present only as sign. The eschatological reversal and the fulfillment of the promise are not simple realities apparent to all. We, too, see only obscure hints of great things hidden in the midst of the ordinary, and we are dependent on signs from the past to help us see them. The text presents us with such a sign. Its power as sign is dependent on the tensive unity of the text, which confronts us with the wonder of a particular event among humble people that has crucial significance for the ages. It is by the power of this sign that we can see signs in our own lives, but the text becomes false to our reality if we take it to be a simple statement of prosaic truth. The text's truth is inseparable from the tensive unity of its poetic language. We lose that truth when we ignore the text's form and dissolve this tension.

3

What Kind of King?
What Kind of Kingdom?

Luke's infancy narrative has been very important in my efforts to understand Luke–Acts as a continuous narrative, united by a consistent understanding of the saving purpose of God. In Luke 1–2 specific expectations of salvation for the Jewish people are aroused, including the expectation that Jesus will be the royal Messiah of David's line who will save Israel from its enemies. These expectations seem to conflict with the actual course of events. I dealt with this issue in my article "Israel in Luke–Acts: A Tragic Story" (included in this collection). Jesus' kingship, emphasized in some key Lukan scenes, is part of the problem, for Jesus does not look like a king in Luke. In "What Kind of King?" I consider the hypothesis that the course of the narrative invites us to revise our understanding of kingship and kingdom as they apply to Jesus. However, the revision does not rob these terms of meaning, for there are some concrete social policies that are distinctive of Jesus' rule.

The following discussion of Luke is the result of an effort to read this gospel holistically as a continuous narrative. This requires us to ask how the beginning sets up expectations and how these initial expectations are realized, not realized, or modified through a process of struggle and conflict. To understand fully any scene within this narrative, we must understand its relation to the rest of the narrative and its function within the whole.[1] When Luke is approached in this way, interesting insights are possible, and aspects of Luke that have been largely ignored take on new importance. Only a few of the results of this approach can be suggested here.

Literary Connections

This approach requires us to ask how the birth narrative prepares for the rest of the story. The birth narrative establishes a horizon of expectations for the rest of the story by telling readers in advance what John the Baptist and Jesus should accomplish to fulfill God's saving purpose. In this way the story sets up its own criteria for the success of Jesus' mission. It will be successful when God's purpose as defined in the birth narrative (and in Jesus' announcement in the Nazareth synagogue) is accomplished.

This way of reading Luke, however, may seem doubtful as soon as we recognize that Jesus in the birth narrative is primarily presented as the royal Messiah who fulfills the scriptural promises to the Jewish people. Although inclusion of the Gentiles is anticipated in Simeon's prophetic hymn (2:30-32), the main focus is on the Jewish people and their Messiah. Furthermore, the birth narrative seems to conflict with the actual course of events. Gabriel tells Mary that Jesus will inherit "the throne of David" and "reign over the house of Jacob forever" (1:32-33). Zechariah expands on this by blessing God for the "horn of salvation" that God has raised up "in the house of David" (1:69). Through this "horn of salvation" God will bring "salvation from our enemies" (1:71; see 1:74) and "guide our feet into a way of peace" (1:79). The theme of peace will be repeated in the birth narrative (2:14, 29), as well as later (see especially 19:38, 42). It should be understood in the broad sense of prosperity and harmony, a harmony both within Israel and between it and its neighbors. But this is not what actually happens to the Jewish people. The catastrophe of the Roman-Jewish war is only a few decades ahead. The reference to "salvation from our enemies" has often been understood vaguely by interpreters, who believe that it could not really indicate foreign oppressors like the

---

[1] For a detailed attempt to read Luke–Acts in this way, see Tannehill, *The Narrative Unity of Luke–Acts: A Literary Interpretation*, 2 vols. (Philadelphia and Minneapolis: Fortress, 1986, 1990).

Romans. But this vague interpretation requires removing these words both from the historical context in which they have been placed by the narrator and from the literary context of Luke, for the related reference to Israel's enemies in 19:43 (a prophecy of the Roman conquest of Jerusalem) shows that the Romans are indeed in view.

The Lukan scene of Jesus' approach to Jerusalem (19:37-40), followed by his words of lament over the city (19:41-44), should be understood in connection with the birth narrative. This passage looks back to the promises and expectations of the birth narrative and repeats a number of its key words. Jesus is again presented as the messianic king (19:38), and the accompanying celebration of peace recalls the angels' words to the shepherds (see 19:38 with 2:14). Now, however, Jesus laments Jerusalem's failure to recognize its opportunity for messianic peace (19:42). Instead of the anticipated "salvation from our enemies," the Roman "enemies" will destroy Jerusalem, because it will not recognize "the time of your visitation" (19:44; in 1:68 Zechariah also spoke of God's visitation). The scene of Jesus' arrival in Jerusalem looks back to the expectations of the birth narrative and indicates that these hopes will not now be fulfilled for Jerusalem because of its blindness. The hopes for the Jewish people and for a kingdom of peace under Messiah Jesus have taken a tragic turn away from the anticipated realization.

Transformed Expectations

What is the effect of these developments on the hopes and expectations of the birth narrative? They are not simply canceled, nor are they lost to the old Israel and transferred to a new Israel. Nevertheless, a significant transformation takes place. Luke affirms that Jesus does become king, being exalted to the right hand of God as ruling Messiah (see Luke 22:69; Acts 2:33-36). Yet his kingship is acknowledged on earth by a limited community. This community remains subject to persecution and extends itself not by the power of earthly kings but by a mission of repentance and conversion.

Narratives permit transformations of expectations. Resisting forces cause twists and turns not anticipated at the beginning. Yet the angels and prophetic men and women of the birth narrative were speaking of the saving purpose of God rooted in Scripture. Their understanding of God's saving purpose reaches to the theological core of Luke and cannot be simply laid aside because the way is hard. Expectations are transformed, but basic hopes persist.

In the terminology of narrative criticism—a recent development in gospel studies—Zechariah is a "reliable character" because his Spirit-inspired hymn (Luke 1:68-79) accurately conveys the perspective of the "implied author," i.e., the views and values affirmed in the writing as a whole. Nevertheless, as Robert Brawley has recently emphasized,[2] narrative commonly works by progressive discovery involving the revision of initial expectations and interpretations. The whole truth is not revealed at the beginning. Although we are expected to take Zechariah's words seriously as an accurate statement of God's saving purpose, they do not fully tell us what kind of king Jesus will be nor what kind of kingdom he will bring. They do not reveal the difficulties that must still be faced by Jesus and his witnesses in establishing this kingdom in a resistant world.

Persistent Hopes

We should try to define with some care what initial expectations are transformed and what initial hopes persist. The hope that the Jewish people will acknowledge Jesus as Messiah persists throughout Luke–Acts, in my opinion, although this view is contested by other scholars.[3] More central to the present essay is the contention that the social hope represented in the birth narrative by references to messianic peace for the Jewish people, including freedom from foreign oppressors and from the oppression of poverty (1:53), has continuing significance.

There is a problem here that should not be ignored. If the messianic kingdom does not arrive through massive acceptance of Jesus as Messiah by his own people nor by force of arms, does it not lose its social effect? In Luke Jesus' disciples are portrayed as having a problem at this point. The narrative emphasizes strongly that they are unable to understand Jesus' announcements of his coming rejection and death (see 9:44-45; 18:31-34). The travelers on the Emmaus road show that, for them, Jesus' death

---

[2] See Robert L. Brawley, *Centering on God: Method and Message in Luke–Acts,* LCBI (Louisville: Westminster John Knox, 1990) 44–51.

[3] See Robert Tannehill, "Israel in Luke–Acts: A Tragic Story," *JBL* 104 (1985) 69–85; Joseph B. Tyson, editor, *Luke–Acts and the Jewish People* (Minneapolis: Augsburg, 1988).

cancels the possibility that he would "redeem Israel," as anticipated in the birth narrative (24:21; see 1:68). The resurrection restores hope, but it does not complete Jesus' task, for the kingdom has still not been restored to Israel, as Jesus' followers remind him in Acts 1:6. The disciples, however, are expected to learn something important from the risen Messiah. They are expected to learn that it was "necessary that the Messiah suffer these things and [thus] enter into his glory" (Luke 24:26). Partly through a new understanding of Scripture (see 24:27), they are expected to learn God's way of working in a resistant world, namely, through allowing God's messengers to be defeated and then creating a victory that humans could not anticipate. They must learn that God works by irony; therefore, God's power is different than human power.

Moreover, the kingdom Jesus is establishing does not retain the structure of other kingdoms, with simply a change in the management. In its portrait of Jesus, Luke reveals a different view of community and of authority within it. Much of this is applied either to Israel or to the original disciples, yet it is significant also for the interim community that arises through the apostles' mission, the church. Therefore, Jesus' kingdom has a social realization even though hopes of social transformation for Israel and the world are largely unrealized.

The relevance of Jesus' teaching for the continuing life of the church is indicated by the fact that an apostle, according to Acts 1:21-22, must be prepared by teaching and experience to transmit the tradition of Jesus' life and teaching to the church. This tradition is not to be forgotten, for it provides the outline of the hidden Messiah's kingdom, the patterns and guidelines by which he intends to rule his community.

Features of the Kingdom

According to Luke, how does Jesus' vision of community differ from the usual patterns? What kind of kingdom is he establishing in the church, and through it, in the world?

First, the kingdom over which Jesus wants to rule must stretch to include people excluded by the holy people as previously defined. Those marginalized by poverty, gender, and purity rules must be included. Jesus brings sinners and tax collectors into his fellowship. This is part of the restoration of Israel to wholeness, as illustrated by someone like Zacchaeus, who, Jesus insists, is "also a son of Abraham" (19:9), a person who rightly belongs within the community of promise, the Israel that the Messiah will rule. This vision of restored Israel also provides guidelines for the church.

Second, the new kingdom requires a new economy. A persistent concern with the poor and a persistent call for a radical change in the rich are widely recognized as strong characteristics of Luke. Most interpreters would probably deny that this constitutes an economic program, but Halvor Moxnes has argued that the material on rich and poor in Luke does present an incipient "economy of the kingdom."[4] The command to "sell your goods and give charity" in 12:33 is part of this program. It may sound like an ordinary charity ethic of limited value. In Luke, however, charity is radicalized, for Jesus is not talking about the surplus that the rich can spare and still maintain their standard of living. According to Moxnes, Jesus in Luke is talking about "outright redistribution," and Jesus' commands to the wealthy are further radicalized by insistence that there be no expectation of return from the recipients (see 6:30, 34-35).[5] The last point is important in light of the prevalence of patron-client relations in ancient Mediterranean culture. The generosity of the patron bound the client indefinitely to be the patron's grateful supporter. Patronage was a way of gaining honor and a loyal retinue. Lukan thought assumes the social patterns of its time in picturing God as the supreme patron and benefactor of humanity, who should be God's loyal clients, but this patron-client relation is used to free persons from the patron-client relations that rich and powerful people use to maintain their status.

A third distinctive feature of the new kingdom appears in the way that community leaders are to function. In Luke the disciples have several persistent failings that bring them into conflict with Jesus. One of these appears in their disputes over who is the greatest. This problem surfaces in 9:46-48. It has not been solved even at the Last Supper, for in 22:24 the same sort of dispute occurs. This is a crucial problem, for the apostles gathered with Jesus on that solemn occasion will be the leaders of the new community. The way that they exercise their role will shape the community as a whole. In correcting them, Jesus first makes clear that the standard

---

[4] See Halvor Moxnes, *The Economy of the Kingdom: Social Conflict and Economic Relations in Luke's Gospel*, OBT (Philadelphia: Fortress, 1988).
[5] Ibid., 154–57.

pattern of kingship in the world will not do in his kingdom. "The kings of the nations are lords over them, and those in authority over them are called benefactors" (22:25), but Jesus insists that authority in his kingdom must be different. Kings may present themselves as generous benefactors, but they are using generosity and power as ways to the highest honor. They want to be *acclaimed* as benefactors. Jesus says, "Let the one among you who is greater become as the younger, and the leader as one who serves," for Jesus himself has taken this servant role (22:26-27). He is speaking specifically of those who wait on tables, as women and servants were expected to do. The point is not merely that the church's leaders should act for the community's benefit rather than using their authority for selfish purposes. Jesus' words disconnect the leadership role from the special honor that customarily goes with it. The leader is to have no more honor in the community than those who perform the lowliest functions. As Moxnes writes, "There is, then, a break with the patron-client relationship at its most crucial point: a service performed or a favor done shall *not* be transformed into status and honor."[6] Jesus also accepts the status of servant. This is demonstrated by his death in faithfulness to his mission, but that is not the end of the matter. The servant role is permanently inscribed in his identity, so that when the heavenly Lord returns to his faithful servants, he acts as he did before, assuming the role of servant to his servants (12:37). This is a distinctive kind of king and kingdom.

Finally, there is the area of foreign relations. Here, too, Jesus' kingdom is distinctive, for he insists on love of enemies. This theme is forcefully developed in 6:27-36. It is, perhaps, hard for us to imagine the author of Luke thinking that, had the people of Jesus' time actually accepted him and his surprising policies, the oppression of Jews by Romans and of the poor by the rich would have given way to the peace of the messianic kingdom. Our cynicism may be justified, but it may rest in part on a misunderstanding. Turning the other cheek is not a policy of submission to the oppressive status quo.[7] Those following this policy will be thorns in the flesh of the

---

[6] See Halvor Moxnes, "Patron-Client Relations and the New Community in Luke–Acts," in *The Social World of Luke–Acts*, edited by Jerome H. Neyrey (Peabody, Mass.: Hendrickson, 1991) 261; emphasis by Moxnes.

[7] Walter Wink has made this point. See "Neither Passivity nor Violence: Jesus' Third Way," in *SBLSP* (Atlanta: Scholars, 1988) 210–24; *idem*, *Jesus and Nonviolence: A Third Way*, Facets (Minneapolis: Fortress Press, 2003).

powers that be. Turning the other cheek is distinctly different than doing nothing or running from danger. Those who keep presenting their cheeks leave the oppressor no peace. They are testing how far the oppressor will go, at great cost to themselves. Eventually they rob oppressors of all legitimacy, even in their own eyes. Especially for the powerless, this is more likely to produce the "salvation from our enemies" of which Zechariah spoke (1:71) than taking up arms.

Our tendency toward passivity receives another jolt when we recognize what a missionary document Luke–Acts is. Luke presents God's saving purpose being realized through the mission of Jesus, as announced in the Nazareth synagogue (4:18-19). At the gospel's end Jesus tells his followers about their mission (24:47), and Acts focuses on crucial steps and central figures of that mission (not on the established church). The church that we know is a provisional arrangement, a group that will be transformed as the Messiah's task is accomplished. If God's purpose is defined as it is in Luke 3:6 ("All flesh will see the salvation of God," quoting Isaiah), God's primary concern is with the world, not the church. A church that has turned inward upon itself is unproductive. Luke–Acts presents a vigorous mission by prophetic figures who continually challenge the world to repentance and conversion. That mission is conducted "in the name of" Jesus (Luke 24:47; Acts 2:38), that is, under his authority and as a sign of his ruling power. But the missioners must not forget what kind of king they serve and what kind of kingdom he wishes to found. These are defined by Luke's story, which vividly presents the unrecognized king revealing through his words and actions the distinctive character of his kingdom.

4

The Lukan Discourse on Invitations

Although I emphasize the continuity of the discourse in Luke 14:7-24 in this essay, I also argue that the parable of the great supper in Luke 14:16-24 has been placed by the Lukan narrator in a double interpretive frame, suggesting two different interpretations of the parable. I am asking whether careful study of a text in its Gospel context still permits more than one interpretation of its message, a question that I will pursue further in some of the following essays ("Should We Love Simon the Pharisee?" "'Cornelius' and 'Tabitha' Encounter Luke's Jesus," "Freedom and Responsibility in Scripture Interpretation"), where I focus more on the role of the reader or hearer. In the present essay I also suggest how two different movements in recent biblical studies—use of literary theory and use of social-scientific theory—may function in a complementary way.

John R. Donahue's book on the parables gives serious attention to the setting and function of the parables within each of the gospels.[1] This is a welcome development, for parable interpreters have often seemed to assume that the use of the parables within the gospels represents a fall from the heights of Jesus' own speech. It is something to be noted so that we can move behind it. We should question this assumption and ask instead

---

[1] *The Gospel in Parable: Metaphor, Narrative, and Theology in the Synoptic Gospels* (Philadelphia: Fortress, 1988).

whether the way that a parable has been set within a particular gospel, rather than limiting and degrading the parable, may actually help it address the reader in a complex and challenging way. I believe that this is the case with Luke's great banquet parable (Luke 14:16-24), for the Lukan setting invites us to understand this parable from two significantly different perspectives.

The following essay can also be understood as an effort to show how two recent developments in biblical studies can be mutually illuminating. I refer to the strong interest in interpreting the Bible in light of literary theory, on the one hand, and in light of social-scientific theory, on the other. These have been independent developments, although some pioneering work has begun, in various ways, to merge the two perspectives.[2] The study of Luke is being affected by these two developments. I have participated primarily in the literary study of Luke[3] but have noted with interest recent studies of Luke from a social-scientific perspective.[4] The following discussion of Luke 14:7-24 illustrates the value of combining the two perspectives in exegesis.

The new literary criticism of the Bible has given birth to various reading strategies, some of which are no longer closely tied to the author's intention.[5] In the following discussion, however, I continue to be concerned both with literary signs of the author's perspective and with historical setting. I am attempting to read the narrative from the perspective of the "authorial audience." The authorial audience is the audience for which the work was originally designed by the author. Author and authorial audience share a set of social and literary conventions that guide reading. These conventions "serve as a kind of assumed contract between author and reader—they specify the grounds on which the intended reading

[2] See Vernon K. Robbins, *Jesus the Teacher: A Socio-Rhetorical Interpretation of Mark* (Philadelphia: Fortress, 1984); Norman R. Petersen, *Rediscovering Paul: Philemon and the Sociology of Paul's Narrative World* (Philadelphia: Fortress, 1985); Burton L. Mack, *A Myth of Innocence: Mark and Christian Origins* (Philadelphia: Fortress, 1988).
[3] See R.C. Tannehill, "Israel in Luke–Acts: A Tragic Story," *JBL* 104 (1985) 69–85; *idem, The Narrative Unity of Luke–Acts: A Literary Interpretation,* 2 vols. (Philadelphia & Minneapolis: Fortress, 1986, 1990).
[4] See Halvor Moxnes, *The Economy of the Kingdom: Social Conflict and Economic Relations in Luke's Gospel,* OBT (Philadelphia: Fortress, 1988); Jerome H. Neyrey, editor, *The Social World of Luke–Acts: Models for Interpretation* (Peabody, Mass.: Hendrickson, 1991).
[5] See the review and proposals of Stephen D. Moore, *Literary Criticism and the Gospels: The Theoretical Challenge* (New Haven: Yale University Press, 1989).

should take place."[6] Even attention to such reading conventions and to historical setting, however, cannot limit the possible reading effects of narrative to simple messages. The author's communication with the authorial audience is mostly indirect, through the medium of a story about other people. As a result, the author must renounce complete control of the significance of the narrative. Since the audience can relate to the persons and actions of the narrative in various ways, strict limits on the story's significance cannot be maintained. Furthermore, the narrator may use literary conventions to suggest that some of Jesus' teaching should *not* be understood in only one way. Such is the case, I believe, with the passage I am about to examine.

Luke 14:1-24 is a single scene, for events take place at a single location with no change of the persons involved. Jesus is invited to a meal in the house of one of the "rulers of the Pharisees." This meal becomes the setting for Jesus' discourse about being invited or inviting others to meals. Thus Jesus' discourse presents his reflection on the narrative setting. After the initial sabbath controversy, Jesus' comments fall into three segments (14:7-11,12-14,16-24), all focusing on invitations to a formal meal, a dinner party.[7] This thematic continuity binds the material together and suggests that the segments may mutually interpret and enrich one another. The theme of invitations is carried by the verb καλέω,[8] which occurs eleven times in 14:7-24. This verb is frequent in Luke–Acts, but it is usually employed to introduce a name or title (e.g., "he will be called . . ."). Apart from Luke 14:7-24, καλέω refers in Luke–Acts to an invitation to dinner or other social occasion only in Luke 5:32 and 7:39. In our passage this word is emphasized and announces the theme.

The introduction of the meal scene in 14:1-24 with a sabbath healing may seem strange. The man with dropsy, however, represents those persons to whom Jesus offers wholeness in spite of religious regulations that would

---

[6] On the value of the concept of authorial audience in literary studies, see P. J. Rabinowitz, *Before Reading: Narrative Conventions and the Politics of Interpretation* (Ithaca: Cornell University Press, 1987). Quotation from p. 43.

[7] X. de Meeûs notes how the atmosphere of a meal is sustained through the introductions to each of the segments of Jesus' discourse (14:7, 12, 15). See "Composition de Lc, XIV et genre symposiaque," *ETL* 37 (1961) 865 [847–70].

[8] A point noted by I. Howard Marshall, *The Gospel of Luke: A Commentary on the Greek Text*, NIGTC (Grand Rapids: Eerdmans, 1978) 581. See also C. F. Evans, *Saint Luke*, TPINTC (Philadelphia: Trinity, 1990) 566–67. Evans notes additional verbal links within the passage.

restrict his ministry. The man with dropsy is comparable to the sinful woman in 7:36-50, who also appears at a dinner in a Pharisee's house, disturbing the occasion. Thus the issue of ministry to such people, even when religious and social restrictions are violated, is made part of Jesus' discussion with Pharisees and lawyers in 14:1-24. This suggests that the man with dropsy may be a specific example of the "poor and disabled and blind and lame" who are mentioned later in Jesus' discourse (14:13, 21). Inclusion of such people in dinner invitations is an important concern of this discourse.

As presented in Luke, the material in 14:7-24 constitutes a little speech by Jesus in the setting of a dinner party. A number of interpreters have noted that the situation fits the Greco-Roman custom of the symposium, in which guests were expected to make speeches—whether humorous or serious—as part of the entertainment after dinner. This could be an occasion for philosophical discourse, and after Plato the symposium developed into a literary genre.[9]

The dinner party is hosted by "one of the rulers of the Pharisees" (14:1), and the other guests are "lawyers and Pharisees" (14:3). Since he is a "ruler" and is able to give a formal dinner party, the host is a person of high social rank and some wealth. Social rank is important in the three situations that Jesus describes in 14:7-24. This subject first appears as Jesus comments on the desire of the guests to get the "first couches" at the dinner. As Dennis Smith explains, the couches in the dining area "had traditional rankings assigned, so that one's position at the table indicated one's rank relative to that of the other guests. This was a regular factor that always had to be addressed at a formal meal: who is to be assigned the position of honor, the second position, and so on around the room."[10] Thus the issue of honor and shame and the social signals used to indicate rank are highlighted by Jesus' comment. He challenges the guests to break with the normal practice and deliberately choose the lowest place. An elevation in status is promised as a reward, and this promise is supported by the

---

[9] On Luke and the symposium see de Meeûs, "Composition," 847–70; J. Ernst, "Gastmahlgespräche: Lk 14,1-24," in *Die Kirche des Anfangs: Festschrift für Heinz Schürmann zum 65. Geburtstag,* edited by Rudolf Schnackenburg et al. (Freiburg: Herder, 1978) 57–78; E. Springs Steele, "Luke 11:37-54—A Modified Hellenistic Symposium?" *JBL* 103 (1984) 379–94; Dennis E. Smith, "Table Fellowship as a Literary Motif in the Gospel of Luke," *JBL* 106 (1987) 613–38.
[10] "Table Fellowship," 617.

maxim "Everyone who exalts himself will be humbled, and the one who humbles himself will be exalted."[11] The use of πᾶς makes this a sweeping claim that ignores the uncertainties of human affairs, hinting already at a more important exalting and humbling, that which takes place before God. This maxim reappears in 18:14, where it clearly refers to one's standing before God, and God's reversal of human claims to greatness is also emphasized by the similar maxim in 16:15: "That which is exalted among humans is an abomination before God."

In Luke the scribes and Pharisees are accused of seeking honor from humans. Mark Powell describes self-righteousness as the "root character trait" of the religious leaders in Luke.[12] Their claim to righteousness is a claim to honor in society. It is righteousness "before humans" (16:15). The narrator also introduces a story about a Pharisee by referring to "some who trust in themselves that they are righteous and despise others" (18:9). The latter reference indicates that such claims for oneself are based on degrading others. The Lukan portrait of the scribes and Pharisees also associates them repeatedly with a desire for public signs of honor. According to 11:43 the Pharisees "love the first seat in the synagogues and greetings in the market places." The scribes and Pharisees choose the first couches at the dinner party in 14:7. The specific accusations of both 11:43 and 14:7 are repeated in 20:46, where the scribes are accused of "loving greetings in the market places and first seats in the synagogues and first couches at the dinners." These words are addressed to the disciples (with the people listening), who are being warned to "beware of (προσέχετε ἀπό)" the scribes who act in these ways. The accusation of the Pharisees in 11:43 is also followed by a warning to the disciples in 12:1: "Beware for yourselves of the leaven of the Pharisees, which is hypocrisy." In Luke the disciples, too, are infected with a desire to be recognized as first, and they squabble over rank.[13] Part of the purpose of pointing to the scribes and Pharisees' desire for social recognition is to warn the disciples not to act in this way. The scribes and Pharisees have largely become stereotypes because they

---

[11] On the thematic use of "bi-polar reversal" in Luke (in both aphorisms and larger texts), see John O. York, *The Last Shall Be First: The Rhetoric of Reversal in Luke*, JSNTSS 46 (Sheffield: JSOT Press, 1991).

[12] Mark Allen Powell, "The Religious Leaders in Luke: A Literary-Critical Study," *JBL* 109 (1990) 95 [93–110].

[13] See Tannehill, *Narrative Unity*, 1.254–57.

are being used rhetorically as negative examples of what the audience should avoid.[14] It is noteworthy that the Pharisees in Luke are also accused of being "lovers of money" who scoff at Jesus' teaching about wealth (16:14). Jesus must warn the disciples and the crowd of the danger of the same entanglement with wealth.[15]

Jesus' teaching at the banquet in Luke 14 is addressed to people of wealth and high status. Both their status and their wealth are significant factors in Jesus' response. Furthermore, the connection between Jesus' criticism of the scribes and Pharisees and his warning to the disciples should alert us to the possibility that Jesus' teaching at the dinner has a double function: it is social criticism of dominant classes in Jesus' society, as the Lukan author understood that society; it is also instruction and warning to members of the Christian community who may have to choose between their social advantages and the call to follow Jesus. This double function will be confirmed by the material surrounding the parable of the great banquet in Luke 14 (to be discussed below). It is important to keep both functions in mind throughout our reading of 14:7-24.

In 14:12-14 Jesus turns from the guests to the host and instructs him on the proper guest list for his dinner parties. The sentences fall into the same pattern as in 14:8-11: "When you . . . , do not . . . , lest . . . , but when you . . . , [positive command followed by a promise], for [rationale for the promise]."[16] In both instances of the pattern, a negative command is followed by a contrasting positive command, resulting in the reversal of behavior that supports the positions of those with high status. Since both of Jesus' comments concern dinner parties, content as well as formal pattern encourage us to consider the two situations together.

In both situations Jesus advocates behavior that sharply conflicts with the social code of ancient society. Guests did not necessarily choose the first couches, since they were probably aware of their rank in comparison with others, but they did not choose the last place if they could do better. In 14:12 Jesus describes the common practice of choosing guests for an

---

[14] See Moxnes, *Economy,* 152. See also Brian E. Beck, *Christian Character in the Gospel of Luke* (London: Epworth, 1989) 131: "Luke has fashioned the Pharisees, who already had a negative image in Christian tradition, so that they embody those faults to which he believes his Christian readers are prone."

[15] See Tannehill, *Narrative Unity,* 1.129–32.

[16] de Meeûs notes this pattern; see "Composition," 868.

important dinner, and it is assumed that the guests at the present dinner were chosen in this way: they are mainly friends, family, and rich neighbors. Instead, Jesus advocates inviting the "poor, disabled, lame, blind." This would conflict with a primary function of a formal dinner in an elite household. One's position as a member of the elite is proclaimed and maintained by receiving invitations from others in this class and having them accept one's invitations in return. The guest list is an important matter, for the invitation is a sign of status. Through mutual invitations the special standing of the elite is maintained. Social obligations are also involved, for accepting an invitation from someone else may obligate the recipient to make a reciprocal invitation. Jesus refers to this social practice at the end of v. 12.

Richard Rohrbaugh, applying a socio-economic model of the ancient urban system, asks us to look at the situation in light of a class system controlled by the urban elite.[17] Class distinctions were clear and rigid. Commenting on the host in the parable of the great banquet, Rohrbaugh says, "A member of the urban elite took significant steps to avoid contact with other groups except to obtain needed goods and services. Such a person would experience a serious loss of status if found to be socializing with groups other than his own."[18] The same would apply to the host addressed by Jesus in 14:12-14. Jesus' words are challenging not primarily because the host is asked to expend a significant amount of money on the poor but because the poor are to be invited to a dinner party in place of members of one's own family and social class. Such strange behavior would both undermine the system of balanced reciprocity by which the host's status is maintained and bind him to a group that would degrade him. The issue of social status, introduced in 14:7-11, is still in the foreground, and it may well be that the maxim in v. 11 applies both to what precedes and what follows it. Those who invite other members of the elite are exalting themselves because they are reinforcing their own position in this

---

[17] Since the excuses in 14:18-19 have to do with agricultural affairs, interpreting the parable in light of a model of the ancient city might seem inappropriate. Rohrbaugh explains that the ancient city and the surrounding agricultural land were part of one system, in which the city was the center of control. The produce of the countryside was exploited by the urban elite, who owned much of the land outside the city; see "The Pre-industrial City in Luke–Acts: Urban Social Relations," in *The Social World of Luke–Acts*, edited by Jerome H. Neyrey (Peabody, Mass.: Hendrickson, 1991) 129–37, 143.

[18] "Pre-industrial City in Luke–Acts," 136.

group. Those who invite the poor and disabled are humbling themselves by associating with them. It could cost them their positions in their families and social class.[19]

A transition in Jesus' discourse is introduced through a remark of one of the other guests: "Blessed is whoever will eat bread in the reign of God" (14:15). This remark is linked to v. 14, where Jesus indicated that the one who invites the poor will be blessed. It would be possible to read the remark in v. 15 as a sign of the guest's discomfort with Jesus' statement, expressed through the counter-assertion that *whoever* shares in the banquet of God's reign is blessed.[20] But the primary function of v. 15 may simply be to shift the level of discussion by explicitly linking banquet invitations to the banquet of God's reign. Thus a well-known religious symbol is introduced as a hermeneutical key to Jesus' discourse. This has both a preparatory and a retroactive effect. It prepares us to interpret the parable that follows, and it invites us to reread the preceding instruction of Jesus in light of invitations to God's banquet.[21] Nevertheless, the application of 14:7-14 to human banquets is not to be lost.

We should consider v. 15 along with v. 24 as an interpretive frame placed around the parable. There is also a larger interpretive frame, as we will see, constituted by 14:7-14 and 25-33. This double interpretive frame helps to give the parable of the great banquet a rich complexity of meaning in Luke. We are invited to hear the parable from several significantly different perspectives.

Verse 15 leads us into the parable by reminding us of the coming banquet in God's reign. Many interpreters who recognize that this introductory verse is Lukan redaction still accept this clue and interpret the parable accordingly. It may well be appropriate to do so, even if we are seeking the meaning of the parable at a pre-Lukan level. Bernard Brandon Scott has suggested that Jesus in his parables "employed stereotyped plots and characters," drawing upon "elements of a traditional thesaurus." In the case of the great banquet parable, the "operative mytheme" is that

---

[19] Moxnes sees 14:12-14 as a basic challenge to the economic system, for the two ways of practicing hospitality represent "two totally different modes of exchange: reciprocity between equals, and redistribution from the rich to the poor." *Economy of the Kingdom,* 129.

[20] See Marshall, *Luke,* 587.

[21] Since the eschatological meal in God's reign, involving a reversal of the expected guests, is presented in 13:23-30, we can also say that 14:15 reinforces an association previously established in the narrative.

"the meal stands for the kingdom."[22] Telling a story enables the traditional material to enter new configurations. A religious teacher of Jesus' time and place who told a story about a master who gives a banquet could probably expect the audience to interpret it in terms of the banquet in God's reign. The teacher could use this expectation, however, to undermine other expectations (e.g., concerning the participants in that banquet) through a surprising twist in the story. This observation relates to the debate about so-called "allegorical" elements in the parables of Jesus. Certain stereotypical identifications are probably presupposed, but these enable the parable to work as a parable. They provide the horizon of expectation that the parable can rework to produce unexpected results.

In any case, the parable of the great banquet in its Lukan setting is introduced by a reference to eating in God's reign.[23] This introduction sets up a particular way of hearing the parable. Since it has to do with the banquet in God's reign, God is the one who is giving the banquet, and the crucial question is who will attend. The parable asks us to compare two different groups in considering this question: a group with property and family responsibilities who, although invited, refuse to come, and a group of beggars who could never expect to attend an important dinner party and yet are invited. The hearer is asked to identify with one of these two groups, and that will determine whether the parable is bad news or good. This identification, however, is not exactly a matter of free choice, for the two groups have clear social profiles: the one group has property and a social status appropriate to grand dinner parties; the other group consists of beggars off the street and outcasts.

That Jesus, too, might be understood as the host of this banquet does not essentially change this way of hearing the parable, for Jesus in this case functions as God's representative. The central issue is still whether one will attend this banquet or not. This issue is highlighted by v. 24 at the end of the parable, which works together with v. 15 to produce the interpretation just mentioned. As frequently noted, v. 24 is puzzling, for

---

[22] *Hear Then the Parable: A Commentary on the Parables of Jesus* (Minneapolis: Fortress, 1989) 18, 172. According to Scott, Jesus' parable subverts the expectations aroused by this mytheme.

[23] This appears, to be sure, in a statement by an anonymous character who has been given no signs of authority by the narrative. (On the issue of when narrative characters represent the views of the narrator or "implied author," see Tannehill, *Narrative Unity*, 1.6–8.) Nevertheless, Jesus in his response does not reject a concern with eating in God's reign. Rather, he tells a story that undermines the guest's assurance that he will be among those sharing in this banquet.

"those men invited" must refer to the first group in the parable, and "my dinner" would appropriately refer to the master's dinner in the parable (see "my house" in v. 23). Yet the "you" in "for I say to you" is plural. We must either imagine that the master is speaking to those brought from the streets to the banquet, as well as to his servant, although v. 23 mentions only the servant, or v. 24 is a concluding statement by Jesus to his audience in the Pharisee's house. Neither view fits easily into the context, the former because of a plural "you" unjustified by the narrative setting, the latter because Jesus would be suddenly introducing a reference to his own dinner. However we solve this problem, v. 24 clearly focuses attention on the exclusion from the banquet of those originally invited. It underscores the fact that they have lost their chance. If the parable has to do with the banquet in God's reign, they have lost their chance for something very important. Thus the parable becomes a warning to such people. We can add, of course, that the parable is also a gracious invitation to street beggars and the outcasts from the city.[24] Verses 15 and 24 work together as a frame that encourages interpretation along these lines.

This interpretation fits the larger Lukan narrative. Jesus is speaking in the home of a ruler of the Pharisees who has invited a group like himself to a dinner party. Jesus is frequently in conflict with such scribes and Pharisees. Their resistance to Jesus' message makes it appropriate to warn them by telling a parable about those who turned down an important invitation. The fact that those who make excuses are people of property and are concerned about its management (see vv. 18-19) also fits the Lukan portrait of the Pharisees, who are accused of being "lovers of money" (16:14). The parable does not mean that the fate of the Pharisees addressed by Jesus in Luke 14 is already fixed. Those who refuse the invitations in the parable are excluded; whether the Pharisees addressed by Jesus have finally refused is an open question, even though the general portrait of Pharisees in Luke does not encourage optimism.[25] Furthermore, the narrative offers other possibilities for identifying those who refuse the invitation. Right before the dinner scene in Luke 14, Jesus was lamenting his impending rejection in Jerusalem. The Pharisees have a very small role

---

[24] Robert W. Funk rightly emphasizes that the great supper is both a parable of judgment and of grace; see *Language, Hermeneutic, and Word of God* (New York: Harper & Row, 1966) 191–92.
[25] Here I am ignoring the references to Pharisees in Acts, which give a more favorable impression of this group.

in the Jerusalem events, being mentioned only at 19:39, but the refusal of Jesus' invitation by Jerusalem and its authorities has a major place in the Lukan narrative.

It is equally easy to identify the "poor and disabled and blind and lame" of the parable with people to whom Jesus ministers, for Jesus' good news to the poor and healing of the disabled are prominent features of the Lukan story. The list in 14:21, in fact, includes the first, second, and last of the list of persons who are the focus of Jesus' ministry according to 7:22. The summary of Jesus' ministry in 7:22, in turn, is confirmation that Jesus is performing the ministry announced in the Nazareth synagogue (4:18).[26]

It is important to notice that the contrast established in the parable is not between self-righteous religious leaders and sinners but between people of property and social rank, on the one hand, and the poor and disabled (people who must resort to begging in the streets), on the other.[27] Thus the issue in Luke 14 is somewhat different than in Luke 15, which begins with a reference to Pharisees and scribes objecting to association with toll collectors and sinners. To be sure, the religious leaders and the people of social rank are overlapping groups in Luke, as are, probably, the poor and the sinners, but the issue of social and economic class is emphasized in 14:7-24.

The Lukan context, however, encourages a second reading of the great banquet parable from a different perspective. While, as we have noted, v. 15 is linked to v. 14 by repetition of the word "blessed" (μακάριος), the great banquet is also linked to v. 13. The four groups that the host in the parable invites (v. 21) are the same groups that Jesus instructs his host to invite in v. 13.[28] The connection with Jesus' instruction in 14:12-14 requires reading the great banquet parable in quite a different way. The issue now is not who will attend the banquet in God's reign. The issue is, rather, who should people of social rank invite to their dinner parties. The host is

---

[26] See Tannehill, *Narrative Unity,* 1.79–81.

[27] In v. 23 the servant is also sent to those outside the city. It is possible that Luke's author and first readers thought of Gentiles at this point, but this is not the only possibility. Rohrbaugh argues that this invitation shows good knowledge of the ancient city. The area immediately outside the city was inhabited by certain outcast groups who were not allowed to live within the city, although they performed certain services for its population. See Rohrbaugh, "Pre-industrial City," 144–45. The invitation in v. 23 also demonstrates the master's determination to have his house filled.

[28] Furthermore, the word ἀνάπειρος occurs only in these two verses in the New Testament, as Herman Hendrickx notes; see *The Parables of Jesus,* rev. ed. (San Francisco: Harper & Row, 1986) 118. The list in 14:21 clearly echoes the one in 14:13.

addressed by Jesus in 14:12-14, and the following parable can be read from the perspective of a first-century host who is being encouraged to flaunt the rigid social rules of his society. Noting the connection between vv. 13 and 21 is nothing new, but interpreters have tended to see here Luke's attempt to "moralize" the parable[29] (an attempt that should be dismissed in order to get at the parable's real meaning), or they simply comment that in vv. 12-14 the host is being told to act as God acts in the following parable.[30] The latter comment ignores the fact that the great banquet parable itself can be understood from a different perspective if we take its connection to vv. 12-14 seriously.

Recently Richard Rohrbaugh has shown that the great banquet parable conveys a message of great challenge when read in light of 14:12-14. Discussing the great banquet in light of the class system of the pre-industrial city, he explains that the original invitations would have gone only to known persons whose social rank could be carefully scrutinized. The elite did not socialize with people they did not know. Those among them who did would be immediately and permanently ostracized because they could not be trusted to protect the system. We come then to what this story is really all about: a member of the elite, a host, making a break with the "system" in the most public and radical sort of way.[31]

Although 14:12-14 is directed to a ruler of the Pharisees, Luke intends Jesus' message to apply especially to rich Christians, according to Rohrbaugh. He rightly points to 14:25-33 to justify this application. To be sure, the scene changes in 14:25. Jesus is now addressing the crowds about the demands of discipleship. Nevertheless, there is thematic continuity with 14:12-24. In v. 26 Jesus states that discipleship requires hatred of one's family, including one's wife. In v. 20 one of those invited excuses himself from the banquet because of his wife. In v. 33 Jesus states that discipleship requires saying farewell to all one's possessions. In vv. 18-19 people excuse themselves because they must attend to their possessions.[32]

---

[29] See John Dominic Crossan, *In Parables: The Challenge of the Historical Jesus* (New York: Harper & Row, 1973) 71.
[30] See Walter Grundmann, *Das Evangelium nach Lukas,* THKNT 3 (Berlin: Evangelische Verlagsanstalt, 1961) 294–95; Gerhard Schneider, *Das Evangelium nach Lukas, Kapitel 11–24,* ÖTK 3/2 (Gütersloh: Mohn, 1977) 315.
[31] Rohrbaugh, "Pre-industrial City," 145.
[32] C. F. Evans rightly points out that there are major problems with the view that the excuses in vv. 18-20 reflect the grounds for exemption from holy war in Deut 20:5-7; 24:5; see *Luke,* 574.

Thus Jesus' comments on discipleship in 14:26-33 can be understood as indication that the preceding parable is not only social criticism of rich Pharisees and lawyers but also a warning that any with ties to possessions and family may have to abandon them in order to share in the banquet of God's reign.

It is also important to note that Jesus' discipleship teaching in 14:26-33 is related to the instructions to the host in 14:12-14. These instructions introduce into the context the problem of attachment to family and rich society that continues through the parable of the great banquet and the following discipleship teaching.[33] They also provide a specific indication of why hatred of family (v. 26) and abandonment of possessions (v. 33) may be necessary. Business and family affairs are not simply a distraction, as the excuses in vv. 18-20 might seem to indicate. Followers of Jesus should not count on attending the party first and then caring for business and family. A choice must be made, for breaking the social code by inviting the poor and disabled to one's parties can destroy family ties and cause the loss of the wealth one gains from family position.

Jesus instructs his host in vv. 12-14 to invite the poor and disabled instead of his family and rich neighbors. But what happens to one's family ties, and one's share in the family wealth, if one invites the poor instead of one's family and those approved by them? In 14:12-14 Jesus is not simply instructing the host to give charity to the poor, which might gain honor for the donor and his family, but to invite the poor and disabled to an important social occasion, thereby giving them the honor normally reserved for family and social peers. Furthermore, the use of present-tense imperatives indicates that this is to be a continuing practice, not a single event. The result could be precisely what Jesus demands in 14:26-33, a firm break with one's family and the abandonment of one's wealth. Thus it is not only the connection between v. 13 and v. 21 that leads us to view the great banquet parable as the story of a wealthy, upper-class person who is willing to abandon class privileges and identify with the poor, thereby demonstrating radical discipleship. The teaching segments in 14:12-14 and 14:26-33 can work together to provide an interpretive frame for the parable that highlights this issue.

---

[33] Evans states that "brothers" and "relatives" in v. 12 are not a natural antithesis to the poor and disabled in v. 13, but these references to family members do prepare for v. 26; see *Luke,* 571.

The conflict of discipleship with family and wealth would be especially acute for persons who came from elite and wealthy families, for becoming involved in the Jesus movement meant associating with people of low status, an offense against the system from which their families benefited. As Jesus indicates in vv. 28-32, such persons must seriously consider whether they can carry through with their initial decision to follow Jesus, for it will surely lead to conflict with family and loss of possessions.

Jesus' teaching in Luke 14, then, is both social criticism of dominant groups in society (represented by the ruler of the Pharisees addressed in 14:12-14) and a sharp challenge to disciples or potential disciples (as in 14:25-33), with this challenge being most difficult for people from elite families. In this interpretive frame the parable of the great banquet becomes the story of a man who was not at first prepared to face social ostracism but encountered it nevertheless. Then he chose to renounce the privileges of his social class and identify with the poor, as Jesus instructed the host in 14:12-14.

Rohrbaugh suggests that the shaky social position of rich Christians might lead to attempts to solidify their social standing by inviting family and elite friends to a banquet. "As a way of reassuring their friends that they had not broken faith with the system, they would invite only the right people."[34] Luke 14, then, would warn of the danger of such attempts and urge Jesus' followers to be willing to pay the full cost of discipleship.

Not only does this reading make sense in the context of Luke 14; it also fits the broader Lukan concern with the need of the rich to renounce their property and helps us understand the social consequences of Jesus' teaching in Luke. Furthermore, it explains one aspect of the parable that is usually not explained. All the previously invited guests change their minds when the servant announces that the banquet is ready. This is very surprising. In the usual interpretation of the parable, this surprise is simply accepted as a way of setting up a conflict situation, forcing the host to take action. Rohrbaugh, however, is doubtless correct that the sudden decision to excuse themselves by all the previously invited guests indicates a coordinated act of ostracism.[35] The host is being informed that he is no longer socially acceptable. The parable story does not tell us why, but Rohrbaugh's description of the shaky position of elite persons attracted to

---

[34] "Pre-industrial City," 146.
[35] Ibid., 141–43.

the Jesus movement indicates how this could happen. It could be a strong sign of disapproval of one's association with this movement and its lower-class members. In the parable the host decides to ratify the break with the elite by a dramatic act of identification with the poor and outcast. This was not his original plan; therefore this host is not a very good representative of a God who is always concerned with the poor. The host's invitation to the poor is his way of dealing with the social problem that he faces. It is only through an unpleasant experience of social controls that this host is led to obey Jesus' instruction in 14:13 to invite the poor, disabled, lame, and blind.

The connection of the parable with the maxim in 14:11 should also be noted. At first the host was trying to exalt himself by giving a party that would confirm his own place among the elite; as a result he was humiliated. Then he chose to humble himself by publicly identifying with the poor and outcast.[36] We should note, however, that 14:11 can also be related to the parable if it poses the question of who will attend the banquet in God's reign, for those who refuse the invitation show their arrogance in presuming that their own affairs are more important than the banquet, while the beggars in the streets are humiliated by their social position and exalted by the unexpected invitation. Because vv. 7-10 discuss a specific case of exalting and humbling oneself, we can say that the great banquet parable is also related to these verses.

My remarks about Rohrbaugh's interpretation are an illustration, I hope, of fruitful interaction between socio-historical and literary exegesis. Careful attention to literary composition in Luke 14 supports the view that Rohrbaugh has proposed, while understanding Luke 14 in the context of ancient social systems underscores the significance of Jesus' words. A purist view of literary interpretation is in danger of allowing the text to hang in the air, preventing us from understanding how it encounters social experience. Attention to socio-historical interpretation can help us guard against this danger.

The reconstruction of the social setting of literature from the distant past is always somewhat speculative, for social history is too complex for us to recapture completely, and literature may shift social settings. Therefore we should be cautious about claiming that we have discovered the only

---

[36] Scott recognizes that the host has humiliated himself. The host "loses his honor and joins the shameless poor," according to Scott; see *Hear Then the Parable*, 174.

appropriate social setting. Nevertheless, it is important for us to imagine what the social effect of our literature might be for an ancient audience, as Rohrbaugh has helped us to do, for this can stimulate further thought about its possible functions in other social settings, including society today.

Rohrbaugh's reading of the great banquet parable is one of at least two basic readings supported by the Lukan context. The commoner interpretation as a story of God's banquet, asking the audience whether they will attend, is also a Lukan reading. It is supported by the immediate frame of the parable in 14:15 and 24. But 14:12-14 asks privileged people to take the role of the host themselves by inviting the poor to their parties, and 14:26-33 indicates the consequences of such behavior. Furthermore, both interpretations find support in the larger Lukan narrative, where Jesus' invitation encounters resistance among the rich Pharisees but freely goes out to the poor and outcasts, and where Jesus strongly challenges people of wealth to abandon their security and give their possessions to the poor. Both interpretations would be relevant to the socio-historical struggles of the late first-century church or would reflect memories that would still be significant then.

Therefore our experience of the great banquet parable in its Lukan setting is somewhat like viewing an optical illusion in which figure and ground interchange. We may view it in one configuration first, but then the relationships must shift so that we can view it in its second configuration.

These two readings of the great banquet parable do not exhaust the possibilities of understanding it within its Lukan context. Looking beyond the immediate context in Luke 14 and considering the Christian mission that is prefigured in 10:1-24, we may surmise that the early missionaries would find some of their own experience reflected in a story of invitations that are rejected. In this case the problem in the story is viewed from the perspective of the inviter, rather than the perspective of those invited, who must decide whether to come. Yet the situation is different than in Rohrbaugh's interpretation. It no longer concerns the social status of rich Christians but the frequent experience of rejection in Christian mission. The parable would encourage the missionary to believe that the banquet will certainly take place, in spite of rejection, and would point the missionary toward those marginal people who may be more willing to respond.

The parables do not yield richness of meaning and deliver sharp challenges only by removing them from their gospel contexts and inserting them into the reconstructed context of Jesus' historical ministry. We should not assume that the gospel writers limit a parable to a single, simple meaning. Careful attention to literary composition, supported by a historically informed imagination, may help us to discover more in their work than we initially expected.

5
The Story of Zacchaeus as Rhetoric

*In various writings on Luke–Acts, I refer to "narrative rhetoric." The term is appropriate, for I am viewing this long narrative as "a system of influence which may be analyzed in literary terms" (*The Narrative Unity of Luke–Acts, *1.8). The following essay is an example of such analysis applied to a single scene. In it I apply insights both from narrative criticism, as I have appropriated and developed it, and from ancient rhetoric.*

The whole of Luke 19:1-10 is rhetorical in that it is designed to persuade readers to view Zacchaeus and Jesus in particular ways and thereby take certain attitudes toward life. The rhetorical dimension is pervasive in language, including narrative. Not only the direct speech of persons can be analyzed for its rhetorical effect. The descriptions of characters, settings, and actions in narrative also have a rhetorical function. The study of narrative rhetoric[1] should embrace more than a concern with how characters speak, for everything that the narrator tells us can be evaluated for its rhetorical significance. To do this well, we must draw on the resources of both ancient and modern rhetoric.

---

[1] See Wayne C. Booth, *The Rhetoric of Fiction*, 2d ed. (Chicago: University of Chicago Press, 1983).

The story of Zacchaeus in Luke 19:1-10 has a number of strongly Lukan features[2] and has an important function in the larger Lukan narrative.[3] These are matters on which the reader should consult the literature just cited in the notes.

Luke 19:1-10 is a pronouncement story in which Jesus' final words rhetorically dominate. For a pronouncement story, however, the narrative gives an unusual amount of attention to another person, Zacchaeus. He is presented as an individual, not merely a character type. We are told his name, one of his physical characteristics (he is short), and an unusual action is narrated (he climbs into a sycamore tree), even though none of this information is strictly necessary for Jesus' final pronouncement.[4] This expansion of narrative detail has a function in the rhetoric of the story. Attention is directed to Zacchaeus as an individual, who begins to stand out as a subject of interest in his own right. Those who become interested in Zacchaeus as an individual will be interested in what happens to him. When he seeks for something, readers are likely to become interested in whether he will find what he seeks and even hope that he will find it, if it is a worthy goal. When Zacchaeus becomes the focus of attention, readers tend to look at events from his viewpoint and to sympathize with his goals. Descriptive detail tends to awaken our interest, and a quest for a worthy goal by a highlighted character tends to awaken our sympathy.

Two important identifying terms are added to Zacchaeus's name in v. 2. We are told that he was a "chief toll collector" and that he was "rich." The impact of this information is likely to be ambiguous, if one is guided by the values affirmed in Luke's Gospel. On the one hand, the toll collectors have been portrayed as responsive to the preaching of John and Jesus, and Jesus has welcomed their company (5:27-32; 7:29; 15:1-2). Not long before the story of Zacchaeus, Jesus told a parable in which a toll collector received God's approval (18:9-14). But Zacchaeus is a *chief* toll collector and is rich. This information may well raise questions about Zacchaeus, for the

---

[2] See William P. Loewe, "Towards an Interpretation of Lk 19:1-10," *CBQ* 36 (1974) 321–31; John O'Hanlon, "The Story of Zacchaeus and the Lukan Ethic," *JSNT* 12 (1981) 2–26.

[3] See Tannehill, *The Narrative Unity of Luke–Acts: A Literary Interpretation,* 2 vols. (Philadelphia & Minneapolis: Fortress, 1986, 1990) 1.107–9, 111–12, 122–25.

[4] Compare the following *chreia*: "Damon the gymnastic teacher whose feet were deformed, when his shoes had been stolen, said: 'May they fit the thief'," quoted from Ronald F. Hock and Edward N. O'Neil, *The Chreia in Ancient Rhetoric*, vol. 1: The *Progymnasmata,* SBLTT 27 (Atlanta: Scholars, 1986) 310. Here an individual physical characteristic is noted, but it is essential for an understanding of the pronouncement.

rich have not been favorably portrayed in Luke. Jesus pronounced a woe upon the rich (6:24), and since Luke 12 the rich have been presented as fools (12:16-21), callous (16:19-31), and incapable of responding to Jesus' call (18:18-23). Thus the indication that Zacchaeus is rich complicates the story and produces uncertainty in expectations. Readers cannot be sure whether this story will follow the pattern of previous stories about toll collectors or whether Zacchaeus will be presented in the manner of other rich men. The importance of Zacchaeus's wealth to the story is indicated by the sentence structure of v. 2. It would have been easy for the narrator to say that Zacchaeus was a rich toll collector. Instead, Zacchaeus's wealth is noted as a separate item and is thereby emphasized (καὶ αὐτὸς ἦν ἀρχιτελώνης καὶ αὐτὸς πλούσιος).[5] Furthermore, he is a *chief* toll collector, one in a position to make big profits.[6]

The fact that Zacchaeus is rich is important to the plot, which deals with the question left dangling by 18:18-27: whether and how a rich man can be saved. The possible negative effect of Zacchaeus's riches, in light of previous descriptions of rich men in Luke, is balanced by strong indications of Zacchaeus's eagerness to see Jesus and responsiveness to him. When the crowd prevents him from seeing Jesus, he runs ahead (rather than walking) and climbs into a tree (probably an undignified thing for an adult to do). When Jesus says, "Hurry and get down (σπεύσας κατάβηθι), "Zacchaeus does exactly that (σπεύσας κατέβη), and he welcomes Jesus to his home "rejoicing." Then v. 8 presents his wholehearted response to the new situation created by Jesus.

Zacchaeus's announcement that he is giving half of his goods to the poor may seem like a halfhearted response when we compare it with 18:22. There Jesus commanded a rich man to sell all and give it to the poor. However, Zacchaeus's statement in 19:8 indicates that he has two important obligations: He, like other rich people, must care for the needs of the poor with his wealth, but he must also restore fourfold what he has gained by false use of his office. The second obligation concerns a different group,

---

[5] The phrase καὶ αὐτός will be repeated by Jesus in v. 9 in another important identification of Zacchaeus.

[6] Luise Schottroff and Wolfgang Stegemann point out that the toll collectors of the synoptic tradition, the people like Levi (Luke 5:27) who actually sat at the toll booths, were underlings. Far from getting rich, they were likely to be people who could find no other work than this thankless task. See *Jesus von Nazareth: Hoffnung der Armen,* 2d ed. (Stuttgart: Kohlhammer, 1981) 17–18; ET = *Jesus and the Hope of the Poor,* trans. Matthew J. O'Connell (Maryknoll, N.Y.: Orbis, 1986).

since the poor are not likely to be moving goods that would be subject to
Zacchaeus's toll. Zacchaeus's wealth is simply divided in half to meet these
two obligations. Thus the reference to "half" is not meant as a limit on
the distribution of wealth, permitting Zacchaeus to keep the rest, but
simply recognizes that he must also compensate those from whom he has
extorted wealth. Of course we cannot know how much Zacchaeus owes
in compensation, but nothing is said about keeping a portion for himself.
Thus it is a mistake to assume that Zacchaeus is trying to strike a bargain,
offering less than Jesus demanded of the rich man in 18:22. Rather, 19:8
is intended to be an enthusiastic announcement of a new life that will be
devoted to the needs of others.[7]

Zacchaeus's announcement is an act of repentance. Joseph A. Fitzmyer
objects to this view, instead interpreting the present tense verbs in v. 8 as
expressing customary action (what Zacchaeus has been doing all along)
rather than a decision made at that moment (which must be carried out
in the future).[8] This view is not required by the present tense verbs and
fits neither the immediate context nor the general Lukan perspective. If v.
8 does not announce a new way of life, the reference in v. 9 to "salvation"
coming "today" does not follow from it, since there is no indication in v.
8 of anything new happening "today." Fitzmyer's view makes the sequence
of thought unnecessarily difficult. Furthermore, 5:29-32, which is closely
related to 19:1-10—indeed, it is another example of the same type-scene[9]
—makes clear that Jesus came to call toll collectors and other sinners "to
repentance" (unique to Luke). The important theme of "salvation" which
reappears in 19:9-10 is closely related to repentance and release of sins in
Luke–Acts (see especially Luke 1:77; Acts 2:21, 38, 40; 5:31). The
announcement in v. 8 indicates the repentance of a man who amassed
wealth through disregarding the needs and rights of others.[10]

---

[7] Compare Walter E. Pilgrim, *Good News to the Poor: Wealth and Poverty in Luke–Acts* (Minneapolis: Augsburg, 1981) 98–102, 132–34. Pilgrim believes that 19:1-10 stands in tension with passages that call for total surrender of possessions, since it indicates that all of one's possessions need not be surrendered.
[8] See *The Gospel According to Luke X–XXIV,* AB 28A (Garden City, N.Y.: Doubleday, 1985) 1220–21, 1225.
[9] See Tannehill, *Narrative Unity* 1.170–71. On type-scenes see Robert Alter, *The Art of Biblical Narrative* (New York: Basic Books, 1981) 47–62.
[10] Dennis Hamm provides further argument for this view of v. 8. See "Luke 19:8 Once Again: Does Zacchaeus Defend or Resolve?" *JBL* 107 (1988) 431–37.

While the reference to Zacchaeus as "rich" may have made the outcome of this scene somewhat uncertain, the portrayal of Zacchaeus's eagerness to see Jesus and responsiveness to him when they do meet suggests a favorable outcome for Zacchaeus. That is strongly confirmed when Jesus announces in v. 9 that "today salvation has come for this house." This announcement controls evaluation of Zacchaeus and the events of this scene, unless the reader is prepared to reject Luke as a whole. For eighteen chapters Jesus has been presented as one who is fulfilling God's purpose in word and deed, which creates a heavy presumption that Jesus' judgment is true in this case also. The authority with which Jesus is endowed in Luke as a whole is a major factor in the rhetoric of each scene in which he appears, for a figure of such authority tends to persuade readers to view events as he does.

This is certainly true when those events are closely tied to Jesus' divinely ordained mission, as in the Zacchaeus story. There is a hint of this in v. 5 when Jesus says, "Today I must stay in your house." Granted, there is no explanation here of why Jesus "must" stay with Zacchaeus, but the repeated use of δεῖ in connection with Jesus' divinely ordained path, which not only includes suffering and death (9:22; 17:25; 24:7, 26) but also other aspects of his mission (2:49; 4:43; 13:16; Acts 3:21), suggests that the necessity derives from Jesus' mission. This is confirmed by Luke 19:10, for Jesus' final statement in the scene relates his encounter with Zacchaeus to Jesus' mission "to seek and to save the lost." Jesus must stay with Zacchaeus in order to fulfill that mission.

Early in the narrative of Jesus' ministry, Luke's Gospel presents a similar scene. There as here Jesus' association with a toll collector produces grumbling from critics, and Jesus responds with a statement of what he has "come" to do, i.e., a statement about his fundamental mission. In 5:32 he says, "I have not come to call the righteous but sinners to repentance." In 19:10 he says, "The Son of man came to seek and to save the lost." These statements in similar scenes, occurring early and late in the narrative of Jesus' mission to the outcasts, bracket Jesus' ministry and interpret it as a whole. The latter statement reminds readers of the former and of the intervening instances of Jesus' ministry to the outcasts in Luke. The reference to "the lost" in 19:10 especially recalls Luke 15, where a similar situation arose (critics grumbling at Jesus' association with toll collectors and sinners) and Jesus responded with parables about the finding of the lost. Thus the general statement about Jesus' mission in 19:10

functions as a summary of the previous narrative. It also underscores the importance of Jesus' encounter with Zacchaeus, which becomes an outstanding example of Jesus fulfilling his central mission.

In the Zacchaeus scene two quests are taking place at the same time. In the end Jesus says that he "came to seek (ζητῆσαι) . . . the lost," but the main sequence of action in the scene begins with the statement that Zacchaeus "was seeking (ἐζήτει) to see Jesus" (v. 3). The scene is enriched by this dual perspective. It can be understood as an example of Jesus seeking the lost. But it can also be understood as a successful quest by Zacchaeus, who happily finds more than he expected. Zacchaeus's successful quest is placed within the context of Jesus' quest for the lost.

Zacchaeus's quest can be understood as the thread that unifies the story. Tension enters the scene as Zacchaeus seeks to see Jesus and is unable. Tension relaxes and the scene ends when Zacchaeus receives what he needs. This is an example of a type of pronouncement story that I have called a "quest story." Quest stories are structured around a person's quest; they give the quester a prominent role alongside Jesus, and do not end without reporting the success or failure of the quest (an indication of the quest's importance in the scene).[11] Such quest stories are especially characteristic of Luke.[12] There is subtlety to the narration of Zacchaeus's quest. It is presented in a limited way at first (Zacchaeus "was seeking to see Jesus, who he was"). This could simply indicate curiosity, but the end of the scene suggests that Zacchaeus comes to a deeper perception of who Jesus is: he is "Lord" (v. 8) and source of salvation (vv. 9-10).[13] The realization repeatedly overshoots expectations. At first Zacchaeus simply wants to see Jesus, but surprisingly Jesus decides to stay at his house. And Jesus not only stays at Zacchaeus's house, but brings salvation to those who are there.[14] The eagerness with which Zacchaeus responds to Jesus shows that

---

[11] On the definition of the quest story see Robert C. Tannehill, "Introduction: The Pronouncement Story and Its Types," *Semeia* 20 (1981) 9.

[12] See Tannehill, *Narrative Unity,* 1.111–27.

[13] See Robert F. O'Toole, "The Literary Form of Luke 19:1-10," *JBL* 110 (1991) 111–16. O'Toole understands the Zacchaeus story as a successful quest to see who Jesus is.

[14] Note the similarity between the two statements of Jesus in v. 5 (σήμερον γὰρ ἐν τῷ οἴκῳ σου) and v. 9 (σήμερον σωτηρία τῷ οἴκῳ τούτῳ). The reference to salvation in the second statement indicates an important progression that deepens the meaning of Jesus' stay in Zacchaeus's house. After Zacchaeus's announcement in v. 8, Jesus can show that his stay with this man was more than a temporary association that left life unchanged.

his real need and desire were deeper than watching Jesus' procession. Consciously or unconsciously he was seeking the salvation that Jesus could bring. Thus the real object of Zacchaeus's quest is gradually disclosed as we learn what he finds through Jesus.

In this quest the crowd functions as a blocking force. This is clearest in v. 7 when "all" grumble at Jesus' decision to stay with Zacchaeus, because he is a "sinner." A negative reaction is a standard element in the stories of Jesus' association with toll collectors and sinners. Even the key word "grumble" (γογγύζω or διαγογγύζω) is repeated (5:30; 15:2). However, in these previous scenes the Pharisees and scribes grumbled at Jesus' association with toll collectors and sinners; in 19:7 "all" grumble. This shift is an indication of another problem that this scene addresses. It is concerned not only with the question of whether a rich man can find salvation through Jesus but also with the relationship of Zacchaeus to the Jewish community. The community rejects Zacchaeus as a sinner, but Jesus intervenes on his behalf, reminding the people of a fact that they have ignored, that "he also is a son of Abraham" (v. 9). This is a relevant remark because Zacchaeus's rights as a Jew, including his right to share in the promises to Abraham and his seed, are being denied. In this conflict between the Jewish community and the outcast, Jesus insists that Zacchaeus must be reinstated as a Jew.

The conflict appears in the contrasting responses of Zacchaeus and the crowd when Jesus announces that he will stay with Zacchaeus. Zacchaeus rejoices at Jesus' proposal (v. 6), but the crowd grumbles (v. 7). The rest of the story is a response to the crowd's objection. In light of the crowd's unfriendly attitude toward Zacchaeus in v. 7, his problem with the crowd in v. 3 may not be as innocent as commonly assumed. In this story the crowd twice acts as a blocking force separating Zacchaeus from Jesus, showing the importance of the issue of Zacchaeus's standing in the community. The open opposition in v. 7 suggests that negative attitudes toward Zacchaeus may also be a factor in v. 3. People might allow a respected member of the community to come to the front in order to see, but they would not do this for Zacchaeus. Zacchaeus's short stature reinforces his helplessness with respect to the crowd, and his position up in a tree symbolizes his isolation from it. When the crowd objects to Jesus' association with Zacchaeus, it is seeking to maintain this isolation. The objection heightens the tension in the story. A strong answer from an authoritative source is necessary in order to persuade readers and hearers that a new attitude toward Zacchaeus is appropriate.

At first glance, however, the response to the objection may seem rather fragmented and unclear. First Zacchaeus makes a statement, not to the crowd but "to the Lord." If this statement does not contribute to a convincing response to v. 7, it will weaken that response by introducing a competing issue. When Jesus speaks, he addresses not the crowd but Zacchaeus. To be sure, some interpreters, noting that Jesus goes on to speak of Zacchaeus in the third person, would like to translate πρὸς αὐτόν as "about him" rather than "to him," but the use of πρός following a verb of speaking to indicate the one addressed is so common in Luke as to make the alternative translation very unlikely. Jesus makes a basic assertion followed by two supporting statements that seem to have little to do with each other, and it may not be clear how the first of these supports the assertion. Thus vv. 8-10 pose a series of questions: why the crowd is not addressed directly, how the declaration of salvation in v. 9 is supported by the following statements, and whether the three verses fit together to present a strong answer to the objection.

We should note first that v. 9, although it rather awkwardly presents Jesus addressing Zacchaeus while referring to him as "he," accurately reflects the fact that Jesus' statement has a double function in the structure of the story. This is a quest story that directs our attention to the successful or unsuccessful outcome of Zacchaeus's quest. The tension of this quest is resolved when Jesus states in v. 9 that this quest has been successful. This concerns Zacchaeus's fate and is properly addressed to Zacchaeus. But the crowd's objection must also be addressed if Zacchaeus's salvation is to be accepted as appropriate. Jesus speaks to the crowd's objection in the brief supporting statements after the announcement of salvation.

Since the story is centrally concerned with Zacchaeus's quest, it is appropriate for Jesus to address him at the climax. However, we can also understand why the narrator would be tempted to modulate into a statement about Zacchaeus in response to the crowd. Furthermore, some comments of ancient rhetoricians may help us to judge the rhetorical appropriateness of the result. In a paper presented to the SBL Work Group on Pronouncement Story, Rod Parrott applied some observations of George A. Kennedy to the pronouncement story in Mark 2:23-28.[15] Kennedy points out that ancient rhetoricians recognized that the speaker's

---

[15] Parrott's paper was published as "Conflict and Rhetoric in Mark 2:23-28," *Semeia* 64 (1993) 117–37; see 127–29.

usual approach must be modified when faced with a hostile or unreceptive audience. "Classical rhetoricians developed a technique of approaching a difficult rhetorical problem indirectly, known as *insinuatio*."[16] The crowd is a hostile audience in the Zacchaeus scene, for it not only denounces Zacchaeus as a sinner but also criticizes Jesus for association with him. The problem is to speak to the issue without alienating this audience still further. The approach taken fits the hostile situation. Neither Zacchaeus nor Jesus speaks to the crowd directly or directly challenges its opinion. Indeed, Zacchaeus and Jesus appear to ignore the crowd's objection, speaking only of Zacchaeus's new situation. But indirectly their statements do speak to the objection. It is difficult to continue to apply the term *sinner* to one who is giving away his wealth to the poor and compensating fourfold those he has injured. This is a changed man who must now be viewed differently. If so, Jesus' declaration of salvation does not seem ridiculous. Furthermore, the people who hope to share in God's salvation as children of Abraham cannot easily reject a repentant man who shares that heritage.

The discussions of ancient rhetoric may help us in another way. The declaration of salvation in v. 9 is followed by two supporting reasons. Thus it is argumentative. Indeed, it has the form of an enthymeme. Enthymeme is the rhetorical form of deductive proof. As Kennedy points out, "An enthymeme commonly takes the form of a statement and a supporting reason." Furthermore, "Behind any enthymeme stands a logical syllogism."[17] However, in speeches part of the logical chain is omitted because, it is assumed, some premises are obvious and the audience will automatically supply them. It is a rhetorical fault to clutter the speech with the obvious.

While vv. 9-10 apparently present arguments, their force may not be clear to modern readers. Two supporting reasons are given, but they do not seem to be related. And the missing premises of the argument may not be obvious to us. Supplying them, of course, does not necessarily mean that modern people will be convinced by the argument, for assumptions may appear that many will find debatable. But supplying them would at least help us to recognize what made sense to the narrator of Luke. Since what is

---

[16] See George A. Kennedy, *New Testament Interpretation through Rhetorical Criticism* (Chapel Hill: University of North Carolina Press, 1984) 36. *Insinuatio* is discussed by *Rhetorica ad Herennium* I.vi.9-11 and by Quintilian, *Institutio Oratoria* IV.i.42–50.

[17] Kennedy, *New Testament Interpretation*, 16.

not stated is assumed to be obvious, unstated premises should be among the basic assumptions of the narrator and the anticipated readers. We will be on the safest ground if we can supply the missing premises from the work that we are studying or the cultural context from which it comes.

Jesus supports his assertion that today salvation has come to Zacchaeus with a double rationale. The logic behind the second rationale (v. 10) is not really obscure. A fuller argument would go like this: The Son of man (Jesus) came to seek and save the lost; Zacchaeus is one of the lost; therefore, Jesus came to seek and save Zacchaeus (and this task has now been fulfilled, bringing Zacchaeus salvation).[18] This argument would be most convincing to someone who shares the Lukan vision of Jesus' work, in which Jesus' saving mission to the oppressed and excluded has a central place.[19] Thus we might say that Luke's larger narrative serves to establish the premise in 19:10, which, in turn, summarizes a major theme of that narrative.

The logic behind the first rationale may be less clear, but again missing parts can be supplied from the rest of Luke–Acts. I would suggest that the logic moves as follows: God has promised salvation to the children of Abraham; Zacchaeus is a child of Abraham; therefore, God has promised salvation to Zacchaeus (and this promise has now been fulfilled through Jesus).[20] Supporting the declaration of salvation by the rationale "for he also is a son of Abraham" presupposes a first premise that connects salvation with the children of Abraham. The narrator's acceptance of such a premise can be supported from parts of Luke–Acts in which authoritative interpreters emphasize God's saving purpose for Israel (see Luke 1:54-55, 68-79; Acts 2:39; 3:25-26; 13:23, 26, 32-33). These passages show how seriously Luke–Acts takes the promise to the Jewish people. This promise is not weakened by the invitation to Gentiles to share in God's salvation. Even awareness that the fulfillment of this promise will encounter rejection does not weaken the narrator's conviction that the promise rightly belongs

---

[18] This is a valid syllogism only if Jesus came to seek and save *all* the lost. Aristotle notes, however, that most propositions in enthymemes will be usually true rather than necessarily true. See *The "Art" of Rhetoric* I.ii.1357a. Arguments with such propositions are used to create a presumption of truth. If detractors wish to exclude Zacchaeus from those sought by Jesus, they would be expected to state a reason.

[19] See Tannehill, *Narrative Unity,* 1.60–68, 103–39.

[20] Again, this is a valid syllogism only if the promise is to *all* the children of Abraham. While some might not accept this, detractors would be expected to give reasons why Zacchaeus, specifically, should be excluded. The preceding statement in v. 8 undercuts the most obvious reason that might be advanced by emphasizing that Zacchaeus is no longer the kind of man that he was.

The Story of Zacchaeus as Rhetoric

to those who are "sons of the prophets and of the covenant which God covenanted with our fathers" (Acts 3:25), the "sons of the family of Abraham" (Acts 13:26; cf. 13:32-33).[21]

Thus attention to the way that logic functions in rhetoric helps us to see that vv. 8-10 are not such a confused response to the challenge in v. 7 as they might appear. The indirectness of these remarks has a rhetorical value in responding to a hostile audience, and the argument, though very compact, raises three significant points which together undermine the critics' charge: Zacchaeus is a new man who can't be dismissed as a sinner; he, too, is a member of the people to whom most of the scriptural promises are directed; and Jesus was sent to bring salvation to the lost, i.e., to just such a person as Zacchaeus.

The story of Zacchaeus combines important Lukan themes: repentance, the responsibility of the rich for the poor, salvation as a present possibility through Jesus' ministry, Jesus' mission of seeking and saving the lost. In particular, it concerns the possibility of a rich man repenting and finding salvation in spite of a past life of oppression. This story continues to be told frequently in church schools, for it is one of the scenes in which a minor character in the gospels stands out as an interesting individual. The interest that Zacchaeus attracts has a rhetorical effect: readers and hearers become involved in his quest, which is stated in a minimal way in v. 3 but deepens in significance. The crowd's rejection of Zacchaeus and resistance to Jesus' association with him are strongly expressed, and the most pointed rhetoric of the story is found in vv. 8-10, in which statements by Zacchaeus and Jesus combine to form an indirect response to the crowd's objection. It may seem surprising that the author of Luke would be concerned with the crowd's acceptance of Zacchaeus as a Jew, but this is one of many signs that salvation for the Jewish people is a continuing concern in Luke–Acts.

---

[21] On the tension in Acts between this promise and Jewish rejection, see Robert C. Tannehill, "Rejection by Jews and Turning to Gentiles: The Pattern of Paul's Mission in Acts," in *Luke–Acts and the Jewish People: Eight Critical Perspectives,* edited by Joseph B. Tyson (Minneapolis: Augsburg, 1988) 83–101, 150–52; on the significance of Jewish rejection in Luke–Acts as a whole, see Robert C. Tannehill, "Israel in Luke–Acts: A Tragic Story," *JBL* 104 (1985) 69–85. My comments about the promise to the Jewish people touch on the controversial issue of the Lukan attitude toward the Jews. The following works provide a sampling of the recent debate: Robert L. Brawley, *Luke–Acts and the Jews: Conflict, Apology, and Conciliation,* SBLMS 33 (Atlanta: Scholars, 1987); Jack T. Sanders, *The Jews in Luke–Acts* (Philadelphia: Fortress, 1987); Joseph B. Tyson, editor, *Luke–Acts and the Jewish People: Eight Critical Perspectives* (Minneapolis: Augsburg, 1988).

6

Repentance in the Context of Lukan Soteriology

Luke–Acts is not commonly viewed as a source of deep theological reflection on soteriology, and its strong emphasis on repentance, in particular, raises some theological questions. The following essay argues that repentance as a Lukan theme is an integral part of the good news of salvation in fulfillment of divine promises that is central to Luke–Acts. Understood in this context, the theme has more theological depth than is often recognized. It also has continuing relevance in the present world.

The following essay is a token of my great respect for Dr. Simon J. DeVries, friend and former colleague on the faculty of Methodist Theological School in Ohio. It is, I hope, in keeping with his lifelong commitment to the development of biblical theology through careful study of the texts. After introductory observations about word usage, this essay will seek to explain the place of repentance within the larger context of Lukan soteriology and explore several noteworthy and unusual aspects of repentance, as this theme is presented in Luke–Acts. It will also discuss the occasional references to specific sins from which some must repent and ask whether all stand in need of repentance, according to Luke–Acts. Finally, the discussion will return to Lukan soteriology, especially the connection of repentance and forgiveness with the historical ministry of Jesus, on the one hand, and with the rule of the exalted Messiah, on the other, instead of with the death of Jesus as a distinct saving event.

The importance of the theme of repentance in Luke–Acts is obvious from a quick review of some key data.[1] Two word groups related to repentance (μετανοέω—μετάνοια and ἐπιστρέφω—ἐπιστροφή) are favored by the author of Luke–Acts. Half of the New Testament uses of the noun μετάνοια ("repentance") are in Luke–Acts (Luke 3:3, 8; 5:32; 15:7; 24:47; Acts 5:31; 11:18; 13:24; 19:4; 20:21; 26:20). The related verb μετανοέω ("repent") occurs seven times in Matthew and Mark, together, but nine times in Luke and five times in Acts (Luke 10:13; 11:32; 13:3, 5; 15:7, 10; 16:30; 17:3, 4; Acts 2:38; 3:19; 8:22; 17:30; 26:20). Beyond the synoptic Gospels and Acts, μετανοέω is found in the New Testament only in 2 Cor 12:21 and in Revelation. The verb ἐπιστρέφω can be used in the sense of physical turning. It is so used in Matthew and Mark, except in a quotation of Isa 6:9-10 (in Matt 13:15 and Mark 4:12). It is also used in this way in Luke–Acts, but sometimes in Luke and frequently in Acts it expresses a turning that is equivalent to repentance: a change in attitude and orientation that results in a new relation to God and fellow humans (Luke 1:16, 17; 22:32;[2] Acts 3:19; 9:35; 11:21; 14:15; 15:19; 26:18, 20; 28:27).[3] To this list we can add Acts 15:3, the only

---

[1]In addition to items cited later in this essay, I note the following bibliography: Peter Böhlemann, *Jesus und der Täufer: Schlüssel zur Theologie und Ethik des Lukas,* SNTSMS 99 (Cambridge: Cambridge University Press, 1997) 96–123; Hans Conzelmann, *The Theology of St Luke,* trans. Geoffrey Buswell (London: Faber and Faber, 1960) 99–101, 227–30; Jacques Dupont, "Repentir et conversion d'après les Actes des Apôtres," in *Études sur les Actes des Apôtres,* LD 45 (Paris: Cerf, 1967) 421–57; *idem,* "Conversion in the Acts of the Apostles," in *The Salvation of the Gentiles: Studies in the Acts of the Apostles,* trans. John Keating (New York: Paulist, 1979) 61–84; Augustin George, "La conversion," in *Études sur l'oeuvre de Luc,* SB (Paris: Éditions Gabalda, 1978) 351–68; Pierre Haudebert, "La *métanoia,* des Septante à Saint Luc," in *La vie de la Parole: Études . . . offertes à Pierre Grelot* (Paris: Desclée, 1987) 355–66; David Lertis Matson, *Household Conversion Narratives in Acts: Pattern and Interpretation,* JSNTSS 123 (Sheffield: Sheffield Academic, 1996); R. Michiels, "La conception lucaniènne de la conversion," *ETL* 41 (1965) 42–78; David Ravens, *Luke and the Restoration of Israel,* JSNTSS 119 (Sheffield: Sheffield Academic, 1995) 139–69; Jens-W. Taeger, *Der Mensch und sein Heil: Studien zum Bild des Menschen und zur Sicht der Bekehrung bei Lukas,* SNT 14 (Gütersloh: Gütersloher, 1982) 105–228; Charles H. Talbert, "Conversion in the Acts of the Apostles: Ancient Auditors' Perceptions," in *Literary Studies in Luke–Acts: Essays in Honor of Joseph B. Tyson,* ed. Richard P. Thompson and Thomas E. Phillips (Macon, Ga.: Mercer University Press, 1998) 141–53.

[2]Luke 17:4 is a doubtful case.

[3]In this meaning ἐπιστρέφω is often completed by the phrase "to the Lord" or "to God" (ἐπὶ τὸν κύριον or ἐπὶ τὸν θεόν).

occurrence of the noun ἐπιστροφή in the New Testament. This second word group, when used to express repentance, is also characteristic of Luke–Acts in the New Testament.[4]

We find more substantial evidence for the importance of repentance in Luke–Acts when we note that this theme is found throughout the two-volume work and is highlighted in key statements about the message and mission of the leading figures in the narrative. The call to repentance is an important part of the mission of John the Baptist (Luke 1:16-17; 3:3, 8; Acts 13:24; 19:4), Jesus (Luke 5:32; 10:13; 11:32; 13:3, 5; 15:7, 10), the apostles, and Paul. It is significant, in connection with the apostles and Paul, that the commission given by the risen Christ to his apostles is to preach repentance and forgiveness "in his name" (Luke 24:47), that repentance and turning to the Lord are repeated themes in the Acts mission speeches (2:38; 3:19; 5:31; 14:15; 17:30) and in summaries of the successful course of the mission (9:35; 11:18, 21; 15:3), and that these themes are repeated in Paul's summaries of his commission from the Lord (26:17-18) and of the actual content of his preaching (20:21; 26:20).

Repentance is often connected with forgiveness of sins in the passages cited above, but the saving benefits may also be expressed by references to the gift of the Spirit (Acts 2:38), being "saved from this crooked generation" (2:40), gaining "life" (11:18) and "light" (26:18). Repentance has an important place in Lukan soteriology—in the understanding of the way of salvation for Jews and Gentiles and, as we will see below, in the understanding of the saving work of God through Jesus Christ.

In Luke–Acts ἐπιστρέφω and μετανοέω are twice used together (Acts 3:19; 26:20; see also Luke 17:4), which may be for purposes of emphasis, since they are largely interchangeable terms. There may, however, be a difference in nuance, μετανοέω and μετάνοια emphasizing a change in thinking and attitude, compared to one's previous life, and ἐπιστρέφω suggesting the positive side of this change: the reestablishment of a harmonious relation to God. This aspect of the word appears in the frequent use of ἐπιστρέφω in references to turning "to the Lord" or "to God" (Luke 1:16; Acts 9:35; 11:21; 14:15; 15:19; 26:18, 20).[5]

---

[4]The verb ἐπιστρέφω is also used in the sense of repentance in 2 Cor 3:16; 1 Thess 1:9; James 5:19-20; 1 Pet 2:25.

[5]Guy D. Nave, Jr., has written the most recent extensive study of repentance in Luke–Acts. See *The Role and Function of Repentance in Luke–Acts,* Academia Biblica 4 (Atlanta: Society of Biblical Literature, 2002). Although this is a valuable monograph, both for its thorough study of the use of

In its use of ἐπιστρέφω, Luke–Acts reflects the language of the LXX and suggests that John the Baptist, Jesus, and Jesus' witnesses revive the message of the Hebrew prophets, who called their people to "turn" back to God, using the Hebrew verb *shuv*. This verb is translated in the LXX by ἐπιστρέφω or ἀποστρέφω rather than by μετανοέω.[6] However, μετανοέω, as well as ἐπιστρέφω, appears in references to human repentance in Jeremiah (see, e.g., Jer 8:6; 24:7; 38[31]:19) and Sirach (see, e.g., Sir 17:24, 25; 48:15; see also Isa 46:8). Also, the noun μετά-νοια, rare in the LXX, does occur in Wis 11:23; 12:10, 19 (otherwise, only in Prov 14:15 and Sir 44:16).[7] A growing tendency to use μετανοέω and μετάνοια for repentance appears not only in Wisdom of Solomon and Sirach but also in later Greek translations of the Hebrew Scriptures and in Philo.[8] The mixed language of Luke–Acts reflects both the wording favored in the LXX and this later tendency.[9]

The Lukan emphasis on repentance, although it continues an important theme in the Hebrew Scriptures, may strike many modern people as odd or repugnant. It may seem too negative in its view of humanity and too closely tied to threats of judgment. In particular, modern Americans have little awareness of a need to repent, either individually or as a society. In an article that appeared shortly before the terrorist attacks on the World Trade Center and the Pentagon, Lewis Lapham compares America's present domination in the world—the American Empire—to

---

μετανοέω and μετάνοια in ancient Greek literature and for its interpretation of Luke–Acts, it is limited by its neglect of ἐπιστρέφω. Nave states that the author of Luke–Acts "did not necessarily consider" the two terms to be "synonymous" (203, n. 262). However, even if we grant that there is a nuance of difference, we should recognize that they function in the same way to refer to the change required in humans in order to share in God's salvation. We can reach a full understanding of the Lukan view of repentance only by studying both.

[6]"For *shuv*, the verbal expression . . . for religious and moral conversion, the LXX never uses μετανοέω but always ἐπιστρέφω (-ομαι) or ἀποστρέφω (-ομαι)." J. Behm in *TDNT* 4.989.

[7]In Wisdom of Solomon note also μετανοέω in 5:3.

[8]See H. Merklein in *Exegetical Dictionary of the New Testament*, edited by Horst Balz and Gerhard Schneider (Grand Rapids: Eerdmans, 1991) 2.416. For Philo's use of these terms see *TDNT* 4.993–94.

[9]Nave provides an extensive discussion of the use of μετανοέω and μετάνοια in classical and Hellenistic Greek literature, Hellenistic Jewish literature, and the New Testament and other early Christian literature. See *Role and Function of Repentance,* 39–144. Nave denies that "the concept of repentance found in the Bible in general, and in the New Testament in particular, was a uniquely Jewish concept that was alien to classical and Hellenistic Greek culture" (71), for the classical and Hellenistic usage is not confined to an intellectual change of mind.

the Roman Empire.[10] He goes on to state that, since we think of ourselves as virtuous, we cannot understand the negative reaction of other parts of the world to American dominance. Since Americans assume that our national character and policies are virtuous (or that the economic decisions of American businesses are exempt from moral judgment), we are unable to face the damaging consequences of our actions and the contradiction between them and our democratic ideals. If this is true, we still need prophetic voices to call us to repentance, and repentance is not an obsolete concern of the Bible.

Considered theologically, an emphasis on repentance may seem to make human action the key factor in salvation. Repentance, to be sure, is closely related to the gracious offer of forgiveness of sins in Luke–Acts, but repentance seems to be the crucial condition that humans must fulfill and the key factor in determining the final outcome for each individual. As a result, it can become the primary focus of the religious life, calling forth the penitent's anxious efforts at improvement in order to achieve salvation. This view may seem to find support in the correct observation that repentance has a moral aspect in Luke–Acts.[11] It is expressed in concrete changes in behavior. In Luke 3:8 the Baptist demands that the crowds produce "fruits worthy of repentance," which are spelled out in some detail in 3:10-14, and this demand is echoed in Paul's summary of his mission and message in Acts 26:20 ("deeds worthy of repentance").[12]

This theological objection will diminish, I believe, if we understand repentance within the larger context of Lukan soteriology. Repentance and forgiveness together refer to the transformation in human lives that results from God's saving action in fulfilling the promises of salvation through Israel's Messiah, Jesus. The reference to "fruits" and "deeds" make clear that this is an ethically transforming event, one that results in changed behavior. But the primary and basic message is not "You must repent" but this good news: the time of fulfillment of the promises, the time of

---

[10]Lewis H. Lapham, "The American Rome: On the Theory of Virtuous Empire," *Harper's Magazine* 303, no. 1815 (August 2001) 31–38.

[11]See Ulrich Wilckens, *Die Missionsreden der Apostelgeschichte*, 3d ed., WMANT 5 (Neukirchen-Vluyn: Neukirchener, 1974) 181.

[12]The nature of these "fruits worthy of repentance" is spelled out in the ethical teaching in Luke–Acts, especially in the teaching of Jesus. But the association of moral transformation with repentance "was not a Lukan invention. Moral and ethical transformation was considered an integral part of repentance in the centuries immediately preceding the Christian era" (Nave, *Role and Function of Repentance*, 110, n. 347).

salvation, has come. God is powerfully at work in the world changing things, and this provides a special opportunity in which you, too, can change. In this context repentance is not isolated human action. It is human action which, theologically discerned, is also divine action in individuals and societies.

Luke's Gospel begins with the infancy narrative, which contains angelic messages and inspired hymns proclaiming the fulfillment of the promises of salvation to Israel through its Messiah, a salvation that the Gentiles will also share (Luke 2:30-32).[13] Then Jesus begins his work by announcing his mission to "preach good news" and "proclaim the acceptable year of the Lord," which is the time of "release" (ἄφεσις)—including the release or forgiveness of sins (Luke 4:18-19).[14] He then proclaims that this special time is "today" (4:21). In following scenes we find narrative development of both the theme of release of sins and of repentance.

Luke 5:17-32 (the healing of the paralytic and the call of Levi, followed by the meal in Levi's house) takes on special importance in Luke's narrative, even though they are found in Matthew and Mark. In this section the Lukan narrative begins to develop Jesus' mission of release as a mission that brings release of sins to those labeled as "sinners." Jesus makes two fundamental assertions about his mission and authority: He has "authority on earth to release sins" (5:24) and he "has not come to call the righteous but sinners to repentance" (5:32). Then, in a process of recall and comparison, later scenes in Luke emphasize and enrich the reader's understanding of these fundamental aspects of Jesus' mission. Through repetition of key words from 5:17-32 in later scenes (see 7:34; 7:48-49; 15:1-2, 7, 10; 19:7, 10), these scenes are linked together as a progressive development of Jesus' role as the one who brings the release of sins.[15]

The important theme of repentance is also progressively developed in the Gospel narrative. It first appears as part of the mission of John the Baptist, who "will turn (ἐπιστρέψει) many of the sons of Israel to the Lord their God," resulting in a people prepared for the coming salvation

---

[13]For the significance of the infancy narrative, in my understanding, see Tannehill, *The Narrative Unity of Luke–Acts: A Literary Interpretation,* 2 vols. (Philadelphia & Minneapolis: Fortress, 1986, 1990) 1.13–44; and *idem, Luke,* ANTC (Nashville: Abingdon, 1996) 35–77.

[14]The word ἄφεσις appears elsewhere in Luke–Acts only in the phrase that is usually translated "forgiveness of sins." On the significance of ἄφεσις in Luke 4:18, see Tannehill, *Narrative Unity,* 1.65–66.

[15]For details, see Tannehill, *Narrative Unity,* 1.103–9.

(Luke 1:16-17). The depiction of John proclaiming a "baptism of repentance (βάπτισμα μετανοίας) for release of sins" and calling for "fruits worthy of repentance" in 3:3-14 shows John fulfilling this prophecy. The proclamation of repentance does not end with John. It continues in the mission of Jesus, and he, in turn, will charge his apostles to preach repentance and forgiveness (Luke 24:47). Repentance is not a concern that passes with the passing of John but is an integral part of the transforming process that continues into the time of the risen and exalted Messiah.

In spite of the fact that Luke refers to repentance more frequently than Matthew or Mark, and mentions it in key statements about Jesus' and the disciples' mission, Luke omits two prominent references in Mark.[16] They occur in Mark's initial summary of Jesus' message (Mark 1:15) and the summary of the message of the twelve, when sent by Jesus (6:12). At these points Luke substitutes statements about "preaching good news" (Luke 4:18; 9:6). Especially the initial description of Jesus' message in the Nazareth synagogue (4:18-21) suggests that repentance is not the fundamental or dominant note in the gospel message. Rather, repentance follows from recognition of God's saving work in fulfillment of prophetic promises, disclosed by the "good news."

Repentance is first mentioned in the ministry of Jesus in 5:32, where Luke's Gospel adds "to repentance" (εἰς μετάνοιαν) to the statement in Mark 2:17 ("I did not come to call the righteous but sinners").[17] This mission of repentance and forgiveness for sinners, resulting in the reinstatement of "sinners" in God's covenant people, is depicted in vivid scenes in 7:36-50, 15:1-32, 18:9-14, 19:1-10,[18] and 23:39-43. As Jesus begins his journey to Jerusalem, however, it becomes clear that the people in general (not just the "sinners") must repent and that failure to repent in response to the mission of Jesus will bring condemnation at the judgment. Woes are pronounced over towns of Galilee because of their failure to repent (10:13-15). The people of Nineveh will condemn "this generation" at the judgment, for the Ninevites repented but this generation has not

---

[16]See Nave, *Role and Function of Repentance,* 159–64, 191–94.

[17]The significance of this addition requires further discussion below.

[18]Some interpreters deny that Zacchaeus is an example of repentance. See Joseph A. Fitzmyer, *The Gospel According to Luke,* AB 28, 28A (Garden City, N.Y.: Doubleday, 1981, 1985) 1220–21, 1225. My reasons for rejecting this view may be found in Tannehill, *Luke,* 277.

(11:32). Recent disasters in the news have not befallen remarkable sinners but are symbolic of what will happen to all, if they do not repent (13:1-5). (To this warning is appended the parable of the barren fig tree, which shows a devoted gardener interceding and laboring to give the barren tree one more chance.) The scriptural prophets' call to Israel to repent resounds in these threatening words.[19]

A closer look at Luke–Acts reveals two noteworthy emphases that differ from common assumptions about repentance. First, the narrative suggests that human repentance should be understood as both divine and human action. The assumption that repentance is the human contribution to salvation and forgiveness is the divine contribution is not only theologically shallow but also ignores indications in Luke–Acts that God's saving purpose and action are manifest in the act of repentance itself. The same act of repentance can be viewed as God's saving action in a person's life and as a human decision. Luke–Acts is a narrative, not a systematic theology, and does not try to explain this puzzle, but there is evidence that both perspectives are important in the two-volume work.

Luke 15 contains three parables. They concern a lost sheep, a lost coin, and a lost son, and they also have in common a communal celebration that expresses joy at recovery of what was lost. There is a significant difference between the first two parables and the third, however. In the first two parables the focus of attention is not on anything that the sheep or coin do (they remain passive figures) but on the determined seekers, the shepherd and the woman. Yet it is these two parables that explicitly speak of repentance (15:7, 10). The parables, then, suggest that the experience of repentance may be more like being found by someone who searches with great determination than like achieving something through our own determination. The parable of the lost son then reflects on the matter from the other side, as a human decision to return.[20]

In Acts repentance is twice described as God's gift. The last of Peter's mission testimonies in Jerusalem contains an important soteriological statement: God has "exalted" Jesus "at his right hand to give repentance to Israel and release of sins" (Acts 5:31). Here repentance and forgiveness

---

[19]Luke 10:13-15 and 11:32, however, presuppose a universal and final time of judgment, which differs from the historical judgment anticipated in most of Israel's prophetic Scriptures.

[20]In 15:17-19 the son rehearses a speech of penitence, but how penitent is he, really? His main motivation seems to be to keep from starving. The parable seems remarkably unconcerned with the "purity" of the son's motivation. The return home is all that matters.

are bracketed together as the gift of the exalted Messiah to Israel, in fulfillment of God's saving purpose. This is not a passing remark of little importance. In 11:18 the important encounter between Peter and Cornelius comes to the moment of insight and resolution for the church when the Jerusalem church is finally convinced by Peter that "to the Gentiles, also, God has given repentance unto life." In this scene there is deliberate reference back to Pentecost and the first preaching to Jews. Peter concludes his argument by emphasizing the similarity between the experience of Cornelius and his household, who received the Spirit, and the experience of the Jerusalem believers at Pentecost, calling the Spirit God's "gift" (11:15-17). The Jerusalem believers respond by confessing that Gentiles share in another gift, the repentance that God gave to Israel, according to Peter's preaching in 5:31. In 11:18 there is deliberate repetition and development of 5:31, helping to express a crucial point in the scene: God is giving the same gifts to Jews and Gentiles, which makes them partners in salvation.

Even if we recognize the importance of these statements about God giving repentance, their significance is debatable. The interpreter can remove some of the oddness and sharpness of these statements by understanding them to mean that God gives the *opportunity* to repent.[21] However, oddities of religious expression may sometimes capture more of the experience of God than the interpreter's effort to rationalize. While it is no doubt true, from the perspective of Luke–Acts, that God is giving people the opportunity to repent, this statement does not sufficiently convey the dynamic view of God in the Lukan writings.

There is considerable evidence in Acts that God is understood to be active in the human conversions that are depicted there. The progress of the mission is described as a process of persons being "added" to the believers (using προστίθημι). In Acts 2:41 this is expressed by using a passive verb ("about three thousand persons were added"), but in 2:47 the underlying theological perspective is expressed clearly ("The Lord was adding day by day those who were being saved"). In Antioch "a great number believed and turned (ἐπέστρεψεν) to the Lord." Once again, this is attributed to divine power: "The hand of the Lord was with" the

---

[21]See Hans Conzelmann, *Acts of the Apostles*, trans. James Limburg et al., Hermeneia (Philadelphia: Fortress, 1987) 42. In support of this interpretation he cites Josephus, *Bell.* 3.127, and Philo, *Leg. all.* 3.106. To these could be added Wis 12:10 (ἐδίδους τόπον μετανοίας).

evangelists (11:21). When Paul and Barnabas return to Antioch, they report "what God had done with them and that he [God] had opened for the Gentiles a door of faith" (14:27). This successful mission is later referred to as "the conversion (ἐπιστροφή) of the Gentiles" (15:3). Similar language is applied to the response of an individual person, Lydia: "The Lord opened her heart" (16:14). Divine intervention is dramatically portrayed in the story of Saul on the Damascus road (9:3-19), and divine guidance leads preachers of the gospel to specific individuals and groups that will respond to the message (8:26, 29; 16:6-10; 18:9-10). The result is sometimes described as a "turning" or "conversion" (using ἐπιστρέφω or ἐπιστροφή), one of the concepts on which this study focuses (11:21, 15:3). Thus, in specific cases the narrative depicts God as actively involved in creating a "turning" in people's lives, that is, in creating repentance. This evidence should be considered when we seek to understand what it means for God "to give repentance" to Israel and the Gentiles. God's gift of repentance refers to a new opportunity to repent, but it also refers to God's dynamic action in people's lives to bring them to repent.[22]

The second noteworthy emphasis in Luke–Acts is the surprising link between repentance and joy rather than mourning, the traditional expression of repentance. It is true that the call to repentance is sometimes motivated by a threat of judgment, a traditional biblical theme. This is true in Luke (3:8-9; 10:13-15; 11:31-32; 13:1-9) and, in less dramatic language, in Acts (10:42-43; 17:30-31; cf. 2:40). However, there are other passages that relate repentance to the joy of a restored relationship, a joy that excludes the demonstrations of sorrow normally associated with repentance. Here the motivation is positive—to share in something that brings joy. Thus each of the three parables of Luke 15 emphasizes joy at finding what was lost, expressed in a public celebration, and the parable

---

[22]Acts 3:26 may express God's active role, but the construction of the sentence, with an articular infinitive (ἐν τῷ ἀποστρέφειν ἕκαστον ἀπὸ τῶν πονηριῶν ὑμῶν), leaves an ambiguity. Grammatically, ἕκαστον ("each") could be either the subject or the object of the turning (ἀποστρέφειν). In the latter case, God is blessing the people through God's servant Jesus "by turning each of you from your wicked ways" (NRSV). In the former case we could translate, "when each of you turns from your wicked ways," which could express a condition; the blessing will take effect only when people repent. The recent commentary by C. K. Barrett chooses the translation that expresses divine action. "In Greek usage generally . . . the intransitive sense seems to be most often expressed by the passive or middle, and the notion of blessing [in Acts 3:26] is more consistent with that of divine than human action." See *A Critical and Exegetical Commentary on the Acts of the Apostles*, 2 vols., ICC (Edinburgh: T. & T. Clark, 1994) 1.214.

of the lost son defends the appropriateness of the celebration against the elder brother, who complains that returning sinners do not deserve such treatment. Perhaps the younger son might be accepted back after appropriate acts of remorse, which would demonstrate his repentance, but the father, in his eager joy, skips all that.

The Lukan redaction in Luke 5:27-35 makes a similar point. This redaction not only involves adding "to repentance" to the Markan statement that Jesus has not come "to call the righteous but sinners" in 5:32. It also involves linking the following question about fasting to the question about feasting with sinners through removal of Mark's indication that a new group approaches Jesus and the scene has changed (Mark 2:18). The complainers of Luke 5:30 press their point by noting that Jesus' disciples "eat and drink" while followers of John and the Pharisees exhibit more appropriate behavior; they are fasting (5:33). This objection is a response to Jesus' festive meals with sinners, which, according to Jesus' statement, result from his call of sinners to repentance. The objectors do not see any sign of repentance. There were customary signs of repentance: weeping and mourning, fasting, donning sackcloth and ashes. Fasting, in particular, is a sign of repentance and accompanies ardent prayer for forgiveness (see Joel 2:12-17; Jonah 3:5-9; *Jos. Asen.* 10:14-17). If Jesus is calling sinners to repentance, why are his followers not fasting? Jesus defends his followers by comparing his ministry to a joyful wedding feast, when fasting would be inappropriate. In Luke 5:29-35 and 15:1-32 repentance is equivalent to the joyful discovery that one is included in God's salvation, making possible a transformed life. Other references to the joy experienced by those who have just encountered Jesus or the gospel (using χαίρω or χαρά) take on deeper meaning in light of these parables and dialogues that present repentance as a joyful discovery (see Luke 19:6; Acts 8:8, 39; 13:48, 52).

Sometimes the narrative indicates specific sins from which people should repent, sometimes not. The question "What should we do?" following John the Baptist's demand for "fruits worthy of repentance" leads to specific instructions to tax collectors and soldiers to avoid oppressive tendencies in their work (Luke 3:12-14). On the other hand, the "sinners" are welcomed by Jesus, and there is no attention in the story to the nature of their sins. These people are socially marginalized but are affirmed by Jesus and the narrative. Their affirmation in the narrative, and the lack of attention to their past behavior, is a protest against this marginalization (see, for example, Luke 7:36-50).

This lack of attention contrasts with the Acts mission speeches to Jerusalem Jews, where there is a sharp focus on a specific reason why the audience must repent, namely, their rejection of Jesus and complicity in his crucifixion.[23] The Pentecost speech in Acts 2 is the first public proclamation of Jesus' resurrection and exaltation, events that reveal him to be Lord and Messiah. These events should change the audience's understanding of its own actions. They share responsibility for Jesus' death, Peter says. They have blindly rejected the one through whom God was bringing salvation to Israel. These accusations of the audience (see 2:23, 36) lead up to the call to repentance (2:37-38), which means accepting Jesus as their Messiah and receiving forgiveness from him. Thus the Pentecost speech, in its narrative context, is a repentance sermon. The temple speech, which follows in Acts 3:12-26, reinforces the accusation and the call to repentance (see 3:13-15, 17-19). Blindly (see 3:17), they have rejected their own Messiah, with tragic results. If they repent, however, the messianic promises can still be fulfilled. The short speeches by Peter in Acts 4:8-12 and 5:29-32 address the same accusation to the Sanhedrin. Remarkably, responsibility for the death of Jesus is laid at the feet of the people of Jerusalem and their leaders also in later speeches (10:39; 13:27-28), where these accusations are not being applied to the audience. The accusation is limited to the people of Jerusalem at the time of Jesus' death.

The repeated emphasis on responsibility for Jesus' death, followed by the call for repentance and offer of forgiveness, shows that rejection of Jesus in Jerusalem is a continuing problem for the implied author of Luke–Acts. The problem grows as the good news about Jesus is rejected by many Jews as the mission unfolds. Believing the scriptural promises of salvation for the Jewish people and affirming that Jesus Messiah has come to fulfill those promises, the author sees the story of Israel taking a tragic turn and encourages us to weep over this, as Jesus wept for Jerusalem (Luke 19:41-44).[24] Recovery from this tragic situation requires repentance, but Paul's anguished words at the end of Acts (28:25-28) indicate that the majority of Israel has not responded to the message of repentance and forgiveness in the name of Jesus Messiah. The theological problem of Jewish rejection remains unresolved at the end of Acts.[25]

---

[23]On these speeches see further Tannehill, "The Functions of Peter's Mission Speeches in the Narrative of Acts," *NTS* 37 (1991) 400–14.

[24]See Tannehill, "Israel in Luke–Acts: A Tragic Story," *JBL* 104 (1985) 69–85.

[25]On Paul's encounter with the Roman Jews, the final scene of Acts, see Tannehill, *Narrative Unity*, 2.344–57.

Gentiles, also, are expected to "turn" in repentance to God (Acts 11:18; 15:3, 19). In their case, they must turn to the "living God," the creator of all, from the worship of "worthless things" (14:15). Paul's Areopagus speech contains a series of implied criticisms of common pagan worship, rejecting the assumption that God dwells in a building of human construction, needs things that humans supply, and can be represented by a manufactured image (17:24-25, 29). The Areopagus speech leads up to a call to repentance: "Overlooking the times of ignorance, God now commands people that all everywhere repent" (17:30). Although there is a reference to philosophers in 17:18, the speech is not directed against the teachings of Greek philosophy. It is an address to the Areopagus council concerning the popular religious rites and shrines over which they have responsibility.[26]

On their face, Paul's words in 17:30 appear to be an emphatic statement of a universal need for repentance ("everywhere" strengthens "all"). It is the clearest such statement. Evidence elsewhere in Luke–Acts, however, does not always support it. In Luke some individuals are described as "righteous" (δίκαιος; Zechariah and Elizabeth, 1:6; Simeon, 2:25; Joseph of Arimathea, 23:50-51), and in the parable of the lost sheep there is a contrast between the repentant sinner and "ninety-nine righteous persons who have no need of repentance" (15:7; cf. 5:32). To be sure, the assumption that there are many righteous persons who do not need repentance is later undermined by reference to those who falsely "justify yourselves before people" (οἱ δικαιοῦντες ἑαυτοὺς ἐνώπιον τῶν ἀνθρώπων, 16:15) and who "trust in themselves that they are righteous" (18:9). Nevertheless, the possibility remains that there are some who are truly righteous.

In Acts there is the special case of Cornelius, who is "righteous and God-fearing" (10:22; cf. 10:2). The speech of Peter to Cornelius and his household contains no call to repentance (and seems to affirm Cornelius as God-fearing and righteous in 10:35), yet Peter ends by stating that everyone who believes in Jesus receives forgiveness of sins (10:43). The reference to *everyone* who believes returns to the thought at the beginning of Peter's speech: God's acceptance of Gentiles. It seems, then, that Peter's final statement assumes that, in general, the Gentile audience stands in need of forgiveness of sins. The reference to forgiveness is supplemented

[26]See Tannehill, *Narrative Unity*, 2.216–17.

by a reference to God's gift of repentance to Gentiles in 11:18, which serves as a theological summary of the whole Cornelius episode. Thus even in the Cornelius episode there is a general assumption that Gentiles need repentance and forgiveness, although there is no clarity about whether this applies to Cornelius himself.

Paul's speech to Diaspora Jews and God-fearers in Antioch of Pisidia also lacks a call to repentance, yet it closes with an offer of forgiveness of sins and the promise that through Jesus "everyone who believes is being justified (δικαιοῦται) from all the things which you were unable to be justified in the law of Moses" (13:38-39). Furthermore, Paul's summaries of his mission preaching in Acts indicate that repentance was a regular part of his message to Jews and Greeks (20:21; 26:20). In Luke–Acts, then, we find a presumption that there is a general need for repentance and forgiveness and that these are important aspects of the salvation that God offers through Jesus Messiah, but there is a lack of clarity as to whether this applies to certain righteous persons.[27] We can also conclude that, even though the mission speeches in Jerusalem are specific about the crime from which the hearers must repent, there are other occasions on which the preacher does not attempt to specify the sins of the audience but relies on their own awareness of their need for repentance and forgiveness of sins.

Finally, I would like to explain further how, in my understanding, repentance and forgiveness fit into the larger Lukan picture of God's saving work in Jesus. One of the most remarkable aspects of the Acts mission speeches is that Jesus' death is not presented as a saving event through which forgiveness of sins is offered to humanity. Salvation through Jesus is not proclaimed by saying that "Christ died for our sins" (1 Cor 15:3).[28]

---

[27]We should not assume that the gospel has nothing to offer the righteous, for the Lukan understanding of salvation includes more than repentance and forgiveness. It includes, for instance, the gift of the Holy Spirit (Acts 2:38), healing (3:16; 4:9-10), the establishment of a unified community devoted to the worship of God in which the destitute are supported through the sharing of possessions (2:44-47; 4:32-35), the restoration of Israel through its Messiah (Luke 1:68-75; Acts 3:20-21), and sharing with Jesus in the resurrection life of God's eternal kingdom (Acts 26:6-8, 23).

[28]Only two passages attribute saving significance to the death of Jesus as a distinct event. They are the words of Jesus at the Last Supper (Luke 22:19-20)—about which there are textual uncertainties—and Acts 20:28. Neither of these references are part of mission speeches, which summarize in careful and compact form the way the gospel was being presented, according to Luke–Acts.

In order to understand why this view of Jesus' death is unnecessary (and, in fact, would fit awkwardly into the Lukan perspective), we first need to recognize that the proclamations of the fulfillment of the promises to Israel with which Luke begins are themselves soteriological statements. There is an unusual concentration of the terms for savior and salvation (σωτήρ, σωτηρία, σωτήριον) in the first chapters of Luke (1:47, 69, 71, 77; 2:11, 30; 3:6), where the coming fulfillment of the promises is celebrated. Because they appear early in Luke and reappear in Acts, three promise traditions are especially important for understanding the Lukan perspective on God's saving purpose. They concern the promise to Abraham, the promise to David, and certain passages in Isaiah that speak of light and salvation.

It is striking that each of these promise traditions of the infancy narrative not only recurs in Acts but is also presented as a promise that includes Gentiles as well as Jews. Thus in the Magnificat Mary celebrates God's saving intervention for Israel in fulfillment of the promise to Abraham (Luke 1:54-55), and Zechariah in the Benedictus elaborates on this theme (1:72-75). Peter, at the end of his temple speech in Acts 3:25, affirms that the Jewish people has a special role as "sons of the prophets and of the covenant" but goes on to cite the Abraham promise in a universal form: "And in your seed all the families of the earth will be blessed" (cf. Gen 22:18; 26:4). This blessing refers to the salvation being offered to the world through Jesus. Similarly, Gabriel's announcement to Mary in Luke 1:32-33 reflects God's promise to David of a successor to his throne, who would be God's son (cf. 2 Sam 7:12-16), and the expectation of the Davidic Messiah is further developed in Luke 1:69-71 and 2:11. Then Peter at Pentecost proclaims that the promise of the Messiah who would inherit David's throne has been fulfilled through Jesus' resurrection (Acts 2:30-31; see also Paul's synagogue speech in 13:22-23, 32-35). The enthronement of the Davidic Messiah is a saving event for Gentiles as well as Jews, as is made clear by Acts 15:16-17 (quoting a version of Amos 9:11-12). The third promise tradition recalls Isaiah's prophecies of "God's salvation" (σωτήριον) revealed to "all flesh" (Isa 40:5 LXX, quoted at Luke 3:6; cf. also 2:30) and of one who will be a "light of the nations" to bring "salvation to the end of the earth" (Isa 49:6; cf. Luke 2:32). These prophecies are not only reflected in the early chapters of Luke but continue to reverberate in

Acts (cf. 1:8; 13:47; 26:23; 28:28[29]). The universal scope of this saving revelation is apparent already in Luke 2:32 and 3:6.[30]

These three promise traditions help shape the Lukan vision of salvation, which is multi-faceted, embracing the bodily, economic, and social dimensions of human life. Even the theme of forgiveness of sins has a social dimension, for, in context, the reference to forgiveness of sins in Luke 1:77 is best understood to refer to the communal sins of the people,[31] and Jesus' ministry to "sinners" has the implication that these marginalized people should now be accepted in Jewish society. Jesus' saving work of forgiving sinners is not postponed until his death, as if it could not happen apart from his death for sins. In the Nazareth synagogue Jesus reveals that he has been sent to proclaim "release," which includes the release of sins, and this is a central aspect of his mission (the word ἄφεσις occurs twice in Luke 4:18). Then in 5:24 Jesus claims the authority to carry out this mission of releasing sins as he encounters specific persons in his historical ministry.

In Jesus' final words to his followers in Luke, he commands that his mission continue through the proclamation of "repentance for[32] forgiveness of sins in his name" (24:47). This is a commission to the apostles, which Paul will later share (Acts 26:16-20). However, we cannot simply say that the apostles and Paul continue Jesus' mission of proclaiming repentance and forgiveness. The apostles are to proclaim repentance and forgiveness *in Jesus' name*, and Jesus has received new authority that makes his name a powerful source of benefits, which are offered through a mission that extends far beyond the previous ministry of Jesus. Thus the saving work of Jesus, including the proclamation of repentance and forgiveness, is raised to a new level. This is the significance of the death, resurrection, and exaltation of Jesus, according to the mission speeches in the early part of Acts. The killing of Jesus is a human act of rejection and denial. By itself it would have no saving significance. But God rejects this human rejection,

---

[29]Use of the rare word σωτήριον—which occurs in the New Testament only in Luke 2:30; 3:6; Acts 28:28; Eph 6:17—indicates that Isa 40:5 is still an influence when Paul makes his final statement in Acts.

[30]For a more detailed discussion of these three promise traditions, see Tannehill, "The Story of Israel within the Lukan Narrative," in *Jesus and the Heritage of Israel: Luke's Narrative Claim upon Israel's Legacy*, edited by David P. Moessner (Harrisburg, Pa.: Trinity, 1999) 327–30.

[31]See Tannehill, *Luke*, 62.

[32]The text is uncertain. Many manuscripts read "repentance and forgiveness."

raising Jesus from the dead, which leads to the public testimony that Jesus is God's Messiah, who will from now on assume the throne of David and reign at God's right hand (cf. Acts 2:23-36).[33]

As ruling Messiah, Jesus has the power to confer benefits.[34] This power is expressed by a repeated pattern of thought in the Jerusalem mission speeches: the exalted Lord Messiah "pours out" or "gives" gifts to those who call upon him. The Pentecost speech focuses on the gift of the Spirit (2:33, "Being exalted at the right hand of God, and having received from the Father the promise of the Holy Spirit, he poured out this that you see and hear"), but other gifts are mentioned in the following speeches. In 4:12 Peter proclaims that Jesus' "name . . . has been given among humans" as a means of salvation (see 2:21). Jesus' name represents his royal power and authority, accessible now as a source of saving benefits. The statement that Jesus' "name . . . has been given" is an extension of the idea that the Messiah gives benefits through his name. These benefits include healing (3:6, 16; 4:7, 10, 30), but through baptism in Jesus' name people will also receive release of sins and "the gift of the Holy Spirit" (2:38). Indeed, the apostles were instructed to proclaim "repentance for release of sins in his [the Messiah's] name" in the commission statement at the end of Luke (24:47; see Acts 10:43). This is the context in which we should understand the prominent statements about "giving" repentance or repentance and forgiveness in Acts 5:31 and 11:18. In 5:31, the fullest statement, the gift is connected directly to Jesus' new status at the right hand of God: "God exalted him as leader and savior at his right hand to give repentance to Israel and forgiveness of sins." Jesus' exaltation has a saving purpose. Enthroned at God's right hand, his ruling power is saving power,[35] for he can confer the benefits of the messianic kingdom on his loyal people. Among these benefits are repentance and forgiveness. Furthermore, Jesus' death, resurrection, and exaltation demonstrate Jesus' faithfulness to God, God's affirmation of Jesus, and God's power to use even human resistance

---

[33]For a more complete discussion of Peter's Pentecost speech, see Tannehill, *Narrative Unity,* 2.29–42.

[34]On the application of the cultural role of "benefactor" to Jesus in Luke–Acts, see Frederick W. Danker, *Luke,* 2d ed., Proclamation Commentaries (Philadelphia: Fortress, 1987) 28–46.

[35]Two of the three passages that designate Jesus as "savior (σωτήρ)" clearly present Jesus as the royal Messiah (Luke 2:11; Acts 13:23). In the third passage also (Acts 5:31), Jesus' exaltation is probably understood as enthronement (see 2:30-35).

to accomplish God's purpose of bringing the nations to repentance and forgiveness.

Luke and Acts are narratives about the past, not messages spoken directly to us. They can be suggestive for our life today, but a leap of insight and inspiration is required to apply the Lukan message to our world. Nevertheless, the strong call for repentance in Luke–Acts, the breadth and depth of reflection on this theme, and the chorus of other biblical voices calling for repentance may set us thinking about our own need for repentance, as individuals and as nations. If we are willing to respond in this way, an understanding of repentance as part of Luke's broader soteriology may help faithful people to embrace repentance as a saving benefit. After all, a transformed life, free of those things that damage ourselves and others, is a great gift.

Part II

Luke and the Jews

Part II

Luke and the Jews

7
Israel in Luke–Acts: A Tragic Story

What is the attitude of the author of Luke–Acts toward Judaism? This has been a controversial question in the interpretation of these writings. I believe that we gain special insight if we consider the story of Israel in Luke–Acts as a unitary plot line within the narrative and compare the expectations of salvation for the Jewish people at the beginning (in Luke's infancy narrative) with the ending of Acts, which highlights the lack of response by Paul's Jewish audience. In between this beginning and this ending, we have a story that takes a tragic turn. The course of events is tragic for the implied author, not just for unbelieving Jews, for it challenges the implied author's conviction that scriptural promises of salvation for both Israel and the Gentiles are being fulfilled through Jesus Messiah.

The following essay is a fairly succinct overview that pulls together large blocks of evidence for my interpretation. Some of the other essays in this collection supplement this one by discussing how Jews are presented or addressed in Luke–Acts. The essays on "Rejection by Jews and Turning to Gentiles" and "The Story of Israel within the Lukan Narrative" are directly related to the theme of the following essay. Further discussion of some of the key passages in Luke–Acts may be found in The Narrative Unity of Luke–Acts *and in my commentary on Luke in the Abingdon New Testament Commentaries series.*

This study[1] is part of an attempt to understand Luke–Acts as a unitary narrative in which the episodes receive their meaning through their function within the larger whole. The encounter between Jesus and his witnesses, on the one hand, and the people of Israel and its representatives, on the other, becomes a major plot development within Luke–Acts, stretching from the beginning to the end of the two-volume work and contributing greatly to its unity. Therefore, it is important that we understand this development clearly.

The episodes in Luke–Acts are part of a unitary story because they are related to a unifying purpose, the βουλὴ τοῦ θεοῦ, to which the writing refers with some frequency (Luke 7:30, Acts 2:23, 4:28, 5:38-39, 13:36, 20:27). This purpose is knowable, and the readers are told what it is. In relation to this purpose individual incidents take on meaning: they represent particular steps in the realization of this purpose or portray human resistance to this purpose.

If we are to understand the narrative in its unity, we must pay particular attention to disclosures of the overarching purpose in light of which individual events take on meaning. Where are these disclosures to be found? I call attention to the following aspects of Luke–Acts. First, recent theoretical discussions of narrative have noted that events in the narrative may be referred to out of chronological order. There may be previews of coming events and reviews of past events, often in a way that interprets these events from some perspective.[2] Luke–Acts makes liberal use of such previews and reviews in interpreting for the reader the overall course of the story. Second, we must pay careful attention to the OT quotations and allusions in Luke–Acts, especially those at major turning points in the narrative and those that appear more than once. Particular OT passages are used to disclose the divine purpose that is being realized in the narrative. These passages not only show in a general way that the law and the prophets are fulfilled in Jesus Christ. They express a particular understanding of

---

[1] This article is a revised and expanded version of my Society of Biblical Literature—Claremont Fellowship Lecture, delivered at the annual meeting of the Society of Biblical Literature, December 1982. I wish to thank the Institute for Antiquity and Christianity at Claremont, the Claremont Graduate School, and the Society of Biblical Literature for support received in 1982, which aided me in the development of the following ideas.

[2] See Gérard Genette, *Narrative Discourse: An Essay in Method* (Ithaca, N.Y.: Cornell University Press, 1980) 33–85.

God's purpose and are programs for action. The discerning reader will ask whether and how this purpose is being realized in the narrative. Third, God's purpose is realized through chosen instruments, persons commissioned by God to carry out some aspect of this purpose. At various points in Luke–Acts there are statements of the commission that has been received by Jesus, by the twelve, by Paul, etc. These commission statements are also disclosures of divine purpose, programs for action by particular characters, and keys to the plot.[3] For instance, at the beginning of his ministry Jesus announces in the Nazareth synagogue what he has been anointed to do, quoting Isaiah (Luke 4:18-19). This is a commission statement, and it is widely recognized that it is programmatic, that is, intended to interpret the subsequent events of Jesus' ministry. Fourth, we must also consider what reliable characters within the story have to say about God's purpose and the meaning of the events being narrated. It is common for an author to present one or more characters as especially reliable, perceptive, authoritative. These characters are likely to become spokespersons for the author in interpreting events of the story.[4] So statements by Jesus in the Gospel, and by Peter, Stephen, and Paul in Acts, may be important for interpreting the narrative as a whole. The four types of material mentioned—previews and reviews, scriptural references, commission statements, and interpretive statements by reliable characters— overlap, for an OT quotation may also be a preview or a commission statement, etc. But mentioning them in series provides some idea of the range of material in which we are likely to find clues to the divine purpose that unifies the story.

Investigation of the role of Israel in the plot of Luke–Acts shows that the study of Luke–Acts as a unitary narrative both sharpens certain questions and

---

[3] A unified narrative sequence results from the acceptance of a commission by a story character and the attempt to fulfill this commission. See Robert C. Tannehill, "The Gospel of Mark as Narrative Christology," *Semeia* 16 (1979) 60–61. My term "commission" is similar to the term "mandate" in some structural analysis of narrative. See Jean Calloud, *Structural Analysis of Narrative* (Philadelphia: Fortress; Missoula: Scholars, 1976) 17, 25, 27; Daniel Patte, *What is Structural Exegesis?* GBS (Philadelphia: Fortress, 1976) 37–44.

[4] See Wayne C. Booth, *The Rhetoric of Fiction* (Chicago: University of Chicago Press, 1961) 18: "The author is present in every speech given by any character who has had conferred upon him, in whatever manner, the badge of reliability." While there are important differences between Luke–Acts and the novels that Booth discusses, in both cases the standpoint of an "implied author" can be inferred from the norms and choices revealed by the construction of the work.

suggests new answers.[5] It also indicates that the message of Luke–Acts lies not merely in its theological statements but also in its feeling tones.

The problem comes into focus when we compare the beginning of Luke with the end of Acts. In a well-formed story of the traditional kind we would expect continuity between the expectations aroused at the beginning of the story and the outcome at the end. There are indeed indications at the beginning of what will happen later. Already in Simeon's response to the baby Jesus (Luke 2:29-32) we are told that Jesus has special meaning for both Israel and the Gentiles. When he sees the baby Jesus, Simeon sees God's salvation (σωτήριον), which will be "light" for Gentiles and "glory" for Israel. This theme of the universal revelation of God's σωτήριον is repeated in the quotation of Isa 40:3-5 in Luke 3:4-6. The only other occurrence of the term σωτήριον in Luke–Acts is in Paul's final statement to the Roman Jews at the end of Acts (Acts 28:28). This seems to be a deliberate inclusion, with the end of the work pointing back to the beginning.[6] But this reference back also emphasizes the difference between the beginning and the end, for in the final scene in Acts Paul declares that the Roman Jews, like the Jews elsewhere, are blind and deaf, while the Gentiles will hear and receive "this salvation of God."

---

[5] In addition to works cited later in this article, the following works are relevant to my topic and provide a sampling of previous opinion: Hans Conzelmann, *The Theology of St. Luke,* trans. Geoffrey Buswell (London: Faber & Faber, 1960) 145–49, 162–67; Walther Eltester, "Israel im lukanischen Werk und die Nazarethperikope," in *Jesus in Nazareth,* edited by W. Eltester, BZNW 40 (Berlin: de Gruyter, 1972) 76–147; Eric Franklin, *Christ the Lord* (Philadelphia: Westminster, 1975) 77–115; Augustin George, "Israel," in *Études sur l'oeuvre de Luc,* SB (Paris: Gabalda, 1978) 87–125; Joachim Gnilka, *Die Verstockung Israels,* SANT 3 (Munich: Kösel, 1961) 119–54; Ernst Haenchen, "Judentum und Christentum in der Apostelgeschichte," *ZNW* 54 (1963) 155–87; Douglas R. A. Hare, "The Rejection of the Jews in the Synoptic Gospels and Acts," *Anti Semitism and the Foundations of Christianity,* ed. Alan T. Davies (New York: Paulist, 1979) 27–47; Jacob Jervell, *Luke and the People of God* (Minneapolis: Augsburg, 1972); Luke Timothy Johnson, *The Literary Function of Possessions in Luke–Acts,* SBLDS 39 (Missoula: Scholars Press, 1977) 38–126; Gerhard Lohfink, *Die Sammlung Israels,* SANT 39 (Munich: Kösel, 1975); Robert Maddox, *The Purpose of Luke–Acts,* FRLANT 126 (Göttingen: Vandenhoeck & Ruprecht, 1982) 31–65; J. C. O'Neill, *The Theology of Acts in Its Historical Setting,* 2d ed. (London: SPCK, 1970) 77–99; Gerhard Schneider, "Der Zweck des lukanischen Doppelwerks," *BZ* 21 (1977) 45–66; Stephen G. Wilson, *The Gentiles and the Gentile Mission in Luke–Acts,* SNTSMS 23 (Cambridge: Cambridge University Press, 1973) 219–38.

[6] See Jacques Dupont, "The Salvation of the Gentiles and the Theological Significance of Acts," in *The Salvation of the Gentiles* (New York: Paulist, 1979) 14–16. The neuter form σωτήριον is found only four times in the NT. The three occurrences in Luke–Acts may all derive from Isa 40:5, quoted in Luke 3:6.

The early chapters of Luke also provide hints of the conflict within Israel that Jesus and his messengers will produce. Mary speaks of God's scattering the proud and sending away the rich (Luke 1:51-53). Simeon adds to his joyful words the somber statement that Jesus "is set for the fall and rising of many in Israel," and Jesus' ministry begins with his rejection at Nazareth (Luke 4:22-30). These indications of conflict fit events of the following narrative. So do the hints that Gentiles will be included in God's salvation. An author who introduces early in the narrative these previews of what is to follow should also be aware that the most strongly emphasized anticipation in Luke 1-2 stands in tension with the course of the narrative in Acts. The few words in the birth narratives suggesting salvation for Gentiles and conflict in Israel are surrounded by much fuller statements about Israel's salvation through Jesus. These statements are phrased in such a way as to make clear that they refer to the Jewish people. The angel Gabriel announces that "the Lord God will give" to Mary's child "the throne of David his father, and he will reign over the house of Jacob forever" (Luke 1:32-33). Both Mary and Zechariah proclaim that God has helped Israel, in fulfillment of the promises to the fathers (1:54-55, 68-75). Zechariah speaks of "redemption" for God's people and "a horn of salvation for us in the house of David" (1:68-69). Specifically, this salvation means "salvation from our enemies and from the hand of all who hate us" and being "rescued from the hand of enemies" (1:71, 74). Consider the impact of such words on readers who are aware of the Jewish-Roman war and its outcome. They would sense the tragic disappointment of this hope. To have a pious man express so poignantly a hope that is later disappointed produces a tragic effect. The narrative about Anna repeats Zechariah's term "redemption" and speaks specifically of the "redemption of Jerusalem" (2:38). The readers of Luke–Acts knew what later happened to Jerusalem.

When we consider the beginning of Luke and look for the type of material which I previously described—previews of the course of the narrative, statements of the commission to be carried out by the main character and his followers, OT quotations or freely formulated reminders of the OT hope, and statements by characters who are presented favorably and therefore seem to be reliable spokespersons for the implied author[7]—

---

[7] The phrase "implied author" is useful for two reasons: (1) it suggests that the values and perspectives of the author implied by the work may differ from those of the author in ordinary life, representing, perhaps, a purified version of the latter; and (2) it indicates that the position of the author must be

we find very strong emphasis on the view that Jesus means redemption for Israel, that is, for the Jewish people. However, in Acts, after the introduction of Stephen, the Jews reject the Word in place after place, and this rejection is highlighted in a series of scenes (two of them lengthy) in which Paul responds by turning to the Gentiles (Acts 13:44-47; 18:6; 28:24-28). So it seems that the expectation most emphasized in Luke 1–2 is largely *not* fulfilled in the following narrative.

There are several possible explanations of what we have found. First, one may conclude that this is evidence that Luke 1–2 has not been integrated into Luke–Acts as a whole. These initial chapters come from a special source and reflect a distinct theological viewpoint. However, since Paul Minear's article "Luke's Use of the Birth Stories,"[8] it should no longer be possible to ignore the many points of contact between the birth stories and the rest of Luke–Acts. The importance of the birth narratives for interpreting Luke–Acts as a whole must be recognized. The possible use of sources for parts of the birth narratives does not undermine this statement, for the selection of source material for inclusion in the work is an authorial choice which may reflect the author's purposes as clearly as freely composed material.

A second possibility: Whether a character is reliable or not can only be judged from the narrative as a whole. We might conclude from the course of the subsequent narrative that Mary and Zechariah, Simeon and Anna, are in some respects unreliable in speaking of God's purpose and the meaning of Jesus. Perhaps they are blinded by Jewish nationalism and by traditional assumptions of God's preference for Israel, while the author intends to lead us beyond their limited perspective. However, the following evidence counts against this view: With the partial exception of Zechariah (cf. Luke 1:20), the four persons named are presented as models of faith within expectant Israel. Furthermore, their words have a poetic quality, rendering them powerful and impressive (see the canticles). These words contain many reminders of scripture, so that they seem to share the authority of scripture. Finally, the first proclaimer of the view that Jesus is

---

inferred from the choices made in writing and the norms suggested in the story for judging events and characters within it. Wayne Booth speaks of "the core of norms and choices [within a work] which I am calling the implied author" *(Rhetoric of Fiction,* 74).

[8] In *Studies in Luke–Acts,* edited by Leander E. Keck and J. Louis Martyn (Nashville: Abingdon, 1966) 111–30. See also Raymond E. Brown, *The Birth of the Messiah* (Garden City, N.Y.: Doubleday, 1979) 241–43.

the messianic redeemer of Israel is the angel Gabriel (1:32-33), who speaks as God's messenger and therefore with unquestionable authority within the implied author's story world. This evidence indicates that the presentation of God's purpose in Luke 1–2 is being affirmed by the implied author.

A third possibility: A narrative may result in the nonfulfillment of expectations and purposes associated with central characters and still be a unified story. Characters may have for themselves, and arouse in the reader, expectations of happiness, while the actual outcome is pain and loss. The more strongly the story arouses the expectation of happiness for a character, presenting this happiness as a possibility within grasp, the more tragic will be the failure to actualize this possibility. Indeed, the sense of the tragic is commonly produced by a sharp shift from happiness or the expectation of happiness to a situation of pain and loss. A vivid sense of happiness present or available is necessary to a vivid sense of tragic loss. It seems to me that the narrative strategy of Luke–Acts takes on meaning if we assume that the author is guiding the readers to experience the story of Israel and its messiah as a tragic story. For this purpose the incongruity we have noted between initial expectation and final reality is highly useful.

I am not implying that Luke–Acts as a *whole* is tragic. Israel's tragic story is an aspect of Luke–Acts, a very important aspect, but there is more to Luke–Acts than this. We are repeatedly told that Jewish rejection does not block the progress of the Word of God, which finds other opportunities. Furthermore, I do not wish to imply that the outcome is tragic for all Jews. The apostles' mission in Jerusalem, up to the narrative about Stephen, is portrayed as very successful (see Acts 2:41; 4:4; 5:14; 6:7; 21:20), and it may be, as some interpreters believe,[9] that the ending of Acts leaves open the possibility that some Jews will still accept Jesus as messiah. However, we must recognize where the emphasis falls as the story in Acts progresses. We must recognize that, from the story of Stephen on, we find repeated emphasis on Jewish rejection, that this is portrayed in major dramatic scenes designed to make an impression on the reader, and that the final statement of Paul in Acts highlights Jewish blindness and deafness, in contrast to the openness of the Gentiles to God's salvation

---

[9] See, e.g., Hermann J. Hauser, *Strukturen der Abschlusserzählung der Apostelgeschichte,* AnBib 86 (Rome: Pontifical Biblical Institute Press, 1979) 108–9; J. Dupont, "La conclusion des Actes et son rapport à l'ensemble de l'ouvrage de Luc," in *Les Actes des Apôtres,* edited by J. Kremer, BETL 48 (Gembloux: Duculot, 1979) 377–80.

through Jesus. When we read of Jewish resistance in city after city and when on three of these occasions (in Antioch of Pisidia, Corinth, and Rome) Paul responds with the announcement that he is turning to the Gentiles, a pattern is established that conveys a general impression of the way things are going. This pattern allows room for exceptions. It is not the same as a general statement about all Jews everywhere. Nevertheless, it indicates a turn in the story away from what we were led to expect by the proclamations of salvation for Israel through Jesus, Israel's messiah, in Luke 1–2.

If it is true that the story of Israel in Luke–Acts is being presented as a tragic story, some common assumptions about Luke–Acts must be reconsidered, especially the assumptions that Luke, as much as possible, emphasizes the success of the mission and is primarily concerned with justifying the Gentile mission and the Gentile church.[10] At least six lines of evidence support the thesis that the author of Luke–Acts is guiding the readers toward viewing the recent history of the Jewish people as tragic. This evidence includes expressions of passionate concern and sorrow by central characters in the story, characters who, being reliable representatives of the author's point of view, express appropriate responses to events in the narrative, according to the standards of the author.

First, consider the series of four texts in the Gospel of Luke that speak of Jerusalem, its rejection of Jesus, and its coming destruction. The importance of this theme is clear from its repeated appearance, first in 13:33-35, then in 19:41-44; 21:20-24; 23:27-31. The destruction of Jerusalem is regarded as divine punishment for the rejection of Jesus, but the tone is pathetic, not vindictive. David L. Tiede, in his book *Prophecy and History in Luke–Acts,* has given the appropriate title "Weeping for Jerusalem" to his insightful discussion of these texts.[11] In two of the passages Jesus speaks directly to the city, using the personal address of the second person in expressions of lament and unfulfilled yearning (13:34-35; 19:42-44). In one of the passages Jesus is depicted as weeping for the

---

[10] See Ernst Haenchen, *The Acts of the Apostles,* trans. Bernard Noble et al. (Philadelphia: Westminster, 1971) 100: Acts "gives the impression of a problem-free, victorious progress on the part of the Christian mission. But in reality Luke the historian is wrestling, from the first page to the last, with the problem of the *mission to the Gentiles without the law.* His entire presentation is influenced by this" (italics in original text). It would be truer to say that the problem for the author is not the Gentile mission but the rejection of Jesus by the Jews, and, when we recognize the importance of this problem, Acts clearly does not present a "problem-free, victorious progress" of the mission.
[11] *Prophecy and History in Luke–Acts* (Philadelphia: Fortress, 1980) 65–96.

city (19:41-44). This is remarkable in light of Luke's general tendency to remove indications of Jesus' emotions found in Mark.[12] The authority attributed to Jesus makes him a reliable guide to the appropriate attitude toward the destruction of Jerusalem. If Jesus weeps, it is appropriate for others, also, to weep for Jerusalem. The last two passages evoke the suffering of women and their children (21:23; 23:28-31), and in 23:27-31 Jesus directly addresses the "daughters of Jerusalem" in a scene of mourning. Here we have the time-tested device of producing tragic pathos by presenting the suffering of helpless women and children.[13] Although Jerusalem's destruction is caused by its blind rejection of Jesus (see 19:44), readers are encouraged to view the city and its inhabitants with the sympathetic pity appropriate to tragedy.[14]

Second, at the transition from Luke to Acts the narrator, through the speech of characters, reminds the reader that the hope for Israel with which the story began has not been fulfilled. That hope is not to be forgotten as if it were unimportant. In Luke 24:21 the disciples on the road to Emmaus say, "We were hoping that he was the one who was going to redeem Israel." They are expressing with sadness the same hope that was proclaimed with joy in the birth narratives. The infinitive λυτροῦσθαι ("to redeem") reverts to a word root that has not appeared in Luke since Zechariah's Benedictus and Anna's words in the temple. In both cases the redemption in question was explicitly for Israel or Jerusalem (1:68; 2:38), just as in the statement by the disappointed disciples. The resurrection, of course, will remove the disciples' disappointment, but it does not immediately and automatically solve their problem, as Acts 1:6 shows. When the disciples ask the risen Jesus, "Will you at this time restore the kingdom to Israel?" they show that the resurrection has revived the hope expressed by the travelers to Emmaus but has not fulfilled it. The disciples are talking about the same hope as the travelers to Emmaus. The reference to Israel is again explicit.

---

[12] See Joseph A. Fitzmyer, *The Gospel according to Luke I–IX,* AB (Garden City, N.Y.: Doubleday, 1981) 94–95. There are a number of similarities in wording between Luke 19:41-44 and Zechariah's Benedictus (1:68-79). Note "visited/visitation," "our/your enemies," "knowledge of salvation/if you knew/because you did not know," "way of peace/the things that lead to peace." With "hid from your eyes" in 19:42 compare 2:30-32; 3:6. Words associated with the fulfillment of Israel's hope in the beginning chapters of Luke return in negative statements in 19:41-44, accentuating the tragic turn in the narrative.

[13] Compare Aeschylus's drama, *The Suppliant Maidens.*

[14] Other aspects of Luke's passion story indicate that it is a tragic narrative in which the Jewish people are involved. See David Tiede, *Prophecy and History,* 103–18.

The restoration of a kingdom to Israel relates to the Davidic messianism of the birth stories, where the language of kingship is clearly used (Luke 1:32-33) and where this messianism is connected with the "redemption" of Israel (1:68-69). In Acts 1:6 the readers are again being reminded of this unfulfilled hope for Israel. Jesus' answer to the disciples' question denies that they can know the time and probably corrects their supposition that the restoration may come immediately, but Jesus' reply is not meant to reject the possibility of a restoration of the kingdom to Israel.[15] This is shown by Acts 3:19-21, where Peter speaks of the "times of restoration," involving the coming of Israel's messiah to the people of Jerusalem, as a real possibility. Not only is Peter's statement linked to the disciples' question in Acts 1:6 by the unusual words ἀποκαθιστάνω and ἀποκατά-στασις,[16] but the words χρόνοι and καιροί occur in the immediate context in both cases. These connections indicate that the times of restoration of which Peter speaks include the restoration of the kingdom to Israel. This is supported by the fact that these times of restoration will bring fulfillment of all things which ἐλάλησεν ὁ θεὸς διὰ στόματος τῶν ἁγίων ἀπ᾽ αἰῶνος αὐτοῦ προφητῶν. The same long and clumsy clause is found in Luke 1:69-70, where it clearly refers to salvation for Israel through the promised Davidic messiah. Peter's sermon shows that the hope of a messianic kingdom for Israel that will fulfill all the prophecies is not dead. However, Acts 3:19-21 makes fulfillment dependent on repentance. After the mission's initial success in Jerusalem, the emphasis in Acts falls on Jewish resistance and rejection. Even this does not mean that the hope for Israel is dead. After all, the kingdom for Israel was promised by God through the prophets, and it is not likely that the author of Luke–Acts would admit that this important aspect of God's purpose has been finally frustrated. However, the story in Acts, so far as the author takes us, is not the story of the fulfillment of this hope but the story of a tragic turn away from fulfillment. The repeated references to Israel's messianic hope during the transition from Luke to Acts remind the reader that this hope is not yet fulfilled and prepare for this tragic turn.

A third kind of evidence is found when we consider repetitive patterns in the mission speeches to Jews in Acts. The great concern of Acts with Jewish rejection of Jesus is indicated by the way that the death of Jesus is

---

[15] In agreement with Hans Conzelmann, *Theology of St. Luke,* 163.
[16] The verb occurs only twice in Luke–Acts; the noun occurs only once in the NT.

presented in these speeches. Jesus' death means the denial and rejection of Jesus by the rulers and the inhabitants of Jerusalem, and this denial and rejection become the basis of repeated accusations of the Jerusalemites (2:23, 36; 3:13-15; 4:10-11; 5:30; 10:39; 13:27-29). Nevertheless, repentance is possible and forgiveness is offered. A sense of passionate concern is added to the call to repentance by a repeated stylistic peculiarity in the use of first- and second-person pronouns. First- and second-person pronouns are used emphatically to stress that Jesus Christ is good news especially for the Jews who are being addressed. This will increase the sense of loss if this good news is rejected. Addressing a Jewish audience, the preacher emphasizes that the promise or the word is "to you," who are the sons of the prophets and the covenant, and this emphasis is made clear by placing the pronoun "you" (or "us") in first position in the sentence or clause. Thus in Acts 2:39 Peter says, *"To you* is the promise, and to your children," and in 3:25-26 he says, *"You* [with the nominative pronoun used for emphasis] are the sons of the prophets and of the covenant. . . . *To you* first God, having raised up his servant, sent him. . . ." Paul speaks in a similar way in 13:26: "Sons of the family of Abraham and the God fearers among you, *to us*[17] the word of this salvation was sent out." Then, following the appearance of Jewish resis-tance, Paul announces, *"To you* it was necessary that the word of God be spoken first" (13:46), echoing the end of Peter's second sermon. These emphatic personal pronouns apply the message to the audience, and this application is accompanied by the idea that the promise was made to the fathers of Israel, announced by the prophets of Israel, and is therefore especially meant for the people of Israel. To them especially it has relevance and meaning, for it is the fulfillment of their hope and history. If, then, this message is rejected by a large part of Israel, the result is tragic, for what was rightfully theirs, what was central to the meaning of Jewish existence, has also been rejected. This tragedy is underlined when the words of Paul to the Jews come back at the end of Acts with one significant alteration. Paul says to the Jews of Antioch of Pisidia, "To us the word of this salvation was sent out" (13:26). He says to the Jews of Rome, "To the Gentiles has been sent this salvation of God" (28:28). In both cases the noun or pronoun indicating the recipient comes first in the clause for emphasis.

---

[17] Alternate reading: "to you."

A related theme is found in the trial speeches of Paul, and this constitutes a fourth line of evidence for a tragic view of Israel. In the narrative of Acts a series of charges against Paul are listed, but in his defense speeches Paul insists that he is on trial for the hope of Israel. This is peculiar. Paul is insisting that the issue of the trial is something quite different from what everyone else thinks it is. The importance of this theme is shown by its gradual development over a series of speeches (see 23:6; 24:15, 21; 26:6-8), coming to a climax in the defense speech before King Agrippa, which is the centerpiece of one of the most fully developed narrative scenes in Acts. Furthermore, Paul repeats this theme in 28:20, when he says to the Roman Jews, "Because of the hope of Israel I wear this chain." This hope is a hope for resurrection of the dead. When introduced in 23:6, it is presented as a Pharisaic hope, rejected by the Sadducees, but in the course of the narrative this hope comes to be identified simply as "the hope of Israel." This hope for resurrection is surely connected in the author's mind with the resurrection of Jesus, who is "first of the resurrection of the dead" (26:23). Yet this connection with Jesus' resurrection is less clearly emphasized than two other points:

(1) Paul's authentic Jewishness in maintaining this Jewish belief, and
(2) the tragic irony that Paul's opponents, in rejecting Paul and his message, are rejecting the fulfillment of their own hope.

Paul's hope is one that Paul's accusers themselves anticipate and await, according to 24:15. It is "hope in the promise made by God to our fathers" (26:6). But this is the bitter irony: "Concerning this hope I am being accused by Jews, O king!" (26:7). This exclamation, the climax of a long development through Paul's defense speeches, reveals the tragic irony of Jewish rejection. The central focus of Jewish hope, the main object of earnest intercession, is rejected by Jews as they reject Paul and his message. The theme of Paul on trial for the hope of Israel highlights the tragic irony of the situation into which Paul's Jewish opponents have blindly stumbled.

The fifth piece of evidence consists in the shifting position of the Jewish people when we consider the course of the plot as a whole. I have already mentioned that the first two chapters of the Gospel, full of previews of the meaning of Jesus, proclaim that Jesus means salvation for Israel. The somber words of Simeon to Mary (Luke 2:34-35) seem only a slight shadow in the midst of all this brightness and joy. However, the end of Acts proclaims that Israel is a people blind and deaf to God's word. There has been a turn in the plot, a reversal of fortunes. Expectations of happiness for Israel as a people, expressed at the beginning of the story, are not realized, for the plot turns in the opposite direction. Aristotle, in his discussion of tragedy in the *Poetics,* speaks of reversal in the plot (περι-πέτεια) as one of the two greatest means by which tragedy wins over its audience (1450a). There is room for debate about the exact kind of reversal Aristotle had in mind. The type of reversal in Sophocles' *Oedipus,* in which the chief character's own quest leads to the tragic reversal of his situation, a reversal that is dramatically disclosed in a key recognition scene, has obvious advantages for dramatic effect. Nevertheless, other reversals of fortune may occur, and, if the shift is from happiness to suffering, the development is tragic.[18] A vivid presentation of great happiness, now enjoyed or within one's grasp, provides a standard for measuring the greatness of loss when that happiness is destroyed. However the reversal of fortune comes about and however it is discovered, vivid presentation of a happiness that was present or possible produces a vivid sense of loss when that happiness is destroyed, which contributes to the emotions of pity and fear which Aristotle regarded as appropriate to tragedy.[19]

In Luke–Acts the downward turn of the plot for Israel is prolonged through a number of stages. It is geographically extended and multi-plied. There is recurrent awakening of hope and recurrent failure of fulfillment. This can contribute to the tragic effect of the whole. The author of Luke–Acts constructs a plot that emphasizes the shift in Israel's fortune and encourages the readers to view this shift as tragic by introducing a pathetic tone into the narrative at key places and by focusing attention on a great possibility of happiness that is being lost. This reading of Luke–Acts is

---

[18] D. W. Lucas, in discussing Aristotle's "complex" plot, which builds up to a scene of reversal and/or recognition, argues "that Aristotle went too far in identifying complexity with the presence of one overriding illusion which is dispelled in a few moments of intense drama; the real difference is that the simple play moves in one direction with minor variations of pace and tension, while a play gives an impression of complexity if there are changes in the trend and direction of the action even without a sudden *volteface*"; *Aristotle Poetics: Introduction, Commentary and Appendixes* (Oxford: Clarendon, 1968) 295.

[19] Aristotle also notes the role of "ignorance (ἄγνοια)" in the tragic plot. See *Poetics* 1453b–1454a. Compare the "ignorance" of the Jews in rejecting Jesus according to Acts 3:17; 13:27. In the light of this, Acts 2:36ff. ("Let all the house of Israel know. . . . They were cut to the heart. . . .") constitutes a recognition scene.

supported by the features of the narrative that I have discussed: the scenes of weeping and lament for Jerusalem; the reminders of the unfulfilled promise to Israel during the transition from Luke to Acts; the insistence in speeches to Jews that this salvation has been sent "to you," the sons of the prophets and the covenant, which accentuates the tragic loss of refusing what is central to their scripture and their life; and the tragic irony that the Jews who accuse Paul are rejecting the hope of Israel.

The remarks about tragic reversal in the plot of Luke–Acts as a whole also help us to understand the significance of Israel's history as presented in Stephen's speech. This will provide a sixth piece of evidence for a tragic view of Israel, for the history of Israel from Abraham to Moses as presented by Stephen follows the same trajectory as the story of Israel from Luke 1 to Acts 28. In both cases it is a story of tragic reversal of fortune. Thus not only does the rejection of Moses prefigure the rejection of Jesus; the whole movement from great hopes to great loss in Stephen's description of Israel's history prefigures the story of Israel and Jesus in Luke–Acts.

Recognizing that Stephen's speech not only prepares for his indictment against his accusers at the end of the speech but also wishes to present Israel's story as a tragic reversal of fortune helps to explain the function of parts of the speech that have seemed irrelevant.[20] The narra-tive of Abraham's election and God's promise to him and his descendants is not irrelevant if the author intends to emphasize that Israel was a people with great expectations who, just when their hopes were about to be fulfilled, tragically opposed that fulfillment. In a straightforward polemic against the Jews, emphasis on God's call and promise is irrelevant or counterproductive, but positive expectations heighten the sense of tragic loss when those expectations fail. A concern to present a tragic reversal is revealed by details of the speech. In describing God's call and promise to Abraham, words are used with positive meaning that later in the speech return with a negative sense. The word μετοικίζω occurs only twice in the New Testament, in Acts 7:4, 43. In both cases God is the one who "resettles" or "deports" Abraham or Israel, but in the first

---

[20] See Martin Dibelius, *Studies in the Acts of the Apostles* (New York: Scribner, 1965) 167: "The irrelevance of most of this speech has for long been the real problem of exegesis. It is, indeed, impossible to find a connection between the account of the history of Israel to the time of Moses (7:2-19) and the accusation against Stephen: nor is any accusation against the Jews, which would furnish the historical foundation for the attack at the end of the speech, found at all in this section."

[21] In Acts 7:43 μετοικίζω is part of the quotation from Amos 5:25-27 LXX. The use of this verb in the quotation may have suggested use of the same verb in 7:4.

case it is *to* the land of promise and in the second case *away* from it.[21] In 7:7 God's promise to Abraham ends with these words: "And they will serve (λατρεύσουσιν) me in this place." However, in 7:42 we read that God "handed them over to serve (λατρεύειν) the host of heaven." These are the only uses of this verb in Acts until 24:14; 26:7; 27:23. Furthermore, 7:8 speaks of the "covenant of circumcision" which God gave Abraham. This, too, returns in negative form, for in 7:51 Stephen describes his audience as "uncircumcised in hearts and ears." The tragic turn is especially dramatic because it is just as the promises to Abraham are beginning to be realized (see 7:17, 32, 34 with 7:6-7) that resistance to God's purpose becomes clear, through rejection of the divinely appointed redeemer. The good things long promised are corrupted just as they are about to be enjoyed (see the promise of the land in 7:4-5 with the deportation in 7:43; the promise of the exodus in 7:7 with the return "in their hearts to Egypt" in 7:39; the promise that they would serve God in 7:7 with 7:42). Thus we find a literary device that points to the tragic disparity between the great promise of Israel's beginnings and the failure of its later history through repetition of key words or word roots, accompanied by a dramatic highlighting of the tragic turn through the appearance of human rejection at the very time of fulfillment.

If the author of Luke–Acts wished only to justify the Gentile mission and a Gentile church, that purpose was already accomplished with the story of Cornelius's conversion (Acts 10:1-11:18) and the decision about the status of Gentile Christians in Acts 15:1-29. There would be no further need to return repeatedly to the problem of the unbelieving Jews. Similarly, the emphasis on the conflict with unbelieving Jews, right to the end of Acts, is not explained by the supposition that the author is concerned with showing the continuity of redemptive history in order to defend the church's claim to be the inheritors of the scriptural promises. Although the emphasis on the Jewishness of the early church and Paul might serve this goal, the even stronger emphasis on conflict with Jews unnecessarily highlights a problem with regard to the church's claim. This claim is contested, and every instance of Jewish rejection makes that more obvious. The concern in Luke–Acts with unbelieving Israel extends beyond the concerns to justify the Gentile mission and show the continuity of redemptive history.

The apparent fixation of the author on the Jews as rejecters of Jesus and his witnesses could support the view that the author is anti-Semitic, a charge that has recently been made by Jack T. Sanders.[22] This view conflicts with my thesis that the author presents the story of Israel as a tragic story. The emotions of anguish, pity, and sorrow aroused by trag-edy are not the same as the hatred of anti-Semitism, nor does the negative stereotyping of anti-Semitism fit the emphasis on the great hopes and honors of the Jews, which is essential to Luke's tragic story. Sanders's position depends on an "epochal understanding" of Acts. The Christian mission is successful among Jews only during the early Jerusalem period, whereas conversion of Jews in the diaspora is rare and Acts 28:25-28 indicates that Jews henceforth have lost all possibility of salvation.[23] The view that this "final solution of the Jewish problem"[24] could be satisfactory to the author of Luke–Acts rests on a mistaken understanding of the divine purpose, as presented in Luke–Acts.[25] Attention to the four types of material listed at the beginning of this article, material in which the author's understanding of the divine purpose is disclosed, shows that there is a strong, repeated emphasis on God's purpose of bringing salvation to "all flesh," which means both Gentiles and Jews. The authority of these statements is indicated by the fact that they are frequently derived from scripture or express the risen Lord's commission to Paul, and the author highlights this material for the reader through repetition, with word links among related statements which serve as reminders. Thus Luke 3:6 quotes Isaiah to the effect that "all flesh will see the salvation of God." This statement has been anticipated by Simeon's declaration in Luke 2:30-32. There the same word σωτήριον is used,[26] and the "salvation" is related to "light," with both Gentiles and "your people Israel" as participants. This understanding of God's purpose in Jesus is still valid in the latter half of Acts. The three accounts of Paul's call repeatedly emphasize that Paul's

---

[22] See Jack T. Sanders, "The Parable of the Pounds and Lucan Anti-Semitism," *TS* 42 (1981) 667: "The entire geographico-theological plan of Luke–Acts is predicated on the simple evangelical premise that the Jews rejected Jesus and that the gospel was then taken to the Gentiles, who accepted it. While such a notion is the backbone of Luke's theology, however, it is hardly reliable history. It is, in fact, so patently untrue . . . that we recognize it for the anti-Semitic lie that it is. Without that lie we would not have Lucan theology."

[23] See Jack T. Sanders, "The Salvation of the Jews in Luke–Acts," in *SBLSP 1982* (Chico, Calif.: Scholars, 1982) 467–83.

[24] Sanders, "Salvation," 479.

[25] For Sanders's view see "Salvation," 476–77.

[26] This neuter form occurs only four times in the NT. Three of these occurrences are in Luke–Acts, where the LXX is the probable source.

mission embraces both Jews and Gentiles (Acts 9:15; 22:15; 26:17-18, 22-23).[27] The narrative of Paul's work corresponds to this view of his call. Paul's speech before King Agrippa provides a comprehensive summary of Paul's mission not only in the past but also in the present (see Acts 26:22: "until this day I stand bearing witness"). The description of that mission in 26:22-23 shows that Simeon's words about "salvation," "light," and "glory" for both the Gentiles and the people of Israel are not obsolete, for Paul bears witness to the Christ who "is going to proclaim light both to the people and to the Gentiles." Even in the final scene in Acts 28:23-28 Paul is still preaching to the Jews.

Since God's purpose in Jesus and the Lord's commission to Paul are presented in these terms, the final words of Paul to the Roman Jews in Acts 28:25-28 cannot represent a satisfying ending for the author of Luke–Acts. The quotation from Isa 6:9-10 shows that the Jews' refusal to see and hear is anticipated in scripture, but the fulfillment of this scripture means that the "hope of Israel" (also founded on scripture) is *not* being fulfilled. To be sure, this situation can be blamed on the Jews themselves, since they have not repented and believed, and our author may still cling to a hope for Israel beyond the situation at the end of Acts (see below). Neither of these observations changes the tragic character of the end of Acts, for the failure to accept the fulfillment of such a great promise is still tragic, even if the Jews themselves are responsible (the tragic hero often has a crucial "flaw"), and the hope beyond tragedy is expressed only in vague hints.

The quotation from Isaiah in Acts 28:26-27 is filled with a tension that expresses the unresolved tension in the plot at this point. It contains repeated and emphatic statements of a highly unnatural situation: ears, eyes, and heart, which are meant for hearing, seeing, and understanding, do not perceive or understand. This unnatural state, in which the organs of perception contradict their own purpose, has blocked God's desire to "heal them," a desire that a perceptive people would gladly embrace. But God is not finished speaking to this people, for it is the prophet's uncomfortable task to hold this self-contradiction before unbelieving Israel. He is told to "go to this people and say" the bitter and anguished words that disclose Israel's failure. Paul takes over this prophetic role of going

---

[27] The other passages cited make clear that the ambiguous εἰς οὓς in 26:17 is meant to refer both to "the people" and "the Gentiles."

and speaking to the people, both by repeating Isaiah's words and by concluding, "Therefore, let it be known to you. . . ." What follows refers to the Gentiles, but his announcement that the Gentiles will hear reemphasizes the preceding words about Israel's failure to hear. Paul continues his witness to Israel by holding its unnatural self-contradiction before it.

The words to the Roman Jews are the last words about Israel within the chosen compass of the author's story. They probably still reflect the predominant experience of the church with non-Christian Jews in the author's situation. Nevertheless, there are a few hints that hope for a happier outcome remains. Probably the most unambiguous indication of this is found in the repeated assertions that salvation and "light" for Israel have been prophesied in scripture, a view that Paul reaffirms as late as Acts 26:22-23. It is hard to imagine that the author of Luke–Acts, for whom the fulfillment of scriptural prophecy is a central article of faith, would ever admit that a primary aspect of prophecy, emphasized in his own work, is finally void. It is not surprising, therefore, that there are a few passages which suggest that the author still hopes that Jewish rejection of Jesus may be temporary.[28] In spite of the rejection of Jesus at the crucifixion, Peter calls the Jerusalemites to repentance, and this call is accompanied by a promise. They are to repent "in order that times of relief might come from the face of the Lord and he might send the Christ appointed for you, Jesus" (Acts 3:19-20). The reference to "times of relief" makes clear that Peter is speaking of a coming of Jesus that will mean salvation, not condemnation, for Israel, and he continues by speaking of the "times of restoration of all things which God spoke" through the prophets (3:21). This includes the restoration of the kingdom to Israel, that is, the coming of Israel's promised messianic kingdom, as the similarities in wording between Acts 3:20-21 and 1:6-7 make clear. Does the author of Luke–Acts regard this promise as still valid at the end of Acts? The formulation in Acts 3:21 already takes account of a delay before the "times of restoration," since there will be a period during which "heaven must receive" Jesus, and there are indications that persistent Jewish rejection is one cause of this delay. Delay in restoration of the kingdom to Israel has

---

[28] For further discussion of these passages see Arthur W. Wainwright, "Luke and the Restoration of the Kingdom to Israel," *ExpT* 89 (1977–78) 76–79; John Koenig, *Jews and Christians in Dialogue: New Testament Foundations* (Philadelphia: Westminster, 1979) 107–15.

already surfaced as a problem in the related passage in Acts 1:6-7. The same problem also appears in Luke 19:11, and the parable that follows explains not only that there will be a delay but also *why* there will be a delay: because the king will be rejected by his citizens (19:14). The disciples are blind to this approaching rejection (Luke 9:43-45; 18:31-34), which results in the false expectation expressed in 19:11. Peter, speaking with new insight in Acts 3:21, takes into account a delay due to persistent Jewish rejection. In spite of this, a hope for "times of relief" and "restoration" is expressed.[29] This hope is important to the author of Luke–Acts, for its complete disappearance would leave him with an unresolvable theological problem. Salvation for Israel has been presented as a major aspect of God's purpose, certified by scripture, but the final outcome would be the opposite. Although the mission to Jews is portrayed as successful in its early days in Jerusalem, the tragic aspects of the narrative previously discussed show that this in itself is not a sufficient and satisfying fulfillment of God's purpose.[30]

Luke 13:34-35, which reflects on the rejection of Jesus by Jerusalem, supports the interpretation of Acts 3:19-21 given above.[31] Jesus says to the city, "You will surely not see me until you say, 'Blessed is he who comes in the name of the Lord.'" Although these words are similar to those used by the rejoicing crowd at Jesus' entry into Jerusalem (Luke 19:38), the author makes clear that it is not the people of Jerusalem who speak of Jesus in this way but the "multitude of the disciples" who had accompanied Jesus during his ministry. Thus the expectation of a positive greeting from Jerusalem in 13:35 is not fulfilled at Jesus' arrival in the city. This verse contains words of judgment but indicates a possible time limit to this judgment. The city is judged by depriving it of its messianic king, whom it cannot "see." But this will last only so long as it refuses to say "Blessed is he who comes in the name of the Lord." This passage also helps us to interpret the time limit in the related passage on the destruction

---

[29] Luke 19:27 may seem to conflict with this hope, since it graphically portrays the judgment of the citizens who oppose their king. In the light of the call to repentance and offer of forgiveness in Acts, this judgment must be understood as an indication of what will happen if those who reject their king do not finally repent.

[30] The simple way to solve the theological problem is to modify the understanding of God's purpose to suggest that the Jewish people are not really very important to God after all. The author of Luke–Acts does not take this easy way out. Living with an unresolved theological problem is a price that the author is willing to pay to remain faithful to Israel and its scriptures.

[31] On Luke 13:34-35 see John Koenig, *Jews and Christians,* 111–12.

of Jerusalem in Luke 21:24, which indicates that the oppression of Jerusalem will last "until the times of the Gentiles are fulfilled." Luke 13:35 suggests that the possibility of the Jews finally accepting their messianic king is a reason for this time limit.

While the passages just discussed indicate a lingering hope for the salvation of the Jews, this remains a hope for salvation through conversion. The passages discussed do not show any shift from the claim of Acts 4:12 that salvation comes exclusively through the name of Jesus. Holding to this position would prevent the author from finding any resolution of his theological problem in the history of Judaism and Christianity to the present. Furthermore, the indications of hope for the salvation of the Jews which point beyond the end of Acts are few and brief, whereas Jewish rejection dominates the final scene in Acts and is emphasized in other major scenes of the narrative. The story of Israel, so far as the author of Luke–Acts can tell it, is a tragic story.

8

The Story of Israel within the Lukan Narrative

The following article returns to the issues discussed in "Israel in Luke–Acts: A Tragic Story" and restates my reasons for viewing the Lukan story of Israel as tragic. It also introduces some new perspectives by emphasizing, for instance, the importance of three scriptural promise traditions that are featured in Luke 1–2 and reappear in significant theological statements in Acts. The two articles supplement each other, for there are points in the earlier article that are not repeated in the later one, points that I still believe to be significant.

Introduction

One of the richest ways of reading Luke and Acts is to read this two-volume work as the story of God's promise to Israel—a promise given to Abraham and made more specific to David—concerning the salvation of Israel through a Messiah who will also be the savior of all nations. This is a rich way of reading because it enables us to interpret the significance of much material emphasized in Luke–Acts. This approach also enables us to link Luke with Acts as two parts of a long and complex story, with enriching cross references.[1]

When we focus on human characters, it is not obvious that Luke–Acts is a unified narrative, for the person central to Luke (Jesus) disappears from the stage in much of Acts. Nor does Acts have a single human protagonist. Yet even a narrative that focuses on a number of characters in turn and is partly episodic may reward our reading it as a unified narrative if we can discern a central purpose behind it all. This central purpose will enable us to understand some episodes as progress toward the goal, other episodes as encounters with resistance. The episodes take on meaning as they relate to the underlying purpose that someone is striving to realize.

In Luke–Acts no single character remains on the human stage, but there is an overarching purpose, the purpose of God. "The purpose of God" (ἡ βουλὴ τοῦ θεοῦ) is an important theological phrase in Luke–Acts, appearing in Luke 7:30; Acts 2:23; 4:28; 13:36; 20:27 (cf. 5:38-39). The narrator and key characters share an awareness that the purpose of God is the dominant reality behind events of the story. At the beginning of Luke this purpose is indicated by references to what God "spoke" to Abraham and David (Luke 1:55, 69-70), namely, promises of salvation that are now coming to fulfillment for Israel and the Gentiles (1:68-71; 2:30-32; 3:6). The Lukan infancy narrative is crucially important because it establishes the theological context for the whole of the following narrative. It introduces the narrative as the story of God fulfilling promises of salvation for Israel and the nations. This introduction is an invitation to the reader to read the rest of the story in this light.

Narrative analysis can be a subtler way of studying what redaction critics call the "theology" of Luke–Acts. Narrative has its special ways of

---

[1] Mikeal Parsons and Richard Pervo have questioned the unity of Luke–Acts and, in particular, have raised questions about my way of interpreting the narrative unity of Luke–Acts. See *Rethinking the Unity of Luke and Acts* (Minneapolis: Fortress, 1993). Parsons and Pervo say that the narrative unity about which I write "is almost exclusively at the level of story and does not reckon adequately with the disunity at the discourse level" (83). The distinction between story and discourse has limited value, in my opinion (it can sharpen our sense of the particular way that the story is told [the discourse] by asking us to imagine other ways in which the same basic series of events [the story] might have been told). Contrary to the quotation from Parsons and Pervo, I am interested in story as discoursed, i.e., in the way that literary techniques are used to present a series of events in a particular light, which may include presenting them as parts of a larger whole. In any case, the points made in this essay will, I think, withstand Parsons and Pervo's skepticism.

projecting what is sometimes called an "ideological point of view."[2] A story is likely to include a number of ideological points of view, expressed by different characters, but one of these may be dominant. The hierarchy of points of view depends on the authority of the voices expressing them. The point of view of the implied author (the evaluating person that we my infer from the norms and values that dominate the story) appears through statements of a reliable narrator and through statements attributed to those characters with highest authority in the story. These are reliable characters, that is, they reliably express the implied author's viewpoint.[3] In the narrative world of Luke–Acts, God is the figure of highest authority. The perspective of God is expressed by scripture references highlighted in the story. It is also expressed through designated spokespersons, first of all by the one whom God designates "my Son" (Luke 3:22), and then by others who are presented as inspired prophets. These persons are granted authority by the narrative. Thus they become the means by which a dominant point of view is expressed. Some of them are also commissioned by God to share in fulfilling God's purpose. Thus commission statements can also be a clue to how God's purpose is understood. In addition, the narrative provides an interpretive overview by previews and reviews of events at certain points in the narrative. Therefore, previews and reviews, highlighted scripture references, commission statements, and interpretive statements by reliable characters provide our best clues to understanding the purpose of God from the Lukan perspective.[4] Looking at events from the perspective of the purpose of God, we can understand how they fit together to create a unified story in two volumes.

God's goal of bringing salvation to both Jews and Gentiles is also the goal of the narrative. This goal defines what is required for a happy or successful outcome to the story. There is resistance to God's purpose, however, introducing tension into the narrative. In particular, developing opposition makes it doubtful whether Israel will participate in the salvation being offered. This problem is highlighted, rather than resolved, at the end of Acts. Luke–Acts is anything but a simple success story. The importance of Jewish resistance within the plot of Luke–Acts led me

---

[2] See Boris Uspensky, *A Poetics of Composition* (Berkeley: University of California Press, 1973) 8–16.
[3] See Wayne Booth, *The Rhetoric of Fiction*, 2d ed. (Chicago: University of Chicago Press, 1983) 18.
[4] See Tannehill, *The Narrative Unity of Luke–Acts: A Literary Interpretation*, 2 vols. (Philadelphia & Minneapolis: Fortress, 1986, 1990) 1.21–22.

elsewhere to interpret the story of Israel as a tragic story.[5] I do not mean that the whole of Luke–Acts is tragic but that there is a tragic aspect to the very important story of Israel within Luke–Acts. The narrative makes use of literary resources to emphasize this tragedy.

The tension between the divine promise of salvation for Israel and resistance by Jewish leaders and some of the people is a major theme that enables us to trace an unfolding plot line encompassing many of the characteristic scenes of Luke–Acts. I will discuss some of the highlights of this plot line in what follows.

Three Promise Traditions as Specifications of the Purpose of God

The Lukan infancy narrative is an extended celebration of the fulfillment of God's promises of salvation to Israel. The infancy narrative also discloses that these promises will include the Gentiles. This disclosure comes, however, only after the strongest affirmations of God's merciful help for Israel. These affirmations are found in the statements of angels (God's messengers) and inspired prophets, figures of high authority in the Lukan narrative world. I will concentrate on three scriptural promises that are important in Luke 1–2 and also in Acts. They are the promise to Abraham, the promise to David, and promises in Isaiah concerning salvation and light. The Lukan understanding of these promises cited in the infancy narrative will be clarified and developed in Acts.

First, the promise to Abraham. In 1:54-55 Mary attributes the help that Israel is now receiving from God, through the coming birth of the Messiah, to God's fulfillment of what God "spoke to our fathers," first of all "to Abraham." The reference to the Abraham promise is picked up and developed by Zechariah in 1:72-75.[6] It is now described as God's "oath" to free the people of Israel from their "enemies" so that they can engage in the cultic service of God without fear. An expanded version of this promise that Abraham's people will be freed for the cultic service of God is found in Stephen's speech (Acts 7:5-7), where it is connected with possession of

---

[5] See Tannehill, "Israel in Luke–Acts: A Tragic Story," *JBL* 104 (1985) 69–85.
[6] On thematic connections among the angelic announcements and prophetic hymns of Luke 1–2, see Tannehill, *Narrative Unity,* 1.42–43.

the promised land. In Mary's and Zechariah's hymns it is made clear that God is acting for Israel in fulfillment of the promise to Abraham. The promise to Abraham also has a prominent place at the end of Peter's temple speech in Acts 3. Peter refers to his audience as "sons of the prophets and the covenant" and then describes the covenant with Abraham. At that point a significant expansion takes place, for the content of the Abraham covenant is described in these terms: "In your seed all the families of the earth will be blessed" (Acts 3:25). The oath or covenant that brings salvation to Israel also brings blessing to the other peoples. Inclusion of Gentiles does not mean Israel's exclusion, for in 3:26 Peter speaks of blessing for his Jewish audience as well. The Abraham promise is a promise of blessing for Israel that will also bring blessing to the Gentiles.

Second, we must consider the promise to David. Gabriel's announcement to Mary in Luke 1:32-33 plays upon God's promise to David of a successor to David's throne who would be acknowledged as God's son, leading to a Davidic kingship that will last "forever" (cf. 2 Sam 7:12-16). Zechariah's hymn combines this promise to David with the Abraham promise (see 1:69-75). Zechariah describes the promised successor to David as a "horn of salvation" (1:69). Later an angel will confirm to the shepherds that the Davidic Messiah who has just been born is a "savior" (2:11). In the first proclamation of the risen Jesus, Peter returns to this promise to David, stating that it has been fulfilled through the resurrection of Jesus as Messiah (Acts 2:30-31). The fulfillment of the promise to David is also the central theme of Paul's synagogue sermon in Antioch of Pisidia (cf. 13:22-23, 32-35). As in the infancy narrative, Jesus, the promised offspring of David, is described as "savior" for Israel (Acts 13:23). The promise to David is similar to the promise to Abraham. It is found in Jewish scripture and benefits first of all the Jewish people. But the enthronement of the Davidic Messiah, which takes place through Jesus' exaltation to God's right hand, will also benefit the Gentiles. This point is made in Acts 15:16-17 through a quotation of Amos 9:11-12 that resembles the LXX. The restoration of the ruined dwelling of David will result in "all the Gentiles" seeking the Lord. Once again, the fulfillment of a central promise of Jewish scripture is understood to bring saving benefits to both Jews and Gentiles. Jewish messianism is not understood as a support for ethnic exclusion. Quite the contrary. Neither is this messianism so torn from its Jewish roots as to lose its special relevance for Jews.[7]

The location of references to the Abraham and David promises within the narrative—at the beginning of both of the volumes and in the most important and extensive theological statements of the beginning chapters—underscores their importance. At the beginning of Luke, the annunciation to Mary centers on fulfillment of the promise to David, the Magnificat ends with fulfillment of the promise to Abraham, and the Benedictus refers to both promises. Similarly, Peter's initial mission speeches in Acts (the Pentecost speech and the temple speech in Acts 2 and 3) refer first to the promise to David and then to the promise to Abraham. The beginning of Luke sets a theological context for understanding the rest of the story. In particular, it leads the audience to understand the story of Jesus in light of these scriptural promises. Then the audience is reminded of the same promises at the beginning of Acts.

But we must also consider a third promise tradition, which stems from Isaiah. Rather than attempting to discuss the numerous references to Isaiah in Luke–Acts, I will concentrate on references to a "light of the Gentiles" (φῶς ἐθνῶν) and to salvation, using σωτήριον, a rare word in the New Testament.[8] Here we can see again how a particular promise tradition is introduced in the Lukan infancy narrative and then is expanded and interpreted in Acts. Both the "light" and "salvation" language appear in Simeon's hymn (see Luke 2:30-32), as he declares to God that he has seen "your salvation" (τὸ σωτήριόν σου) and then describes this salvation as a "light for revelation of Gentiles" (φῶς εἰς ἀποκάλυψιν ἐθνῶν). The reference to light for the Gentiles comes from two similar texts, Isa 42:6 and 49:6. The use of σωτήριον probably reflects Isa 40:5 LXX, since this verse is quoted a little later in Luke 3:6. This verse is the result of a Lukan extension of a quotation found in Matt 3:3 and Mark 1:3. The primary purpose of the Lukan extension is probably to include the sentence "and all flesh will see the salvation (τὸ σωτήριον) of God," a promise of inclusive salvation that fits the Lukan perspective. Simeon's words are the first mention of the Messiah's significance for the Gentiles. Previously it

---

[7] The interpretation of scriptural promises in Luke–Acts involves a revisionary process that is discussed by Robert Brawley in "The Blessing of All the Families of the Earth: Jesus and Covenant Traditions in Luke–Acts," in *SBLSP 1994* (Atlanta: Scholars, 1994) 252–68.
[8] This word is found only in Luke 2:30; 3:6; Acts 28:28; Eph 6:17.

has been said repeatedly that Jesus Messiah means salvation for the Jews. The introduction of Gentiles in 2:32 does not mean that they are replacing the Jews, for the one who is "light" for the Gentiles is also "glory of your people Israel." The careful inclusion of both Jews and Gentiles is important. It is typical of Luke–Acts. Paul's commission will be described in a similar way: he is sent to both Jews and Gentiles (see Acts 9:15; 20:21; 22:15; 26:16-17).

When we follow this promise tradition into Acts, we find that it is influential at key places in the narrative. The commission of the apostles to be witnesses "to the end of the earth" in Acts 1:8 picks up a phrase from the rest of Isa 49:6 LXX, which reads, "I have set you for a covenant of the people, for a light of the Gentiles, so that you may be for salvation to the end of the earth." That Isa 49:6 is indeed the source of the phrase in Acts 1:8 is shown by a fuller quotation of Isaiah in Acts 13:47. "The end of the earth" is the final destination of a mission that begins in Jerusalem and Judea, i.e., with Jews. Acts 1:8 might lead one to believe that the Jewish phase of the mission will close early, leaving only a Gentile mission from that point on. The narrative contradicts such an interpretation. When Paul leaves Jerusalem and Judea, he still preaches to Jews as well as Gentiles, regularly beginning his mission in a Jewish synagogue. Indeed, the Jews deserve to hear about Jesus first, since he is their Messiah. (According to 3:26 and 13:46, the preachers had to speak "to you [the Jews] first.") This priority is seen not only in Jesus' requirement that his witnesses begin in Jerusalem but also in Paul's mission, which regularly begins in the local synagogue.

The quotation of Isa 49:6 in Acts 13:47 justifies Paul's turning to the Gentiles. He does so, however, only when Jewish opposition makes further work among the Jews impossible. Until then, he is under obligation to preach to the Jews. ("It was necessary that the word of God be spoken first to you," Acts 13:46.) The pattern of Paul's mission contradicts the supposition that Isa 49:6 is being read as warrant for an exclusively Gentile mission. Paul provides a retrospective summary of his mission in Acts 26:12-23. His statement comes to a climax by another appropriation of the light imagery from Isaiah: the risen Messiah "is going to proclaim light both to the people [i.e., the Jewish people] and to the Gentiles." In Jesus' name, Paul has been delivering this two-fold proclamation. We could also say that Simeon was already proclaiming light to Jews and Gentiles in Luke 2:30-32. The reading of Isa 49:6 is consistent from Luke 2 through

Acts 26. This text proclaims God's will that the saving revelation be taken to the Gentiles, but this is to happen as part of a double mission that includes the Jews.

Of course, one may ask whether Paul's concluding statement in Acts 28:25-28 marks the end of the Jewish mission. This statement is linked to the passages we have been discussing, for v. 28 refers to "this salvation (σωτήριον) of God," which has now been sent to the Gentiles. This term σωτήριον, probably borrowed from Isa 40:5 LXX, has not been used since the salvation proclamations of Luke 2:30 and 3:6, where it was tied to references to saving light for both Gentiles and Israel, and to the proclamation of salvation for "all flesh."[9] The fact that this term returns at the end of Acts shows its thematic importance in Luke–Acts, and the thematic importance of the Isaiah passages which it brings to summary expression. But in Acts 28:25-28 Paul says to the Roman Jews that they have been blind and deaf; therefore "this salvation of God" has been sent to the Gentiles. Does this mark a change in the previous pattern of mission? From now on will this salvation be offered to Gentiles only? I think not. However, this announcement does highlight a tragic turn in the narrative, for the hopes for the Jewish people in the infancy narrative are not coming to fulfillment. (For further discussion of the end of Acts, see below.)

We have now discussed three promise traditions taken from Jewish scripture that have an important place in the infancy narrative of Luke and also link Luke with Acts, where these promise traditions are further developed and interpreted. These three promise traditions make important contributions to the Lukan understanding of God's purpose in the world, which is the underlying project that turns the many episodes of the story into a unified, developing plot.

We have been studying some important indications of the unity of Luke–Acts, both a theological unity and a unity of narrative plot. Now we must consider more carefully the place of Israel in this story, starting with a few comments about the resistance Jesus faces.

---

[9] Jacques Dupont recognized the significance of this link between the end of Acts and the beginning of Luke. See *The Salvation of the Gentiles: Essays on the Acts of the Apostles* (New York: Paulist, 1979) 16.

Resistance to Jesus in Luke

The resistance that Jesus will face within Israel is indicated already in Simeon's oracle to Jesus' parents (Luke 2:34-35), and in the first scene of Jesus' public ministry, the rejection in Nazareth (4:16-30). This rejection could be understood as a purely local event of limited significance. Yet the people of Nazareth are especially inflamed by Jesus' reference to prophets sent to help Gentiles (4:25-28), which seems to be an early signal of a later problem. Paul, like Jesus, preaches in a synagogue, which leads to conflict when Jews become jealous of the outsiders who are attracted (see Acts 13:44-45). As portrayed in the narrative, there are Jews who don't want to hear about salvation for all flesh because they believe the benefits belong to them. Inevitably, the mission will come into conflict with these people.

There are also conflicts over other issues, especially with the scribes and Pharisees. The Pharisees are regularly presented as Jesus' opponents in the Gospel. They have a rhetorical function: they represent the view that Jesus wishes to correct, thus making Jesus' view stand out more sharply. Therefore, it is easy to read them as negative stereotypes. There are, however, some scenes in Luke in which the narrative allows us to view Pharisees as round characters, capable of favorable development, not as negative stereotypes. Simon the Pharisee in Luke 7:36-50 can be viewed as a round character, if we wish.[10] This observation indicates the need for caution about the more thoroughly negative view of Pharisees that some interpreters attribute to Luke.[11]

Some developments are discernible in the relation between Jesus and the religious authorities in Luke, and the record of Jesus' relation to the Jewish people or crowds shows shifts in emphasis: on the one hand, there is strong support for Jesus; on the other hand, Jesus delivers strong warnings because of an inadequate response. However, I cannot pause here to discuss

---

[10] See Tannehill, "Should We Love Simon the Pharisee? Hermeneutical Reflections on the Pharisees in Luke," *CTM* 21 (1994) 424–33.

[11] See Jack Dean Kingsbury, *Conflict in Luke* (Minneapolis: Fortress, 1991) 21–28; *idem*, "The Pharisees in Luke–Acts," in *The Four Gospels 1992: Festschrift Frans Neirynck*, edited by F. Van Segbroeck et al. (Leuven: Leuven University Press, 1992) 1497–512; John A. Darr, *On Character Building: The Reader and the Rhetoric of Characterization in Luke–Acts*, LCBI (Louisville: Westminster John Knox, 1992) 85–126.

the developing relations between Jesus and the religious authorities or between Jesus and the people.[12]

Something must be said, however, about the major crisis in the relation of Jesus to Israel that increasingly dominates the narrative as Jesus approaches Jerusalem. Jesus comes to claim his place as messianic king, but he is rejected by the Jewish leaders in Jerusalem, and even the people, who support Jesus strongly while he is teaching in the temple (19:47-48; 20:19; 21:37-38), cry for his death before Pilate (23:13-24). Later the attitude of the people again changes. By the time of Jesus' death the people are showing signs of remorse (23:48), and when Peter calls them to repentance, many will respond (Acts 2:38-41; 4:4). Nevertheless, when Jesus is rejected by the Jewish authorities in Jerusalem, they are rejecting "the things that lead to peace" (19:42), according to Luke, with fateful consequences for Jerusalem and the Jewish people. The four passages that address Jerusalem and prophesy its fate have an important role in the plot (see 13:33-35; 19:41-44; 21:20-24; 23:27-31). It is important to catch the dominant feeling tone of these passages. Jesus speaks words of anguished longing and lament (13:34; 19:42). He is depicted as weeping (19:41), although Luke, in comparison to Mark, tends to avoid references to Jesus' emotions.[13] There is a strong sense of pathos here, and the last scene (23:27-31) adds to it by presenting women weeping for Jesus, who are then told that they must weep for themselves and their children. The suffering of innocents clearly increases the pathos. These four scenes, which build up to the crucifixion and help to set the tone for it, constitute one major reason for interpreting the story of Israel in Luke–Acts as tragic. The tragic aspect is even clearer when we realize that Jesus in 19:42-44 is using key terms previously used by Zechariah in celebrating God's salvation for Israel (1:68-79).[14] The same key terms are being used, but now in a lament because what was promised is being lost. The contrasting use of the key terms indicates the tragic turn in the plot.

We are encouraged to read Luke and Acts as a continuous narrative not only by the reference back to the previous book in the preface to Acts

---

[12] On Jesus and the authorities, see Tannehill, *Narrative Unity,* 1.167–99. On Jesus and the people, see ibid., 1.141–66.

[13] See Joseph A. Fitzmyer, *The Gospel According to Luke,* AB 28 (Garden City, N.Y.: Doubleday, 1981) 95.

[14] See the references to "peace," "enemies," "visitation," and "knowledge." Note also the connection between 19:38 and 2:14. For discussion, see Tannehill, *Narrative Unity,* 1.159–60.

(1:1-2) but also by the commission statement at the end of Luke (24:47-49), which summarizes key themes that anticipate the narrative in Acts.[15] Following these literary clues and reading Luke and Acts in continuity has consequences for our understanding of Luke. It is more than the story of Jesus. It is part of a larger story concerning the fulfillment of God's purpose of salvation for "all flesh" (Luke 3:6). More specifically, the larger story relates the fulfillment of the divine promises discussed earlier in this essay. These promises are in process of fulfillment, but the process is not complete. Indeed, there seems to be a major obstacle to this fulfillment. Jesus was rejected in Jerusalem. With him Jerusalem rejected the messianic "peace" being offered to it (19:42). The divine purpose of salvation for Jerusalem appears to be blocked. And Jerusalem is the symbolic center of the Jewish people.

If we take account of the specific promises to Israel that are highlighted in the infancy narrative, the end of Luke does not provide a satisfactory resolution. The narrative makes us aware of this lack of resolution through comments of disciples that remind us of these promises in the infancy narrative. These comments also provide a connecting thread between Luke and Acts. The Emmaus disciples express their disappointed hope: "We were hoping that he was the one who was going to redeem Israel" (Luke 24:21). The phrase "redeem Israel" (using λυτροῦσθαι) takes us back to the infancy narrative, for this stem has not been used since Zechariah proclaimed that God "has visited and redeemed (ἐποίησεν λύτρωσιν) his people" (1:68) and Anna spoke of the "redemption (λύτρωσιν) of Jerusalem" (2:38). However, this redemption has not happened, and the disciples' sad comment reminds the reader of this. The theme continues in Acts 1:6. Jesus has been raised from the dead and has appeared to the disciples. But the disciples' question in Acts 1:6 reflects the fact that there is still something outstanding in the biblical promises. They ask when the kingdom will be restored to Israel. In reply, Jesus rejects their desire to specify a time, but his response need not be understood as a rejection of the basic hope of a restored kingdom for Israel. Indeed, the angel Gabriel promised that the Messiah would "rule over the house of Jacob forever, and of his kingdom there will be no end" (Luke 1:33). Thus the infancy narrative's anticipations of salvation for Israel as a nation, which include rescue from oppressor nations (cf. 1:71, 74),

---

[15] See Tannehill, *Narrative Unity,* 1.295.

reappear in the narrative as unfulfilled hopes as we make the transition from the end of Luke to the beginning of Acts.

Paul and Israel

The rejection of Jesus in Jerusalem is not the last word. Peter's speeches at Pentecost and in the temple call the residents of Jerusalem to repentance for their share in Jesus' death, offering them forgiveness (Acts 2:37-40; 3:19-20, 26). The first two mission speeches in Acts are basically repentance speeches directed to a particular audience—the residents of Jerusalem at the time of Jesus' death—in light of their rejection of Jesus. Thus they are responses to a problem that has surfaced in the plot.[16] These speeches have a powerful effect (2:37, 41; 4:4). The tide appears to be turning. But the temple authorities intervene, the opposition increases, Stephen is killed, and the Jerusalem disciples are scattered by a "great persecution" (8:1). Thus the bitter opposition that caused Jesus' death reappears in Acts.

It continues as Acts turns to Paul as the principal figure. There are repeated references to Jewish opponents as Paul moves from place to place. The drama of the Jewish people and its Messiah continues to be played out through the story of Paul in Acts. Two aspects of this story deserve special attention: 1) The scenes in which Paul announces that he is turning to the Gentiles in the face of Jewish opposition. 2) The series of interrogation and trial scenes in which Paul responds to Jewish accusers after his arrest in Jerusalem.

Paul's Announcements of Turning to the Gentiles

The first of the scenes in which Paul announces a turn to the Gentiles is set in Antioch of Pisidia.[17] This is also the setting of a major speech in a synagogue setting, which provides the fullest account of Paul's missionary preaching to Jews. In order to provide a balanced interpretation, it is

---

[16] On the narrative significance of Peter's mission speeches, see further Tannehill, "The Functions of Peter's Mission Speeches in the Narrative of Acts," *NTS* 37 (1991) 400–14.

[17] On this scene see further Tannehill, "Rejection by Jews and Turning to Gentiles: The Pattern of Paul's Mission in Acts," in *Luke–Acts and the Jewish People: Eight Critical Perspectives*, edited by Joseph Tyson (Minneapolis: Augsburg, 1988) 83–89; *idem, Narrative Unity,* 2.164–75.

important to pay attention to the speech in 13:16-41 as well as to the later announcement in 13:46-47. In the speech Paul affirms the election of Israel by God (13:17) and announces the fulfillment of the promise of a Messiah for Israel, a fulfillment that has taken place through the resurrection of Jesus (13:22-23, 32-33). Paul emphasizes that his message is a word of salvation for his audience of Jews and God-fearers (13:26). Thus the Paul of Acts is aligned with the promise traditions—which are first of all promises to Israel—that first appear in the Lukan infancy narrative and that reappear in Acts. But on the following sabbath, when "nearly the whole city" gathers to hear Paul, Jews become jealous and oppose Paul, who then announces that "we are turning to the Gentiles" (13:46). This announcement is justified by a citation of Isa 49:6, which reintroduces the "light of the Gentiles" tradition.

In the narrative context Paul's announcement cannot mean that he will never again preach to Jews, for he immediately does so in the next city (14:1). The announcement of turning to the Gentiles must be taken with the rest of 13:46, where the statement of Paul and Barnabas begins, "To you [the Jews] it was necessary that the word of God be spoken first." Turning to the Gentiles is a special event because Paul and the other missionaries are under obligation to speak to the Jews first. When bitter opposition makes it impossible to continue, Paul is released from this obligation and can begin a mission that no longer centers in the synagogue. Thus the fact that a turning to the Gentiles takes place at a special time is a result of the priority of the Jews as God's special people, to whom the promises first of all apply. (Peter's preaching agrees with this perspective, for he says that God's servant was sent "to you first," you who are "the sons of the prophets and the covenant" [Acts 3:25-26].) Paul's preaching in Antioch of Pisidia is a major scene in Acts that highlights the tension between God's saving purpose for Israel, now being fulfilled, and rejection of that fulfillment by many Jews. The mission is able to move forward by turning to the Gentiles, but God's saving purpose will be incomplete so long as the covenant people do not accept God's salvation.

Brief episodes similar to the scene in Antioch of Pisidia are placed in Corinth and Ephesus (18:5-6; 19:8-10). When Paul announces that he is turning to the Gentiles in 18:6, he also says, "I am clean" (or "innocent"), indicating that he has been under an obligation that, if previously abandoned, would have rendered him guilty. The major scene that we must consider, however, is the final one of Acts, Paul's encounter with the

Roman Jews (28:17-28).[18] The fact that the last major scene of Acts presents Paul in conversation with Jews indicates how important the issues raised by Jewish resistance are in Acts.

Paul's discussion with the Roman Jews is actually a double scene (28:17-22, 23-28), for Paul makes statements on two different days. The first statement is a summary of Paul's arrest and the defense scenes that follow (21:27—26:32). Paul insists strongly that he has done nothing against the Jewish people or their customs. He is a loyal Jew. It is ironic that the very chain he wears is a sign of his loyalty. He wears this chain "for the sake of the hope of Israel" (28:20; the hope of Israel is an important theme of the defense scenes discussed below). Thus Paul denies that either he or his mission is anti-Jewish. This statement is further response to accusations raised against Paul in 21:20-21, 28, accusations that hover behind much of the narrative that follows.

The Roman Jews are not presented as hardened opponents. They are willing to hear Paul's message (28:22). Furthermore, their response is not wholly negative. "Some were being persuaded," even though others were not (28:24). It may be surprising, then, that Paul responds with what seems like a scathing denunciation. In evaluating Paul's response, we must note several things: 1) Paul was evidently seeking a communal response, recognition by the Jewish community in Rome that Jesus is the fulfillment of God's promises. The division among the Roman Jews is sufficient indication that there will not be a favorable communal response, and Paul reacts to this situation. 2) The quotation from Isa 6:9-10 includes the instruction to the prophet, "Go to this people and say." This is a reminder that Paul's way of speaking at this point has biblical precedent, that he is, in fact, assuming the prophetic role previously assigned to Isaiah. Seen in biblical perspective, Paul is not being anti-Jewish (the charge he denied in 28:17). 3) The words from Isaiah are deeply ironic. They speak of ears, eyes, and heart, organs of perception and understanding, that contradict their own purpose. The extreme rhetoric is an attempt to get the Roman Jews to hear their deafness and see their blindness. 4) The announcement of turning to the Gentiles in 28:28 has a similar purpose. It is not primarily an attempt to justify a Gentile mission. The rights of the Gentiles are well established by the time of the Jerusalem council in Acts 15. They are not

---

[18] On this scene, see further Tannehill, "Rejection by Jews," 92–101; *idem, Narrative Unity,* 2.344-57.

the issue here. The statement that the Gentiles will hear contrasts with the Roman Jews' failure to hear and is part of Paul's rebuke of their deafness.

This strong rebuke does not mean an end to the Jewish mission. To be sure, the fact that Acts ends on this note gives the scene extra weight. If we were to consider this scene in isolation from Acts as a whole, we could only say that Paul is rebuking the Roman Jews. However, there have been other scenes of Jewish rejection, leading to a turning to the Gentiles. Although there have also been positive responses from Jews, a pattern has developed in the narrative, indicating a trend. When the narrative ends with Paul's rebuke of a Jewish community, the conflict with Jews assumes a certain permanence. There is no more narrative that might end this conflict.

Perhaps the scene suggests a change from the conditions of Paul's mission. This change is not the end of a Jewish mission but the end of the possibility of preaching to Jewish assemblies, as Paul has done. Witnessing to individual Jews is still possible. This possibility is suggested by the concluding summary of Paul's two years in Rome. The statement in v. 24 that some of the Jews were being persuaded provides a motive for visits to Paul by some of these Jews. They were already favorably impressed and would want to discuss Paul's message further. Then the remark in v. 30 that Paul was welcoming "all" who were coming to him would indicate that he is continuing his mission to both Jews and Gentiles, within the limits possible as a prisoner. In doing so, Paul is being faithful to his commission, which was a charge to carry the word to both Jews and Gentiles (9:15; 20:21; 22:15; 26:16-17).

Paul's commission comes from the Lord Jesus, who speaks with the authority of God, according to the norms of the implied author. This commission gives Paul an important role in the realization of God's purpose of salvation for "all flesh" (cf. Luke 2:30-32; 3:6). The negative trend in the narrative, represented by repeated scenes of Jewish rejection, is a frustration of the divine will for Israel. It is contrary to the divine purpose announced in Luke 1–2, which remains the underlying purpose behind the whole narrative. Thus Acts ends on a negative note for which the prediction of success among the Gentiles does not adequately compensate. The story of Israel, so far as the narrator could tell it, is tragic. The beginning of the narrative aroused great hopes for Israel, but these hopes are not being realized. The resulting tragedy is highlighted in the words of Jesus, when he weeps over Jerusalem, and the words of Paul, when he speaks of the tragic irony of ears that refuse to hear. Emphasis on these scenes does not mean that the narrator has no hope for change. Indeed, faith in God and belief in the scriptural promises requires such hope. But the narrative does not point to any concrete signs of change in the response of Jews. It can only point to Paul as a model of faithful witness in difficult times (28:30-31).

Paul's Defense Scenes

Some hope of success in a Jewish mission may be found in the scenes of Paul's defense that dominate 21:17—26:32. In this major section of Acts, Paul is primarily defending himself against accusations that he has betrayed the Jewish people and their faith. Devotion of so much space to this issue shows its importance to the implied author. The issue is important because the implied author regards the Jewish people as important and believes the divine promises made to them.

This long section of Acts begins by highlighting two sets of charges against Paul.[19] Paul is responding to them throughout the series of defense scenes (and even in 28:17-20, when he is in Rome). The sum of these charges is that Paul has betrayed the Jewish people, for his mission is an attack on Judaism. The first of these charges comes from Christian Jews who believe that Paul is teaching diaspora Jews "apostasy from Moses, saying that they should not circumcise their children nor walk by the customs" (21:21). The Christian opponents of Paul drop out of the narrative, but their charge merges with the charge of the Jews who mob Paul in the temple, shouting "this is the fellow who is teaching everyone everywhere against the people and the law and this place [the temple]" (21:28). The opponents are referring to three marks of Jewish identity: they are a people chosen by God, governed by God's law, with a divinely established temple in Jerusalem. The opponents believe that Paul is attacking Judaism in his teaching by rejecting all three of these identity markers.

The defense scenes are framed by two major speeches by Paul (22:1-21; 26:1-23). In the first Paul is defending himself before the mob of

---

[19] On the scenes of Paul's defense, see further Tannehill, "The Narrator's Strategy in the Scenes of Paul's Defense," *Forum* 8.3-4 (1992) 255–69; *idem, Narrative Unity,* 2.268–329.

Jewish attackers, and he emphasizes, in an autobiographical statement, his Jewish roots and the Jewish roots of his mission. This emphasis will continue in later scenes, but there are also important developments. In 23:6 Paul makes a short statement to the Sanhedrin: "I am a Pharisee, a son of Pharisees. I am on trial concerning hope and resurrection of the dead." This statement is more than a tactical move to cause dissension between Pharisees and Sadducees in the Sanhedrin, for it is the first expression of a theme that will be developed in following chapters of Acts. We can only understand its importance by tracing its development in the narrative. As a defense strategy, we can say that Paul is trying to change the main issue in his coming trial, but I believe that there is a second motive behind this statement, a missionary motive that will become apparent in Acts 26. For the moment, we should note that Paul makes no reference to the resurrection of Jesus in his statement to the Sanhedrin. He speaks only of a resurrection hope shared with other Pharisees. This reticence, not characteristic of Paul previously, continues into the following scenes. In 24:14-15, in the trial before Felix, Paul again insists that he shares with other Jews the hope in resurrection, and the speech ends by referring back to Paul's statement about resurrection to the Sanhedrin (24:21). It is also remarkable that christological argument from scripture, important in previous speeches, is largely absent from Paul's defense speeches. (There is a general reference to scripture in 26:22.) If, as many believe, the purpose of these scenes is to assure Christian believers that their faith is firmly linked to Jewish roots and Jewish scripture, a major source of arguments is being ignored. Nor can these scenes be explained as apologetic directed to the Roman world. Romans would find much of the argument irrelevant but would probably be impressed by one detrimental fact highlighted by the narrative: the claim of many Christians to Judaism is sharply contested by Jewish authorities acknowledged by Rome. A different explanation of these scenes is necessary. Paul is being defended; he is also being presented as a model of a resourceful missionary who seeks and finds common ground with suspicious and antagonistic Jews.[20] Because of the antagonism, Paul develops a circuitous witness that builds on a base acknowledged by many Jews. This second purpose appears in the climactic defense scene before King Agrippa (Acts 26).

---

[20] Paul's speech to the Ephesian elders (20:18-35) makes clear that Paul is presented, in part, as a model for later church leaders.

In 25:19 Festus indicates that the previous talk of resurrection included Paul's claim that Jesus had been resurrected. This remark anticipates the end of Paul's speech to King Agrippa (26:23) but does not preempt its climactic impact, since the remark is relegated to a report by Festus. The speech of Paul in Acts 26 has multiple functions. For the reader it is a review and summary of Paul's role in the unfolding purpose of God. Thus it has great importance in understanding the Lukan view of Paul. In the immediate context, it is a defense speech that, at the end, turns into a missionary appeal. There is a literary signal of this shift in function. In v. 2 Paul refers to making his defense and in v. 6 he says, "I stand being judged" (or "on trial," ἕστηκα κρινόμενος), but in vv. 22-23 he says, "I stand bearing witness" (ἕστηκα μαρτυρόμενος) and gives his witness to the risen Messiah. Agrippa recognizes the shift to an evangelistic appeal, as the following dialogue shows (vv. 25-29).

The theme of resurrection hope has an important role in this evangelistic appeal. This theme is inserted into Paul's autobiographical narrative when Paul refers to himself as a Pharisee (see vv. 6-8). In a short digression, Paul declares that he is being accused concerning the very hope and promise that the Jews eagerly hope to attain. This is ironic. Indeed, it is tragic irony, for it means that Jews are rejecting what they deeply desire and what rightly belongs to them. The hope in question is hope in resurrection of the dead, as v. 8 indicates. It may seem strange that hope in resurrection is viewed as the central hope of Judaism. However, more than individual life after death is at stake. In the Lukan perspective, the Jewish hope in resurrection is tied to the Jewish hope for a messianic kingdom. Resurrection life is an aspect of the Messiah's kingdom, which has consistently been presented as central to Jewish hope. Already in the first chapter of Luke, the angel Gabriel said that the Messiah Jesus would "reign over the house of Jacob forever, and of his kingdom there will be no end" (Luke 1:33). The Messiah's kingdom is eternal because the resurrected Jesus does not die. This point was emphasized by Paul in Acts 13:34-35. The speech of which these verses are a part proclaims that the promise of the Davidic Messiah for Israel has been fulfilled through the resurrection of Jesus (13:32-33). The promise of the messianic kingdom to which Paul refers in this his first major speech includes the promise of resurrection life to which he refers in his last major speech. A peculiar phraseology provides evidence for this connection. In 13:32 Paul refers to "the promise made to the fathers" (τὴν πρὸς τοὺς πατέρας ἐπαγγελίαν γενομένην); in 26:6 the phrase is repeated, including the word order (τῆς εἰς τοὺς πατέρας ἡμῶν ἐπαγγελίας γενομένης). The promise of a messianic kingdom and the promise of resurrection life flow together in Lukan thought, for the Messiah is "first of the resurrection of the dead" (26:23). He is the first of many. More than his own resurrection is at stake, for through him comes resurrection life for others (cf. Acts 3:15; 4:2). Thus Paul in the trial scenes is able to move from hope in a general resurrection to hope in a messianic kingdom for Israel established by a resurrected Messiah.

Conclusion

Luke and Acts are a unified narrative because the different events reported there relate to a single underlying purpose, God's purpose of bringing salvation to all flesh. This purpose remains constant and is presented consistently through use of three promise traditions that appear in the infancy narrative and reappear in Acts. Each of these promise traditions is used to indicate that Gentiles are included in God's salvation, but the implied author does not lose sight of the fact that these are first of all promises to Israel. The Pauline portion of Acts does not show a loss of interest in Jews and Judaism. Indeed, the issue of Paul and Judaism dominates Acts 21:17—28:31. The point of the lengthy defense scenes is not to prepare for a final rejection of Judaism but to defend Paul against the view that he has betrayed Judaism and to provide through him an example of how a resourceful missionary might appeal to Jews, in spite of growing antagonism. The ending of Acts does not imply that the Jews have finally lost their chance. The negative response of many Jews is a major theological problem for the implied author, for God has promised salvation to the Jews. This problem is not solved at the end of the narrative. Much of the narrative will be misunderstood if we do not recognize that the fate of the Jewish people remains a central concern throughout Luke–Acts.

The persistent concern with Jewish rejection in Luke–Acts shows that the implied author is not content with salvation for a remnant. God's promises are understood to apply to Israel as a people, not to a remnant. These promises are being fulfilled through Jesus Messiah, the implied author believes, but many Jews refuse to recognize Jesus as their Messiah.

The acceptance of Jesus by a Jewish minority is not a satisfactory solution. The anguish of Paul as he speaks his final words to the Roman Jews reflects the anguish of the implied author, who cannot accept this situation as a satisfactory fulfillment of God's promises to Israel.

Whether there should be a Christian mission to the Jews is a subject of debate among Christians today. In my view, concern for the Jewish people and belief in the scriptural promises would have led the author of Luke–Acts to continue mission to the Jews. Today, however, Christians must consider whether almost two millennia of history lead to a different conclusion: that God has a continuing purpose for Jews as a separate people. This conclusion permits respectful dialogue that need not lead to conversion.

9

Rejection by Jews and Turning to Gentiles: The Pattern of Paul's Mission in Acts

The volume in which this essay was published was largely the result of exchanges at the annual meeting of the Society of Biblical Literature and illustrated the controversies swirling around the issue of Luke's attitude toward the Jewish people.

"Rejection by Jews and Turning to Gentiles" develops further the perspective introduced in "Israel in Luke–Acts" by considering the Pauline mission in Acts. In Paul's preaching to Jews, we find a pattern of public Jewish opposition, followed by announcements that the mission is turning to the Gentiles, and Acts ends with a strong example of this pattern. What does this imply about the author's attitude toward the Jews? I argue that we must carefully consider the larger context of these announcements, especially Paul's synagogue sermon in Acts 13:16-41 and the complete scene of Paul at Rome (Acts 28:17-31). Scripture references in Luke–Acts and the leading preachers of the gospel highlight promises of salvation for Israel. The increasing emphasis on Jewish rejection in the Pauline portion of Acts dramatically presents a theological problem that Acts does not solve: the tragic contradiction between the saving purpose of the sovereign God and the resistance of God's chosen people. The importance given to this problem in the narrative is a sign of the importance of scriptural promises to the Jewish people for the implied author.

The passages in Acts discussed here are also discussed in The Narrative Unity of Luke–Acts, *vol. 2, but in this essay related scenes scattered through Acts are considered together in a way that sharpens the issue and clarifies my response.*

Paul's announcements in Acts that he is turning to the Gentiles in response to Jewish rejection have strongly influenced scholarly assessment of the Lukan attitude toward Judaism. It will be useful to take a new look at these announcements in their contexts.[1]

Antioch

Following Paul's speech in Antioch of Pisidia, Paul and Barnabas encounter Jewish opposition and solemnly declare that they are turning to the Gentiles (Acts 13:46). Awareness of the rest of the narrative should lead us to eliminate certain interpretations of this event that might otherwise be advanced. The announcement cannot mean that Paul will never again preach to Jews, for as soon as he reaches the next town, he begins his mission by preaching in the synagogue to Jews (14:1). He preaches to Jews repeatedly in his continuing mission. Paul's announcement also cannot mean that Gentiles are offered the word of God only because of Jewish rejection, as an afterthought or as a second choice. The narrator of Luke–Acts has made clear ever since the birth narrative that the purpose of God shaping this story intends to work salvation for all peoples. This was announced by an inspired prophet (Luke 2:30-32) and proclaimed as God's purpose in a banner quotation of Scripture (Luke 3:6). Then an inclusive mission of preaching was entrusted by the risen Messiah to his apostles (Luke 24:47; Acts 1:8). Preaching to the Gentiles is part of God's saving purpose announced long ago in Scripture, and it is a task entrusted by the risen Messiah to his witnesses. It is also part of the commission that Paul received from the risen Lord, governing his ministry (Acts 9:15; 22:15; 26:16-18). It is not an afterthought, nor does it need to be justified by Jewish rejection. In the narrator's view, salvation for the Gentiles is firmly rooted in Scripture, the witness to God's ancient purpose, as the Antioch

---

[1] Comments on other aspects of the Lukan attitude toward the Jews may be found in a previous article. See Robert C. Tannehill, "Israel in Luke–Acts: A Tragic Story," *JBL* 104 (1985) 69–85. The present essay provides further support for the position broadly sketched in the previous article.

scene also makes clear. In Acts 13:47 Paul and Barnabas quote from Scripture a command of the Lord that governs their ministry, obligating them to bring light to the nations and salvation "to the end of the earth" (ἕως ἐσχάτου τῆς γῆς, as in the command to the apostles in 1:8).

In order to understand why turning to the Gentiles is nevertheless a special event deserving a dramatic announcement, we must consider the first part of the declaration in Antioch: "To you it was necessary that the word of God be spoken first" (13:46). The mission is universal, but it must follow a prescribed order. The Jews must be addressed first. If they reject the gospel, the missionaries are free to begin the second phase of their mission. But why was it "necessary" that the preachers speak to the Jews "first"?

The message that Paul delivered in the Antioch synagogue provides some clues. In order to appreciate the narrator's perspective, it is important to keep the complete Antioch episode in mind, giving full weight both to the synagogue speech and to the announcement on the following Sabbath, for the poignancy of the announcement depends on the content of the synagogue speech. Interpretation that forgets the speech when interpreting the announcement will miss the unresolved tension in the narrator's attitude toward unbelieving Jews, a tension to which the total scene gives powerful expression.

Not only the setting but also the content makes clear that this is a speech by a Jew to Jews, for it concerns God's promise to the Jewish people. Paul addresses his audience as "Israelites" and "sons of the family of Abraham" (13:16, 26). He also stresses his own position in this family by calling his audience "brothers" (13:26, 38). The speech is addressed to this particular people and those who have chosen to associate with it ("those who fear God," 13:16, 26). The review of Israel's history at the beginning of the speech is more than a "reference to the depicted situation," a repeated feature of the mission speeches in Acts.[2] This introduction to the speech affirms the election of Israel (13:17) and God's faithful care for the elect people. The raising up of David as king and the promise concerning his offspring continue this faithful care. Once David is mentioned, the speech focuses on him and his promised heir. The speech is basically the announcement, with supporting argument, that the promised heir has

---

[2] See Ulrich Wilckens, *Die Missionsreden der Apostelgeschichte,* 3d ed., WMANT 5 (Neukirchen-Vluyn: Neukirchener, 1974) 53.

come and has been installed as Messiah through resurrection. The turning point of the speech is 13:23, where, following statements that almost any Jew would accept, Paul announces something new: the promise has now been fulfilled through Jesus. The word "promise" (ἐπαγγελία) in this verse becomes a theme word when it reappears in 13:32-33 in a more forceful proclamation of the fulfillment of the promise. The narrative concerning Jesus (13:27-31) leads up to this proclamation that the promise has been fulfilled through Jesus' resurrection, and 13:33b-39 develops the significance of this event through Scripture and an invitation to forgiveness. Thus the fulfillment of the promise to Israel of an heir to David's throne is the leading idea of the speech.[3]

After announcing that Jesus is the promised "Savior" from David's line (13:23),[4] Paul emphasizes the special importance of this announcement for his Jewish audience: "To us[5] the word of this salvation has been sent out" (13:26). The placement of the personal pronoun in initial position in the clause indicates the stress. When Paul again relates his message to his audience in 13:32-33, the stress on the special significance of this message for the Jewish people reappears. He is announcing the fulfillment of the promise made to their fathers concerning a king for Israel.

Paul in 13:32-33 is speaking of the promised king of David's line, as is shown by the further references to David in 13:34, 36, and by the close connection of this section of Paul's sermon to Peter's Pentecost sermon. The reference to Ps 16:10 (15:10 LXX) in 13:35-37 is a brief reminder of the more extensive quotation and application of this psalm in Acts 2:25-31. There Peter argued that David was not speaking of himself but of his descendant, concerning whom God had sworn an oath to seat him on David's throne (2:30). It is Jesus, risen and seated at God's right hand, who fulfills this promise. The oath of which Peter spoke is equivalent to the promise of which Paul speaks; both refer to the expected Davidic king for Israel. Peter connected the resurrection of Jesus to the oath that God would seat David's descendant on David's throne and proclaimed Jesus, seated at God's right hand, as the promised Lord and Messiah. Similarly,

---

[3] Acts 13:23, 32, 33a formulate the *Leitgedanken* of the speech, as indicated by Matthäus Franz-Josef Buss, *Die Missionspredigt des Apostels Paulus im Pisidischen Antiochien,* FB 38 (Stuttgart: Katholisches Bibelwerk, 1980) 29.

[4] The association of Jesus' role as "Savior" with his role as Davidic Messiah is typical of Luke–Acts. See Luke 1:69; 2:11.

[5] Variant reading: "to you."

Paul proclaims God's resurrection of Jesus (ἀναστήσας Ἰησοῦν, 13:33) as the fulfillment of the messianic promise. Through resurrection and exaltation[6] Jesus is declared to be God's Son, which is equivalent to the enthronement mentioned in 2:30. The context strongly supports the view that 13:33 refers to Jesus' resurrection as the fulfillment of the messianic promise, for Jesus' resurrection is the subject throughout 13:30-37.[7]

The messianic significance of Jesus' resurrection is developed through the scriptural quotations in 13:34-35.[8] There Paul indicates that the risen one is "no longer going to return to corruption." This places emphasis on continuing freedom from death, an emphasis that is supported by reference to "the holy things of David that are faithful," i.e., lasting.[9] The emphasis in 13:34 fits well with the description of the Messiah in the angel's announcement to Mary. He will not only be called God's Son and receive "the throne of David his father." He will also "reign over the house of Jacob forever, and of his kingdom there will be no end" (Luke 1:32-33).[10] Since the Messiah has been enthroned through resurrection, he is no longer threatened by corruption, and his kingdom will have no end.

The significance of this messianic promise for the Jewish people is expressed by the quotation of Isa 55:3 in Acts 13:34, a quotation which usually receives too little attention. The plural pronoun ὑμῖν shows that this promise is not a promise to the Messiah but to the Jewish people (in the context of the speech, to Paul's audience). The application of Paul's message to his audience is strongly stressed through first or second person

---

[6] The narrator distinguishes between the resurrection and exaltation of Jesus in Acts 1 in order to emphasize Jesus' careful instruction of the apostles. However, when Jesus' messianic enthronement is the main concern, this distinction can be ignored.

[7] For further argument supporting the view that 13:33 refers to Jesus' resurrection, see Evald Lövestam, *Son and Saviour: A Study of Acts 13, 32-37*, ConNT 18 (Lund: Gleerup, 1961) 8–10; Emmeram Kränkl, *Jesus der Knecht Gottes: Die heilsgeschichtliche Stellung Jesu in den Reden der Apostelgeschichte* (Regensburg: Pustet, 1972) 137–38; and Robert F. O'Toole, "Christ's Resurrection in Acts 13, 13-52," *Bib* 60 (1979) 361–72.

[8] Marcel Dumais compares the scriptural interpretation in the speech to Jewish midrash, arguing that the methods of interpretation as well as the themes are appropriate to the Jewish synagogue. See *Le langage de l'évangélisation: L'annonce missionnaire en milieu juif (Actes 13, 16-41)* (Tournai: Desclée , 1976).

[9] See Hans Conzelmann, *Die Apostelgeschichte,* HNT 7 (Tübingen: J. Mohr/Siebeck, 1963) 77: "τὰ πιστά wird als 'unvergänglich' aufgefasst." E. Lövestam detects a double aspect to the promise in 13:34: "The covenant promise to David had . . . a *firm* and *irrevocable* nature. This promise similarly concerned *permanent* dominion"; see *Son and Saviour,* 79 (emphasis in the original).

[10] Buss emphasizes the close terminological and thematic connection of the Antioch speech with Luke 1–2; see *Die Missionspredigt,* 146.

plural pronouns, sometimes in emphatic position, in 13:26, 32, 33, 38. The pronoun in the quotation in 13:34 fits with these other pronouns and refers to the same group. Since the verb in the quotation has been changed from the verb in Isa 55:3 LXX and the pronoun is the indirect object of that verb, it could easily have been changed if it did not serve the narrator's purpose. Instead, the pronoun has been allowed to stand. Paul through this quotation affirms the promise of the messianic kingdom for the Jewish people and again acknowledges that this promise is firmly rooted in Scripture.

The verb in the Isaiah quotation has been changed so as to match the verb in the psalm quotation that follows. The words which these two quotations have in common, as well as the way that they are introduced, indicate that they are to be interpreted together. Indeed, they are understood to be the positive and negative expression of the same basic promise, and the parts correspond: "I will give to you" / "You will not give"; "the holy things of David" / "your holy one"; "that are faithful" / "to see corruption." The connection between the last two phrases, which is not apparent in the wording, is established by the introduction to the Isaiah quotation in 13:34: the messianic kingdom is "faithful" because the risen Messiah is "no longer going to return to corruption" but will rule over an eternal kingdom. The reference to "the holy things of David" helps to make clear that "your holy one" refers to the Davidic Messiah. While the strange phrase τὰ ὅσια Δαυίδ is open to several interpretations, the reference to something belonging to David in a promise applying to people of Paul's time naturally calls to mind the promised kingdom of David's heir, especially after 13:22-23, 32-33.[11]

The Antioch scene repeats themes from both of Peter's first two speeches, an example of the common Lukan practice of sounding important themes more than once. The Pentecost speech helps us to

---

[11] Walter Bauer interprets τὰ ὅσια as divine decrees, in contrast to human ones. See *A Greek-English Lexicon of the New Testament and Other Early Christian Literature,* translated and adapted by W. F. Arndt and F. W. Gingrich (Chicago: University of Chicago Press, 1957) s.v. Jacques Dupont objects to this. He says that use of the phrase to mean religious duties, in contrast to social duties, is well established, but the meaning "divine decrees" is doubtful. See "ΤΑ ΟΣΙΑ ΔΑΥΙΔ ΤΑ ΠΙΣΤΑ (Ac XIII 34 = Is LV 3)," *RB* 68 (1961) 95. Dupont's criticism leads me to suggest that the narrator may have understood τὰ ὅσια to refer to the religious duties of David as king and therefore to what we would call the "office" of king. This royal office will be established for the Jewish people through the coming of their Messiah, according to 13:34.

understand Paul's reference to Jesus' resurrection as the fulfillment of God's oath to David. The speech in Solomon's portico helps us to understand the necessity of Paul's speaking first to the Jews (see 13:46). After making clear that God will still send the "times of refreshment" and "restoration" associated with the Messiah if the people of Jerusalem repent (3:19-21), Peter ends his second speech by saying, "God, having raised up his servant, sent him to you first" (3:26). This is explained by the preceding reference to his hearers as "sons of the prophets and of the covenant that God covenanted with our fathers" (3:25). The covenantal promise is described as a blessing that "all the families of the earth" will share, but it is clear that the Jewish people are meant to share in this blessing as "first" (3:25-26). The way that this priority is highlighted in Acts and its connection with the Jewish people as "sons of the prophets and of the covenant" show that the narrator still understands the scriptural promises quite concretely as promises to the Jewish people, even though Jewish Scripture also promises salvation for all nations. The narrator affirms God's promise to the Jewish people found in Scripture and is therefore willing to have one of his chief characters say that God sent his servant "to you first." This determines the course of the mission. If God sent the risen Messiah and his blessings to the Jews first, in fulfillment of promises to their ancestors, Paul must speak to the Jews first, as he indicates in 13:46.

The risen Messiah's instructions to his apostles also recognize this. The extension of the mission to the Gentiles is clearly stated in the two versions of the commission to the apostles, but both also indicate where the mission must begin: in Jerusalem, the center of Jewish life (Luke 24:47; Acts 1:4, 8).

The preceding discussion should make clear that the narrator of Acts is not merely giving a Jewish coloring to Paul's Antioch speech to make it fit the synagogue setting. Paul's preaching reflects a view that characterizes Luke–Acts from its beginning, the view that Jesus is the Davidic Messiah who fulfills specific promises of God to the Jewish people. These promises are found in Scripture, which the narrator accepts as the revelation of God's saving purpose for Israel and the world. To assume that Jewish rejection will permanently block the fulfillment of these promises for the synagogue audiences addressed by Paul is to assume that a major aspect of God's saving purpose can be defeated. This defeat would not be complete, perhaps, for Acts affirms the success of the mission among some Jews, especially in Jerusalem. But Acts also makes us aware that the mission is not successful among many Jews; indeed, the sequel to Paul's Antioch sermon will highlight Jewish rejection. The Antioch sermon views Israel from the viewpoint of God's saving purpose and scriptural promise. The theological problem is how that purpose and promise can remain valid in the face of Jewish rejection. In my opinion, this is a problem that Acts never resolves. Nevertheless, it does not mitigate the problem and reduce the tension by weakening the witness to God's saving purpose and scriptural promise to the Jewish people. Apparently, living with the tension is preferable to ignoring either of two fundamental realities: God's promise to Israel, fulfilled in Jesus, and Israel's rejection.

Furthermore, Paul's sermon at Antioch is the primary place where the narrator reveals the content of Paul's mission preaching to Jews. The later brief summaries of Paul's preaching to Jews are to be understood in light of this fuller statement. This sermon, then, has a key role in indicating the place of Israel in Paul's gospel, according to Acts.

What, then, of the announcement in 13:46 that, since the Jews are rejecting the word of God, Paul and Barnabas are turning to the Gentiles? Several aspects of the context need to be noted to help us understand more clearly what is happening. First, Paul began by speaking in the synagogue to the Jewish assembly. Turning to the Gentiles means the end of such preaching in the Antioch synagogue. Second, the situation changes because Jews "were contradicting the things being said by Paul, reviling them" (or "blaspheming" the Lord Jesus; the object of βλασφημοῦντες is not specified). Resistance is openly expressed and involves personal attacks that would make continued preaching in the synagogue difficult or impossible. Third, when they are thrown out, Paul and Barnabas shake off the dust from their feet and go to another city. In doing this, they are following the instructions Jesus gave to the 12 and the 72 (Luke 9:5; 10:11), instructions that apply when a *city* fails to receive the mission. The context in Acts 13:51 is the same, for this gesture is used as the missionaries leave one city and go to another, where the mission to the Jews will begin again. So the announcement of turning to the Gentiles applies first of all to the city of Antioch. Of course, we must also note that the narrator has given a great deal of space to what happened at Antioch, suggesting that it may have special importance for understanding Paul's mission.

Corinth, Ephesus, and Jerusalem

It is widely recognized that the announcement of turning to the Gentiles in Antioch is the first of a series of similar scenes in Acts. These are often reckoned to be three in number,[12] although there are several additional scenes that should be noted. The second of these scenes, set in Corinth (18:5-6), will help us to clarify the understanding of Paul's mission to Jews and Gentiles. The sequence of events begins with Paul "testifying to the Jews that the Messiah is Jesus." This summary recalls an important aspect of Paul's message as previously presented in the Antioch synagogue. In the next verse Paul announces, "From now on I will go to the Gentiles." The cause of the announcement closely parallels the situation in Antioch. The announcement is made when the Jews are "resisting and reviling" (or "blaspheming"). Paul shakes out his garments as he makes his announcement, a gesture that parallels the shaking off of dust from the feet in 13:51. However, this gesture has a slightly different meaning here, for it does not take place as Paul leaves the city. Indeed, a vision of the Lord makes clear that Paul is to stay in this city (18:9-11). But the announcement and gesture are still accompanied by a change of location. Paul has been preaching in the synagogue (18:4). When he begins to encounter strong resistance, he transfers to the house of Titius Justus (18:7). The practical effect of Paul's gesture and announcement is that Paul no longer uses the synagogue as his place of preaching. Paul's announcement indicates a shift from a synagogue-based mission, addressed to Jews and to those Gentiles attracted to Judaism, to a mission in the city at large, where the population is predominantly Gentile. The narrator makes clear that Paul's mission to Jews and Godfearers had some success, mentioning Titius Justus (who presumably has become a believer, since he offers his house for Paul's use) and Crispus, a synagogue ruler, who "believed the Lord with all his house" (18:7-8).

Paul's announcement in 18:6 includes the words, "Your blood is [or 'will be'] on your head; I am clean." These words are to be understood in light of the necessity laid on Paul to speak the word of God first to the Jews, as stated in 13:46. References to blood-guilt as responsibility for someone else's death, as in Matt 23:35; 27:25; Acts 5:28, are not close

[12] See Ernst Haenchen, *The Acts of the Apostles,* trans. Bernard Noble, et al. (Philadelphia: Westminster, 1971) 729.

parallels, for here the Corinthian Jews are responsible for their own blood. *They* are responsible, not Paul, as he emphasizes with the statement, "I am clean." The situation is like that of the prophetic "watchman" described in Ezek 33:1-9, and Paul borrows the language of Ezek 33:4 (τὸ αἷμα αὐτοῦ ἐπὶ τῆς κεφαλῆς αὐτοῦ ἔσται). The watchman is one who hears a word from God and is obligated to speak it to the people. If he does not, the blood of those who perish will be demanded from the hand of the watchman; if he does, the blood of those who perish will be on their own heads. Paul is declaring that he has fulfilled his obligation to speak God's word to God's people.[13] They are now responsible for their own fate. The pattern of speaking first to Jews and only later turning to the Gentiles testifies to Paul's sense of prophetic obligation to his own people. He is released from this obligation only when he meets strong public resistance within the Jewish community. Then he can begin the second phase of his mission within a city, a phase in which the conversion of individual Jews is still possible, although Paul is no longer preaching in the synagogue or addressing Jews as a community.

In Acts 19:8-10 (Ephesus) there is no announcement by Paul that he is turning to the Gentiles, but we are told of a shift from the synagogue to the school of Tyrannus as the location of Paul's work. The circumstances are similar to the texts previously discussed. The change takes place when "some were becoming hardened and were disbelieving, speaking evil (κακολογοῦντες) of the way before the multitude" (19:9). Note that these attitudes and actions are attributed only to "some" (τινες). Nevertheless, Paul ends his preaching and discussing in the synagogue. While it comes from only some of the Jews, the opposition is vocal and public. It could include heckling and disruption of the assembly. Under these circumstances Paul moves his mission to another setting. Indeed, we are told that he not only withdrew but also "separated the disciples" (19:9). This remark suggests permanent consequences to the shift of mission locations in response to Jewish rejection: Christian disciples are becoming a separate religious community. The repeated references to resistance in the synagogue, followed by a shift to a Gentile location, suggest that the narrator is adjusting to a hard fact. The Christian message belongs in the synagogue, since it is first of all a message to Jews about their Messiah,

---

[13] In Acts 20:26-27 Paul declares that he is "clean from the blood of all" because of his dedicated preaching.

but, under the circumstances, the synagogue cannot be a place of Christian preaching.

We have now observed that on three occasions (13:45-46; 18:4-7; 19:8-9) a shift from the synagogue to another location for preaching is the result of "reviling" (or "blaspheming") and "speaking evil" by Jews. Two of the announcements that Paul is turning to the Gentiles are found in these settings, indicating that they announce a shift from a synagogue-based mission to a mission at large because public opposition by Jews no longer allows preaching in the synagogue.

At the end of his first imprisonment speech, Paul reports a message that he received from the Lord during his first preaching in Jerusalem. The Lord commanded Paul to leave Jerusalem, since "they will not receive your witness about me," and go "to nations [or 'gentiles'] afar" (22:18, 21). Here we have the same pattern: Jewish refusal leads to a mission among the Gentiles. To be sure, there are also differences: Paul does not announce what he is going to do; he is commanded by the Lord. Paul even seems to protest when the Lord orders him to leave. Paul is portrayed as reluctant to abandon his mission in Jerusalem.

The story implies, of course, that the Lord knows better. Paul here begins to learn how things will frequently go in his preaching: Jews will often reject his witness, and he should then turn to the Gentiles. This pattern of mission, which is here traced back to a command of the Lord, is presented in a simplified way. Paul does not preach only to Gentiles when he leaves Jerusalem. He repeatedly begins by preaching to Jews. In this temple vision the many experiences of Jewish rejection and continuation of the mission in a Gentile setting are reduced to a single movement: from Jerusalem into the Gentile world. But the vision scene also maintains a symbolic contact with Judaism (it takes place in the temple) and expresses Paul's reluctance to abandon his mission in Jerusalem. The temple location may hint at the irony of the situation: Jews are rejecting a message that originates from the core of their own faith. It may also recall Isaiah's temple vision (Isa 6:1-8), a prophetic call that leads directly into the bitter message that Paul will quote in 28:26-27 (= Isa 6:9-10), although the indications of this connection to Isaiah's vision are not very clear.

Acts 22:17-21 does not provide a setting for the Lord's command by reporting actual resistance to Paul's witness. However, the narrator's understanding of the situation is indicated by the earlier report of Paul's preaching in Jerusalem in 9:29-30. Paul left Jerusalem, we are told, because of a plot against his life. "The brothers" learned about this and "sent him out" to Tarsus. The ἐξαπέστειλαν in 9:30 apparently describes the human execution of what is presented in 22:21 as the Lord's command (ἐξαποστελῶ).

Rome

The final scene to which we must give some detailed attention presents Paul speaking to the Jews in Rome. Since this is the last major scene in Acts, followed only by a brief two-verse summary of Paul's continuing preaching, it has special importance. The final scene of a narrative is an opportunity to clarify central aspects of plot and characterization in the preceding story and to make a final, lasting impression on the readers. The fact that the narrator has chosen to end the work with a scene that focuses on Paul's encounter with Jews shows how extraordinarily important the issues of this encounter are to the narrator. We must recognize, however, that this final scene of Acts is actually a double scene (28:17-22, 23-28), in which Paul makes two important statements to the Roman Jews. When we acknowledge the importance of both of these statements and allow them to resonate against each other, we will see that Acts' portrait of Paul in relation to Israel is richer and more complex than often thought.

Paul's statement in 28:17-20 is a summary of the preceding trial narrative and imprisonment speeches in Acts 22–26. It presents what the narrator most wants readers to retain from that long narrative. Paul claims that he was recognized as innocent of any serious crime when examined by the Romans (28:18; cf. 23:28-29; 25:25; 26:31-32). Primary emphasis falls, however, on Paul's claim that he has "done nothing opposed to the people or the customs received from the fathers" (28:17). Such charges were made in 21:21, 28; 24:5-6, and Paul previously denied them in 25:8,10. He also assures the Roman Jews that in his appeal to Caesar he does not intend to bring an accusation against his own nation (28:19). Thus considerable stress is placed on Paul's loyalty to Israel and its way of life.[14] In 28:17 Paul is not merely saying that he is a loyal Jew like many

---

[14] It is interesting that Paul is presented here as directly denying anti-Judaism on his part. While this does not settle the modern question of whether the Paul of Acts is anti-Jewish, it at least lets us know how the narrator wishes to present Paul.

others. He is asserting that his mission has not been an anti-Jewish movement. Furthermore, he remains loyal to his people in spite of the opposition that he has experienced from many of his fellow Jews. Indeed, he says, "Because of the hope of Israel I wear this chain" (28:20). This statement shows the narrator's talent for presenting a vivid picture in words. It is meant to be a memorable picture that conveys the narrator's message: Paul's mission and imprisonment are acts of loyalty to Israel. In the first sub-scene Paul's statement begins with his claim that he has done nothing opposed to Israel or the law; it ends with his claim that he is a prisoner for the hope of Israel, thus emphasizing these two related claims of loyalty.

Acts 21:17—26:32, which contains the "final cycle" of speeches in Acts,[15] is carefully constructed as a continuous narrative that builds up to Paul's climactic speech before King Agrippa. The speeches in this section are a series of related, interlacing statements about the issues between Paul and his accusers. Defense against accusations that might concern the Roman authorities plays a relatively minor role, for the primary focus is on the issues between Paul and his fellow Jews.

The hope of Israel is a central theme in this cycle of speeches.[16] I will confine my remarks about the imprisonment speeches to this theme, which is introduced in 23:6 as Paul speaks before the Sanhedrin. There Paul claims that the issue of his trial is "hope and resurrection of the dead." This is strange, for no accusations on these matters have been leveled against Paul. As Paul introduces this subject, he identifies himself as a Pharisee, and his reference to resurrection immediately produces a dispute between the Pharisees and the Sadducees in the Sanhedrin. At this point the reference to hope and resurrection looks very much like a clever ploy to disrupt the proceedings, especially when we note that Paul's statement seems to ignore the real theological issue between himself and his Jewish accusers, namely, his claim that Jesus is the Messiah. However, if we follow this theme of hope and resurrection into the other speeches, we will see its significance grow.

---

[15] See Paul Schubert, "The Final Cycle of Speeches in the Book of Acts," *JBL* 87 (1968) 1–16.
[16] See Klaus Haacker, "Das Bekenntnis des Paulus zur Hoffnung Israels nach der Apostelgeschichte des Lukas," *NTS* 31 (1985) 437–51. Haacker's interpretation, developed as a critique of Haenchen, is in many ways congenial with the interpretation I am about to offer. Haacker rightly places Paul's loyalty to the hope of Israel in the broader context of the Lukan emphasis on the fulfillment of Israel's hope, an emphasis that begins with the birth narrative (Luke 1–2). On the significance of the birth narrative for our theme, see Robert C. Tannehill, *The Narrative Unity of Luke–Acts,* 2 vols. (Philadelphia & Minneapolis: Fortress, 1986, 1990) 1.15–44.

In part it grows through ignoring the initial indication that resurrection is expected by only one branch of Judaism. In 24:15 (cf. 24:21) Paul claims that his hope of resurrection is a hope that "these men themselves await," even though the high priest Ananias, presumably a Sadducee, was among the accusers present. In 26:6-7 it is described as hope in "the promise to our fathers" and the hope of "our twelve tribes" (τὸ δωδεκάφυλον ἡμῶν). In 28:20 it is simply called the hope of Israel. Resurrection is not finally a special doctrine of Pharisees or an optional element in Judaism but represents the fulfillment of a promise that is central to Jewish existence, as understood by the narrator.

The impression that Paul is harping on a minor and irrelevant theme also begins to wane when we realize that his reference to the hope of the resurrection has a hidden Christological core. There is a hint of this Christological core in 25:19, but it becomes explicit at the end of Paul's major address before King Agrippa, when Paul speaks of the Messiah who, as "first of the resurrection of the dead, is about to proclaim light both to the people and to the Gentiles" (26:23). It is the resurrection of Messiah Jesus that fulfills the Jewish hope for the resurrection of the dead. His resurrection initiates a resurrection that others will share.

In the Antioch synagogue Paul previously proclaimed that Jesus' resurrection fulfilled the promise to Israel of a Davidic Messiah. The hope of resurrection is such a weighty matter in Acts because it is also the hope of the messianic kingdom. The "hope of the promise" of resurrection in 26:6-8 is a variation on the "promise" to David of a successor to his throne, which was fulfilled through Jesus' resurrection, according to 13:22-23, 32-37. This connection is supported by a peculiarity of shared language between 13:32 and 26:6. In the one case the promise is τὴν πρὸς τοὺς πατέρας ἐπαγγελίαν γενομένην; the other verse refers to hope τῆς εἰς τοὺς πατέρας ἡμῶν ἐπαγγελίας γενομένης. The only use of ἐπαγγελία between these two passages is a reference to the Roman tribune's promise in 23:21. The last major speech of Paul is echoing a theme of his first major speech. According to 26:23 it is "the Messiah" who, through being "first of the resurrection of the dead," proclaims light to the people and the Gentiles. These connections make sense because resurrection life is one of the benefits of sharing in the Messiah's eternal kingdom.[17] This insight explains how

---

[17] On the Messiah's kingdom as an eternal kingdom, recall the preceding discussion of Luke 1:32-33; Acts 13:34.

Paul can describe resurrection as "the promise to our fathers" for which "our twelve tribes" hope (26:6-8). This is not an individualistic hope for life after death but a hope for the messianic kingdom, which is established through resurrection and characterized by resurrection life.

Paul's emphasis on the hope of Israel is designed to show the continuity between his Pharisaism and his present role as witness of Jesus Messiah. However, this does not explain Paul's reticence (until 26:23) to state that he now believes this hope for resurrection to be fulfilled in Jesus. Jesus is a divisive issue. Paul begins by emphasizing what he has in common with his many Jewish critics. As a good missionary he seeks a point of contact with his audience and from that point of contact attempts to lead them to understand the importance of Jesus. This strategy is indicated by the way that the defense speech before King Agrippa gradually turns into a mission speech. By the end of the speech Paul is no longer talking about his call and his past faithfulness to that call. His past witness to Jesus merges into a present witness: "Until this day I stand bearing witness both to small and to great" (26:22). The missionary significance of the speech is underlined by the concluding dialog with Agrippa, in which Paul appeals to Agrippa's belief in the prophets and Agrippa recognizes that Paul is trying to make him a Christian (26:27-28). Paul is appealing to others as well (26:29). His message is especially designed to appeal to Jews, for it is addressed to those who believe in the prophets, and it concerns the hope of Israel.

These observations raise questions about the view, sometimes asserted on the basis of the end of Acts, that the mission to Jews is a thing of the past for the author of Acts. In his farewell speech to the Ephesian elders (20:18-35), Paul is presented as a model for church leaders, in his dedicated witness to Jews and Greeks (20:21) as well as in other ways. If this is so, it is highly likely that the picture of Paul in the imprisonment narrative, where he is presented as a bold and resourceful missionary who continues his appeal to Jews even in difficult circumstances, is part of the model that the later church should follow.

Nevertheless, the theme of Israel's hope also helps to reveal the tragic irony of Israel's situation. In 26:7 Paul first emphasizes the Jews' intense hope in the promise and then says that he is now being accused by Jews concerning this same hope. The very hope so eagerly sought is rejected when it appears. This is ironic; it is also tragic, for Israel is losing what rightly belongs to it. The same tragic irony is conveyed in 28:20 by the image of Paul in chains for the hope of Israel. The messenger who proclaims the fulfillment of Israel's hope should be honored by Israel. Instead, Paul wears a chain because of his faithfulness to Israel's hope. This means suffering for Paul. It is an even greater tragedy for Israel.[18] This sense of tragic irony carries over into the second sub-scene (28:23-28) of Paul's encounter with the Jews of Rome and is forcefully expressed through the quotation from Isaiah.

This second sub-scene reminds us of previous occasions when Paul responded to Jewish resistance by announcing that he was turning to the Gentiles. However, there are some differences. Paul is not preaching in a synagogue. This change, to be sure, simply reflects Paul's imprisonment. It is still clear that Paul is addressing a Jewish assembly. The difference in the description of the Jews' reaction may be more significant. Instead of a report that Paul turns to the Gentiles when there is public reviling or blaspheming, we are simply told that the Jews disagreed among themselves, some being persuaded and some disbelieving (28:24). Paul's reaction makes clear that his intensive efforts ("from early morning until evening") have not been successful, so it is unlikely that the reference to some "being persuaded" (ἐπείθοντο) means that they have committed themselves to the Christian way. Probably the use of the imperfect is significant: they were in process of being persuaded but had made no lasting decision.[19] Why would the narrator want to say this when the scene is building up to the bitter words of Isaiah? Use of the quotation would seem most justified if the rejection is total. Furthermore, if the scene's purpose is to show that there is no longer any hope of convincing Jews and that the church must now concentrate exclusively on the Gentile mission, the point is undermined by portraying part of the Jewish assembly on the verge of acceptance. The reference to some being persuaded indicates that there is still hope of convincing some Jews in spite of what Paul is about to say about the Jewish community. While the Jewish community (controlled by its leadership) is deaf and blind, there are still those within it who are open to the Christian message. To indicate this, the narrator chose not to make the Jewish reaction as completely negative as we might expect.

---

[18] The significance of both the broad contours of the story and details of its presentation become clearer when we recognize the tragic aspect of Israel's story in Luke–Acts. See Tannehill, "Israel in Luke–Acts," 69–85.

[19] This is the conclusion of Hermann J. Hauser, *Strukturen der Abschlusserzählung der Apostelgeschichte (Apg 28, 16-31),* AnBib 86 (Rome: Pontifical Biblical Institute, 1979) 64–66.

The harsh words of the quotation are nevertheless appropriate. Paul's preaching on this day was a special opportunity to speak to the Jewish community of Rome, which is now departing without accepting Paul's witness. The presence of disagreement among the Jews is enough to show that Paul has not achieved what he sought. He was seeking a communal decision, a recognition by the Jewish community as a whole that Jesus is the fulfillment of the Jewish hope. The presence of significant opposition shows that this is not going to happen. Previous scenes have shown that the opposition of some can make preaching to the Jewish assembly impossible. Paul's closing statement in 28:25-28 is a response to this hard fact.

In spite of their failure to accept his witness, Paul still has a message for the Roman Jews. He must take the role of the prophet Isaiah and re-speak his words,[20] words so bitter for both prophet and people that Isaiah cried out, "How long?" (Isa 6:11). Isaiah's words are full of ironic tension that expresses the tension in the plot of Acts at its end. Through repeated and emphatic statements, the people are told of a highly unnatural situation: ears, eyes, and heart, which are meant for hearing, seeing, and understanding, have lost their power to perceive. This unnatural state, in which the organs of perception contradict their own purpose, has blocked God's desire to "heal them," a desire that a perceptive people would gladly embrace. But God has not finished speaking to this people, for it is the prophet's uncomfortable task to show unbelieving Israel its self-contradiction. He is told to "go to this people and say"[21] the bitter and anguished words that disclose Israel's failure. Both prophet and people are caught in this situation of tragic irony, for the prophet is commanded to speak to a people that cannot understand. Paul assumes this prophetic task. He again speaks to Israel, trying to make the people see their blindness and hear their deafness.[22]

---

[20] Paul is portrayed as a prophet on the model of the scriptural prophets through applying Septuagintal language from prophetic calls to him. See Acts 18:6 (cf. Ezek 33:4); 18:9-10 (cf. Jer 1:7-8); 26:16-18 (cf. Ezek 2:1, 3; Jer 1:7-8; Isa 42:6-7). In speaking the harsh words in Acts 28:26-27, Paul is fulfilling a prophetic role well-established in Israel's Scripture, where prophetic indictments of the people are common.

[21] These words are addressed to the prophet, not to the people, and it would not have been necessary to include them in the quotation. However, their inclusion emphasizes the divine command behind the prophetic role that Paul is fulfilling at this point in the story.

[22] Part of the preceding paragraph is adapted from my article, "Israel in Luke–Acts," 83.

Acts ends on a tragic, not a triumphant note. This is not lessened by 28:28. The function of these concluding words about the Gentiles is not to justify the Gentile mission, which has been done long ago, but to jar the Roman Jews by the contrast between their deafness and the gentiles' readiness to hear. This is a message to the Roman Jews ("Let it be known to you . . ."). It says, "They will hear," but you will not. This ironic reversal is strengthened by noting that Paul's announcement is a striking shift from his earlier announcement in the Antioch synagogue. There he proclaimed, "To us the word of this salvation has been sent out" (ἐξαπεσ-τάλη) (13:26). But to Jews who are deaf and blind he says, "To the Gentiles has been sent (ἀπεστάλη) this salvation of God; *they* will hear."

Paul is speaking to the Jews of Rome, not to Jews everywhere. Yet the theme of Jewish rejection, followed by mission to the Gentiles, is highlighted in major scenes at the beginning and end of Paul's mission and is repeated in other scenes. These connected scenes suggest a pattern or trend, even though there are exceptions. Building a pattern through individual scenes allows the narrator to avoid the implication that Jewish response was always the same, while suggesting the direction in which events are moving.

In previous scenes the announcement of turning to the Gentiles did not exclude renewed Jewish mission in other cities. Nothing prevents us from understanding the announcement in 28:28 as applying to Rome, leaving open the possibility of preaching to Jews elsewhere. Yet such an announcement at the end of a narrative carries extra weight. Just because the narrative ends, the narrator grants the final situation a certain permanence. The narrator may have been willing to do this because of awareness that the possibility of Christians preaching to a Jewish assembly, such as Paul addressed in Rome, has become very remote.

Nevertheless, there are signs of the narrator's concern to keep a mission to Jews alive in spite of this situation. Even after Paul is forced to abandon his preaching in the synagogues of Corinth and Ephesus, the narrator indicates that the mission reaches Jews of those cities (18:8; 19:10, 17-18).[23] In Ephesus, especially, there is indication of a preaching mission to Jews after Paul leaves the synagogue. There Paul preached for two years, with the result that "all those inhabiting Asia heard the word of the Lord, both Jews and Greeks" (19:10). This remark is placed after Paul's

---

[23] These passages are noted by Hauser, *Abschlusserzählung,* 109.

withdrawal from the synagogue. The Jews mentioned cannot be limited to those encountered in the synagogue of Ephesus before Paul's departure. Even if we allow for exaggeration, we must recognize that Paul's continuing preaching brings him in contact with a much wider circle of Jews than those who attended the synagogue of Ephesus.[24] Paul's continuing mission to both Jews and Gentiles in Ephesus provides a precedent for understanding his continuing mission in Rome, described in 28:30-31.

We have already noted that there are individuals within the Jewish community in Rome who show openness toward the Christian message (28:24). We have also noted that the lengthy imprisonment narrative presents Paul as a Jew who continues to witness to Jews in spite of their vigorous attempts to do away with him, and I have suggested that in this as in other respects Paul is a model for later evangelists. The summary of Paul's continuing preaching in 28:30-31 provides some additional evidence. After the preceding contrast between Jews and Gentiles, the reference in 28:30 to Paul welcoming "all" those coming to him should not be dismissed as an idle remark. According to 28:24, some of the Jews Paul had addressed were being persuaded by his message. This provides a motivation for some of them coming to talk to him later. Acts 28:30 makes clear that any Jews or Gentiles who did come were welcomed by Paul, who continued to preach to them and teach. Note that Paul's preaching and teaching focus on "the reign of God" and "the things concerning the Lord Jesus Messiah." These are the themes of Paul's preaching to the Roman Jews in 28:23. The distinctive speeches in Lystra (14:15-17) and Athens (17:22-31) show awareness that the mission cannot begin with pure Gentiles in the same way as Jews. Yet Paul in Rome continues to preach the themes with which he had addressed the Jews, suggesting that Jews are at least included in his audience.

The special connection of "the reign of God" and "the Lord Jesus Messiah" with a Jewish setting is indicated by some other observations. While Acts twice refers to God's reign in statements to established Christian communities (14:22; 20:25), which could include Gentiles (and in which Gentile members could have been instructed in such Jewish matters), the

---

[24] See Francis Pereira, *Ephesus: Climax of Universalism in Luke–Acts: A Redaction-Critical Study of Paul's Ephesian Ministry (Acts 18:23—20:1)* (Anand, India: Gujarat Sahitya Prakash, 1983). Pereira emphasizes that Paul's lengthy mission in Ephesus is, according to Acts, a universal mission, directed at the same time to Jews and Gentiles.

term is used elsewhere in addressing Jews or Samaritans (1:3, 6; 8:12; 19:8; 28:23). This is especially appropriate because the theme of God's reign is connected in Luke–Acts with Jesus' own reign as the Davidic Messiah. Lukan interest in Jesus' kingship appears in Luke 19:38 (which differs from Matthew and Mark); 22:29-30; 23:42, and in the passages that present Jesus as the successor to David's throne (Luke 1:32-33, 69-70; Acts 2:25-36; 13:22-23, 32-37). The centrality of Jesus' kingship in God's reign explains the repeated dual description of the preacher's message in Acts 8:12; 28:23, 31. It concerns both God's reign and Jesus. The missionaries are not preaching about two separate things. They are preaching about the realization of God's reign through the enthronement of Jesus at God's right hand as royal Messiah. It is sometimes noted that the reference to "the reign of God" in 28:31 forms an inclusion with the similar reference in 1:3.[25] The reference in 28:31 to the "Lord Jesus Messiah" also forms an inclusion with the climax of the Pentecost speech in 2:36. "The Lord Jesus Messiah" briefly summarizes Peter's proclamation of Jesus as "both Lord and Messiah," Messiah because he fulfills God's oath to David, and Lord because he is seated at God's right hand, a proclamation that Paul repeated (with variations) in his synagogue sermon in Acts 13. At the end of Acts, Paul is presented as faithfully continuing the message that he and Peter preached to the Jews in the major sermons near the beginning of the narratives about their ministries.[26] The situation has changed in that Paul can no longer speak in synagogues or to the Jews assembled as a community. But he continues to welcome all people who are willing to hear his message, including Jews.

The indication in 28:24 that some Jews are receptive and the description of Paul's activity in 28:30-31 both suggest that Paul's audience continues to include Jews, and this view is supported by the precedent of Paul's preaching in Ephesus after leaving the synagogue (19:10). Furthermore, this interpretation fits the portrait of Paul's mission as a whole. To the very end Paul remains faithful to the Lord's calling to bear

---

[25] See, e.g., Hauser, *Abschlusserzählung*, 118.

[26] Jacques Dupont, in "La conclusion des Actes et son rapport à l'ensemble de l'ouvrage de Luc," in *Nouvelles études sur les Actes des Apôtres* (Paris: Cerf, 1984), discusses the relation of the end of Acts to Paul's sermon in the Antioch synagogue. He remarks (p. 487), "Le long discours de 13, 16-39 donne une idée de ce que Luc peut avoir dans la tête quand, en 28,23, il résume en deux mots le contenu d'une prédication qui a duré 'depuis le matin jusqu'au soir'." I would add that Paul is still repeating the same message in 28:31.

witness to both Jews and Gentiles (9:15; 22:15; 26:16-18 [cf. 26:23]). Neither Jewish rejection nor Roman imprisonment prevent him from preaching "with all boldness" in response to this call. The final verses of Acts picture Paul doing what he told the Ephesian elders he must do: complete his ministry from the Lord in spite of the threat of death, a ministry of witnessing to both Jews and Greeks (cf. 20:21, 24). This is the image of Paul with which the narrator chooses to leave us.

Discussion of the Lukan attitude toward Israel must take account of two fundamental points: a persistent concern with the realization of scriptural promises which, the narrator recognizes, apply first of all to the Jewish people, and the stinging experience of rejection of the message that the hope of Israel is now being fulfilled. The resulting tension, especially apparent in the tension between the promise in the Antioch sermon and the bitter words at the end of Acts, is not resolved in the narrative. Acts offers no solution except the patient and persistent preaching of the gospel in hope that the situation will change.

The situation has not changed. Therefore, the assumption that the promises to the Jews will be realized primarily through their acceptance of the Christian message is now doubtful not only to Jews but also to many Christians. The passionate concern in Luke–Acts that God's salvation be realized comprehensively—for both Jews and Gentiles—is still important, but, in my opinion, it is now necessary to recognize the diverse ways in which different groups will find that salvation and express its meaning for their lives.

Part III

Acts as Narrative

10

The Functions of Peter's Mission Speeches in the Narrative of Acts[1]

My essay on "Peter's Mission Speeches" introduces a narrative critical perspective by viewing the speeches as actions within a developing plot. Although there are repeated themes within these speeches, each speech is more closely related to its specific setting than is commonly recognized. Each responds to a specific situation and has results within that situation. This is true of the Pentecost speech, not only because it comments on the coming of the Spirit but also because it addresses the critical situation of its audience, who have rejected their Messiah and now must repent. Although the mission speeches are the fullest theological statements in Acts, they are not addressed directly to the readers of Acts. Rather, readers are allowed to overhear skilled interpreters of the gospel addressing a particular audience in a particular situation of the past. I also discuss Peter's mission speeches in The Narrative Unity of Luke–Acts, *vol. 2, but the following essay clarifies my approach by discussing five speeches together and concentrating on their functions within their narrative settings.*

---

[1] A main paper delivered at the 45th General Meeting of SNTS, held in Milan, Italy, 23–27 July, 1990.

The repeated elements in the mission speeches of Acts have attracted considerable attention. Some scholars believe that these repeated elements reflect a pattern of early Christian preaching;[2] others see in them a pattern of Lukan theology.[3] Narrative criticism, the study of biblical narratives in light of literary theories of narrative,[4] suggests that past study should be balanced by a different approach. It suggests that we should investigate the functions of the individual speeches within their narrative settings. Despite the repeated themes, the speeches differ significantly in emphasis and function. These differences relate to the narrative setting in which each speech is found, and the setting influences the speech more profoundly than is commonly recognized. It is illuminating to think of each of the speeches as an action in the unfolding narrative plot. In speaking, Peter acts to influence a particular audience at a particular point in the plot. This action and the hearers' decision about how to respond will determine the direction in which the plot develops. When studied in this way, we can appreciate the differences among these similar speeches and understand why each is appropriate to its setting. This aspect of the Acts speeches is ignored when we concentrate primarily on abstracting a common pattern from them.[5]

---

[2] See C. H. Dodd, *The Apostolic Preaching and Its Developments* (Chicago: Willett, Clark & Co., 1937) 19–49; Martin Dibelius, *Studies in the Acts of the Apostles,* trans. Mary Ling (London: SCM, 1956) 165–66, 184; *idem, Die Formgeschichte des Evangeliums,* 4th ed. (Tübingen: Mohr/Siebeck, 1961) 15–16.

[3] See Ulrich Wilckens, *Die Missionsreden der Apostelgeschichte,* 3d ed., WMANT 5 (Neukirchen-Vluyn: Neukirchener, 1974); Eduard Schweizer, "Concerning the Speeches in Acts," in *Studies in Luke–Acts,* edited by Leander E. Keck and J. Louis Martyn (Nashville: Abingdon, 1966) 208–16. Jacques Dupont also recognizes the strong role of the Lukan author in forming the speeches but remains cautiously open to the presence of pre-Lukan tradition. See *Nouvelles Ètudes sur les Actes des Apôtres,* LD 118 (Paris: Cerf, 1984) 61–96.

[4] On narrative criticism as a method, see David Rhoads and Donald Michie, *Mark as Story* (Philadelphia: Fortress, 1982); R. Alan Culpepper, *Anatomy of the Fourth Gospel: A Study in Literary Design* (Philadelphia: Fortress, 1983); Stephen D. Moore, *Literary Criticism and the Gospels: The Theoretical Challenge* (New Haven: Yale University Press, 1989); Mary Ann Tolbert, *Sowing the Gospel: Mark's World in Literary-Historical Perspective* (Minneapolis: Fortress, 1989); Robert C. Tannehill, "Narrative Criticism," in *A Dictionary of Biblical Interpretation,* edited by R. J. Coggins and J. L. Houlden (Philadelphia: Trinity, 1990) 488–89. My application of narrative criticism to Luke–Acts may be found in *The Narrative Unity of Luke–Acts: A Literary Interpretation,* 2 vols. (Philadelphia and Minneapolis: Fortress, 1986, 1990).

[5] Martin Rese, in studying the statements about Jesus' death and resurrection in the Acts speeches, rightly notes that the "Grundschema" is not simply repeated but varied according to the situation. He cautions against neglecting "diese situationsbezogenen Differenzierungen." See "Die Aussagen über Jesu Tod und Auferstehung in der Apostelgeschichte—Ältestes Kerygma oder lukanische

I will quickly enumerate certain general functions in the narrative that Peter's mission speeches share,[6] although these general functions are not the main focus of this essay: 1) These speeches provide reviews of key events in the Jesus story and previews of important new events,[7] interpreting these events theologically, i.e., as manifestations of God's purpose interacting with human purposes. 2) Not only events of the past and future are interpreted; a speech may also interpret the significance of events taking place at the time of the speech. 3) The speeches as a group have a reinforcing function, reminding readers of certain themes and emphasizing their importance through repetition. 4) The speeches are also complementary, for they supplement each other, one expanding a particular theme and providing supporting detail, another expanding a different theme. Thus the full picture appears only when we consider all of the mission speeches. 5) The speeches present the new interpretation of Scripture in light of Jesus' death and resurrection disclosed by the risen Messiah to his first followers, according to the last chapter of Luke.[8]

Now we must consider the individual speeches as actions within the plot. The first four speeches that we will consider (Peter's speeches in Acts 2–5) are part of a developing conflict in Jerusalem that climaxes with Stephen's death. The first of these is the Pentecost speech. A critical situation for the people of Jerusalem already exists at the beginning of Acts, and this observation is important for understanding the function of the Pentecost speech in the narrative. Repeated references in Luke have emphasized the rejection of Jesus in Jerusalem.[9] Ironically, this rejection has led to God's installation of Jesus as ruling Messiah.[10] Peter and his

---

Theologumena?" *NTS* 30 (1984) 344. I agree and hope to explain more fully the contextual functions of these variations. Isolating the common pattern from the narrative settings of the speeches encourages the idea that these speeches are really directed to a general audience, including the readers of Acts. However, the reading experience is truncated if we do not recognize that the individual speeches are actions within particular situations and produce particular effects. Although Acts as a whole may have significance for its readers, the speeches are not made directly to them. Readers experience a speech along with its situation and result in the narrative, which are part of the total reading experience and rightly affect one's understanding of a speech's significance.

[6]Paul's synagogue speech in Antioch of Pisidia (Acts 13:16-41) could also be included at this point.

[7] On the significance of reviews and previews in Luke–Acts, see Tannehill, *Narrative Unity*, 1. 21.

[8]See Luke 24:26-27, 44-46 with Acts 2:25-36; 3:22-26; 4:11; 5:30; 13:32-37.

[9]See Luke 13:32-35; 19:11-27, 41-44; 20:9-19; 23:27-31.

[10]On the ironic aspect of the death and resurrection of Jesus in Luke–Acts, see Tannehill, *Narrative Unity*, 1.282–84, 288–89; 2.37.

companions know this, but his audience does not, nor have they faced the critical situation that results. If the residents of Jerusalem have supported their leaders in rejecting and killing their Messiah, these people must now face the fact that they have opposed God's saving purpose for Israel. At Pentecost Peter reveals to the people of Jerusalem what they have done, calling them to repentance. It is this situation that justifies the strong note of accusation in the speech.

When this situation is taken into account, we can recognize that there are multiple connections between the Pentecost speech and its setting and that these connections concern the core of the speech. We are not dealing with superficial splices used to insert a standard speech into its context. The speech is connected to its narrative setting not only by the brief response to the charge of drunkenness in 2:15 and by the commentary on the gift of the Spirit in the quotation from Joel (Acts 2:16-18; see 2:33, 38) but also by the emphasis on Jesus' resurrection and exaltation in this speech, the scriptural argument that the risen and exalted one is Lord and Messiah, and the sharp accusation of the audience in the statements that "you" killed or crucified Jesus (2:23, 36). Special emphasis on Jesus' resurrection is appropriate because this is the first public announcement of this event, and the scriptural argument that the risen Jesus is Lord and Messiah highlights the crime of the audience in rejecting him. Precisely these features constitute the core of the Pentecost speech, and the special emphasis on them fits the situation and audience addressed.

I do not mean to imply, of course, that proclaiming the resurrection of Jesus, or proclaiming him as Messiah, is only appropriate in this context. Other passages show that these are repeated features of the missionary message. The Pentecost speech also reflects the fact that it is the beginning of a mission directed to all Jews (note the reference to 'the whole house of Israel' in 2:36), Nevertheless, this speech brings the message of the risen Messiah to bear upon a specific audience in a specific situation, as the conclusion and climax of Peter's argument shows. In 2:36 Peter concludes his account of Jesus' resurrection by repeating and emphasizing his earlier accusation of his hearers.

Peter will continue to accuse his hearers of responsibility for the death of Jesus, but this accusation applies only to the Jewish rulers and people of Jerusalem. Paul's synagogue speech (13:16-41) resembles Peter's Pentecost speech in important respects, which makes differences between the two speeches more remarkable. To be sure, some of the differences between Paul's speech and the Pentecost speech simply show the tendency to supplement the previous message by making a similar point in a different way,[11] but some of the differences reflect the special situation of the Pentecost speech.[12] Paul does not make his audience responsible for the death of Jesus. Like Peter, he attributes Jesus' death to "those dwelling in Jerusalem and their rulers" (13:27). Therefore, Paul must approach his audience differently than Peter. The death of Jesus cannot be used as a basis for calling Paul's audience to repentance. Instead, Paul calls for faith, supported by a general, and therefore rather bland, reference to sins that need forgiveness (13:38-39). In Jerusalem the crime needing forgiveness is specific, and Peter's emphasis on this crime introduces a high degree of tension into the narrative. This tension grows as the conflict between the apostles and the Sanhedrin develops in Jerusalem.

Peter's accusation is appropriate neither to humanity in general nor to Jews in general. The impact of Peter's words in 2:36 depends to a considerable extent on the prior involvement of the audience in the death of Jesus. The inhabitants of Jerusalem[13] are being told something new that should radically change not only their view of Jesus but also their understanding of their own situation. Because of this, it is helpful to speak of the Pentecost episode as a "recognition scene." Aristotle wrote of the importance of "recognitions" or "discoveries" (ἀναγνω-ρίσεις) in tragic plots.[14] People who have acted blindly[15] against their own best interest may at a later time discover the truth in a recognition scene. Peter is the messenger who discloses the uncomfortable truth.[16]

---

[11]See the appeal to Ps 2:7 in Acts 13:33, which takes the place of Ps 110:1 in Acts 2:34-35.

[12]The introduction to Paul's speech provides little information except that Paul is speaking in a diaspora synagogue. The speech in Antioch of Pisidia can be taken, in most respects, as Paul's standard speech to diaspora Jews.

[13]Peter is speaking to Jews "from every nation under heaven," but these Jews have been "dwelling in Jerusalem," according to 2:5. They serve a dual function in the narrative. On the one hand, they represent Judaism as a whole, which is here being told about its Messiah; on the other hand, they are distinct from other Jews because they were present when Jesus was condemned and crucified and bear some responsibility for these events. The speech also has a dual function. It calls a specific group to account for what they have done; it also initiates the mission to Israel as a whole.

[14]See Aristotle, *Poetics* 1450a.

[15]That is, "in ignorance" (κατὰ ἄγνοιαν); see 3:17. Aristotle also notes the role of "ignorance" (ἄγνοια) in the tragic plot *(Poetics* 1453b-4a). On the tragic aspect of the story of Israel in Luke–Acts, see Tannehill, "Israel in Luke–Acts: A Tragic Story," *JBL* 104 (1985) 69–85.

[16]Note that the speech in 2:14-36 begins and ends by referring to what the audience must now know through Peter.

The narrator of Acts seems to recognize the dramatic value of a recognition scene within the plot and constructs the narrative accordingly.

The Pentecost speech, building up to its climax in 2:36, is well-designed to produce the effect described in the next verse. The listeners are "stabbed in the heart," the narrator says. They are shocked to recognize what they have done and immediately cry out for some remedy, which leads to Peter's call to repentance and offer of forgiveness. The narrative indicates that Peter's speech is powerfully effective. Peter at Pentecost is calling his audience to repentance for a specific, recent crime, and his words have the desired effect.

Furthermore, the Pentecost speech anticipates and interprets the following narrative through the quotation from Joel in Acts 2:17-21. This quotation is not only a comment on the Spirit's arrival at Pentecost but expresses a divine promise that will be progressively realized through the course of the mission. God promises to pour out the Spirit "on all flesh" (2:17), and the narrative traces the partial fulfillment of this promise as Samaritans (8:15-17) and Gentiles (10:44-46) receive the Spirit.[17] The final words of the Joel quotation ("Everyone who calls on the name of the Lord will be saved") also anticipate the following narrative, which shows the realization of this promise through repeated references to the powerful name of the Lord and to salvation through him.[18] The speech provides clues in advance for interpretation of the subsequent narrative, and the narrative, in turn, interprets the speech. God's promise in Joel may even be said to motivate the mission, contributing to the vision of God's saving purpose for the world that guides Jesus' witnesses in their work.[19]

Peter's second mission speech, which is associated with the temple, complements rather than simply repeats the Pentecost speech. After speaking in some detail about Jesus' resurrection in the Pentecost speech, Peter treats it very briefly in the temple speech.[20] The accusation, however, is developed, using details out of the Lukan passion story (3:13-15; see Luke 23:13-25). Both speeches cite Scripture, but the Pentecost speech cites a prophetic book and the Psalms, while the temple speech cites the

---

[17]See further Tannehill, *Narrative Unity,* 2.30–31.
[18]See Acts 2:38, 40; 3:6, 16; 4:7-12, 17-18, 30; 5:28, 31, 40-41.
[19]Charles Cosgrove notes that the divine δεῖ, revealed through Scripture, functions, in part, "as an imperative, a summons to obedience." See "The Divine ΔΕΙ in Luke–Acts," *NovT* 26 (1984) 183.
[20]See 3:15 and perhaps 3:22, 26. Some scholars also interpret "glorified his servant" in 3:13 as a reference to Jesus' resurrection and exaltation. See, e.g., Jürgen Roloff, *Die Apostelgeschichte,* NTD 5 (Göttingen: Vandenhoeck & Ruprecht, 1981) 74.

Pentateuch.[21] There are other differences between the Pentecost speech and the temple speech that show a desire to broaden the perspective on central themes with supplementary detail.[22]

The accusation of responsibility for Jesus' death is emphasized in 3:13-15 by double use of the emphatic nominative pronoun "you" (ὑμεῖς). This emphasis on the negative involvement of the audience is balanced at the end of the speech by emphasis on their positive involvement. Again using emphatic second-person plural pronouns, Peter emphasizes that the promises coming to fulfillment particularly concern his audience. "You (ὑμεῖς) are the sons of the prophets and the covenant. . . . To you (ὑμῖν) first . . . God sent" his servant (3:25, 26).[23] Thus the application of the message to Peter's audience is strongly emphasized especially at the beginning and ending of the speech.

The speeches in Acts 2 and 3 are both designed to call the people of Jerusalem to repentance, yet they do this in different ways. The Pentecost scene portrays the shock caused by Peter's announcement that the rejected and crucified Jesus is actually the Messiah chosen by God. The temple speech can no longer rely on the initial shock of recognition to produce repentance. Instead, it presents a series of supporting motivations. The call to repentance occurs in the middle of the temple speech (3:19), rather than at the end, because this call is followed by a series of supporting motivations for repentance in 3:19-26, emphasizing what the audience may gain or lose by its decision. The call to repentance is followed by two purpose clauses. The first refers to sins being wiped out, a variation on the offer of forgiveness of sins. The second goes further. It links repentance with "seasons of refreshment," the coming of the chosen Messiah, and the "times of restoration" of all that God promised through the prophets (3:20-21). This hope for fulfillment of all the scriptural promises, including, I think, the promise of restoration of Israel as a nation,[24] is a powerful motivation for repentance. Peter's audience must repent in order that God may send the Messiah, whose coming is associated with the final fulfillment of the promises to Israel. The images here are hopeful ones. The possibility of the fulfillment

---

[21]Acts 3:13 may allude to Isa 52:13, but there is no citation. The prophets are mentioned in 3:25. Again there is no prophetic citation.

[22]See Tannehill, *Narrative Unity,* 2.58.

[23]The pronoun in 3:26, although not nominative, is still emphatic because of its position.

[24]See Tannehill, *Narrative Unity,* 1.34–37 on the Benedictus and 2.14–17, 55–56 on Acts 1:6 and 3:19-21.

of God's promises to the Jewish people is still open, but the outcome depends on repentance. These hopeful words are followed by a threat of exclusion from the people for anyone who refuses to listen to the prophet like Moses (3:22-23). Then Peter again emphasizes the biblical hope of the prophets and Pentateuch. The quotation from Genesis in Acts 3:25 expresses this hope in universal terms: "all the families of the earth will be blessed." Yet the people of Israel have a special role in the fulfillment of God's purpose. They are the "sons of the prophets and of the covenant," and the promised blessing is being sent to them "first" (3:25-26). The final words of the speech again link this promised blessing for the people of Jerusalem to repentance (3:26). Thus the temple speech is the repentance speech *par excellence.* Although other speeches also contain a call to repentance, this speech expands the call and gives it extensive support through reference to the positive and negative possibilities between which Peter's audience must choose.[25]

This passionate call for repentance continues to reflect the special situation of the people of Jerusalem, who have rejected their Messiah. The temple speech is also related to its narrative context through references to the healing of the lame man at the temple gate.[26] The people gather because they are amazed at this healing, and Peter first responds to their amazement by denying that the healing happened by the apostles' own power (3:12). A few verses later he explains, in an emphatic if somewhat awkward statement, that it happened by faith in Jesus' name (3:16). This sign of healing now becomes additional evidence for Jesus as Israel's savior. The theme of salvation through the name of the Lord, based on the end of the Joel quotation in the Pentecost speech (2:21), is being developed through the healing and speech in Acts 3, and this theme will be further developed in the short speech in Acts 4.

Arrested and interrogated, Peter in 4:8-12 tells the authorities by what name the lame man was healed. This short speech is clearly connected with the surrounding narrative, providing crucial comment on salvation through the name of the Lord (see 2:21) and on the significance of the lame man's healing. Nevertheless, it is also a mission speech, not only

---

[25]The conclusion of the Pentecost speech (2:38-40) has a comparable function but is briefer.

[26]Dennis Hamm sees a very close relation between the speech and the healing, for he understands the healing to be symbolic of the restoration of Israel and the speech to be an interpretation of the healing. See "Acts 3:12-26: Peter's Speech and the Healing of the Man Born Lame," *PRS* 11 (1984) 199–217. The healing does have a symbolic aspect, but this is more clearly revealed in 4:9-12 than in the temple speech.

because it briefly repeats the contrast, found in the previous mission speeches, between what "you" did (crucify Jesus) and what God did (raise him from the dead) but also because it ends with a proclamation of Jesus' exaltation and the saving power of his name (4:11-12). Furthermore, Peter indicates that his statement about the name of Jesus is important not only for the assembled religious authorities but also for "all the people of Israel" (4:10). Peter is not merely responding to a legal interrogation; he is proclaiming Jesus. The strong influence of the narrative context does not eliminate Peter's response from the set of mission speeches, for we have discovered that the previous mission speeches are more closely tied to specific contexts than has generally been recognized.

Peter reveals that the name of Jesus is the power by which the lame man "has been saved" (σέσωται), but Peter ends his statement by speaking of salvation available to all through the name of Jesus (4:12). This development in thought from a specific act of salvation in healing to salvation as a general possibility gives to the healing of the lame man a symbolic dimension. The healing of the lame man is symbolic because it represents a salvation that extends to many other persons and includes more than physical healing. The name given for salvation in 4:12 must be understood in light of the larger narrative, especially the quotation from Joel in Acts 2:21 concerning the name of the Lord which may be called upon for salvation. In the Pentecost scene this reference to salvation was the basis not of an offer of physical healing but of Peter's call to the people of Jerusalem to repent and "be saved from this crooked generation" (2:40).

Peter and John have been arrested and are being called to account by powerful authorities. The function of Peter's speech is not only to reveal the full significance of previous events and statements in order to proclaim salvation through Jesus but also to show Peter's reaction to the threat that he and John face. Following the speech, the narrator comments on the "boldness" (παρρησία) of Peter and John (4:13). The speech is important to the narrative because it dramatically demonstrates this boldness. Repeating the message in this situation, including the accusation of crucifying Jesus, shows the bold persistence of Peter and John in spite of danger. The narrative emphasizes this trait, which contrasts sharply with the apostles' faithless reaction to danger in the Lukan passion story.[27]

---

[27]See Tannehill, *Narrative Unity*, 1.262–74. Reminders of the passion story in Acts 4–5 help to underscore the difference in the apostles' behavior. See Tannehill, *Narrative Unity*, 2.68–72.

There is a repetitive pattern of arrests, interrogations, and releases in Acts 4-5.[28] In Acts 5 apostles are arrested and interrogated a second time, and Peter delivers a second short speech before the Sanhedrin (5:29-32). This speech is the last presentation of Peter's message to Jerusalem Jews. It is an important summary statement. It not only reemphasizes the contrast between God's act of raising Jesus and the authorities' violent rejection of him (5:30) but also specifically recalls the Pentecost speech by referring to Jesus' exaltation at the right hand of God (5:31; see 2:33). The concluding reference to the Holy Spirit recalls both Pentecost and the second outpouring of the Spirit in 4:31, following the church's prayer in the face of danger. The Spirit is given to those who "obey" God, that is, those who persist in the mission in spite of danger (5:29, 32).

The specific connections with the Pentecost speech indicate that themes of the beginning are being repeated at the end of Peter's Jerusalem mission speeches, creating an *inclusio* or envelope structure. Peter's mission speeches repeatedly link the exalted Jesus to the pouring out or giving of gifts (see 2:33; 4:12; 5:31-32). This theme is important in the soteriology of Acts.[29] Among these gifts are the Spirit ("poured out" by the exalted Jesus, according to 2:33; "given" by God to Jesus' followers, according to 5:32). Other important gifts are the name "given" for salvation (4:12) and repentance and forgiveness of sins given to Israel (5:31). The emphasis on the "gift" of the Spirit in the Pentecost speech (see 2:38) fits the Pentecost scene. The emphasis on the gift to Israel of repentance and forgiveness in 5:31 may also fit the situation in which these words are spoken. The conflict between the apostles and the Sanhedrin is developing. The Sanhedrin's angry reaction to Peter's second statement shows that the apostles are now in danger of death (see 5:33). The persistence of Peter in this situation not only reveals something about Peter—he is now a bold witness for Jesus—but also reveals something about God's purpose in relation to the Jewish people. In previous speeches Peter has called for repentance, but here he speaks of repentance as God's gift to Israel and the purpose of God's exaltation of Jesus, strengthening previous

---

[28]Repetitive patterns (parallel sequences of events) in Luke–Acts have been studied by Charles H. Talbert in *Literary Patterns, Theological Themes and the Genre of Luke–Acts,* SBLMS 20 (Missoula, Mont.: Scholars, 1974). There is a complex set of parallels in Acts 4–5 and between these chapters and other parts of Luke–Acts. See Tannehill, *Narrative Unity,* 2. 63–77.
[29]See Tannehill, *Narrative Unity,* 2.39–40.

statements.[30] That purpose still holds despite the opposition of Jewish leaders to the mission. Indeed, the offer is still valid for the leaders to whom Peter is now speaking. The mission must persist because it is still God's purpose to offer forgiveness to the Jewish people through Jesus. The need for forgiveness is all the clearer as the opposition to God's offer hardens.[31]

The offer of repentance and release of sins in 5:31-32 is given climactic position among the statements of the apostles in Acts 4–5. The following speech by Gamaliel is, of course, important. However, the final statement by the apostles is made by Peter in 5:31-32, and it centers on their witness to the gift of repentance and forgiveness to Israel through its exalted savior. The placement of this message appears to be significant. Although the first and second arrests and interrogations in Acts 4–5 are roughly parallel, the first and second speeches before the Sanhedrin do not occupy the same position in the sequence. In the first interrogation sequence the mission speech comes first (4:8-12), followed by the authorities' command not to speak in the name of Jesus (4:18) and the apostles' refusal, with a declaration of obedience to God rather than human authorities (4:19-20). In the second interrogation sequence the authorities must deal with the fact that the apostles have disobeyed. The sequence begins with the high priest's accusation (5:28), followed by the apostles' second declaration of obedience to God rather than humans (5:29) and then the second mission speech to the Sanhedrin (5:30-32). The relative position of the mission speech and the declaration of obedience to God has shifted in Acts 5. The proclamation of the exalted savior who gives repentance and forgiveness to Israel has become the climax of the apostles' response, Peter's last word to the Sanhedrin. Although the Sanhedrin reacts with anger, Peter's speech emphasizes the continuing availability of repentance and forgiveness of sins for Israel, an important point in light of the developing

---

[30]The active purpose of God working through repentance is also presented in 3:26 if the verb in the infinitive construction is transitive: "God sent him as a source of blessing for you in turning each from your wicked ways."

[31]The statement that "God exalted him as leader and savior" in 5:31 resembles the statement in 2:36 that "God made him both Lord and Messiah," although the titles differ. The titles in 5:31 summarize affirmations about Jesus in Acts 3-4, for the title "leader" (ἀρχηγός) was introduced in 3:15 and salvation through Jesus was emphasized in 4:12. "The God of our fathers" in 5:30 also repeats a phrase from 3:13. These observations add to the evidence for the summary function of 5:30-32.

resistance to the mission. Once again, the placement of the speech in the developing plot of Acts suggests that there is a reason for the special emphasis in the speech.

Finally, we must consider Peter's speech to Cornelius and his companions in 10:34-43. Ulrich Wilckens stressed the difference between this speech and the previous mission speeches, insisting that it is not really a mission speech but a sketch of Luke's own Gospel that would be more appropriate to a group of converted Christians.[32] This speech is indeed a sketch of Luke's own Gospel, more clearly so than Wilckens recognized, and it does differ significantly from the preceding mission speeches. However, each of the mission speeches is different, reflecting its special functions in its narrative context, as we have seen. To be sure, there is a special problem with the speech in Acts 10, for it is not immediately obvious that the narrative setting calls for this kind of speech. Why should the meeting with Cornelius call forth a summary of the Lukan story of Jesus, and why should preaching to Gentiles put such emphasis on the Jewish setting of Jesus' life?

There is no problem in recognizing the connection between the introduction to Peter's speech and the preceding narrative, for Peter begins by commenting on what he has learned through the events that brought him to Cornelius' house. Peter now recognizes in a new and deeper way that God does not play favorites, for Gentiles who fear God and do righteousness are not unclean, as Jews have supposed, but are acceptable to God and therefore should be accepted into the fellowship of believers. Peter continues to express his new insight in 10:36, although we here encounter a well-known grammatical difficulty that creates various interpretations. It is clear that the statement "He is Lord of all" in this verse relates to the inclusion of Gentiles, the subject of Peter's statement in the two preceding verses. Furthermore, this is the main statement of v. 36, in my view, and should not be translated as a parenthetical remark.[33] I would translate v. 36 as follows: "With respect to the word which [God] sent to the sons of Israel, preaching good news of peace through Jesus Messiah, he is Lord of all," understanding the initial τὸν λόγον as an

---

[32]See "Kerygma und Evangelium bei Lukas (Beobachtungen zu Acta 10. 34-43)," *ZNW* 49 (1958) 223–37.

[33]As was done in the RSV.

accusative of respect.[34] Peter is drawing two conclusions from his recent experience. He first draws a theological conclusion concerning God's impartiality and the significance of this for Gentiles. He then draws a christological conclusion concerning the scope of Jesus' lordship: "He is Lord of all." It may seem puzzling that this affirmation is preceded by a reference to the word sent to the sons of Israel. This reference to a message to Israel is part of the striking Jewishness of the universal Lord who is presented in this speech to Gentiles.

Before addressing this problem, I want to add that the end of Peter's speech emphasizes the availability of forgiveness of sins to "everyone who believes in him" (10:43). This is another way of speaking of God's acceptance of Gentiles. Thus the end of the speech returns to the thought of the beginning, and this frame clearly relates the speech to its narrative context.[35] Is the rest of the speech, however, appropriate to its Gentile audience?

It is important to recognize that the main part of the speech is a summary in chronological order of the story of Jesus as presented in Luke's Gospel, including specific reference to three major scenes: the announcement to the shepherds in the birth narrative, Jesus' interpretation of his mission in the Nazareth synagogue, and the risen Jesus' commission of his followers at the end of the Gospel. Most scholars will recognize the reference in Acts 10:38 to Isa 61:1 and Jesus' announcement in the Nazareth synagogue (Luke 4:18). It is less common to recognize that "the word which [God] sent to the sons of Israel," mentioned in Acts 10:36, is a reference to the Lukan birth narrative.[36] The angel speaking to the shepherds said, "I announce good news" (εὐαγγελίζομαι) concerning the birth of the "Messiah Lord" (Χριστὸς κύριος), and the angel chorus proclaimed peace on earth (Luke 2:10-11, 14). Peter summarizes this message to the sons of Israel in these terms: "announcing good news of peace through Jesus Messiah." The announcement of good news, the reference to peace, and the reference to the Messiah all fit the shepherd scene in the Lukan birth story. The angel's description of Jesus as Messiah

[34]Following Christoph Burchard, "A Note on ῬΗΜΑ in JosAs 17:lf.; Luke 2:15, 17; Acts 10:37," *NovT* 27 (1985) 293.
[35]A universal perspective also appears in 10:42, for Jesus is "judge of the living and the dead," i.e., judge of all persons.
[36]See, however, Burchard, "Note on ῬΗΜΑ," 290–94; Gerhard Schneider, *Die Apostelgeschichte,* HTKNT 5 (Freiburg: Herder, 1982) 2.75, n. 149.

Lord is also important. At this point Peter makes a significant modification: Jesus is not only the Messiah Lord of the Jewish people but "Lord of all."

If we recognize this reference to the birth narrative in 10:36, Peter's account of Jesus unfolds in chronological order. The announcement at Jesus' birth is followed by references to John's baptismal proclamation, Jesus' anointing with the Spirit and acts of healing, his crucifixion, resurrection, and resurrection appearances, and his command to proclaim and bear witness. The prophets also bear witness that everyone receives forgiveness of sins through Jesus' name. The command to proclaim and bear witness, and the link between Scripture and the message of forgiveness through Jesus' name, recall the scene at the end of Luke in which Jesus commissions his witnesses (Luke 24:46-48).[37]

Ending with Jesus' commission to his witnesses to begin a world mission in his name is appropriate to this scene in which Peter preaches to Gentiles. Up to this time the apostles have neglected the task of preaching repentance and forgiveness to "all the nations" (Luke 24:47).[38] Even now Peter speaks of the apostles' proclamation "to the [Jewish] people" (10:42). He adds, however, the witness to Jesus as universal judge and source of forgiveness for "everyone who believes in him" (10:42-43). The formulation at the end of the speech reflects, in part, the actual role that Peter plays in Acts. Apart from this scene, he preaches to Jews, while also defending the rights of Gentile believers (15:7-11). A division of labor, not anticipated in the commission at the end of Luke, is arising. Peter supports the Gentile mission, but it is largely carried out through Paul and his companions, according to Acts.

We should also consider the special emphasis placed on Jesus' witnesses in the speech before Cornelius. Although three of the four previous mission speeches of Peter contain references to these witnesses (see 2:32; 3:15;

---

[37]Note that the proclamation of forgiveness of sins in Jesus' name to all the nations, beginning from Jerusalem, is part of what "is written," according to Luke 24:46-47. Acts 10:43 rests on the same interpretation of Scripture. On the Christology and interpretation of Scripture behind Luke 24:46-47, see Dupont, *Nouvelles Ètudes,* 37–57.

[38]Wilckens cites the absence of repentance or conversion in the speech as evidence that the missionary proclamation has here been turned into "Gemeindepredigt." See "Kerygma und Evangelium," *ZNW* 49 (1958) 237. However, the reference to "forgiveness of sins" in 10:43 presupposes that the Gentiles addressed are also involved in sin, and the whole Cornelius story is summarized in 11:18 by the statement "Then God has given repentance unto life also to the Gentiles." Dupont states that outside Jerusalem forgiveness of sins is related to faith, as in 10:43, rather than repentance. See *Nouvelles Ètudes,* 76. Acts 26:18-20, however, shows that faith for Gentiles includes repentance.

5:32), only here is there repeated reference to their role. They are witnesses both to Jesus' ministry (10:39) and to Jesus' resurrection (10:41), a twofold witness that corresponds to the requirements for an apostle indicated by Peter when Judas was replaced (1:21-22). Furthermore, these witnesses were specially chosen and ate and drank with the risen Lord, and they have been commissioned by the Lord to proclaim forgiveness in the Lord's name (10:41-43).[39]

The emphasis on the witnesses in this speech corresponds to the unusual fullness of the Jesus story, stretching from the announcement to the Jewish shepherds to the commission by the risen Lord. While Paul is also called a witness (see 22:15; 26:16), the scope of his witness is not the same. Peter and the apostles, because of their participation in the ministry of Jesus, are the ones appointed to bear witness to it, as well as to Jesus' resurrection. We still should ask, however, why the story of Jesus prior to the crucifixion receives such emphasis just here. This leads to a second observation: the emphasis on these witnesses corresponds to the position of this speech in the development of Acts. The speech to Cornelius and his companions is the last mission speech by an apostle in Acts. Peter represents the apostles, who can bear witness to the story of Jesus in its full scope. We are reminded of the importance of that story by the summary of it presented in the last mission speech given by one qualified to bear witness to it. Thus the function of this speech relates in part to the conversion of Gentiles in the Cornelius episode, but it also relates in part to a larger narrative context: the transition taking place between the mission of Peter and the mission of Paul. During this transition the Lukan story of Jesus is summarized and interpreted for the benefit of both Cornelius and the readers.

The placement of this type of speech at this point in the narrative implies that it is important for Cornelius to hear the story of the Jewish Messiah. Contrary to what we might expect in a speech to Gentiles, the Jewish context of Jesus' ministry is emphasized in Peter's account. He begins the story with the birth announcement to "the sons of Israel." As he continues, he makes repeated references to the Jewish regions of Jesus' work: "the whole Jewish land" (καθ᾽ ὅλης τῆς Ἰουδαίας), "Galilee," "Nazareth," "the land of the Jews," "Jerusalem." This story of the Jewish Messiah is placed in a universal

---

[39]Although 10:43 refers to the witness of the prophets, it also indicates the content of the message given to the apostles, as Luke 24:46-48 shows.

frame, which affirms God's acceptance of Gentiles as well as Jews. The speech thereby becomes an affirmation of the significance of the Jewish Messiah for Gentiles also. Jesus, however, does not cease to be the Jewish Messiah in this sermon to Gentiles.[40] He is the Jewish Messiah who graciously offers the benefits of his peaceful reign to all, thereby becoming "Lord of all" (10:36).[41] Acts will later emphasize that Paul, too, is a loyal Jew in his life and in his message. The concern to make this point suggests that Peter's presentation of the Jewish Messiah to Cornelius may also have an underlying theological purpose. The "Lord of all" must remain the Jewish Messiah and the apostles' missionary witness, presented for the last time in this speech to Cornelius, should ensure this.[42]

Peter's words at Pentecost include a call to baptism and an invitation to receive the Spirit (2:38). Although these elements are absent from the speech to Cornelius, the following narrative indicates that the Gentiles received the Spirit, and then Peter commands that they be baptized (10:44-48). The close connection between the speeches and their narrative settings is also shown by the fact that some of the repeated elements may occur in one case in the speech, in another case in the setting.

We have examined the mission speeches of Peter in Acts and have noted that, despite their repeated themes, they differ significantly in their emphases. These different emphases reflect the varying functions of the individual speeches in their narrative settings. Careful study of the speeches as part of the narrative results in a better understanding and appreciation of their different emphases and varying functions.

---

[40]The Areopagus speech differs markedly, but it does not represent the full missionary message. Rather, it suggests the special preparation necessary with those not yet ready to understand "Jesus and the resurrection" (17:18). To comprehend the Lukan message, it would be necessary to bring Gentiles to the level of Cornelius' understanding. Cornelius not only knows about Judaism and supports it with gifts (10:2) but also knows something about Jesus. See "you know" in 10:37. In the context of the Lukan narrative, it is not strange that Cornelius should have some knowledge of Jesus, for the narrative emphasizes the spreading fame of Jesus, reaching as far as "the seacoast of Tyre and Sidon" (Luke 6:17; see also Acts 26:26). See Ulrich Busse, *Die Wunder des Propheten Jesus,* 2d ed., FB (Stuttgart: Katholisches Bibelwerk, 1979) 348–50; Tannehill, *Narrative Unity,* 1.85–86.

[41]The quotation from Amos in Acts 15:16-17 implies a similar view of Jesus as the Davidic Messiah whose reign will include the Gentiles.

[42]The underlying concern could arise from some combination of the following: 1) criticism of the church from outside because it is not being faithful to Judaism; 2) the author's own fear that the church is losing its Jewish heritage and the scriptural context of its message; 3) a desire to keep the mission to the Jews alive and to avoid presenting the church and its message in ways that create additional obstacles for this mission. Many would judge the last concern to be foreign to Luke–Acts. See, however, Tannehill, *Narrative Unity,* 2.286–90, 328, 350–53.

11

The Composition of Acts 3–5: Narrative Development and Echo Effect

My essay on Acts 3–5 moves a significant step beyond the previous essays in this collection because I discuss literary patterns in an extensive narrative, rather than focusing on a single scene or type of material. This essay is a stage in the development of narrative criticism as a method of interpreting Luke–Acts. It assumes that we can and should read Luke–Acts as a unitary narrative with significant plot development and that in doing so we can apply observations about narrative developed by literary theorists outside of biblical studies. It anticipates the discussion of Acts in volume 2 of The Narrative Unity of Luke–Acts. *The two parts on "Narrative Development" and "Echo Effect" suggest that good reading will engage in two activities simultaneously: tracing the forward movement of the plot through a series of causally connected events and listening for the enriching echoes of similar events in other parts of the narrative. In the final section of this essay I summarize the significance of repetitive narrative patterns, an extensive summary not found in my other writings.*

This paper is a piece of a larger work on Luke–Acts, which might be called a commentary but not of the traditional kind, for it will focus on features of Luke–Acts ignored or treated lightly in traditional commentaries. It will study Luke–Acts as a unitary narrative. This requires attention to continuous plot lines that unify the story. But, as we will see below, linear plot development is overlaid with patterns of recurrence that enrich the context in which individual events can be viewed, helping to give them imaginative resonance. I am trying to keep the two-volume work continually in view as the interpretive context for understanding each part of it. The significance of particular features of an episode may only appear when we note connections with other sections of Luke–Acts. The work as a whole is the best guide to the special perspectives and values of the implied author. Apart from an understanding of Luke–Acts as a unitary narrative, judgments about these perspectives and values are hazardous, for in narrative it is always possible to qualify or undermine the supposed implications of earlier scenes through later developments.

I am not just searching for theological themes, if by that is meant a set of static statements about God, Jesus, and humanity that are supposedly the essence of the author's message. The implied author does have theological perspectives that limit and control the intended meanings of the story, and these must be understood in order to interpret it. But the author's methods also give the story imaginative impact, stimulating an imaginative response from readers that cannot be entirely controlled. A "narrative world" is being created,[1] an imaginative world, both in the sense that it is the product of a human imagination and also in the sense that it engages others imaginatively. This creative act is both power and risk, for basic perceptions of readers may be changed through this imaginative engagement, but no author can completely control what readers will make of the work once the imagination is let loose.

Furthermore, we must always be sensitive to how repeated themes function within a narrative as a developing whole. Themes which, isolated from their narrative context, appear to be constant may actually shift significantly in meaning through some new development in the plot. Thematic expectations at the beginning may be recalled to highlight their disappointment or their fulfillment in some unexpected way. Thus we

---

[1] See Norman R. Petersen, *Literary Criticism for New Testament Critics,* GBS (Philadelphia: Fortress, 1978) 40.

must keep in mind where we are in a story that may be full of twists and turns, rather than reducing Luke–Acts to a set of static theological themes.

Although we will focus primarily on Acts 3–5, we must recognize that Acts 1:1-8:3 is carefully composed as a unified narrative of the mission in Jerusalem. Continuity is maintained as events develop from one scene to the next, finally reaching a climax with Stephen's speech and death. In the course of this development, the crucial decision faced by the people of Jerusalem and their leaders is revealed with clarity, and the opposition to the apostles' message gradually develops to the point of drastic action. Along with this major plot development there is a minor theme of the unity of the church expressed through sharing of possessions (2:44-45, 4:32-37), a unity of heart and soul that is threatened but, through prompt action, restored (5:1-11, 6:1-6).[2] The scenes at the beginning of chapters 3 and 6 may seem to introduce new material that causes a major break in the narrative, but when we read on, we discover that these scenes will contribute to the continuous plot uniting Acts 1:1-8:3. The healing of the lame man causes a series of important events, and the choice of the seven in 6:1-6 introduces Stephen, the key figure in the next stage of the conflict that dominates Acts 4-7.

Narrative Development in Acts 3–5

Healing and Speech to the People

The healing of the lame man instigates a series of encounters among the apostles, the "people," and the Sanhedrin in 3:11—5:42. The healing causes "all the people" to gather (3:11), which becomes the occasion for Peter's speech in 3:12-26. This speech in turn provokes the temple authorities to arrest Peter and John (4:1-3). The whole sequence of events in 3:1—4:22 takes place on an afternoon and the next day and is directly caused by the healing of the lame man and by Peter's speech to the crowd attracted by this event. There are repeated references to the healing of the lame man in this section as Peter and John explain what it reveals about the "name" of Jesus Christ and the Sanhedrin struggles with the question

---

[2] See Joseph B. Tyson, "The Problem of Food in Acts: A Study of Literary Patterns with Particular Reference to Acts 6:1-7," in *SBLSP* (Missoula, Mont.: Scholars, 1979) 1.69–76.

of how to respond to what has happened (3:12, 16; 4:7-12, 14, 16). The section ends as it began with a reference to the healing of the lame man and its effect on the people (4:21-22). Thus the sequence of events in 3:1—4:22 is unified causally, one event provoking the next. It is united temporally by the short span of time. It is also unified by the persistent presence of the healed man with Peter and John. Remarkably, the lame man is physically present even at the hearing before the Sanhedrin after the apostles' arrest (4:14). He is a persistent reminder of the power of Jesus' name.

The causal chain does not end at 4:22. The hearing of Peter and John before the Sanhedrin concludes with the threats of the Sanhedrin, who are trying to force the apostles to stop speaking in the name of Jesus. The prayer of the church that follows in 4:23-31 is a response to this threat, and, following a second arrest and hearing, the complaint of the Sanhedrin is that the apostles have disobeyed the command not to teach in Jesus' name (5:28). They attempt again to enforce their order, but their efforts are ineffectual. So 5:17-42 is tied to 4:5-31 because it is the continuation of the story of the church's response to the threats of the Sanhedrin. The one section also reduplicates the other, each moving from arrest to hearing to release, thereby emphasizing the courage of the apostles and the inability of the Sanhedrin to respond effectively.

Acts 2–5 is also united by the frequent references to the "name" of the Lord or of Jesus Christ, references that are especially characteristic of this section of Acts. This begins with the reference to the "name of the Lord" at the end of the Joel quotation in 2:21, followed by the reference to being baptized "in the name of Jesus Christ" in 2:38. Then the name of Jesus Christ is presented as the effective power behind the healing of the lame man (3:6, 16; 4:7, 10, 12), and there are repeated references to Jesus' name as the apostles encounter the rulers' threats (4:17, 18, 30; 5:28, 40, 41). In following chapters the "name" of Jesus is also important. Indeed, Christians are described as those who "call upon the name" (9:14, 21; 22:16), a reminder of the Joel quotation in Acts 2:21 with which the theme is introduced. Following Acts 2–5 references to the name of Jesus are first associated with the mission of Philip in Samaria (8:12, 16) and then with Paul's call and early preaching (9:14, 15, 16, 21, 27, 28), perhaps as a deliberate means of emphasizing the continuity of the preaching of Philip and Paul with the preaching of the apostles. After Acts 9, however, references to Jesus' name become less frequent and concentrated, occurring at 10:43, 48; 15:26; 16:18; 19:5, 13, 17; 21:13; 22:16; 26:9. The comparative infrequency of references to Jesus' name in Acts 10–28 suggests that the frequent references in Acts 2–5 and 8–9 are not merely the result of habits of expression but show deliberate emphasis in a section of Acts where this theme contributes to narrative continuity. The lame man becomes a paradigm of salvation through the name of the Lord, in fulfillment of the Scriptural promise quoted in 2:21, and the promised salvation then passes to others through the missions of the apostles, Philip, and Paul.

The narrator places some emphasis on the lame man's "leaping" immediately following the healing, using the rare word ἅλλομαι and its compound form ἐξάλλομαι together in 3:8.[3] This not only demonstrates the healing vividly but, for those as familiar with the prophecies of Isaiah as our author is, recalls Isa 35:6, part of a passage which probably influenced the summary description of Jesus' mighty acts in Luke 7:22. In the context of Acts 3, this allusion to Isaiah would support Peter's claim that "all the prophets . . . proclaimed these days" (3:24).

Peter's second speech is given in response to the amazed crowd that gathers after the healing of the lame man. Peter begins by correcting a possible false impression, that the apostles had "made him walk by our own power or piety" (3:12). In Acts, Peter and Paul do mighty works similar in kind to those of Jesus in the Gospel. Therefore, it is important to make clear that these mighty works are performed not by the disciple's own power but by the power of Jesus' name, as Peter will explain in 3:16. The same sort of correction is made more dramatically when Paul heals a lame man, for Paul and Barnabas must stop the people of Lystra from sacrificing to them as gods (14:14-15). Peter, too, must correct a Gentile who treats him as more than human (10:25-26). The care with which Peter and Paul distinguish between themselves and the power at work through them contrasts with the claims of religious charlatans like Theudas and Simon Magus who claim that they themselves are "somebody" or "somebody great" (5:36; 8:9). The sensitivity that Peter and Paul show on this issue is also an indication of the change that has taken place in Jesus' followers through the appearance of the risen Christ and the gift of the Spirit. While in Luke the disciples engaged in disputes over who was the

---

[3] Ἐξάλλομαι occurs only here in the NT. Ἅλλομαι is used in Acts 14:10 in a scene that parallels the healing of the lame man in Acts 3. Elsewhere in the NT it is found only at John 4:14.

greatest, even at the Last Supper (Luke 22:24; cf. 9:46), Jesus' warning that "everyone who exalts himself will be humbled, and the one who humbles himself will be exalted" (Luke 14:11; 18:14; cf. 9:48; 22:26) has now taken hold in the lives of Jesus' witnesses.

Even more clearly than the Pentecost speech, the speech in Solomon's portico aims to awaken repentance. It must be understood in its narrative context, for it addresses a specific audience, the Jerusalem Jews who lived at the time of Jesus' death and (in the eyes of Peter and the implied author) were responsible for it. The special involvement of the audience in what has happened and is happening is stressed. They are involved in two ways: (1) They "delivered up and denied" him, asked for a murderer in his stead, and "killed" him (3:13-15). The accusation is made vivid by the repeated verbs and by descriptive details from Luke's passion story (Pilate's decision to "release" [ἀπολύειν] Jesus—cf. Luke 23:16; the crowd asking for Barabbas, the "murderer"—cf. Luke 23:18-19), and the involvement of the audience receives further stress through the double use of the emphatic nominative pronoun "you" (ὑμεῖς). (2) Emphatic second person plural pronouns return at the end of the speech, now in order to emphasize the audience's involvement in the promised blessing (3:25—emphatic nominative pronoun; 3:26—dative pronoun in emphatic position at the beginning of the sentence). This emphasis may suggest that the rather frequent use of the second person plural pronoun throughout 3:19-26 is also significant.[4] The reference in 3:20 to Jesus as "the Messiah chosen for you" is also a significant indication of the concern to make clear that it is precisely their Messiah and their promises concerning which they must now make a decision. Thus the application of the message to this audience is especially emphasized, and this is particularly clear at the beginning and end of the speech. The audience is involved in God's work through Jesus both negatively and positively. They bear responsibility for rejecting and killing Jesus. Nevertheless, God is working through Jesus and his witnesses to fulfill the covenantal promise to them. To be sure, there is a hint at the end of the speech that the promised blessing is not for them alone, but it is for them *first,* for they are "the sons of the prophets and of

---

[4] The three occurrences in the following sentence are especially striking: "The Lord *your* God will raise up a prophet for *you* from *your* brethren, a prophet like me" (3:22) (my emphasis). The first *your* is textually uncertain. The LXX of Deut 18:15 has singular rather than plural pronouns in all three cases.

the covenant" (3:25-26). Peter makes clear that the promised blessing is still available to them, if they repent.

The stress on the audience's involvement, negatively and positively, in God's work through Jesus heightens both danger and opportunity. It discloses a situation of high tension, a tension that can only be released through turning away from past rejection and accepting the promised blessing through Jesus. The speech is shaped to fit its narrative setting and to move its audience in the narrative to action. It is meant to call the people of Jerusalem to repentance. Thus Dibelius was mistaken when he concluded that the author of Acts is presenting the type of Christian sermon customary in his own day, with the implication: "This is how the gospel is preached and ought to be preached!"[5] The author has composed a speech that, in his opinion, was appropriate to the speaker and the audience. This is not surprising, for appropriateness was an important criterion of good speech in Greco-Roman rhetoric, and in Greco-Roman education students were trained in the art of "impersonation" (προσωποποιΐα).[6] Thus the speech has narrative significance. It is meant to move characters in the story to action. It directs the readers' attention forward to indications of how the people of Jerusalem will respond to Peter, for fateful decisions are being made.

Peter still hopes, and encourages the people of Jerusalem to hope, that they will share in the "times of the restoration of all that God spoke" through the prophets. This will include the sending of their Messiah to them, provided they repent (3:19-21). Since the birth stories in Luke, readers have been led to expect that Jesus would establish a Messianic kingdom for Israel. Gabriel told Mary that her son "will reign over the house of Jacob for ever" on the throne of David (Luke 1:32-33), and Zechariah blessed God for the "horn of salvation . . . in the house of David" whom God has "raised up" (Luke 1:69). This fulfills what God "spoke through the mouth of his holy prophets from of old" (1:70), a

---

[5] Martin Dibelius, *Studies in the Acts of the Apostles,* trans. Mary Ling (London: SCM, 1956) 165.
[6] See Donald L. Clark, *Rhetoric in Greco-Roman Education* (New York: Columbia University Press, 1957) 100: "Language should be appropriate to the speaker, to the audience, and to the subject." Training in "impersonation" was one of the prescribed "elementary exercises" in Greco-Roman education. Students were asked to "compose an imaginary monolog which might appropriately be spoken or written by a historical, legendary, or fictitious person under given circumstances" (ibid., 199). See also William S. Kurz, "Hellenistic Rhetoric in the Christological Proof of Luke–Acts," *CBQ* 42 (1980) 186.

statement repeated almost verbatim by Peter in Acts 3:21. Peter's statement includes the same hope of the Messianic kingdom promised in Scripture, a kingdom that, according to Zechariah, will bring political freedom for the Jewish people (Luke 1:71, 74). Acts 1:6-7 also supports the view that the hope which Peter holds out to the Jews of Jerusalem in 3:20-21 includes the Messianic kingdom for Israel. The disciples ask the risen Jesus, "Are you at this time restoring the kingdom to Israel?" Peter's statement in 3:21 is not only linked to the disciples' question about the kingdom for Israel by the unusual words "restore" and "restoration" (ἀποκαθιστάνω, ἀποκατάστασις),[7] but also by the references, to "times" and "seasons" (χρόνοι, καιροί) in both passages (1:7; 3:20-21). While Jesus in 1:7 indicates that his followers cannot know the times and seasons, he does not reject the hope for Israel's restored kingdom. So authoritative speakers at the beginning of Luke (Gabriel and Zechariah) declare that the Messianic kingdom for Israel is part of God's promises in Scripture that are being realized through Jesus, and this hope remains alive at least through Peter's speech in Acts 3. If this hope is not fulfilled, the story has taken a tragic turn, and the high hopes and expectations for Israel's redemption encouraged in the story itself will emphasize the tragedy.[8]

The Jews of Jerusalem must repent in order to share in the promised times of relief and restoration (3:19-21). Even though there is no indication yet of the reaction of Peter's hearers, his speech contains some hints of what will happen. The statement with which Peter closes, "To you first . . . God sent his servant," indicates that the offer of salvation to the Jerusalem Jews is only the first stage of a longer process. This should be no threat to Peter's audience, for those who know the prophecies of Isaiah should know that God intends to bring salvation to Gentiles as well as Jews. Nevertheless, the inclusion of Gentiles will, in fact, become a cause of Jewish rejection in later scenes (13:44-48; 22:21-22). This cannot be a cause of rejection in Acts 3–5, for the reference to the Gentile mission in 3:25-26 can only be understood in the context of Luke–Acts as a whole.[9] Here we have a

---

[7] Ἀποκαθιστάνω or ἀποκαθίστημι is used once more in Luke–Acts, of the restoration of a hand (Luke 6:10), and occurs six times in the rest of the NT. Acts 3:21 is the only occurrence of the noun in the NT.

[8] See Robert C. Tannehill, "Israel in Luke–Acts: A Tragic Story," *JBL* 104 (1985) 69–85.

[9] In 3:25 the use of πατριαί ("families") instead of ἔθνη ("nations," "Gentiles")—the reading of Gen 18:18 LXX—introduces ambiguity, permitting an application to the Jewish "families of the land."

subtle hint of a future development that will involve Jewish resistance. In 3:23 the harsh warning about the possibility of being "destroyed from the people" may also anticipate a downward turn of the plot for some of Peter's audience. Immediately following Peter's speech the temple officials will demonstrate their refusal to hear the prophet like Moses and Peter, his witness (4:1-3). Such anticipation of rejection in the speech of a major character prior to its actual appearance is typical of Luke–Acts (see Luke 4:23-30; Acts 13:40-47).

In 3:17 Peter says, "Brothers, I know that you acted in ignorance, just as also your rulers did." This failure to recognize and accept God's servant requires repentance, as Peter goes on to say, but it is something that can be forgiven. Paul, too, will refer to the ignorance of the inhabitants of Jerusalem and their rulers, as well as the Gentiles' ignorance—ignorance of the true God—which requires repentance from them (13:27; 17:23, 30). The mission speeches in Acts are efforts to overcome this ignorance, which amounts to an ideologically caused blindness leading to the denial that God and God's Messiah can be what Luke–Acts proclaims them to be. Faced with this ignorance and blindness, the preachers repeatedly cry, "Let this be known to you" (2:14; see 2:36; 4:10; 13:38; 28:28). For the inhabitants of Jerusalem, both the people and their rulers, enlightenment involves recognition of their own responsibility for Jesus' death. When this happens (as in 2:37), we have a recognition scene similar to the recognition scenes in tragic drama, in which characters, acting in ignorance, recognize a tragic event after it has happened.[10] However, Peter makes clear that it is still possible to correct their error. The denouement need not be tragic.

The new possibility is dramatized by the story of Jesus' followers in Luke, for until they encountered the risen Christ, the disciples shared the ignorance of the people of Jerusalem. They did not understand (ἠγνόουν) Jesus' statements that he must be rejected and killed (Luke 9:45; see 18:34). The ignorance of both the disciples and the people of Jerusalem includes a failure to understand what was written by the prophets (Luke 18:31; 24:25-27, 32, 44-46; Acts 13:27; cf. 3:17-18). Thus Peter, in speaking to the people of Jerusalem, is trying to convey the new and revolutionary understanding which removed his own blind ignorance when

[10] On the role of "ignorance " (ἄγνοια) in the tragic plot see Aristotle, *Poetics* 1453b–1454a. On "recognition" (ἀναγνώρισις) see *Poetics* 1450.

he was instructed by the risen Christ.[11] The issue is whether his hearers will recognize what they have done and repent or whether their blindness will continue and harden.

The narrator emphasizes strongly that the "people," indeed, "all the people," saw the healed man and heard Peter's speech, the term λαός appearing no less than five times just before and just after the speech in Acts 3. This term is especially frequent in Acts 2:47—6:12 and plays a role in a significant development. In 2:47 we are told that the Jerusalem Christians were viewed favorably by "all the people." This favor continues. The temple authorities, who in 4:1-3 begin to oppose the apostles, are unable to act effectively because the apostles enjoy the people's support (4:21; 5:13, 26). The rulers are annoyed because the apostles are teaching the people (4:2), usurping their own authority. They try to stop this by threats but fail. The situation mirrors the passion story, where the people support Jesus as he teaches in the temple, preventing the authorities from taking action against him (Luke 19:47-48; 20:19, 26; 21:38; 22:2). In Acts the people are a fertile field for the Christian mission (see 2:41, 47: 4:4; 5:14), yet, just as in the passion story, they are fickle and easily swayed by false charges. The opposition turns deadly when opponents are finally able to arouse the people by false charges against Stephen (6:11-13). In Jesus' trial before Pilate the people, despite their previous support, suddenly shift their attitude and join in calling for Jesus' death (Luke 23:13-25).[12] Readers will be reminded of this in Acts 4:25-28. The role of the people in Stephen's death is not as clear as in the passion story, but, following this event, the Jewish people appear frequently as an opposing and threatening group, which represents a significant shift from the way in which the people was presented in Acts 2–5. The converted Saul must escape a conspiracy by "the Jews" of Damascus (9:23) and then encounters in Jerusalem the same opposition that Stephen faced (9:29). In 12:3-4, 11 "the people of the Jews" is a threatening group, from which Peter must be rescued. In this passage Herod and the Jewish people stand together as persecutors, just as another Herod and the people of Israel joined together

---

[11] This point is noted by M. Dennis Hamm, "This Sign of Healing, Acts 3:1-10: A Study in Lucan Theology" (dissertation, Saint Louis University, 1975) 156. Hamm also notes that Peter, who accuses the Jerusalem Jews of having "denied" Jesus (3:13-14), is himself "a denier only recently reformed" (p. 119).

[12] On the role of the people in Luke's passion story, see David L. Tiede, *Prophecy and History in Luke–Acts* (Philadelphia: Fortress, 1980) 103–18.

against Jesus, according to Acts 4:25-28. As the mission of Paul develops, the Jews of Antioch turn against him (13:45, 50), and in Acts 14 we begin to hear of Jews who are persistent persecutors, even following Paul from city to city (14:19). Such opposition by Jews appears repeatedly. It is significant that in the scene of Paul's arrest in Jerusalem, references to the "people" (λαός) reappear with sudden frequency (21:28, 30, 36, 39, 40). Here we find reminders of the passion story in Luke, including the cry "Away with him!" (21:36; 22:22; cf. Luke 23:18, which differs from Matthew and Mark). It is the "people" who shout for Paul's death, just as they supported Herod's persecution of the church according to Acts 12:3-4, 11. The charge that the Christian mission endangers the Jewish people and its way of life is false, as Paul will reiterate as late as 28:17. Nevertheless, the Jewish "people," who are presented as supporters of the Christian mission in Acts 2–5, will act primarily as opponents following the death of Stephen. This shift in attitude has a major effect on the course of the narrative.

First Arrest and Interrogation

Conflict first arises with the temple authorities. This involves a split between the people and their religious leaders. The leaders feel threatened by the apostles and their message; the people regard them favorably. The conflict between the early church and nonbelieving Judaism evolves by careful stages and only after there are strong indications of the powerful impact of the works and words of the apostles on the people of Jerusalem.

This arrest and the following release is the first of a series of arrests and releases of the preachers of the Word in Acts. The extensive development of the theme of rescue in Acts suggests that the implied author believes in the possibility of rescue of the missionary by divine intervention, either miraculously or through a human instrument, but also knows that the missionary does not always escape. The basic belief is in the power of God's purpose to fulfill itself in the world in spite of, or even by means of, the suffering caused by human opposition.

It is only as the apostles stand before the Sanhedrin, facing the first powerful opposition, that the full significance of the Joel quotation in 2:21 and of the healing of the lame man is made clear. The promise from Scripture quoted in 2:21, "Everyone who calls on the name of the Lord will be saved," is reflected in the exhortation of Peter to "be saved" in 2:40 and in the reference to "those being saved" in 2:47. But these general references are not enough. In Acts 3–4 the healed lame man, who in his leaping demonstrates the fulfillment of the prophecies (see Isa 35:6), becomes a paradigm of salvation through Jesus' name. The healed man takes on this significance through the speeches that follow the healing. Peter's statement in 3:12 that he and John had not healed the man "by our own power" raises the question of whose power is behind this wonder. A first answer is given in 3:16. Acts 3:16 is an overloaded and awkward sentence, but close inspection suggests reasons for its awkwardness. It places great emphasis on faith and on Jesus' name as the keys to the healing of the lame man. First a prepositional phrase linking the two key concepts is placed at the beginning of the sentence as a heading: "On the basis of faith in his name." This is followed by two linked sentences with "his name" and "faith" as subjects, arranged chiastically so that these two key terms are brought together ("this one . . . his name, and the faith which is through him . . ."). The result is emphasis on "faith" and "his name," and on their close connection with each other, through repetition, through making them active causes of the healing, and through word order.[13] The emphasis on faith does not fit the healing story itself. The lame man did not show faith prior to being healed; indeed, he was expecting alms, not healing (3:5-6). The emphasis on faith is the belated addition of an element that is necessary if the healing of the lame man is to be understood as a paradigm of salvation through Jesus, for "those being saved" (2:47) are "the believers" (2:44).

The first hearing before the Sanhedrin continues the development of the paradigmatic significance of the healed lame man. The question of the Sanhedrin in 4:7 borrows the language previously used by Peter in connection with the healing ("by what power"—cf. 3:12; "by what name"—cf. 3:6, 16), thereby connecting this scene to the preceding narrative and providing a perfect setup for Peter's disclosure of the full meaning of the healing.[14] In answer to the question by whom this man "has been saved" (σέσωται), Peter proclaims that it was "by the name of Jesus Christ." The verb σώζω can, of course, be applied to healing, but the choice of this word here is an important indication that the healing is being transformed into a symbol of something greater. The combination of salvation and the name of the Lord first appeared in 2:21, and in 2:38-

---

[13] On 3:16, see Gerhard Schneider, *Die Apostelgeschichte* (Freiburg: Herder, 1980) 1.320–21.

[14] Admittedly, this is a bit too neat for modern ideas of verisimilitude in narrative.

40 salvation was related to the release of sins, the gift of the Spirit, and the fulfillment of the promise. While the reference to the lame man being saved (or healed) in 4:9 may be calculated ambiguity, Peter's climactic statement in 4:12 makes clear that the healing is a symbol of a multidimensional salvation that includes all the benefits previously promised to those who repent and call on Jesus' name. Peter tells the Sanhedrin that the name of Jesus is the means "by which we must be saved." The salvation that the lame man received represents a greater salvation offered to all: the apostles, the Sanhedrin, and "all the people of Israel" (4:10). Indeed, Jesus' name is the inescapable decision point concerning salvation for Peter's hearers, because "there is no other name under heaven" given to people for salvation.[15] For Peter's audience this salvation does not mean healing of lameness but the gifts of repentance, release of sins, and the blessings of the Messianic kingdom. The healed lame man is the continuing symbol of the salvation for all offered in Jesus' name.

According to 4:13, Peter's words in 4:8-12 are a demonstration of παρρησία ("boldness," especially boldness of speech in circumstances that might inhibit frank speech). Peter demonstrates boldness both in his proclamation of the name of Jesus and in his blunt accusation of the rulers for their rejection of Jesus. The short speeches in 4:8-12 and 5:29-32 are important because, in the former, the theme of salvation in Jesus' name is developed, and, in the latter, readers are reminded of themes from the Pentecost speech, thus rounding off the series of speeches by the apostles in Jerusalem. But these short speeches are also important because they dramatically demonstrate the *persistent* speaking of the Word in the face of opposition. It is dramatically important that the apostles repeat what they have said in spite of threats from the powerful. The importance of boldness in the face of opposition is made clear by the church's prayer for such παρρησία and by the answer to that prayer (4:29, 31), as well as by the repeated declarations of allegiance to God's command, rather than the Sanhedrin's, in 4:19-20 and 5:29.

The authorities command the apostles to stop teaching in the name of Jesus and back this command with threats (4:17-18). This threatening

---

[15] The δεῖ in 4:12 probably refers, as elsewhere, to a necessity that derives from God's purpose, in this case God's saving purpose through Jesus Christ that aims at salvation for "all flesh" in accordance with the promise of Isa 40:5 (cf. Luke 3:6).

command heightens the tension in the situation and provides a further test of Peter and John, a test that they immediately pass, defiantly announcing that they will not stop preaching (4:19-20). Their defiant words are a reaffirmation of the commission that they received when the risen Christ charged them to be his witnesses (Luke 24:48; Acts 1:8). The statements in 4:19-20 epitomize the apostles' stance in a dramatic situation, which helps to give the declaration impact. This declaration will be repeated in 5:29, again drawing the contrast between God and human authorities, and even Gamaliel will warn the Sanhedrin that it must respect the difference between what is "from God" and what is "from humans," lest they become foolish "fighters against God" (θεομάχοι) (5:38-39). The repetition of this contrast between divine and human authority in several dramatic scenes and from the mouths of both the apostles and Gamaliel indicates emphasis, suggesting that we are encountering narrative rhetoric meant to convey a message not only between characters in the story but also from the implied author to the reader. This message indicates approval of those who, in proclaiming the name of Jesus, obey God rather than humans and suggests their boldness as a model for others. It is also a message about how the story is to be interpreted. This is a story about what happens when a purpose "from God" is recognized by persons willing to obey God in spite of human hostility.

The defiance of Peter and John in 4:19-20 reveals the impotence of the Sanhedrin, for it can only make additional threats and release the apostles. Nevertheless, the narrative leaves open the question of what the Sanhedrin will do if the apostles not only state their defiance but also disobey the Sanhedrin's command to stop preaching. This uncertainty enables the conflict to develop, moving to a new stage in 5:17ff.

The prayer scene in 4:23-31, in which the church prays for boldness in preaching in the face of threats, makes clear the source of the boldness already demonstrated by Peter and John. This scene also places the developing conflict in the context of sacred paradigms provided by Scripture and the passion story of Jesus, a matter that I will discuss below. The church appeals to God both for the power to speak the Word boldly and for the continuation of the signs and wonders through Jesus' name (4:29-30). The importance attributed to the healed lame man as a sign of Jesus' saving power, a sign recognizable even by outsiders and opponents, suggests why signs and wonders have an important role in strengthening a mission under pressure, in the author's eyes. Both aspects of the church's appeal are answered. Bold and powerful speaking is recorded in 4:31, 33. "Many signs and wonders" are reported in 5:12-16, along with the addition of new believers to the church. Individual healings are not reported, but some details emphasize the eagerness of the multitude, who come even from surrounding cities, bringing their sick, all of whom were being healed. This leads into the next stage of the conflict with the Sanhedrin. Just as the healing of the lame man and Peter's preaching to the crowd led to the first arrest, so now the continued preaching and healing which is attracting multitudes leads to a second arrest and the attempt of the high priest's party to enforce the previous prohibition of preaching in Jesus' name.

Second Arrest and Interrogation

The importance of the conflict with the temple authorities is made clear by the space devoted to it in Acts 4-7. The conflict develops in three stages (the third focusing on Stephen), and each stage is dramatized through a face-to-face confrontation between the temple authorities and Jesus' witnesses, with speeches in direct discourse.[16] The narrative makes the similarity between the confrontations in Acts 4 and 5 especially clear. Similar wording is used in 4:1-3 and 5:17-18 to introduce the two episodes. In both cases we have a sequence of arrest, imprisonment, hearing before the Sanhedrin with a short speech by an apostle, deliberation by the Sanhedrin while the apostles are outside, and release of the apostles, even though they continue to defy the ban placed on their preaching.

The narrator makes use of these similar sequences to present an evolving conflict that moves toward a crisis. The repetitive sequences contribute to the development, for the situation in Acts 5 is not exactly the same as in Acts 4. Both parties must deal with the fact that the apostles have defied the command not to teach in Jesus' name (see 5:28). The previous threats by the high priestly party would seem to require them to take punitive action or else acquiesce in the loss of their own authority. The stakes have increased since the first encounter. Certain differences in detail between Acts 4 and 5 show this increase in tension. In Acts 5 the apostles in general, not just Peter and John, are arrested. There is imminent

---

[16] A narrator can highlight material by presenting it in a dramatic scene or subordinate it in a brief summary. This material is highlighted in dramatic scenes.

danger of death (5:33), and the apostles do not escape without physical suffering through flogging (5:40). Furthermore, the high priest and his party are reacting not only to the apostles' refusal to keep silent but also to the accusation that the Sanhedrin is responsible for Jesus' death and must repent (5:28). The teaching that they are trying to suppress is not only a word about Jesus but also a stinging word about themselves. The apostles repeat their charge and their offer of repentance and forgiveness (5:30-31), bringing the narrative to the brink of crisis, for the hearers are infuriated and want to do away with them (5:33). But then the tension relaxes as Gamaliel intervenes.

This, however, is not the end of the conflict. After a brief narrative introducing Stephen, we find a third scene in which a witness of Jesus[17] is brought before the Sanhedrin (6:11-8:1). To be sure, a new protagonist has been introduced, the accusations against him are new, and Stephen's speech develops the accusation against his hearers at great length. Nevertheless, this is a new phase of the same conflict, with the Sanhedrin still trying to suppress the witness to Jesus. This time the conflict comes to the brink of crisis and spills over. The action contemplated in 5:33 is carried out against this new witness: Stephen is killed. The continuity is made clear to the reader by the use of the same verb of strong emotion, the verb διεπρίοντο (literally, "they were being sawn through," Acts 5:33, 7:54, and only there in the New Testament). In the one case this leads to the desire to "do away with" the apostles (5:33). In the other case it leads to the actual "doing away with" Stephen (8:1). Thus in Acts 4–7 we have a continuous narrative that depicts a series of similar confrontations, each representing a surge toward the crisis marked by Stephen's death and the great persecution that accompanied it.

The arrest and hearing in Acts 5 also exceeds the similar sequence of events in Acts 4 in that the apostles are rescued from prison by an angel of the Lord. This is narrated briefly and without dramatic emphasis. As much attention is given to the angel's command to continue speaking in the temple as to the opening of the prison. Furthermore, the rescue from prison does not affect the course of the plot, for the apostles are still in danger and must still appear before the Sanhedrin. The rescue from prison does, however, provide the basis for the following scene (5:21b-26), which

---

[17] Stephen, like the apostles and Paul, is called Jesus' "witness" in 22:20.

is developed with direct discourse and dramatic detail despite the fact that the apostles are not present. This scene is an ironic description of the embarrassment and confusion of the high priest and his party when they discover that the imprisoned apostles have vanished. The scene is introduced with a solemn formality that contributes to its burlesque quality ("the Sanhedrin and all the senate of the sons of Israel," 5:21). The scene focuses on the reports of messengers who tell the Sanhedrin what the reader already knows, provoking smiles at their surprise and confusion. In 5:23, part of the first messenger's report, we find some of the descriptive detail that we might have expected in the earlier narrative of the rescue from prison. The messenger makes clear that the expected security measures were carried out, yet the apostles are gone. The narrator's focus on the report to the Sanhedrin, rather than on the rescue itself, shows that the primary interest here is not in miraculous rescues as such but in the impotence of human authorities to control the course of events. Although the apostles end up just where they would have been apart from the prison release—standing before the Sanhedrin accused of disobedience—the threat from the Sanhedrin has been undermined by irony and burlesque. The point that Gamaliel will later make ("If it is from God, you will not be able to destroy them"; 5:39) has already been made by the narrator through the rescue from prison and the ensuing scene of discovery. Here we have an instance of reinforcement through reiteration. A message is first suggested by an event and then clearly stated in the interpretive commentary of a story character.[18]

The rescue from prison by an angel in 5:19-20 is accompanied by the command to continue speaking to the people in the temple, an activity and place that directly challenge the authority of the high priest. So, in spite of their release, the apostles are brought before the high priest and must answer his charges. The release of the apostles in 5:40 shows that there are two rescues in Acts 5, one by the intervention of an angel, one by the intervention of a human being, Gamaliel. Gamaliel, a person of insight and reason, intervenes as the plot moves toward crisis and corrects

---

[18] Susan Rubin Suleiman presents an elaborate classification of types of narrative "redundancy" in her article "Redundancy and the 'Readable' Text," *Poetics Today* 1 (1980) 119–42. Among the types are cases in which "an event is redundant with the interpretive commentary made by a C [character] . . . concerning it" (p. 128). Gamaliel may not be interpreting the prison rescue directly, but it is at least an illustration of his point.

those carried away by their murderous passions (5:33). The speech of Gamaliel shows that there are still cool heads within the Sanhedrin. He is persuasive; he is able to convince the Sanhedrin that the apostles should not be put to death. There are several indications that Gamaliel, although he does not speak as a Christian, serves as spokesman for the implied author. As I have indicated, the point made by Gamaliel in 5:39a has already been supported by the narrator, who chose to highlight the impotence of the temple authorities in 5:21-26. Furthermore, in speaking of the two possibilities of "this purpose or this work" being "from humans" or "from God," Gamaliel shifts from the conditional sentence with ἐάν and subjunctive to εἰ and indicative. The latter construction often, as here, comes close to the causal meaning "since."[19] The shift in construction suggests that "this purpose" really is from God, showing that the implied author is placing his own view in the mouth of Gamaliel.[20] Also, the contrast between what is "from humans" and what is "from God" in 5:38-39 continues a theme that has already appeared in the responses of the apostles before the Sanhedrin, who have demonstrated which side they stand on by declaring, "It is necessary to obey God rather than humans" (5:29, cf. 4:19). Gamaliel also seems to recognize that Jesus and his followers are different from the followers of Theudas and Judas the Galilean, who disappeared with the death of their leader. Gamaliel's warning to "take care . . . what you are about to do" and to beware of becoming "fighters against God" emphasizes the significance of the decision about to be made by the Sanhedrin. Gamaliel's argument is persuasive on this occasion, but the danger of which he warns will reappear in the trial of Stephen.

Again the bold persistence of the apostles is expressed in a brief speech in which they repeat the proclamation concerning Jesus (5:30-32). This, the last speech by the apostles to the people of Jerusalem or their leaders, briefly summarizes themes from previous speeches, including some that have not been mentioned since Acts 2 ("God exalted him at his right hand," cf. 2:33; "the Holy Spirit which God gave," cf. 2:33, 38). The

---

[19] See F. Blass and A. Debrunner, *A Greek Grammar of the New Testament and Other Early Christian Literature,* translated and revised by Robert W. Funk (Chicago: University of Chicago Press, 1961) §372, 1.

[20] This is the opinion of Hans Conzelmann, *Die Apostelgeschichte* (Tübingen: Mohr/Siebeck, 1963) 42; and Ernst Haenchen, *The Acts of the Apostles* (Philadelphia: Westminster, 1971) 253.

authorities are again accused of killing Jesus, but this is still followed by the proclamation of repentance and release of sins, a still valid gift of God for Israel through the exalted Messiah.[21] The sermons with their persistent themes demonstrate the persistence of the apostles, who neither crumble before powerful opponents nor despair of the possibility of repentance.

Echo Effect in Acts 3–5

To this point I have followed a consecutive reading of Acts, noting how the story is building up to a point of crisis and decision, although there have been references to related material in other parts of Luke–Acts that help us understand the narrative lines developing in Acts 3–5. The story is comprehensible through such a consecutive reading. However, our experience of the story is greatly enriched when we note that Acts 2–5 (as well as other material) can produce a complex echo effect. Characters and events in this section of Acts echo characters and events already presented in the Gospel, and recall of these earlier characters and events suggests a complex set of similarities, differences, and fulfillments that contribute to the significance of the story. Therefore, the text takes on resonance. The previous story resonates with the new events, so that meanings are both amplified and enriched. We can also say that the previous story provides commentary on the current story. At some points this commentary seems clear and specific, so that the echo effect serves to control interpretation. The echo adds emphasis, helping to specify and ensure communication of central meanings. But the echoes multiply, producing tantalizing hints of meaning which are difficult to control. Echo added to echo produces a resonance that surrounds the central meanings with overtones the writer cannot fully control and the reader cannot easily exhaust.

We are discussing what is often called "parallels" within Acts and between Acts and Luke's Gospel.[22] In discussing such parallels, we should

---

[21] Luke Timothy Johnson believes that the offer of repentance and release of sins no longer applies to the leaders, who have already rejected Jesus a second time. See *The Literary Function of Possessions in Luke–Acts* (Missoula, Mont.: Scholars, 1977) 69. However, no distinction is made between the leaders and the rest of Israel in 5:30-32. Whether the leaders' rejection of Jesus is final and irrevocable, bringing upon them the curse of 3:23, is unclear at this point in the narrative. The apostles speak to them as if there were still hope of repentance.

[22] For a recent discussion of such parallels see Charles H. Talbert, *Literary Patterns, Theological Themes and the Genre of Luke–Acts,* SBLMS 20 (Missoula, Mont.: Scholars, 1974). The study of

remember that they serve to enrich narrative lines that keep moving into the future. Absolute sameness would bring movement to a halt. The "parallels" always suggest *similarity* in events that are not the *same,* each event retaining the uniqueness that contributes to a sense of verisimilitude. Furthermore, the discovery of similarity may also accent important differences, and exploring these differences may also contribute to the significance of the story. We become aware of similarities and differences together as comparisons come to mind. Significant comparisons may multiply. The discovery of similarities between two events does not preclude connections with other events as well. Nor do the events that resonate together all occur between the birth of Jesus and Paul's preaching in Rome. The story also awakens echoes of Old Testament figures. Here, however, I will confine myself to echoes within Luke–Acts, discussing features of composition and wording suggesting that conscious or unconscious choices were made by the author, enabling one scene or statement to echo another within this literary work.

Echoes of the Beginning of Jesus' Mission

A first set of similarities appears when we compare the beginning of the mission of the apostles with the beginning of the mission of Jesus.[23] In each case we must consider not single scenes but a development through several chapters, encompassing a group of scenes with thematic connections. Both the mission of Jesus and the mission of the apostles begin with prayer and the coming of the Spirit, followed by an inaugural speech that relates the coming of the Spirit to the new mission through a Scripture quotation. The inaugural speech also proclaims "release" (ἄφεσις). Soon afterwards we are told of the healing of a paralytic or lame man, which becomes the occasion for a fundamental disclosure concerning Jesus' saving significance. The disclosure also involves the

---

G. W. Trompf on *The Idea of Historical Recurrence in Western Thought: From Antiquity to the Reformation* (Berkeley: University of California Press, 1979) provides further evidence that patterns of recurrence are widespread in writings of the ancient Mediterranean world and that ancient readers would not be surprised by them. Trompf discusses Luke–Acts at length and believes that it reflects notions of recurrence from both Hebraic and Greco-Roman tradition.

[23] See Talbert, *Literary Patterns,* 16.

interpretation of something from the Scripture quotation in the inaugural sermon. This same healing is the occasion for the appearance of the first opposition to the new mission from Jewish leaders.

To explain this series of similarities in greater detail: In Luke 3–4 we are told that Jesus, praying, received the Holy Spirit (3:21-22) and later delivered an inaugural speech which, through a Scripture quotation, related his mission both to the coming of the Spirit and to the proclamation of "release" (4:18-19). In Acts 1–2 the apostles, having been told by Jesus of the coming of the Spirit, pray (1:14) and on Pentecost receive the Spirit, which leads to Peter's inaugural speech containing a Scripture quotation that relates the apostles' mission to the coming of the Spirit (2:17-21). In his speech Peter also offers "release of sins" to his hearers (2:38).

The first opposition from Pharisees and teachers of the law appears when Jesus offers release of sins to a paralytic (Luke 5:17-26), an important fulfillment of Jesus' commission to proclaim release, announced in 4:18. This scene is both the beginning of a continuing conflict with the scribes and Pharisees and an occasion for highlighting Jesus' authority to release sins (5:24), an authority basic to his ongoing ministry, as is made clear by the narrator's tendency to link later scenes with Luke 5:17-32.[24] The narrative in Acts 3–4 is linked to Peter's inaugural sermon by the theme of the saving power of Jesus' name (2:21; 3:6, 16; 4:7-12). The development of this theme begins with the healing of a lame man. While there are some similarities of expression between the story of Jesus' healing of the paralytic and the story of the healing of the lame man at the temple gate, these similarities might simply reflect the fact that both stories report the healing of a man who could not walk.[25] The connection between the two stories becomes striking, however, when we consider the function of the stories in the larger narrative. Both stories, placed early in the missions of Jesus and the apostles, are associated with a basic proclamation of Jesus' saving significance, a proclamation that has continuing importance for the mission, and both provoke opposition from Jewish leaders, which will continue into following chapters. We have seen how the healing of the

---

[24] In *The Narrative Unity of Luke–Acts: A Literary Interpretation,* 2 vols. (Philadelphia & Minneapolis: Fortress, 1986, 1990) 1.103–9, I argue that the narrator uses the stories of the healing of the paralytic and the meal in the tax collector's house to interpret Jesus' ongoing ministry through a series of reminiscences of these stories in later episodes of the Gospel.

[25] The similarities in wording are clearer between Acts 3:1-10 and 14:8-11 (Paul's healing of a lame man) than between Acts 3:1-10 and Luke 5:17-26.

lame man in Jesus' name leads up to the general proclamation about salvation in Jesus' name in 4:7-12, thereby explaining the offer of salvation to those who call upon the name of the Lord in the Scripture quotation in 2:21. The healing of the paralytic in Luke 5:17-26 is also linked to the preceding inaugural sermon (through the theme of "release") and develops the understanding of Jesus' salvific work found there by presenting a general claim about Jesus' authority to do what he has done for the paralytic (5:24). This general claim is made in the face of opposition already expressed by Jewish leaders, just as Peter speaks to the temple authorities about Jesus after he and John have already been arrested and must defend themselves. In both cases the opposition from Jewish leaders has just appeared but will continue in closely following scenes.

Thus the similarity between Jesus' healing of the paralytic and Peter's healing of the lame man lies less in the healing itself than in the function of these scenes in the larger narrative. In both cases the healing becomes the occasion for a fundamental claim about Jesus' saving power, emphasizing its importance and general scope ("on earth," Luke 5:24; "under heaven," Acts 4:12). In both cases it is the occasion for speaking of a salvation that encompasses more than physical healing. In both cases the claim is made in the face of new opposition and develops the significance of the mission announced in the Scripture quotation in the inaugural sermon.

One feature of Acts 3 resembles the scene in which Jesus is rejected in Nazareth more closely than it resembles Luke 5:17-26. Before Jesus is rejected in Nazareth, he announces that he is a prophet who will not be accepted in his homeland and hints that God's saving work will extend to the Gentiles (4:24-27). His statement that he will not be accepted is immediately confirmed by the response of the people. Before the opposition from the temple authorities appears, Peter warns of the consequences of failing to hear the prophet like Moses and hints that God's servant will be sent elsewhere, having been sent to the people of Jerusalem "first" (Acts 3:23, 26). Immediately afterwards, the authorities show that they are not willing to accept the prophet like Moses proclaimed by Peter.[26]

---

[26] Opposition to Jesus, from different parties, appears in both Luke 4:28-30 and 5:21. Acts 2–4 refers to only one group of opponents, and parts of these chapters resemble both Luke 4:16-30 and 5:17-26.

Conviction that these similarities are not accidental increases when we note that the sequence appears a third time at the beginning of the section of Acts devoted to Paul.[27] After prayer and fasting, Paul and Barnabas are set aside for their mission, according to the command of the Holy Spirit, the divine power behind this mission (13:2-4). Shortly thereafter we find a major scene in which Paul gives a speech that resembles Jesus' speech at Nazareth in its setting and resembles Peter's speech at Pentecost in significant points of content. The speech contains Scripture quotations, but the quotation corresponding most closely with those at the beginning of Jesus' and Peter's inaugural speeches, because it discloses the nature of the speaker's mission, is found in 13:47. There Paul, a week later but still speaking to the same group, says, "Thus the Lord has commanded us, 'I have placed you for a light of Gentiles, so that you may be for salvation to the end of the earth.'" Paul discloses this commission in the face of Jewish opposition, opposition about which he warned in advance at the end of his synagogue speech (13:41). In light of the other similarities to the narratives of the beginning of Jesus' and the apostles' missions, it is not surprising that a healing of a lame man by Paul occurs shortly after the speech in Antioch of Pisidia. The connection between Peter's and Paul's healings of lame men is emphasized by the narrator through repetition of words and phrases (compare 3:2 with 14:8; 3:4 with 14:9; 3:8 with 14:10; 3:12 with 14:15).

Although the narrator in 14:8ff. recalls the earlier healing of a lame man by Peter through use of similar wording, the scenes are only partially similar in function. They agree in referring to the healed man's leaping, recalling the prophecies of Isaiah, and in the negative point that the power to heal does not reside in the healer himself. The positive side of this, the saving power of Jesus' name, is not repeated in 14:8-18, and the opposition that appears following Peter's healing and preaching has already been encountered by Paul before 14:8. Nevertheless, we have found a bundle of similarities stretching across a sequence of scenes near the beginning of the sections that focus on Jesus, Peter, and Paul. It is hard to believe that these similar combinations in analogous locations in the narrative are accidental.

The similarities between Luke 6:17-19 and Acts 5:12-16, which include summary description of the coming of multitudes and of works

---

[27] See Talbert, *Literary Patterns,* 23.

of healing and exorcism, even through touch or shadow, suggest that another element from Luke's narrative of Jesus' early ministry has been repeated in Acts. There is similar material in the story of Paul, but it is divided between 14:3 (which also recalls Acts 4:29-30) and 19:11-12.

Echoes of Luke's Passion Story

We have noted similarities between Acts 1–5 and a series of important events reported near the beginning of Jesus' ministry in Luke. There are also a number of similarities between the Jerusalem section of Acts and the Jerusalem section of Luke. Thus there is a second set of echoes of the Jesus story. Reading Acts 3–7 against the background of both the beginning and ending of Jesus' ministry in Luke adds greatly to the resonance of the Acts account.

There is explicit recall of the rejection and death of Jesus in the four speeches of Peter in Acts 2–5, and we have already noted the close connection between Acts 3:13-15 and the trial scene before Pilate, especially Luke 23:16-19.[28] Furthermore, there is continuity of characters between the passion story in Luke and the Jerusalem section of Acts. Peter in his speeches is addressing people who were directly involved in Jesus' death, and he emphasizes their guilt. The high priest and the Jerusalem Sanhedrin play key roles in both the confrontation with Jesus and with the apostles. This provides an opportunity for the narrator to suggest that similar situations are recurring, and the narrator takes advantage of this opportunity. After Peter has recalled the circumstances of Jesus' death in his first two speeches, a sequence of events takes place that partially reduplicates the passion story. Like Jesus, Jesus' witnesses are arrested, they are called to account before the Sanhedrin, and the third sequence of arrest and trial in Acts leads to a death. The report of Stephen's death both recalls and parallels the narrative of Jesus' death in Luke. Stephen's speech ends by recalling Jesus' death (7:52). Stephen's next words recall Jesus' words to his accusers about the exalted Son of Man (Luke 22:69; Acts 7:56). His final words parallel Jesus' words from the cross (Luke 23:34, 46; Acts 7:59-60).[29] Thus the sequence of arrests, trials, and death in Acts

---

[28] See the section above: Healing and Speech to the People.
[29] On the textual problem in Luke 23:34, see Tannehill, *Narrative Unity*, 1.272, n. 126.

4-7 reaches its climax in a scene in which the connections with Luke's passion story are quite clear.

Details of description indicate a desire to suggest such connections not only at Stephen's death but also in the series of events leading up to it. Note the following similarities between the description of the arrest and examination of the apostles in Acts 4 and the arrest and examination of Jesus in Luke: Acts 4:1 refers to "the captain (στρατηγός) of the temple"; Luke 22:52 also refers to "captains of the temple" (differs from Matthew and Mark). The temple officials "laid hands on" (ἐπέβαλον τὰς χεῖρας) the apostles (4:3, 5:18); the same phrase is used in reporting the frustrated attempt of scribes and high priests to arrest Jesus in Luke 20:19 (differs from Matthew and Mark). Acts 4:5 places the examination on the morning after the arrest, as with Jesus (Luke 22:66, differs from Matthew, Mark), and Acts 4:5-6 agrees further with Luke 22:66 in referring to the groups constituting the Sanhedrin having been "gathered together" (aorist passive of συνάγω). The reference to "rulers" (ἄρχοντας) in Acts 4:5 corresponds to Luke 23:13, 35; 24:20 (differs from Matthew and Mark).

Most of Jesus' speaking in Jerusalem is done prior to his arrest, and the primary location of his teaching is the temple. The narrative in Acts recalls some of this material in shaping the dialogues between the rulers and the apostles, who also teach in the temple. In Luke 20:2 Jesus was asked, "By what authority are you doing these things?" In Acts 4:7 Peter and John are asked, "By what power or what name did you do this?" The same group poses the question in the two instances. Peter, in responding to the question, refers to the stone scorned by the builders which has become head of the corner (Acts 4:11), repeating (with some variation in wording) a Scripture quotation used by Jesus in Luke 20:17 in a scene which ends with the attempt of the scribes and high priests to arrest Jesus. In this scene Jesus has just accused the rulers of killing God's greatest messenger, using the indirect form of a parable. This accusation will become explicit in the Acts speeches. So the Scripture reference to the stone in Acts 4:11 recalls the rejection and vindication of Jesus in imagery already used by Jesus. In both Luke and Acts the "people" (λαός) support Jesus or the apostles, preventing the rulers from taking action against them (Luke 19:47-48; 20:19; 22:2; Acts 4:21; 5:26). This will delay, but not prevent, the death toward which the narrative is moving.

The similarities between Acts 4–5 and the Jerusalem narrative in Luke help to make clear that the conflict in Jerusalem over Jerusalem's Messiah has not been resolved. It simply enters a new phase, with the apostles as Jesus' witnesses. The apostles now assume the risky role of proclaiming Jesus and of calling the people of Jerusalem and their rulers to repent of their blind error. Their new role shows that the apostles have changed in important ways. The similarity of the situation (arrest and trial) and the continuity of the opposition (from the high priests and others associated with the temple or Sanhedrin) highlight the difference in the behavior of the apostles before and after the resurrection and sending of the Spirit. Luke alone reports Peter's declaration that he was ready both to die and to go "to prison" with Jesus (Luke 22:33). He failed to keep this promise when he denied Jesus. In Acts Peter no longer denies Jesus, though threatened by powerful people, and he does go to prison. His boldness before the rulers is the opposite of his previous denial. The boldness of the apostles helps the rulers to recognize that Peter and John "were with Jesus" (Acts 4:13). This is what Peter denied, according to Luke 22:56, 59.

Having been transformed by the risen Jesus and the Spirit, the apostles are now able to follow the instructions about facing opposition that Jesus gave during the journey to Jerusalem. In following his instructions, they also experience the fulfillment of his promises. A number of descriptive details in the narrative of the apostles' arrests recall Jesus' teaching about persecution in Luke 12:11-12 and 21:12-15. Jesus prophesied in Luke 21:12 that "they will lay their hands on you" (see Acts 4:3; 5:18), "handing you over . . . to prisons . . . because of my name" (see the emphasis on Jesus' name in Acts 3–4). Jesus promised, "It will lead to witnessing" (Luke 21:13; see Peter's witness before the rulers in Acts 4:8-12 and 5:29-32). The promise that the opponents will not be able to "contradict" (ἀντειπεῖν) them (Luke 21:15) is fulfilled in Acts 4:14, and the related promise that they will be taught by the Holy Spirit what they should say (Luke 12:12) is fulfilled in Acts 4:8.[30] The inability of the opponents to reply to or contradict the apostles also fits an emphasis within stories of Jesus, for Jesus had silenced his opponents both during his temple teaching (Luke 20:26, 40) and earlier (Luke 13:17; 14:6). The points that we have noted show that the similarities between the situation of Jesus in the passion

---

[30] It is possible that the rulers' judgment that the apostles are uneducated and untrained (Acts 4:13) in part reflects the fact that they did not plan a polished oration in advance, since they were following Jesus' instructions in Luke 12:11; 21:14.

story and the situation of the apostles in Acts 3–5 serve in part to highlight the transformation of the apostles, who were unable to face danger courageously but now are able. This, in turn, makes possible the fulfillment of some specific promises of Jesus to his witnesses.

The theme of persecution because of Jesus' "name," developed as a prophetic preview in Luke 21:12-19, reappears at the end of the narrative of the apostles' arrests and releases (Acts 5:40-41), and there may be additional points of contact between these verses in Acts and Jesus' teaching about persecution in Luke. The apostles leave "rejoicing (χαίροντες) . . . because they were counted worthy to be dishonored on behalf of the name" (Acts 5:41). In Luke 6:22-23 Jesus instructed his disciples to "rejoice" (χάρητε) at persecution, a strikingly odd response shared by these two passages in Luke–Acts. The verb "dishonor" (ἀτιμάζω) is found not only in Acts 5:41 but also in the parable of the wicked vineyard tenants (Luke 20:11). Since it is a rare word in Luke–Acts, occurring only twice and on both occasions associated with beatings, this link suggests that Jesus' parable of the wicked tenants may still be working in the imagination of the author,[31] who sees the beaten and dishonored servants of the vineyard owner as an apt image for the apostles. These points of contact reveal particular aspects of the story of Jesus which had sufficient appeal to the author's imagination to shape the vision of the early church in Acts.

The connections that we have noted between Acts 4–5 and the passion story become explicit when the church responds to its first crisis by turning to God in prayer (4:23-31). The church prefaces its petition with a reference to the passion story, interpreted as fulfillment of Scripture. This recall of Jesus' passion is relevant because Jesus' situation, threatened by rulers and peoples, is viewed as essentially the same as the church's situation, faced with the threats of the Sanhedrin. The prayer moves directly from a reference to "Herod and Pontius Pilate with the Gentiles and peoples of Israel," those who gathered against Jesus the Messiah, to a petition concerning "their threats," meaning the threats of the Sanhedrin that the apostles have just encountered. Ernst Haenchen speaks of a "rift between verses 27 and 29," since "their threats" does not refer to threats by Herod and Pilate, as vv. 27-28 would seem to suggest.[32] However, the distinction important to Haenchen is not important in the prayer; indeed, it is deliberately eliminated. The

---

[31] We have already noted reminiscences of Luke 20:17, 19, which conclude this scene.

[32] See Haenchen, *Acts*, 228.

opponents of Jesus and of the church are viewed as one continuous group, a simplification facilitated by the fact that the Sanhedrin had a leading role in both situations.[33] Although the connection drawn in 4:27-29 may seem strange to some modern interpreters, these verses disclose a mode of thought presupposed throughout Acts 3–7, as is shown by the repeated parallels drawn between the passion story in Luke and the experience of the early church. The prayer of the church (and later the speech and death of Stephen) reveals that there are actually two levels of echoes that may be heard in the story. The conflict of the mission with the Sanhedrin is echoed by the passion story in Luke, and both are echoed by Scripture.

The explicit parallel between Jesus' passion and the church's situation that is basic to the structure of the prayer provides important evidence that the similarities with the passion story that we have already noted are not accidental. It should also stimulate us to ask whether the church's prayer has a more specific connection with material in the passion story. In Luke 22:39-46, just before Jesus' arrest and just after Peter's assertion that he is ready to go with Jesus to prison and death, Jesus urged the disciples to pray in order that they might not enter into temptation. Instead, the disciples fell asleep and were unprepared for the crisis that immediately followed. In Acts 4:23-31 Jesus' followers are again confronted with the dangerous opposition of the Sanhedrin. Now they pray as they had been told to do when Jesus and his followers first faced this threat. As a result they receive power from God to continue the mission despite the opposition. We have already noted that Peter's boldness before the Sanhedrin in Acts contrasts with his denial of Jesus in Luke. The church in Acts which finds power for bold witness in prayer also contrasts with the disciples who sleep when they should pray in Luke. These contrasts support the narrator's picture of the dramatic transformation that has taken place in Jesus' followers.

The Acts speeches repeatedly affirm God's active presence in the story of Jesus. It is clear that the implied author believes that God continues to be active in the life of the church, and the narrative has various ways of signaling this active presence of God: angels, visions, messages from the

---

[33] Rather than Herod representing the "kings" and Pilate the "rulers" of 4:26 (so Haenchen, *Acts*, 227), there is some evidence that the "kings" are political authorities and the "rulers" religious authorities, i.e., the Sanhedrin, which is otherwise not mentioned in 4:26-27. Compare 4:26 with 4:5, where "rulers" appears in a reference to the Sanhedrin. Both verses use the aorist passive of συνάγω.

Spirit, etc. One further way of bringing God into the narrative is to report a prayer and answer to prayer. This is an opportunity to show how God responds to the characters and events of the narrative.

This is also an opportunity to characterize God more fully, so that readers have a clearer impression of the God who is acting through the human events of the story. The church's petition in 4:29-30 is preceded by a five-verse preface that is basically characterization of God. God is creator of all things and therefore sovereign (δεσπότης) over all. This sovereignty is revealed as God announces in Scripture a preordained purpose and brings this to fulfillment. God's sovereignty is even more clearly revealed when opponents of God's purpose become instruments of its realization. The chief instance of this is celebrated in 4:25-28: Jew and Gentile gathered in opposition to God and God's Messiah but ironically fulfilled God's purpose.[34] This is a theological vision of a God who works by irony. Human actors do not see truly what is happening, for reality is in conflict with appearance. Blind human actors commit themselves to a course of action, only to discover that its meaning and results are quite different than they thought. The implied author traces the work of God in a series of such ironies. The irony of the realization of God's purpose through the blind rejection of God's Messiah provides the interpretive key. The church at prayer recalls this event, which enables it to trust in the sovereign God when it must face human opponents. It prays for the power to continue the mission of preaching and healing in the face of the Sanhedrin's threats, and its prayer is answered. Remaining faithful to its mission, it will discover again that the sovereign God can twist the human purposes of opponents to fulfill the divine will, as the "great persecution" in Jerusalem (8:1) leads to the spread of the Word to new areas and Saul, the most devoted persecutor of the church, becomes a witness of Jesus to all people.

The first opposition to the mission comes from the Jewish rulers in Jerusalem. But the Psalm quotation in 4:25-26 refers also to Gentiles, and Gentiles are included among the opponents of God's Messiah when the Psalm is applied to Jesus' death in 4:27. The church has not yet experienced opposition from Gentiles, but it will. Paul's arrest and imprisonment in Philippi (16:16-24) and the riot in Ephesus (19:23-40)

---

[34] Note that 4:28 repeats and reemphasizes the assertion in 2:23 that God's preordained purpose was realized in the death of Jesus.

are dramatic accounts of such opposition. I am suggesting that the church's prayer in 4:23-31 relates not only to the specific situation of the apostles' arrest by the Sanhedrin and the previous situation of Jesus' rejection and death. It also anticipates the recurrent opposition from Jews and Gentiles that the mission will encounter from this point on. Furthermore, the church's prayer for power to speak the word with "boldness" (παρρησία) and for signs and wonders is not answered solely by the outpouring of the Spirit in 4:31. These characteristics of bold and powerful speech, accompanied by signs and wonders, are passed on from the apostles to Stephen (6:8-10), Philip (8:4-7), and Paul (9:27-28; 14:3) as the narrative progresses. Indeed, Acts ends with the picture of the imprisoned Paul faithfully preaching "with all boldness" (28:31). The powerful and hardy witness that the Spirit inspired in response to the church's prayer persists to the very end of Acts and appears in the narrator's last statement. It is in 4:23-31 that we learn that the Spirit not only inspired the mission in the beginning (2:1-21) but also inspires the bold speaking that maintains the witness despite all opposition and danger.

Echoes within Acts 1–5

We have discussed similarities between the early chapters of Acts and (1) the beginning of Jesus' ministry in Luke, (2) Jesus' temple teaching and the passion story in Luke. We have noted that themes associated with the beginning of Jesus' and the apostles' mission also appear in the story of Paul's mission.[35] Paul's final journey to Jerusalem, arrest, and trials will also be told in ways that echo Jesus' journey to Jerusalem and final days there,[36] so that the Pauline section of Acts echoes two sections of the Jesus story, just as Acts 1–7 does.

In Acts 1–5 the similarities with the Gospel that we have discussed are overlaid with a third pattern of similarities, for there is reduplication within Acts 1–5 itself. This is clearest when we compare 4:1-22 with 5:17-42, the two narratives of the arrest of the apostles, their appearance before the Sanhedrin (including short speeches which both reaffirm the apostles' message about Jesus [4:10-12; 5:30-32] and declare that the apostles will

---

[35] See the section above: Echoes of the Beginning of Jesus' Mission.
[36] On this see Walter Radl, *Paulus und Jesus im lukanischen Doppelwerk* (Frankfurt: Lang, 1975).

obey God rather than the Sanhedrin [4:19-20; 5:29]), deliberation by the Sanhedrin without the apostles being present (4:15-17; 5:34-39), resulting in the release of the apostles, although the Sanhedrin prohibits speaking in Jesus' name. Although the sequence of events is so similar, it is clear that the second arrest and hearing builds upon the first, for the second interrogation by the Sanhedrin begins with the accusation that the apostles have disobeyed the rulers' command in the first hearing (5:28), and the second response of the apostles to the Sanhedrin puts them in danger of death (5:33).

Charles Talbert believes that the pattern of correspondences is more extensive. He compares 1:12-4:23 with 4:24-5:42.[37] It does seem significant that in both of these sections of Acts we hear of the church gathered at prayer (1:14; 4:24-30), then filled with the Holy Spirit and speaking by the Spirit's power (2:4; 4:31). The two descriptions of the communal life of the church that follow the Pentecost scene and the renewed outpouring of the Spirit are also closely related (2:42-47; 4:32-35), and the signs and wonders of the apostles are noted before each of the arrests (2:43; 3:1-10; 5:12-16). This pattern of reduplication contributes to the story of the developing conflict between the church and the Sanhedrin. It helps to build suspense as the resolve of both parties in the conflict is tested under increasing pressure. It shows the apostles and the church holding firm under this pressure. That the apostles and church continue or repeat what they have already done makes the point of their firmness in the face of the threats. But tension also increases, for the rulers, frustrated in their attempts to silence the apostles, must either give up their authority or take more drastic action. That the narrative is building to a climax through these patterns of reduplication becomes clear when we have a third sequence of arrest and trial before the Sanhedrin (6:8-7:60), this time resulting in the death of Jesus' witness and the scattering of the church (8:1).

The Significance of Repetitive Patterns in Luke–Acts

Various types of repetition in narrative have been discussed by some recent theorists under the heading of "redundancy." Redundancy, far from being

---

[37] See *Literary Patterns,* 35–39.

strange and unusual, is a necessary aspect of effective communication. In narrative it may take many forms.

Susan Rubin Suleiman has proposed an elaborate "classification of the types of redundancy possible in realistic fiction."[38] Many of her types of redundancy occur in Luke–Acts. In our discussion we have noted as especially important the repetition of the same type of event or sequence of events happening to different characters (Jesus, Peter, and Paul are filled with the Spirit and deliver inaugural sermons that comment on the missions which they are beginning), similar events or sequences of events happening to the same characters (apostles are twice arrested and appear before the Sanhedrin), and similarity between an event as presented and interpreted by the narrator and an interpretation offered by a character. Examples of the last type of redundancy are the narrator's declaration in 2:4 that the church was "filled with the Holy Spirit," an interpretation repeated in Peter's speech (2:15-17), despite brief reference to an alternative view (2:13, 15), and the ironic portrayal of the Sanhedrin's impotence in 5:17-26, followed by Gamaliel's statement, "If it is from God, you will not be able to destroy them" (5:39).

What is the function of the rather elaborate patterns of repetition or "redundancy" that we have noted? Why would one compose a story in this way? The answer must be complex, embracing at least the following points:

1. Information theorists note that every channel of communication is subject to "noise," i.e., "disturbances . . . which interfere with the faithful transmission of signals," and "a certain degree of redundancy is essential . . . in any communication system in order to counteract the disturbing effects of noise."[39] In Luke–Acts one major source of "noise" is the length of the narrative, offering the reader a large opportunity to forget what has already happened. Redundancy combats the tendency to forget.

2. Repetition is a means of emphasis. Selective emphasis enables authors to convey the views that they regard as most important for arriving at the correct interpretation of the events being narrated. Thus emphasis serves the "education of the reader"[40] in what is central to understanding

[38] "Redundancy and the 'Readable Text,'" *Poetics Today* 1 (1980) 126–32.
[39] John Lyons, *Semantics,* 2 vols. (Cambridge: Cambridge University Press, 1978) 1.44. See Fred W. Burnett, "Prolegomenon to Reading Matthew's Eschatological Discourse: Redundancy and the Education of the Reader in Matthew," *Semeia* 31 (1985) 93–94.
[40] A phrase used by Burnett; see the preceding note.

the story. Since a particular interpretation is being suggested, other options are being rejected, reducing the amount of indeterminacy in the text. However, the closing of options may guide the reader to an interpretation that the author regards as particularly rich, with its own broad field of meanings, a field not likely to be explored if the reader is not led to it. Since repetition conveys interpretation through emphasis, it is important for the reader to take careful note of what is repeated. Interpretation takes place through selective repetition.

3. Repetition has a persuasive effect. The events, characters, or assertions seem "right" because they fit what is already known. Or, as Susan Wittig says,

> The creation . . . of a multi-level set of expectancies not only allows the audience to predict the occurrence of successive items, but also provides for that audience's *assent* to the sequence, for if the listener can predict the next item (perhaps he may even repeat it silently before it occurs) he will be more likely to accept it and agree to it.[41]

4. Characters in Acts who show qualities and patterns of behavior similar to Jesus and to scriptural models take on some of the authority of these authoritative figures. This is true of Peter, Stephen, and Paul, whose missions and sufferings resemble those of Jesus, while Jesus' mission and rejection reflect the experience of Moses with the rebel- lious Israelites (see Acts 3:22; 7:22-39).[42]

5. Reading is a constant process of forming and revising expectations, both focal expectations, relating to the immediate context, and global expectations, stretching over large sections of the work.[43] The need to continually revise expectations involves the reader actively in the work

[41] Susan Wittig, "Formulaic Style and the Problem of Redundancy," *Centrum* 1 (1973) 131. Emphasis by Wittig. See Janice Capel Anderson, "Double and Triple Stories, the Implied Reader, and Redundancy in Matthew," *Semeia* 31 (1985) 84.

[42] Johnson, *Possessions,* 38–78, discusses similarities among Moses, Jesus, and Jesus' witnesses, who are portrayed according to a common model that Johnson labels "men of the Spirit." Furthermore, Talbert understands the parallels between Jesus and his witnesses in Luke–Acts as a way of indicating who are the authentic successors of Jesus; see *Literary Patterns,* 125–36.

[43] See Frank Smith, *Understanding Reading: A Psycholinguistic Analysis of Reading and Learning to Read,* 2d ed. (Holt, Rinehart and Winston, 1978) 168–72. Smith's work is discussed by Anderson in "Double and Triple Stories."

and can be a major means of holding the reader's interest. To be most effective, the reader must have some basis for anticipating events, perhaps through suggestive patterns of repetition, but must lack certainty. The lack of certainty pertains not only to what will happen but also to how, when, and why it will happen. Furthermore, the process of building and revising expectations in reading can be used effectively to guide readers toward a climax in the narrative. Confirmation of expectations through a growing repetitive pattern allows the reader to anticipate a climactic instance of the pattern, which will fulfill expectations in the highest degree, as in the triple pattern of arrests and confrontations with the Sanhedrin that lead up to Stephen's death.[44]

6. The same or related characters may be presented in similar situations in order to highlight an important change. The similarities make the differences stand out sharply, suggesting an important development in the narrative. In Acts 4–5 Peter and the other apostles face situations similar to those in Luke's passion story. The contrast in behavior highlights their transformation. Now Peter faces the threat of the Sanhedrin by boldly confessing Jesus, while this threat causes the church to turn in prayer to God, the source of power to withstand opposition.

7. The use of repetitive patterns preserves a sense of unity of purpose and action in spite of significant developments. Very important changes take place as the mission moves from Nazareth to Jerusalem to the Gentile world, but the author succeeds in presenting all this as the manifestation of a single purpose of God, in part through the recurrence of unifying patterns in different sections of the narrative. The author seems to be especially careful not to allow innovations to disrupt the continuity of the narrative.

8. Repetitive patterns in narrative encourage interaction among characters and events in the reader's experience. The character or event is experienced not in isolation but against a background that gives it "resonance." That is, we are able to detect overtones and echoes of other characters and events that add suggestive richness to the narrative episode now being read. Such resonance is not entirely controllable by an author.

---

[44] See the discussion of "building" (along with emphasizing, echoing, and complicating) in chap. 2 of Bruce F. Kawin, *Telling It Again and Again: Repetition in Literature and Film* (Ithaca: Cornell University Press, 1972).

Once some parallels have been suggested in the narrative, other related ones may occur to the reader, whether intended by the author or not. This is especially true when possible interconnections are multiple, with several systems of echoes working at once, as in Acts 1–7. The thick layers of background that produce resonance appeal to the reader's imagination. The reader is sent actively exploring the rich associations, involving both similarity and contrast, which may exist among characters and events. In reading, resonance is a cumulative experience. Connections among narrative materials build up, so that more and more is available as background for exploring those nodal points of narrative where many lines of connection cross. When an author emphasizes certain images and patterns through repeated use, much will depend on the capacity of the selected material to grow in significance through the creative work of the author. Repetition without growth soon becomes monotonous. On the other hand, an author may convince us of the value of central images and patterns if we discover that they expand in meaning. This may happen as we find that they encompass more and more of human experience, including, perhaps, the reader's experience. It may also happen as we are led to a deeper grasp of their implications. The discovery of an expanding symbol is a powerful enticement to explore a new perspective on life. Repetition may lead us to deepening discovery of such symbols, as familiar material returns in new contexts and with new significance. Having experienced the power of the symbol to expand in the story, the reader is more likely to believe that it hides residues of meaning that call for further exploration.[45]

In Acts 3–5, it seems to me, the repetitive patterns help to give resonance to a vision of the God who works by irony, subverting and overruling the human powers who appear to be in control. Because of this God, there can be a mission in which courageous people speak boldly of realities denied and rejected by these human powers.

---

[45] The remarks concerning the expanding symbol were suggested by E. K. Brown, *Rhythm in the Novel* (Toronto: University of Toronto Press, 1950) 33–59. According to Brown, "the expanding symbol is repetition balanced by variation, and that variation is in progressively deepening disclosure" (57). "By the use of an expanding symbol, the novelist persuades and impels his readers towards two beliefs. First, that beyond the verge of what he can express, there is an area that can be glimpsed, never surveyed. Second, that this area has an order of its own which we should greatly care to know" (59).

12

Paul outside the Christian Ghetto: Intercultural Conflict and Cooperation in Acts

The next two essays focus on the Pauline portion of Acts. (See also "Rejection by Jews and Turning to Gentiles: The Pattern of Paul's Mission in Acts.") "Paul outside the Christian Ghetto" discusses the interaction of the Christian mission with non-Christian culture by examining four examples of the "public accusation type-scene" in Acts, stories that illustrate the conflict between the mission and the surrounding culture. In their variety, they suggest some of the complexity of issues and outcomes. I also discuss the story of the sea storm in Acts 27 as an example of beneficial cooperation across religious lines, resulting in the salvation of all.

In *Theology out of the Ghetto,* Hendrikus Boers prompted New Testament exegetes to consider the dangers of religious exclusiveness and to search for resources within the New Testament that can lead us beyond this exclusiveness. "In religious exclusiveness," he reminded us, "a captive God functions to isolate the believer" from nonbelievers.[1] There is a prophetic

---

[1] See *Theology out of the Ghetto: A New Testament Exegetical Study Concerning Religious Exclusiveness* (Leiden: Brill, 1971) 105.

quality to Boers' book. He saw ahead of time that a dormant issue was in fact a key issue. The role of religion in the present political scene underscores the correctness of his insight, for we can now see clearly that exclusive religion, religion that encourages imperial attitudes by believers and consigns nonbelievers to the hostile darkness, makes peaceful settlement of political disputes almost impossible. To survive, the world needs a large infusion of tolerance.

Concern over religious exclusiveness has been one motivating factor in my study of Luke–Acts. I am convinced that Luke–Acts has a vision of God's saving purpose that can help Christians to embrace the world, for, guided by Second Isaiah, it understands God's saving purpose as potentially universal, encompassing "all flesh." This saving purpose underlies the whole narrative and is emphasized for the reader at the beginning through Simeon's oracle (Luke 2:30-32) and the banner quotation from Isa 40:3-5 in Luke 3:4-6. God's salvation is for both Jews and Gentiles, that is, for all. But it is being brought to the world through the mission of Jesus and his witnesses. Here problems arise, problems that Luke–Acts does not hide. The mission produced conflict and rejection, both among Jews and Gentiles. The Christian mission moved out of its ghetto into the larger world, but partially for this reason, it became separated from its Jewish parent. Christianity became a threat to Judaism and strong barriers were the result. Far from being a simple success story, Acts highlights the tragedy of Jewish rejection.[2] Instead of uniting Jews and Gentiles, Christianity became a religion in competition with Judaism, and the protective barriers on both sides became strong.

The culture and government of the Greco-Roman world, guided by values quite different than the Christian movement, were also potential sources of conflict. This essay concerns the ways in which Paul interacts with Greco-Roman culture and government according to Acts. I hasten to add that I cannot discuss this subject fully here. Full discussion would obviously require treatment of Paul's response to the religion of Lystra (Acts 14:11-18) and the idols and philosophers of Athens (17:16-34), and consideration of Paul's relation to Roman officials after he is seized in Jerusalem (21:27-26:32).[3] Instead I wish to focus on some other passages,

---

[2] See Tannehill, "Israel in Luke–Acts: A Tragic Story," *JBL* 104 (1985) 69–85.

[3] For comment on these passages, see Tannehill, *The Narrative Unity of Luke–Acts: A Literary Interpretation* (Philadelphia & Minneapolis: Fortress, 1986, 1990) vol. 2.

which I will approach in a different way than commentaries usually do in order to highlight their importance for our subject. I am referring to 1) four passages in Acts 16-19 in which Paul and other Christians are publicly accused and 2) the sea voyage to Rome in Acts 27. The first four passages are scenes of conflict. The last passage is a suggestive example of cooperation across religious lines. In both cases attention to certain aspects of narrative composition will help us to understand the importance of the material.

The Public Accusation Type-Scene

In four sites of Paul's later missionary work—Philippi (16:19-24), Thessalonica (17:5-9), Corinth (18:12-17), and Ephesus (19:23-40)—we find scenes that present a similar sequence of events. The sequence contains three basic elements: 1) Christians are forcefully brought before officials or a public assembly. 2) An accusation is made, and this accusation is highlighted by direct quotation. 3) The result of this attempt to curb the Christian mission is narrated. Thus in Philippi the owners of the girl with the oracular spirit drag Paul and Silas to the magistrates (16:19) and state their accusation (16:20-21). As a result, Paul and Silas are beaten and imprisoned (16:22-24). In Thessalonica Jews raise a mob and come looking for Paul and Silas (17:5). Not finding them, they drag "Jason and some brothers" to the magistrates (17:6) and make their accusation (17:6-7). The officials are disturbed and require Jason and the others to post a bond (17:8-9). In Corinth the Jews bring Paul before the tribunal of Gallio, the proconsul (18:12), and accuse Paul (18:13), but Gallio refuses to accept the case (18:14-16). The scene in Ephesus is the most independent in construction. Here the narrator presents a longer and more dramatic scene, and the first two elements of the type-scene are rearranged. The accusation is stated first, in a speech by Demetrius to other members of his trade (19:25-27). In this case the accusation motivates action against Christians, which follows. People rush together into the theater, seizing Gaius and Aristarchus, companions of Paul, along the way (19:29), and forming an impromptu public assembly (ἐκκλησία, 19:32). After much confusion and uproar, the secretary (γραμματεύς) of Ephesian government succeeds in calming the people and dissolving the assembly.

The similarities among these scenes justify speaking of a public accusation type-scene. We may speak of a type-scene when a basic situation, with similar characters and plot-elements, recurs several times in a narrative. The analysis of type-scenes is similar to the analysis of genres in form criticism, but my interest, like that of Robert Alter, who introduced the term,[4] is not in the pre-literary history of traditional genres but in a narrator's employment of type-scenes to suggest similarity, with variation, in a narrative. Type-scenes can be used as an important literary technique. The recurrent type-scene suggests that the situation is common or characteristic, while the variations in the type-scene both fight monotony and teach us to look for similar situations in varying costume. The public accusation type-scene in Acts, with its four examples in four consecutive chapters, shows the narrator's strong concern with the way that the Christian mission appears to the outside world and the effect those perceptions may have on Christians.[5]

The accusation is a central element in the scene. It is highlighted through direct discourse and expresses what Paul and his supporters represent to opponents, both Gentiles and Jews. These opponents see the Christian mission as a threat to established society. In most cases they express their accusation in a way likely to arouse their audience and move them to action against the Christians. This public accusation may not completely coincide with their private motives, as indicated by the narrator. Thus in Philippi the narrator first indicates that Paul's opponents, when they seize Paul and Silas, are reacting to their financial loss through the exorcism of the slave girl. But in their statement to the magistrates they present Paul and Silas as a threat to society. They say, "These men, who are Jews, are unsettling our city, and they are proclaiming customs that it is not lawful for us, who are Romans, to accept or practice" (16:20-21). The customs that made Rome great are being threatened by some troublesome Jews, who, it is well known, follow a very distinct set of customs. Paul and Silas, the accusers claim, are openly advocating Jewish customs in a Roman colony. Note that Paul and Silas are attacked as missionaries of Judaism. By Jews Paul is attacked for failing to uphold the Mosaic customs (21:20-21, 28). Thus he is caught between two

---

[4] See *The Art of Biblical Narrative* (New York: Basic, 1981) 47–62. On type-scenes in Luke, see Tannehill, *Narrative Unity*, 1.18, 105, 170–71.

[5] In her dissertation, Marie-Eloise Rosenblatt discusses "the public confrontation type-scene" in Acts. Her category overlaps with mine, although it is defined somewhat differently and includes a somewhat different list of passages. See "Under Interrogation: Paul as Witness in Juridical Contexts in Acts and the Implied Spirituality for Luke's Community" (Ph.D. dissertation, Graduate Theological Union, 1987) 193–205.

suspicious communities, each regarding him as an advocate of the opponent's position. In Philippi the charges are accepted by the local magistrates. Paul and Silas are beaten and imprisoned.

While Paul has frequent disputes in synagogues, in the four cases we are examining the dispute either does not begin or does not remain in the synagogue community. It spills over into the public sphere and is brought to city officials, the provincial governor, or the public assembly. Jews may or may not be involved as accusers. Of the four scenes under consideration, Jews are accusers in the second and third (Thessalonica and Corinth), while Gentiles are accusers in the first and fourth (Philippi and Ephesus). This provides a neat balance that may be deliberate. Jews are not the sole source of trouble for Paul's mission. Gentiles also feel threatened by his mission and take action against him. To both Jews and Gentiles Paul is a troublesome outsider who advocates teachings and behavior that threaten their way of life.

From Philippi Paul travels to Thessalonica. Here the public accusation scene grows out of his preaching in the synagogue. Paul has some success there, but jealous Jews form a mob, set the city in an uproar, and appear at Jason's house in hopes of capturing Paul. When they can't find Paul, they drag Jason and some others to the magistrates. Just as the validity of the accusation in Philippi was undermined when the narrator indicated that the accusers were acting out of selfish economic motives, so the accusation of these Jews is undermined by indications that they are acting out of jealousy (17:5). Furthermore, they form a mob from "some evil men" hanging around the market place and set the city in an uproar. When they then accuse Christians of "upsetting the world," the lack of evidence of deliberate disturbances by Christians contrasts starkly with the accusers' own behavior. The Jews have their private reasons for opposing Paul and his supporters, while the public accusation is designed to move Gentile magistrates to action. It portrays Christians as a threat to Roman society. It goes a step further than the accusation in Philippi. Christians are not only a threat to social stability because they are "upsetting the world"; they are also a direct threat to Caesar's rule, for "all these persons are acting against the decrees of Caesar, saying that there is another king, Jesus" (17:7). This charge and the preceding one in Philippi would be plausible to outsiders with little acquaintance with Christianity. Clearly the narrator intends this extreme charge to be an expression of either ignorance or malice. However, Acts also shows awareness of realistic reasons for tension between the Christian way and its Roman environment, including government officials.[6] In the scenes we are examining, the accusations are not followed by defense speeches. We are left to speculate about the grains of truth that may lie behind the charges that arise from ignorance and malice.

In Thessalonica the magistrates are disturbed by the charges and require Jason and the others to post a security bond. While the charges have some effect, the result is not nearly as severe as in Philippi. The four public accusations in Acts 16–19 have varied results, and they illustrate various attitudes among officials. The Philippian magistrates are fully taken in by the charges, with serious results for Paul and Silas. The Thessalonian magistrates are more cautious. In Corinth the proconsul Gallio will dismiss the charges out of hand, probably with contempt for the accusers. In Ephesus the charges lead to a large public protest but no legal action or bodily harm, due in part to the intervention of a city official. There is no attempt in Acts to stereotype officials. They may or may not protect Christians against attacks. The variety of the local scene is retained in this aspect of the narrative. A sense of the varied local situation is further encouraged by the use of titles appropriate to the particular locations (στρατηγοί for Philippi [16:20],[7] πολιτάρχαι in Thessalonica [17:6]), naming a particular proconsul in Corinth, and referring to the temple of Artemis and the theater in Ephesus. The accusations, the attitudes of the officials that respond to them, and the results vary from place to place.

The officials of Roman society do not form a monolithic front of opposition to the Christian way, but those who protect it may have their own reasons for doing so. The scene before Gallio in Corinth may well be intended to illustrate the Lord's protection of Paul, promised in the vision in 18:9-10. At the same time, it is probable that Gallio's own motives in this scene are less than admirable. The Jews bring Paul to Gallio and make their charge: "This fellow is inciting people to worship God contrary to the law" (18:13). There is some uncertainty here whether Roman law or Jewish law

---

[6] Richard J. Cassidy provides a helpful discussion of Paul and Roman authorities in Acts, showing that the picture does not fit the theory of political apologetic. See *Society and Politics in the Acts of the Apostles* (Maryknoll, N.Y.: Orbis, 1987) 83–157.

[7] See Walter Bauer, *A Greek-English Lexicon of the New Testament,* translated and adapted by W. F. Arndt and F. W. Gingrich, 2d edition revised and augmented by F. W. Gingrich and F. W. Danker (Chicago: University of Chicago, 1979) 770: "This title was not quite officially correct" for the officials of the Roman colony of Philippi, "but it occurs several times in inscr[iptions] as a popular designation for them."

is meant, and Hans Conzelmann believes that Luke pictures the Jews as deliberately ambiguous in an attempt to deceive Gallio.[8] This strains credulity, however. Jews speak of worshiping God (using the singular). It is unlikely that any official would forget that Jews have their own way of worship according to their own law. It seems, then, that the Jews are straightforwardly appealing to Gallio for protection of their religious community against a disturbing intruder. The Jewish concern may have a basis in the earlier narrative. Paul left the Corinthian synagogue for the house of Titius Justus, a "worshiper of God" (σεβομένου τὸν θεόν) (18:7). This devout Gentile would not be bound to observe the Jewish law as a Christian, while the local Jews may have hoped that he and others would accept the life of Judaism. The complaint in 18:13 could be a direct result. According to the complaint, Paul is telling people like Titius Justus that it is possible "to worship God" (σέβεσθαι τὸν θεόν) apart from the law, robbing the Jewish community of present supporters and potential converts.

Gallio's refusal to intervene may have been the correct decision, but the final verse of the scene suggests that he is acting less from legal wisdom than from contempt for Jews. He not only refuses to intervene in Jewish disputes but also refuses to rescue a Jew being attacked in his presence. While the attackers are not clearly specified, the Jews as a group are driven away from Gallio's tribunal in 18:16. Therefore, when Sosthenes is attacked before the tribunal in 18:17, it would seem to be the work of Gentile onlookers who share Gallio's attitude toward Jews, not the work of Jews taking out their frustrations on their leader. Paul benefits from Gallio's refusal of the Jews' appeal, but not because Gallio is a virtuous governor. A sense of the complexities of good and evil in human affairs appears in this scene.[9]

The effect of Christianity on Greco-Roman religion is a thematic issue in the last of the public accusation scenes. The episode begins with the speech of Demetrius and ends with the speech of the secretary. In both cases we must understand the speech in light of the person who is speaking. Demetrius the silversmith, speaking to the people of his trade, brings the

[8] See *Acts of the Apostles,* trans. James Limburg et al., Hermeneia (Philadelphia: Fortress, 1987) 153.

[9] It is wrong to interpret Luke–Acts itself as anti-Jewish. See Tannehill, "Israel in Luke–Acts," 69–85; and *idem,* "Rejection by Jews and Turning to Gentiles: The Pattern of Paul's Mission in Acts," in *Luke–Acts and the Jewish People,* edited by Joseph B. Tyson (Minneapolis: Augsburg, 1988) 83–101, 150–52.

accusation against Paul, and his speech is carefully crafted to move his audience to action. He cites the threat to their trade from Paul's influence and adds that reverence for the temple of Artemis and for Artemis herself is threatened (19:25-27). Here, as in the Philippi scene, the commercial motive of the accuser undermines his moral stance. However, the concern about Artemis and her temple is picked up by his hearers and the larger population of Ephesus. Inspired by a mixture of local pride and devotion to Artemis, the crowd in the theater spends hours shouting "Great is Artemis of the Ephesians." Then the government secretary intervenes. He rejects the position of Demetrius and denies that the Christians apprehended by the crowd have committed sacrilege against Artemis' temple or blasphemed her (19:37). Although he defends Christians, he does not speak from a Christian point of view but as a city official who shares its dominant culture. He points out the danger to the city of being accused of riot or revolt, a concern that would weigh heavily on a city official. His remarks about Ephesus and Artemis also reflect his place in the local establishment. He refuses to take the concern of Demetrius and the crowd seriously. He is sure that no one fails to recognize Ephesus' claim to fame as "temple keeper of the great Artemis." These things are "undeniable," he says (19:35-36).

These opening words of the official's speech can be interpreted either as strategic flattery to quiet the crowd or as the smug assurance of an establishment figure who thinks that Paul's mission cannot possibly affect the dominant culture. In the latter case, he is naive, from the perspective of Acts as a whole. Demetrius pointed to Paul's strong influence in Ephesus and the province of Asia and reported that Paul has been saying, "Gods created by hands are not gods" (19:26). Here Demetrius' report fits what we find elsewhere in Acts. In 19:10 we were told that Paul worked in Ephesus for two years, "so that all those inhabiting Asia heard the word of the Lord, both Jews and Greeks." In an earlier example of his preaching, Paul stated that human attempts to represent the divine by images of gold, silver, or stone are signs of pagan ignorance of God (17:29-30). Thus the larger narrative indicates that Demetrius has good reason to be worried about Paul's effect on his trade and Ephesian religion, while the city official is either blind to the problem or chooses to ignore it in order to soothe the crowd. The worried reaction of Demetrius and the crowd hints at the potentially shattering effect of the Christian mission on the religious culture of a place like Ephesus. The episode is remarkable in that Christians have a very small role in it. We are asked to view the effect of the mission through the eyes of Demetrius, the crowd, and the city secretary, an approach that requires subtle sifting of characters' points of view in order to discern the implied author's.[10]

These four examples of the public accusation type-scene in Acts provide narrative images of conflict between the Christian mission and both Jewish and Gentile society, conflict important enough to demand the attention of government officials. While the accusations may reveal ignorance and malice, and arise from self-interested motives, there is a core of hard reality behind the conflict. In some ways the Christian movement does threaten both Jewish and Gentile society, raising the question whether peaceful coexistence is possible.

The Storm at Sea

It is remarkable that the implied author chooses to tell in such vivid detail the story of storm and shipwreck in Acts 27. It is doubly remarkable when we note that Paul is only intermittently in the focus of attention. It will be helpful to begin with the hypothesis that Acts 27 is a unified narrative in which the parts contribute fittingly to the whole, for we will discover good evidence to support this view. Furthermore, this approach will help us to recognize that this story of a storm at sea is more conducive to theological reflection than commonly assumed.

In the early part of the chapter there are numerous signs of a difficult and dangerous voyage.[11] These include Paul's explicit warning of loss of the ship and loss of life (27:10). This warning is not heeded, and the ship is caught by the great storm. As the storm continues, the "we" narrator indicates that "all hope of our being saved" was dissolving (v. 20). At this low point in the narrative, Paul intervenes a second time.[12] Although he

---

[10] The implied author is a mental construct, based on a reading of the work, of the kind of person who would write this work, which affirms certain values, beliefs, and norms. The implied author may closely resemble the real author, but there may also be differences, for authors may write in order to purify themselves, becoming more consistent, noble, radical, etc., than they are in real life.

[11] The following discussion parallels much of my treatment of Acts 27 in *Narrative Unity*, 2.330–39.

[12] Reinhard Kratz notes that Acts 27 shifts between scenes that heighten the danger and scenes in which Paul responds to this danger. See *Rettungswunder: Motiv-, traditions- und formkritische Aufarbeitung einer biblischen Gattung*, Europaeische Hochschulschriften 123 (Frankfurt: Lang, 1979) 323.

reminds his audience of their failure to listen to his previous advice, his main purpose is to revive the hope and courage of a company that has lost hope.[13] He urges them "to cheer up" or "take heart" (εὐθυμεῖν, v. 22; cf. v. 25). Paul can encourage others because he himself has been encouraged by an angel, who said, "Do not fear" (v. 24), and assured him that it is still God's plan for him to reach Rome and stand before Caesar. Furthermore, the angel said, "God has granted you all those sailing with you." The whole ship's company will be rescued, a major modification of what Paul expected according to his earlier warning in v. 10. If the author were simply interested in bringing Paul to Rome under divine protection, it would be an unnecessary complication to refer to the rescue of all, especially since this requires correction of Paul's previous warning. This announcement is a key to understanding the rest of the episode, for it determines what must happen, and the acts of sailors, soldiers, and Paul are to be judged in light of it. From this point on, no method of escape is acceptable that doesn't include all. Opportunities arise for the sailors to escape, abandoning the rest (v. 30), and for the soldiers to escape after killing their prisoners (v. 42). These plans are thwarted, in spite of the risk involved in trying to get the large ship close to shore and allowing prisoners to swim for their lives when they might escape. These plans are wrong not only because they endanger Paul but also because they offend against the divine plan of saving all.

Paul identifies the angel as "an angel of the God whose I am, whom I also serve" (or "worship," v. 23). He refers in this way to his own God because the majority of his audience has other gods. Thus the "all" who are promised rescue consist primarily of pagans who do not worship the one God. Nevertheless, God has decided to rescue them.

There is no indication that Paul's encouraging message has an immediate effect on his audience. The narrative continues with the approach of the island, which, although it fits Paul's prediction in v. 26, produces fear (v. 29), not encouragement. The sailors are afraid that the ship will run aground against sharp rocks. Paul's efforts to revive hope are successful only after a further intervention, when the ship's company finally

---

[13] A speech in the midst of the storm is a convention of storm scenes, as Susan Marie Praeder indicates. She says, "The usual place for such speeches is at a high point in the storm and a low point in the fortunes of the sea travelers." Paul's speech is unusual in conveying a message of hope. See "Acts 27:1—28:16: Sea Voyages in Ancient Literature and the Theology of Luke–Acts," *CBQ* 46 (1984) 696 [683–706].

does take heart (εὔθυμοι . . . γενόμενοι, v. 36), as Paul had earlier urged (vv. 22, 25). With the approach of land, the technical skills of the sailors, also noted previously in the narrative, come into play. They sense the approach of land. They confirm that shallows are approaching by taking soundings. Then they throw out four anchors from the stern to keep the ship from drifting onto rocks in the middle of the night. In all of this they are acting for the benefit of the whole ship's company. Then, however, they do something that both demonstrates disloyalty to the rest of the seafarers and failure to trust Paul's promise that God would provide a way for all to be saved. They try to "flee" from the ship in a small boat, on "pretext" of stretching out further anchors from the bow. Paul recognizes their plan in time, tells the centurion and soldiers, and the soldiers cut the ropes, letting the boat drift ashore. This is a drastic move, since the boat might have been useful the next day. If nothing is done, however, the boat will only help the fleeing sailors, who are abandoning the others in a ship they cannot handle. The ship can carry all, and the divine plan is that all should be saved. The sailors are needed to sail the ship. Without them there is no hope of bringing it safely to shore. The boat must be sacrificed so that all will have a chance. Paul's alertness and the soldiers' swift action make it possible for all to reach safety.

Already in v. 21 we were told that the ship's company was not eating. Seasickness in the storm could have been the cause, but there may also be a link between the loss of hope in v. 20 and the failure to eat in v. 21. The latter view is strengthened by the scene in vv. 33-38, for which v. 21 is preparation. Paul urges all to eat and begins to eat himself. The decision of the others to eat is accompanied by a change of mood; all were "taking heart" (v. 36). It is Paul who causes this change. So we find Paul, shortly before the final effort to reach shore safely, urging all to take nourishment and break their long fast. He supports his exhortation with a reason, which includes a renewed promise that all will be saved. They must eat, for it will contribute to their "salvation, for a hair from the head of none of you will perish" (v. 34). It is finally this promise plus Paul's own action that overcomes the hopelessness indicated in v. 20, replacing it with new hope and courage.

Paul takes the lead and begins to eat. The description of this is remarkable, for it echoes accounts of other significant meals in Luke–Acts: "Taking bread, he gave thanks (εὐχαρίστησεν) to God before all, and breaking it, he began to eat" (v. 35). The sequence of taking bread, giving thanks or blessing, and breaking the bread is also found in Luke 9:16 (Jesus feeding the multitude), 22:19 (the last supper), and 24:30 (the meal at Emmaus). Furthermore, the church's meal celebration in Acts is called the breaking of bread (Acts 2:42, 46; 20:7, 11). The reference to giving thanks makes Acts 27:35 particularly close to Jesus' last supper, while the reference to the number of participants and the indication that they were filled in vv. 37-38 are reminiscent of the feeding of the multitude (Luke 9:14,17). The details of Paul's actions in Acts 27:35 are not necessary parts of the narrative. They could easily have been omitted if they did not have special significance. The narrative invites us to picture Paul doing what Jesus did and what the church does: give thanks to God by breaking bread and eating.

Paul's meal, then, is as sacramental as any other meal in Luke–Acts. However, the fact that Paul is eating with pagans has proved troublesome for this interpretation. Bo Reicke, who argued for the sacramental associations of this scene in 1948, nevertheless added that it could not be a real Lord's Supper, since Paul is eating with pagans. Rather, Paul is allowing the people in the ship to participate in a prefiguration of the Christian Lord's Supper as preparation for later discipleship.[14] The absence of an indication that Paul distributed the bread over which he had given thanks is probably significant. Gerhard Schneider, who recognizes the eucharistic associations of this scene, is technically correct in saying that it does not depict a common meal, for Paul eats his food and the rest of the company other food.[15] To that extent the privacy of the church's celebration is maintained. The remarkable thing, however, is the effect that Paul's eucharist has on his non-Christian companions. By eating before them, Paul finally achieves his goal of encouraging them. They take nourishment and strengthen themselves for the final effort to reach shore safely.

The promise of rescue for all in v. 24 is echoed by repeated references to all in vv. 33-37. Paul urges all to take nourishment (v. 33). He promises that a hair of none of them will perish (v. 34). He gives thanks before all (v. 35). Then all take heart (v. 36). Finally, v. 37 indicates, "All the lives in the ship, we were two hundred seventy six." The "we" in the voyage to

---

[14] See "Die Mahlzeit mit Paulus auf den Wellen des Mittelmeers Act. 27,33-38," *TZ* 4 (1948) 408–9.

[15] See *Die Apostelgeschichte,* 2 vols., HTKNT 5 (Freiburg: Herder, 1980–82) 2.396.

Rome generally refers to a small group of Christians. Here, however, the entire ship's company becomes a single "we" as the narrator numbers the company so that readers will know what "all" means. Even though the boundary of the church is not completely eliminated, the meal on the ship is an act that benefits all, Christian and non-Christian, and an act in which community is created across religious lines.

The meal can do this because of its association with God's promise for all. In v. 34 Paul repeats the angel's promise of v. 24 in other language. Then Paul takes bread and gives thanks to God. In the present context Paul's thanksgiving has particular significance. It is thanksgiving especially for God's promise of the rescue of all. Therefore, it is also an act of trust in this promise in spite of the immediate danger. There may even be a play on words to support a connection with the promise. The angel announced that God "has graciously granted" (κεχάρισται) all to Paul. In response Paul "gave thanks" (εὐχαρίστησεν).[16] Paul's gratitude and trust are infectious. The others take heart and eat, showing the first signs that they, too, believe in the promise.

Even though the others do not share Paul's food, celebrating eucharist "before all" so that all will eat shows a remarkable concern to benefit non-Christians through a central Christian practice. The use of the hyperbole of the hair of the head in v. 34 is also remarkable. It parallels a promise of Jesus in Luke 21:18, but there the promise applied to persecuted disciples. Here the promise is stretched to include all, in accordance with the repeated references to the salvation of all in the voyage narrative.

Paul told the centurion and soldiers, "Unless these [sailors] remain in the ship, you cannot be saved" (v. 31). Paul also urged the others to eat because this would contribute to their "salvation" (v. 34). He is referring, of course, to being saved or rescued from the sea. These verses are part of an emphasized theme, for there are seven references to being saved from the sea in this section of Acts, using the verbs σῴζω (27:20, 31) and διασῴζω (27:43, 44; 28:1, 4), and the noun σωτηρία (27:34). The rapid repetition of the same word in 27:43, 44; 28:1 is a particular sign of emphasis. These words are found in other accounts of sea voyages in ancient literature.[17] Therefore, ancient readers would not find them to be unnatural

[16] See Praeder, "Sea Voyages," 698.
[17] See Susan Marie Praeder, "The Narrative Voyage: An Analysis and Interpretation of Acts 27–28" (Ph.D. dissertation, Graduate Theological Union, 1980) 245–56.

232

in their context. But Susan Praeder rightly discerns a double sense in these words. She emphasizes that narratives are both created from and read in light of a real world context of "experience and imagination" that enters literary expression. Two such contexts have taken literary shape and are particularly relevant to reading Acts 27:1-28:15: the imaginative experience of ancient sea voyages expressed in sea voyage literature and the imaginative experience of first century Christianity as expressed in Luke–Acts.[18] These two contexts suggest a double reading of the thematic emphasis on salvation or rescue. In the former context the hope for rescue from the sea is a natural part of the experience of a sea voyage, when danger arises. The salvation or rescue may come from various human and divine sources. In the latter context salvation takes on a special significance. It is not only the hope of those in a storm at sea but the purpose of God for all humanity, as announced at the beginning of Luke (2:30-32, 3:6). The emphasis on salvation in Luke–Acts gives to the emphasis on salvation in this sea voyage a second, symbolic sense.[19]

The narrative hints at a second sense by emphasis within the story of the voyage and by the theological importance of the terms "save, salvation" in Luke–Acts as a whole. However, the narrative does not determine for us how far we should take its suggestion. Even if we wish to remain close to the Lukan world of thought, there are two interesting possibilities to consider. First, not only does the emphasis on salvation in the voyage echo the emphasis on salvation in Luke–Acts as a whole, but the insistence that all the ship's company must be saved echoes the promise that "all flesh will see the salvation of God" in Luke 3:6.[20] Thus the fulfillment of God's promise to Paul that all those in the ship will survive the storm becomes a sign in miniature of God's promise of salvation for all flesh, which has not yet been fulfilled. Paul is conscious that he is speaking

---

[18] See "Narrative Voyage," 95–99, 183–312.

[19] G. Schneider, *Apostelgeschichte,* 2. 396, n. 107, recognizes that the use of the term elsewhere in Acts suggests that σωτηρία in v. 34 is "transparent" to a meaning larger than rescue from the sea. On the use of the word group "save, salvation" in Luke–Acts, see Augustin George, *Études sur l'oeuvre de Luc,* SB (Paris: Gabalda, 1978) 307–20. George, however, regards the occurrences in the voyage to Rome as simply profane uses.

[20] On Luke 3:6 see Tannehill, *Narrative Unity,* 1.40–42, where I argue that seeing God's salvation means recognizing it and responding to it, which shades over into personal participation in it. In the Lukan context Luke 3:6 (= Isa 40:5) refers to participation in salvation by both Jews (including Jewish outcasts) and Gentiles.

mainly to pagans when he shares God's promise with those on board the ship.[21] This unconverted audience is promised salvation from the sea. Paul makes no reference to faith in Jesus Christ as a precondition. God graciously grants salvation to all on the ship, not because of their works or their faith, but simply because it fits God's purpose. In fact, the whole narrative of the voyage to Rome is remarkable for the absence of any indication that Paul proclaimed Jesus either to his companions on the ship or to the people of Malta. The benefits that God brings through Paul do not depend on acceptance of this message. In Rome Paul will continue his work as a missionary. He has not changed his mind on the importance of this work. But the voyage narrative presents a more comprehensive vision of God's saving work, which is not limited to those who hear and accept the gospel. The mission continues within the context of this vision.

To be sure, there is little evidence outside Acts 27 that Luke–Acts anticipates the salvation of every individual. One could argue that in the context of Luke–Acts the promise to "all flesh" is a promise to large numbers of people of all kinds, but not necessarily to every individual. Indeed, the reference to "as many as were ordained to eternal life" in Acts 13:48 suggests that there are some who are not ordained to eternal life. However, if salvation in Paul's voyage to Rome does have a second level of meaning, this section of Acts represents a new boldness of hope that anticipates salvation (in some sense) for every individual of a pluralistic community and views persons such as Paul as mediators of this promise. We cannot assume that the implied author reached theological clarity on this issue and held one view consistently. Furthermore, the nature of this salvation is not clarified. The larger Lukan context suggests that it has a second level of meaning that exceeds rescue from a storm, and the voyage narrative indicates that this salvation reaches even unconverted pagans. These observations still leave various options of interpretation, stretching from the view that Christianity is an occasional benefactor of society at large to a universalism that includes every creature in God's ultimate salvation.

Reflection on this story of the salvation of all may also move in a second direction. In the voyage narrative a remarkable amount of attention is given to the cooperative relationship between Paul and Julius the centurion and to the contributions that various parties—the sailors, Julius,

---

[21] As noted above, Paul in v. 23 must distinguish the God he is talking about from other deities.

and Paul—make to finally reaching safety. God's role in events is explicit only at one place: Paul receives a message from God through an angel (vv. 23-24). This message is important because it conveys a promise that enables humans to take heart and because it points to the goal toward which humans must work. Human decision and action are crucial in reaching this goal. As Paul said to the centurion, "Unless these [sailors] remain in the ship, you cannot be saved" (v. 31). Therefore, the soldiers must act. Human actions that work toward the rescue of all are acceptable contributions to the realization of God's purpose, while actions that seek the safety of one's own group while abandoning others will block this purpose until corrected. When the parties in the ship work together cooperatively for the good of all, dangers are avoided and the ship's company is finally saved. In the ship Paul and his Christian companions are a small minority within a largely pagan company, but survival depends on each party acting for the good of all. Paul does this when he warns Julius that the sailors are abandoning the ship and when he eats before all. Julius does this when he stops the soldiers from killing the prisoners, who might escape (vv. 42-43). The sailors do this when they stick to their tasks in the ship. Working together and for each other, they reach the safety that God had promised.

The implied author's interest in such a narrative could arise from concern about the role of a Christian minority in Roman society. The Christian movement is very important in the eyes of the implied author, but it will remain a minority for the foreseeable future. The possibility of salvation in the social and political sphere depends on Christians and non-Christians being willing to follow the lead of Paul, Julius, and the sailors, when they are acting for the good of all. Perhaps the Christian prophet, like Paul, will have a special role in conveying an understanding of what is possible and promised by God, but non-Christians also have important roles.

Following the meal the rejuvenated company moves into action. Remaining cargo is cast overboard so that the ship will have the best chance of passing over shoals. The efforts of the sailors (mentioned simply as "they" in vv. 39-41) are described in detail. In spite of their previous attempt to abandon the ship, they now do their duty for the good of all and steer the ship toward a beach. But this is not a familiar harbor. The ship runs aground, and the stern begins to break up. Paul has helped by prophetic encouragement, enabling the company to respond to their situation in light of the divine promise. The sailors have done their part by protecting the ship in the storm and taking it as far as possible toward the beach. But still there is danger. Not only is the ship breaking up, but the soldiers decide to kill the prisoners, lest they escape. The soldiers, like the sailors, forget in the crisis that God's promise is for all, and they plan to save themselves by eliminating others. The community of all with mutual responsibilities is about to be violated a second time. At this point Julius the centurion makes an important contribution to the rescue. "Wishing to save Paul," he stops the soldiers and organizes the escape from ship to shore, making it possible for all to reach safety. Julius' friendship with Paul makes a crucial difference at this point, saving not only Paul but the other prisoners. His friendly attitude was demonstrated at the very beginning of the voyage (v. 3), and the relationship was probably strengthened when Paul helped the soldiers and then the whole ship's company in vv. 31 and 33-36. Paul is a benefactor of the others on this voyage,[22] but he is also benefited. His benefits return to him as the centurion intervenes to save his life. Of course, this is part of God's care for Paul, who must stand before Caesar (v. 24), but the narrative gives careful attention to the ways that other persons contribute to and are benefited by this aspect of God's purpose. The storm narrative ends with a significant summary: "And thus it happened that all were saved (διασωθῆναι) upon the land" (v. 44). "Thus," i.e., through these human actions, God's promise was fulfilled.

In the narrative of Paul's mission in Acts, we find stories of inter-cultural conflict and also a remarkable story of cooperation. The stories of conflict are, of course, narrated from a Christian point of view and tend to present Paul's opponents in a negative way. The opponents act from commercial motives (16:19; 19:25-27) or cause civil unrest while accusing Christians of upsetting the world (17:5-6). Nevertheless, it would be naive to assume that a religion can be vital without causing conflict. If avoidance of conflict is the primary value, the status quo is ratified and the prophetic function of religion is nullified. The stories of conflict we have examined (and other parts of Acts) provide images of a bold messenger who is willing to challenge religious cultures that have become tired or corrupt, while accepting the negative reaction that will follow. These narrative images

---

[22] Emphasized by Gerhard Krodel, *Acts*, ACNT (Minneapolis: Augsburg, 1986) 470.

have continuing usefulness. But one of the results of such a missionary challenge may be the revival of the other religion in reaction, and religious conflict easily gets out of hand. Therefore, it is important that there is also a model of interreligious cooperation in Acts, encouraging us to find a way to bring all to safety from the dangers that threaten our world. This narrative also reminds us that the divine promise ultimately is for all; it therefore transcends all of the religious perspectives that inspire and divide us.

13

The Narrator's Strategy in the Scenes of Paul's Defense

Paul's defense scenes are a commonly neglected but important part of Acts. In this essay I consider them from the perspective of narrative rhetoric. The interconnected scenes are part of a narrative process that follows a rhetorical strategy that only becomes clear in Acts 26. The underlying purpose is not simply to provide political apologetic or to reassure Christian believers that their faith is rooted in Jewish scripture. When accused of being anti-Jewish, Paul responds as a resourceful missionary who carefully builds a basis for communication with a suspicious audience and thereby provides a model for others.

Although Paul's defense scenes are also discussed in The Narrative Unity of Luke–Acts, *vol. 2, the following discussion is a clearer and more compact account of the narrator's rhetorical strategy as I understand it.*

I was a young teacher, my dissertation not far behind me, when I encountered Robert Funk's book *Language, Hermeneutic, and Word of God.*[1] It made a lasting impact on my scholarly work, for it forced me to recognize

---

[1] Robert W. Funk, *Language, Hermeneutic, and Word of God: The Problem of Language in the New Testament and Contemporary Theology* (New York: Harper & Row, 1966).

that one cannot deal with issues of New Testament theology without careful consideration of the literary forms in which New Testament writers communicate. In my scholarly pilgrimage from parables through synoptic sayings and pronouncement stories to the gospels and Acts as narratives, the question of how these literary forms communicate, raised with urgency by Funk's work, has never left me. Those of us who are currently studying the gospels and Acts as narratives are now also indebted to Robert Funk for *The Poetics of Biblical Narrative*.[2] Here Funk clarifies the rules of narrative grammar assumed by biblical writers, enabling us to analyze biblical narrative precisely. This book appeared while I was completing my volume on Acts, and it provided a clear statement of important rules of narrative composition encountered in my work on Acts.[3] In thanks for these and other benefits, I offer the following study of the narrator's strategy in Paul's defense scenes in Acts.

In spite of the high drama of these scenes, they are seldom appreciated as a unified development carefully shaped according to a controlling strategy. When referring to the narrator's "strategy," I am focusing on the rhetorical shaping of a narrative to make a particular kind of impression on its readers or hearers, or to appeal to them in a particular way.[4] Conclusions about the narrator's strategy must, of course, be based on careful observation of literary composition, but the literary data are being read as clues to a purposeful appeal to readers to view a problematic situation in a particular way. In order to understand the narrator's strategy, we must be clear about the main problem being addressed. In the scenes of Paul's defense we must also recognize that the narrator can develop central themes over a complex series of scenes, with the point being scored coming to full clarity only at the end. Thus it is vital that we study the defense scenes not in isolation from each other but as a broad development coming to its climax in Paul's appearance before King Agrippa.

---

[2] Funk, *Poetics of Biblical Narrative,* Foundations and Facets (Sonoma, Calif.: Polebridge, 1988).
[3] See Tannehill, *The Narrative Unity of Luke–Acts: A Literary Interpretation,* 2 vols. (Philadelphia & Minneapolis: Fortress, 1986, 1990) 2.6, 26, 48, 130, 275.
[4] Elsewhere I use the phrase "narrative rhetoric"; see Tannehill, *Narrative Unity,* 1.8.

The Jewish Charges

Since Paul is a prisoner of the Romans, we might expect political charges to dominate the defense scenes. Actually they play a subsidiary role. The charges are initiated by Jews before Paul becomes a Roman prisoner, and these initial charges shape the debate throughout. Indeed, Paul is still responding to these Jewish charges when he arrives in Rome and speaks to the Roman Jews (28:17-20). The relevance of the speeches will only be clear if we are clear about the basic charge with which the speeches are dealing. This is the charge that Paul is anti-Jewish, that his mission is a fundamental attack on the Jewish people and its faith. Charges punishable by Rome are mentioned, and at points Paul responds to them, but the overriding issue is one between Paul and his Jewish attackers.

The new problem that requires solution, or the "state of disequilibrium" that requires search for equilibrium,[5] surfaces in the narrative through these Jewish charges. They appear in two related scenes before Paul's arrest and express the reason Paul is attacked in the temple and opposed thereafter. These charges are expressed by two different parties, but in content they are related. Immediately following Paul's arrival in Jerusalem, James and the elders indicate what Jewish Christians have been told about Paul, namely that "you teach all the Jews among the Gentiles apostasy from Moses, telling them not to circumcise their children nor walk by the customs" (21:21). To prove this charge false, Paul is willing to perform a public act demonstrating his loyalty to the law. He is willing in spite of the fact that publicly announcing when he will participate in a temple ritual puts him in jeopardy, since his enemies will know when they can locate him in a public place. The result is the attack on Paul in the temple. Paul risks his life to demonstrate his support of Christian Jews who want to live according to the law and share in the temple worship.

Although Paul's relation to Judean Christians receives no attention after his arrest, their charge does not disappear. It is absorbed into a second, closely related charge, made by the Asian Jews who instigate the attack in the temple. They call out to the crowd, "This is the person teaching all everywhere against the people and the law and this place" (21:28). To this is added the specific charge that Paul has defiled the temple by bringing Greeks into it. The specific charge plays some role in the following defense

---

[5]See Funk, *Poetics of Biblical Narrative*, 23.

240

scenes, but the general charge is more important. It is a charge that Paul is anti-Jewish, attacking the very foundations of Judaism, the special role of the chosen people, called to live by the law and worship in the Jerusalem temple. The charge refers to Paul's teaching. That is, it relates not just to Paul's personal behavior but to what he advocates in his mission. His mission is an anti-Jewish movement, the accusers claim. This charge is taken so seriously by the narrator of Acts that it shapes the extensive series of defense scenes that follow.

Paul's Speech to the Jerusalem Mob

Only two of the scenes can properly be called trials, the trial before Governor Felix in 24:1-23 and the trial before Governor Festus in 25:6-12. Paul's most extensive defense speeches appear in other settings. The defense sequence is framed by two major speeches, the first delivered by Paul to his Jewish opponents immediately after the attack in the temple (22:1-21), the last delivered to King Agrippa in the presence of Festus and other prominent persons (26:2-23). These two related speeches are the major means by which Paul replies to the charge of anti-Judaism. The scenes between contribute to a significant development (to be discussed below). The audiences of the two major speeches differ. The first speech is delivered to determined opponents who have just tried to kill Paul. In spite of their hatred, Paul tries to explain why a zealous Jew, one like themselves, could be involved in the mission that he has conducted. King Agrippa differs from this audience not only in rank but in attitude. Paul addresses him as a Jew. However, he is not identified with Paul's Jewish opponents and is open to Paul's message. Indeed, before Agrippa Paul boldly moves from a defense speech into a missionary appeal. While Agrippa is not willing to accept Jesus as Messiah in so short a time, faith remains a possibility for such a Jew, and Agrippa is willing to affirm that Paul is innocent of serious charges. Thus the grim picture of Paul attacked in Jerusalem develops into a scene suggesting that there are still some Jews willing to consider his message.

The strong emphasis on Paul's Jewishness in his speech to the Jerusalem mob is obvious. This emphasis is a direct response to the preceding charge of anti-Judaism (21:28). Paul begins by stating, "I am a Jew," followed by his credentials in upbringing and education. He asserts that he is "a zealot for God just as you all are this day" (22:3). Then he must explain how such a Jewish zealot could be involved in a mission so provocative to his audience. Paul tries to be persuasive even though his audience is hostile. He tells his own story in a way that repeatedly highlights the basis of his mission in the faith that he shares with his audience. Ananias is not presented as a Jewish Christian, as in 9:10-18, for the dominant issue has shifted. It no longer concerns Paul and persecuted Christians but Paul and the Jews. Therefore, Ananias is presented as "a devout man according to the law, attested by all the Jewish inhabitants" (22:12), and he affirms that Paul's call has come from "the God of our fathers" (22:14). Even the vision that sends Paul forth to the nations occurs in the temple. The speech shows how Paul's life story can be rhetorically shaped to respond to those who attack Paul as anti-Jewish.

Paul attempts to form a bond with his audience by emphasizing his own Jewishness, claiming that he is a "zealot for God just as you all are today," and supporting that claim by describing his persecution of Christians. Paul's audience is now the persecutor. The old Paul and his present audience are alike in their understanding of the implications of zealous loyalty to the God of Israel. Therefore, Paul's autobiography is particularly relevant to this audience.[6] Paul is testifying to the power of the Lord to change persecutors. His story of the radical change that took place in his own life is an invitation to present persecutors to reevaluate Paul and Jesus, and thereby be changed themselves.

However, the conflict is not so easily resolved. At the end of the speech the crowd breaks out anew in shouts for Paul's death. Paul is here addressing hardened opponents. The conclusion of Paul's speech, which focuses on his vision in the temple, takes that into account. The temple vision not only authorizes Paul's mission among the nations but gives a warning to his audience concerning the result of their attitude. In the face of hardened opposition, the mission is directed elsewhere. This was the case when Paul first preached in Jerusalem, and the rejection that he experienced then is being repeated now. Later, however, there will be indications that not all Jews are hardened opponents.

---

[6]See Karl Loening, *Die Saulustradition in der Apostelgeschichte,* NTAbh 9 (Münster: Aschendorff, 1973) 175–76.

The Hearing before the Sanhedrin

The hearing before the Sanhedrin in Acts 22:30-23:10 continues to emphasize that Paul is a dedicated Jew. Paul's retraction of his words when told that he was speaking against the high priest shows how far the narrator is willing to go in demonstrating Paul's loyalty to the law. The hearing before the Sanhedrin also adds an important new note. Paul says to the council, "Brothers, I am a Pharisee, a son of Pharisees; concerning hope and resurrection of the dead I am on trial" (23:6). This seems a strange remark. No one has accused Paul concerning such matters. Nevertheless, Paul's statement should not be dismissed as a tactical maneuver, intended merely to disrupt the council proceedings, for this is the first sounding of a developing theme whose full significance will be disclosed only in Paul's speech before King Agrippa.

Paul, in effect, is trying to substitute his own definition for his opponents' definition of the central issue of the conflict. Jerome Neyrey, in his treatment of Paul's defense speeches against the background of the forensic defense speech in ancient rhetoric, notes that definition of the "main question" is an expected part of the statement of facts or *narratio* in a defense speech.[7] It is appropriate for a speaker to consider the main question carefully, for its definition is an important persuasive move in debate. It defines the case that one wants to argue, and the outcome will depend to a considerable degree on whether one has chosen to argue the right issue. Paul's restatement of the issue of his trial in 23:6 is the beginning of a persistent effort to shift the focus of debate.

Roman officials will later conclude that the real issue of the trial does not concern matters punishable under Roman law but rather disputes concerning Jewish religion (25:18-19, 25; 26:31-32). Paul's strategy may contribute to this conclusion. However, Paul's effort to shift the focus of debate does not have Romans alone in mind. As the theme of hope and resurrection develops, it becomes a way of appealing to Jews to reconsider their rejection of Jesus. Even to the Jews of Rome, who have no role in the legal proceedings, Paul will insist that he is a prisoner "because of the hope of Israel" (28:20), another statement of the claim that the hope of

---

[7]See Jerome H. Neyrey, "The Forensic Defense Speech and Paul's Trial Speeches in Acts 22–26," in *Luke–Acts: New Perspectives from the Society of Biblical Literature Seminar,* edited by Charles Talbert (New York: Crossroad, 1984) 214–15.

Israel is the real issue of his prolonged trial. Paul will also make the hope of the Jewish people in God's promise the basis for his witness and missionary appeal to King Agrippa. Paul before the Sanhedrin is laying a basis not merely for his defense before Roman officials but also for a continuing missionary witness to Jews, who are suspicious of Paul and the Christian way but who might still be reached by a resourceful witness.

Especially through this redefinition of the issue of the trial, Paul's personal defense becomes a witness to his Lord. This intention is not apparent in Paul's statement before the Sanhedrin, for Paul does not speak there of Jesus' resurrection but of the hope of Pharisees, the general resurrection (ἀνάστασις νεκρῶν—"resurrection of dead people," using the plural). There is nothing distinctly Christian about this, and that is part of Paul's point at the moment. Later the speech before Agrippa will show that there is a missionary strategy behind this emphasis. The connection between resurrection, Israel's hope, and Jesus will be disclosed in the speech before Agrippa, in which the theme of hope and resurrection will play a key role. For the present, note that the Lord Jesus, in the night vision following the Sanhedrin scene, counts Paul's words before the crowd and the Sanhedrin as witness for his cause (23:11). Note also that Paul by his witness will fulfill Jesus' words in Luke 21:12-13, which indicated that Jesus' followers would be led before kings and governors and this would result in witnessing. Paul does not refer to Jesus when the theme of hope and resurrection is introduced in Acts 23 and 24. Nevertheless, his approach serves a purpose if it is being presented as a model of a resourceful and gradual appeal to suspicious Jews. For the later witness to be effective, it is first necessary to establish the fact that Paul and many Jews share a common hope. Paul makes this point before the Sanhedrin and will come back to it later in a context that includes an appeal to faith in Jesus.

The portrayal of the Pharisees' reaction in the Sanhedrin shows that they are not viewed as part of the hardened opposition. They are not converted by Paul, but they are willing to come to Paul's defense. The narrative suggests that there is a basis for communication with some Pharisees.

The Purpose of the Defense Scenes

Recent scholarship has been inclined to read the scenes we are considering in light of other concerns. The narrator, many believe, is concerned to assure Christians that they are valid heirs of the scriptural promises in the face of doubts raised by the disappearance of obvious connections with Judaism.[8] I agree that reassurance of Christians may have been one of the purposes of Acts. However, I do not think that it is an adequate explanation of Paul's defense scenes. I call attention to two aspects of Paul's defense speeches that are not easily explained on the basis of this theory.

First, it does not explain why Paul is pictured as initially avoiding christological controversy with his Jewish opponents. If the real purpose is to reassure the church of its Jewish roots, there is no need to be reticent on this point. Placing Jesus Christ in a Jewish and scriptural context would provide the roots that the community needs. Instead of doing this, Paul refers vaguely to "hope and resurrection of the dead" in Acts 23 and 24, using the plural for "dead." This reticence concerning Jesus' resurrection (a reticence that does not disappear until 26:23, the end of the last defense speech) is strange and unnecessary if the narrator is only concerned with the reassurance of Christians. It makes sense, however, if the narrator is presenting Paul as a model of a resourceful missionary who believes in God's promise to Israel and, in spite of opposition, patiently attempts to build a basis for common understanding with Jews. The tendency of interpreters to overlook Paul's christological reticence in the defense scenes results from a failure to study them as a narrative process and rhetorical strategy. This strategy seeks to build a bridge to suspicious outsiders before speaking of Jesus' resurrection. This insight is lost if we immediately interpret all of Paul's references to resurrection in light of the final christological affirmation in the speech before Agrippa. We must attend to what Paul does not say as well as what he says.

Second, we should note that the kind of christological argument from Scripture found in earlier mission speeches to Jews is remarkably absent from Paul's defense speeches. This absence is especially remarkable in the major speeches at the beginning and end of the defense sequence. The speech before Agrippa leads up to a point where argument from Scripture might be appropriate (see 26:27), but the speech itself follows a different strategy. There are general references to Scripture in 24:14 and 26:22, but there is no attempt to mount a scriptural argument that Jesus is the Messiah.

---

[8]See Robert Maddox, *The Purpose of Luke–Acts,* FRLANT 126 (Göttingen: Vandenhoeck & Ruprecht, 1982) 187: Luke "writes to reassure the Christians of his day that their faith in Jesus is no aberration, but the authentic goal towards which God's ancient dealings with Israel were driving."

This fact is hard to explain if the real purpose of these scenes, and of the very Jewish Paul presented in them, is to reassure Christians that they are the true heirs of the scriptural promise. The narrator has no trouble finding Jesus Christ in Scripture, and repeating the church's christological interpretation of Scripture would be effective reassurance for those who share the church's presuppositions. However, it is not effective witness among those likely to reject the church's presuppositions. The strangely circuitous witness that Paul presents in the defense scenes shows awareness of this fact. It also presents Paul as one who is sensitive to his audience in the narrative and concerned to find ways of breaking through the wall that is rapidly rising between Judaism and Christianity.

My argument does not imply that the author of Acts anticipated non-Christian Jews as readers. It does imply that there is a continuing concern in Acts with a mission to Jews, even though relations have been poisoned by conflict. Paul is being presented to Christians as a model from whom later missionaries may learn. This model includes Paul's exemplary efforts to speak even to hostile and suspicious Jews through building a basis for mutual understanding.

Some scholars find an apologetic motive behind the scenes of Paul's defense. They are thinking of an effort to present Christianity favorably to suspicious Roman officials. It is possible that the narrator wishes, among other goals, to supply Christians with themes and an example that will help them respond to suspicious officials,[9] but this theory of political apology does not, by itself, adequately explain the defense scenes. Christians might find it politically advantageous to deny "disrespect for ancient and venerable religious traditions"[10] and claim continuity with Judaism, a religious community that had certain rights in many cities of the eastern Mediterranean.[11] If this is the goal, however, the defense scenes begin by putting the Christian apologist at a strong disadvantage. As I pointed out, the narrator first highlights charges of anti-Judaism against Paul, charges made by both Christian and non-Christian Jews. Paul's speeches are largely a response to these charges. Paul denies them, but in apologetic to Roman

---

[9]This view is more likely than the hypothesis that the author expected Roman officials to read Acts.

[10]See Helmut Koester, *Introduction to the New Testament*, Vol. 2: *History and Literature of Early Christianity* (Philadelphia: Fortress, 1982) 323.

[11]See Robert F. Stoops, Jr., "Riot and Assembly: The Social Context of Acts 19:23-41," *JBL* 108 (1989) 76–79.

officials it would be best to avoid or minimize this conflict, not only because the officials might not understand the details of it but because they would easily understand one detrimental point: many Jews, including Jewish officials recognized by the Romans, deny that Paul and his followers are true Jews. This point is likely to weigh heavily with the Romans. If there is a political benefit in claiming continuity with Judaism, the story of Paul in Acts is not well shaped to secure that benefit, for it highlights the fact that this continuity is contested. The defense scenes, introduced by the Jewish charges in 21:21, 28, speak primarily to suspicious Jews, while an apologetic to Romans would be better presented in a different way. Although the scene of Paul before Agrippa ends with acknowledgment of Paul's innocence, its dramatic climax is not found there nor in an appeal for political tolerance of Christians but in an evangelistic appeal to Agrippa, a relatively unprejudiced Jew (26:25-29). These observations indicate that a concern with political apologetic does not adequately explain the composition of the defense scenes.

The Trials before Felix and Festus

In the trial before Felix the charges against Paul are restated by the orator Tertullus. In this setting the charges have a stronger political accent. Paul is portrayed as the leader of a movement that causes dangerous disturbances in the Roman empire. Then the charge of attempting to defile the temple is added (24:5-6). In his defense speech Paul replies to these charges, but he also returns to the issue of hope and resurrection. He insists that he serves the ancestral God and believes what is written in the law and the prophets, "having a hope in God which these people themselves await, that there will be a resurrection of both righteous and unrighteous" (24:14-15). This statement combines the emphasis on Paul's authentic Jewishness, found in the speech before the Jerusalem crowd, with the theme of hope and resurrection in Paul's statement before the Sanhedrin. We should also note that Paul specifically emphasizes that he shares the expectation of resurrection with his accusers. Paul is deliberately pointing out to his accusers the common ground that he shares with them. He is speaking to them as well as to Felix, and the speech includes the main lines of thought developed in the first two defense scenes, where Paul was addressing Jews.

The theme of resurrection returns a second time at the end of the speech before Felix. Since the Asian Jews are not present to provide evidence about Paul in the temple, let the high priest and elders testify about the only "crime" that they personally witnessed, namely, his outcry in the Sanhedrin, "Concerning resurrection of the dead I am on trial today before you" (24:21). In the course of a short speech Paul twice shifts from rejecting the charges to an emphasis on hope and resurrection, and the speech ends with this emphasis. Paul is still trying to define the main issue of the trial in his own way by emphasizing the hope that he shares with other Jews. This emphasis will become the basis for a shift from defense to missionary witness when Paul appears before Agrippa.

The report of the trial before Felix is followed by a report of Paul's missionary witness to Felix at a later time (24:24-26). Paul, who has been called as Jesus' witness to both Jews and Gentiles, presents his missionary message first to a Gentile ruler and then a Jewish ruler in the course of the defense scenes.

Both the accusations and Paul's reply are much abbreviated in the trial before Festus. The narrator encourages us to assume that the arguments in the trial before Felix were simply repeated before the new governor. When Festus later reports on the trial to Agrippa, however, he mentions that the disputes included "a certain Jesus who had died, whom Paul was claiming to be alive" (25:19). This is the first indication in the defense scenes that Paul's emphasis on resurrection has anything to do with Jesus, and it appears only in a report by Festus. It provides a hint of what is to come in Paul's speech before Agrippa, but it does not preempt the later climax. Through concealing the full significance of the emphasis on hope and resurrection until the final defense speech, the narrator makes the speech before Agrippa a climactic disclosure of Paul's strategy and purpose.

Paul and King Agrippa

The speech before Agrippa is not simply a defense speech. It also provides for the reader a review and summary of Paul's role in the unfolding purpose of God. Furthermore, when Paul's life story reaches the present, Paul shifts adroitly from an account of his past mission to a present missionary witness, which develops into a missionary appeal to Agrippa in the following conversation.

Paul's introductory compliment to King Agrippa indicates that Paul's case requires knowledge of things Jewish, which Agrippa possesses. Paul then proceeds with an autobiographical statement similar to his statement before the crowd in Jerusalem. Again he emphasizes his Jewish roots. Again he speaks of his persecution of Christians. Again he reports the call on the Damascus road that led to his mission. Among the variations from the Jerusalem speech, we should note the more fully developed statement of the mission to which Paul is called (26:16-18) and the report of the fulfillment of this calling (26:19-20). Furthermore, the theme of hope and resurrection, introduced in Acts 23, is inserted into the autobiographical narrative that was first presented in Acts 22. Thus we have a combination of important themes from the first two defense scenes.

At the point where Paul mentions his life as a Pharisee, a digression is inserted (26:6-8), commenting on the hope in resurrection to which Pharisees are committed. Once more Paul asserts that he is on trial for this hope. This hope is presented not as a secondary and optional aspect of Judaism but as central to Jewish existence. It is "hope in the promise made to our fathers by God." It is the hope "to which our twelve tribes, earnestly worshiping night and day, hope to attain." Paul the Pharisee has been consistently loyal to this hope of the Jewish people, while his opponents are strangely inconsistent. What they earnestly desire, the focus of their hope, is rejected when it arrives, and, ironically, the messenger who brings word of fulfillment is accused of being anti-Jewish. The irony is underscored by emphasizing that the very hope that the twelve tribes so earnestly seek is now the cause of accusations against Paul. This is tragic irony because many Jews are in danger of losing what has been promised to them by God. This passage is part of the Lukan story of Israel, which emphasizes the fulfillment of its great hope and then traces a tragic turn away from that fulfillment. This story line stretches from the beginning of Luke to the ending of Acts.[12]

Paul in his defense speeches makes much of this issue of hope and resurrection. This emphasis may seem strange for two reasons: 1) It seems to ignore the real source of controversy between Jews and Christians, the Christian claim that Jesus is the Messiah. 2) The hope for resurrection was not as important in early Judaism as Paul seems to imply. The first of these assumptions dissolves at the end of Paul's speech before Agrippa,

---

[12]See Tannehill, "Israel in Luke–Acts: A Tragic Story," *JBL* 104 (1985) 69–85.

where Paul bears witness to the Messiah who is "first of the resurrection of the dead" (26:23). Here the Christian witness to Jesus, the resurrected Messiah, falls into place, and we realize that the repeated emphasis on hope and resurrection has been preparation for this witness.

There is also a reason why the narrator believes the hope for resurrection to be crucially important for Judaism. If we assume that resurrection of the dead simply means life after death for individuals, we will miss the point. We have already noted that Paul's speech before Agrippa picks up and develops themes from the earlier defense speeches. In order to understand fully the theme of hope and resurrection, we must look even further back in Acts. In this Paul's last major reported speech, he is developing a theme from his first major reported speech, the speech in the synagogue of Pisidian Antioch. The theme of the promise to the Jewish people was central in that speech (13:23, 32-33). The promise concerns the Davidic Messiah, but this promise is tied to resurrection because Jesus is established as ruling Messiah through resurrection and his rule is characterized by resurrection life. In the birth narrative the angel told Mary that Jesus "will rule over the house of Jacob forever, and of his rule there will be no end" (Luke 1:33). Similarly, Paul reminded the Jews in the synagogue that God had made this promise to them: "I will give you the holy things of David which are faithful" (i.e., lasting), for the risen Messiah is no longer subject to "corruption" (Acts 13:34).[13] The Messiah's eternal rule is a result of his resurrection, and others will be freed from corruption to share the benefits of his eternal rule, for the Messiah is only the "first of the resurrection of the dead" (26:23; see also 3:15; 4:2). Thus the hope and promise of which Paul speaks before King Agrippa is not merely a hope for individual life after death but a hope for the Messiah's rule with all its benefits for the Jewish people. This hope is realized through resurrection.

The connection that I am making between the promise to the Jewish people in Paul's first and last major speeches is supported by the repetition of a complex phrase. Both speeches refer to "the promise (ἐπαγγελία) made to the fathers" (13:32; 26:6), with both using the verb γίνομαι and the same word order. It is the same promise,[14] and Paul's synagogue speech

---

[13]On Acts 13:32-35 see Tannehill, *Narrative Unity*, 2.170–72.

[14]The only use of ἐπαγγελία between these two passages is a reference to the Roman tribune's promise in 23:21. Robert O'Toole, *Acts 26: The Christological Climax of Paul's Defense (Ac. 22,1—26,32)*, AnBib 78 (Rome: Pontifical Biblical Institute Press, 1978) 86, notes the similar wording

makes clear that it concerns the Davidic Messiah who will bring to the Jewish people all the benefits of his rule. Thus the intense hope that Paul describes in 26:7 is not confined to an individualistic hope for life after death. It is a hope for the Messiah's promised rule, which is established through resurrection and characterized by resurrection life corporately shared. That is why it is so important to Israel.

After speaking of his call to be the Lord's witness, Paul summarizes his fulfillment of this calling in a mission among Jews and Gentiles. When his life story reaches the present, he says, "I stand bearing witness both to small and to great" concerning the fulfillment of the scriptural promise of the Messiah (26:22-23). The past story of being called to witness merges into the present act of witnessing, and the defense speech becomes a missionary speech. This shift in function is reflected in Paul's language. In 26:6, on the one hand, Paul describes his situation by saying, "I stand being judged" (ἕστηκα κρινόμενος); in 26:22, on the other hand, he says, "I stand bearing witness" (ἕστηκα μαρτυρόμενος). The shift in self-description reflects the shift in the function of the speech.

The missionary aspect of the speech is developed in the following conversation between Paul and Agrippa. Speaking boldly, Paul appeals to Agrippa personally on the basis of belief in the prophets.[15] Paul refers to the prophets because the promise emphasized in Paul's preceding speech can be found in their writings. Agrippa protests that Paul is trying to make a Christian of him too quickly. In his closing remark Paul affirms that it is, indeed, his desire that Agrippa, and the rest of his audience, share the Christian faith. The final and climactic defense scene shows Paul continuing his witness to a Jew on the basis of the prophetic promise to the Jewish people, a witness most fully expressed in the synagogue speech in Pisidian Antioch. Thus the emphasis on the resurrection hope, repeated in the defense scenes since Acts 23, is not only defensive but also evangelistic in purpose, a fact that at first was concealed.

Does the narrator believe that a mission to Jews is still possible, or have the Jews been written off as hopeless? Paul's final statement to the

---

in 13:32 and 26:6 and rightly concludes that the promise realized in the resurrection of Jesus in 13:32f. is the same as the promise in 26:6-8. See also Klaus Haacker, "Das Bekenntnis des Paulus zur Hoffnung Israels," *NTS* 31 (1985) 442.

[15]Agrippa's belief in the prophets and Paul's inclusion of him in the reference to Jewish disbelief in 26:8 (cf. "you") make clear that Agrippa is not only acquainted with Jewish matters but is approached by Paul as a Jew.

Jews in Rome has persuaded many interpreters that no further mission to the Jews is anticipated. In discussing this final scene of Acts elsewhere in my writings,[16] I have tried to show that this is a hasty and unjustified conclusion. To confine myself to one point: the statement that Paul welcomed all who came to him (28:30) should be taken seriously. It means all, whether Gentiles or Jews, for the preceding narrative provides a basis for expecting some Jews among Paul's visitors. The narrator told us that the reaction to Paul's preaching was mixed. Some were being persuaded, although others were disbelieving (28:24). This conflict prevents the Jews from accepting Jesus as a community, which was Paul's goal, but the partially positive response provides a basis for anticipating that some Jews will seek out Paul later. If the narrator's intention at the end of Acts is to say that further mission among Jews is hopeless, inclusion of the statement that some Jews were being persuaded makes no sense, for this statement provides a ground for hope of fruitful mission. It indicates that some Jews are still open to the Christian message. Probably the narrator recognizes that mission preaching to a Jewish community, the kind of preaching that Paul did in synagogues and at Rome, is no longer possible, but there is still hope that Jewish individuals can be reached. Paul's speech before Agrippa not only defends Paul from Jewish criticism but also suggests how Jews might still be reached, in spite of the accusations that they are making against Paul and the Christian movement.

Thus Paul is in part a model for later evangelists in his speech before Agrippa. The use of Paul as a model for the later church is nothing new in Acts. In the section of Acts that most clearly refers to the post-Pauline church, Paul's farewell address to the Ephesian elders, Paul is presented as a model for church leaders. Paul is a model not only in his refusal to take church support but also in his work as a pastor. When he mentions the coming troubles that church leaders will face, Paul also reminds them of his own dedicated work as a pastor (20:29-31). The elders must show the same dedication in order to preserve the church. Earlier in the same speech Paul reminded the church leaders of his dedicated work of witnessing both to Jews and Greeks (20:20-21). The way that Paul is presented in Acts suggests that he is a model in this respect, too. This is the impression made by the final verses of Acts, which present Paul, in spite of Roman imprisonment and Jewish rejection, boldly carrying on his witness to all

---

[16]See Tannehill, *Narrative Unity*, 2.346–53.

who would come to him. The speech before Agrippa is a fuller dramatic presentation of Paul witnessing to a Jew in spite of the same difficult circumstances. Agrippa is not only a high official who can testify to Paul's innocence but also represents the individual Jews who might still be reached by the Christian mission.

This persistence in mission is necessary if the narrator is to be faithful to the vision of God's saving purpose announced at the beginning of Luke and periodically reaffirmed thereafter. When Simeon received the baby Jesus in the temple, he spoke prophetically of God's salvation prepared for all the peoples, both the Gentiles and Israel (Luke 2:30-32), and his words were supported by the reference in Luke 3:6 to "all flesh" seeing the salvation of God. As the narrative unfolds, it becomes clear that this salvation for Jews and Gentiles is to be concretely realized through the missions of Jesus and his witnesses. Therefore, the mission of Paul must include both Jews and Gentiles, as the commissioning words in the three Damascus road scenes make clear (Acts 9:15; 22:15; 26:17, 23). Paul's words of bitter pathos at the end of Acts show that the Jews converted so far are not a satisfactory fulfillment of God's saving purpose for Israel. Since the narrator recognizes no other way in which God is now working for Israel's salvation (cf. 4:12), continuation of a mission to Jews is a theological necessity in order that God's saving purpose may be realized.

Theological Postscript

Modern Christians will react in different ways to this story of missionary commitment. Some will understand it as a call to continue an evangelistic mission to the Jewish people. Others will affirm the Lukan vision of God's salvation for all people, Jews and Gentiles, but also acknowledge that the long painful history of Jews and Christians, together with the continuing vitality of non-Christian religion, has changed the situation substantially. These Christians need not deny that they still have good news to announce, but they will do it more humbly, recognizing that mission must now become dialogue in which Christians have as much to learn as to teach about the various ways that the peoples of the world encounter the saving power of God.[17]

---

[17]See Michael Barnes, *Christian Identity and Religious Pluralism: Religions in Conversation* (Nashville: Abingdon, 1989).

Part IV

Hermeneutical Experiments

14
Should We Love Simon the Pharisee? Reflections on the Pharisees in Luke

In this essay I begin to consider the important role of the reader (or hearer) and recognize that the reader has considerable freedom, even when he or she wishes to respect the text. I also discuss the ethical implications of that freedom.

How should we as readers understand the Pharisees in Luke–Acts (a character group that is commonly viewed as a negative stereotype)? I discuss both the debate over the Pharisees in Luke–Acts as a whole and the particular case of Simon the Pharisee in Luke 7:36–50. I argue that the text permits us to view Simon as an "open" character, one who is not totally evil and is capable of change. Therefore the text does not prevent us from recognizing that Simon is a "neighbor" whom we must love.

Recent literary interpretation of the Gospels may avoid old issues about historical accuracy, but in its own way it seems to rob the Gospels of their innocence. Rather than simply telling stories about Jesus which are "natural" because "that's just the way it was," the new literary criticism explores the subtle ways in which literature advocates "ideological" positions. In presenting characters in the narrative, the Gospels seldom take a neutral stance.

The Pharisees in Luke, for instance, frequently resist what Jesus says and does, and since the Gospel of Luke is so strongly pro-Jesus, a negative view of the Pharisees seems the inevitable result. Does Luke as a literary work necessarily cause negative stereotyping of the Pharisees, if we accede to its point of view? If by negative stereotyping we mean viewing people as having only negative traits that are unlikely to change, I would say that this is a possible but not a necessary result of Lukan descriptions of the Pharisees. The text does not constrain the respectful reader to negative stereotyping. It leaves the reader a significant area of freedom in interpreting characters.

Stereotyping, then, becomes an issue of how we read, and how we read becomes an ethical test. The way that we treat people in daily life may not be exactly the same as the way that we interpret characters in a story, but there is likely to be significant overlap. If we are content with prejudice in the one case, we are more likely to show prejudice in the other. Awareness of this possibility should make us more careful preachers. I will explore this issue first in relation to recent studies of the Pharisees in Luke–Acts and then by focusing on the story of the sinful woman in the Pharisee's house (Luke 7:36-50).

There has been considerable debate in recent scholarship over Luke's view of the Pharisees. J. A. Ziesler, working within a redaction-critical perspective and so emphasizing Luke's differences from Matthew and Mark, concludes that Luke "finds it possible to depict them [the Pharisees] favourably at least in part."[1] More recently Robert Brawley has argued that Luke responds to Jewish antagonism not only with apologetic but also with efforts at conciliation. Reflecting this, "the Gospel already tends to present the Pharisees in comparatively favorable light," while "in Acts, Pharisees and Christians are kindred spirits."[2] Jack T. Sanders goes so far as to accuse Luke–Acts of anti-Semitism, yet his treatment of the Pharisees is not completely negative, for, in Sanders' opinion, the Pharisees who oppose Jesus on *halakah* are representatives of "traditionally Jewish Christians" and "the friendly, non-Christian Pharisees in Acts underscore

---

[1] "Luke and the Pharisees," *NTS* 25 (1978–79) 156.
[2] *Luke–Acts and the Jews: Conflict, Apology, and Conciliation,* SBLMS 33 (Atlanta: Scholars, 1987) 84, 155.

the linkage between Christianity and the ancestral Israelite religion."[3] According to David Gowler, "The portrait of the Pharisees in Luke is primarily negative, whereas the portrait of the Pharisees in Acts is primarily positive." In Luke "signs of hope occur infrequently, but overall their characterization is rigorously closed off. They reject the purpose of God for themselves. . . . Yet in Acts the various levels of response to Christianity generate a sense of openness" and hope for the Pharisees.[4]

Two other scholars interpret Luke's portrait of the Pharisees as more consistently negative. According to Jack Dean Kingsbury, the religious authorities have the role of "antagonists" in Luke's story. They can be treated as a "group character," for "they are the stereotypical opponents of Jesus."[5] Kingsbury denies that Luke is more favorable toward the Pharisees than Matthew or Mark, even in Acts. Thus Luke's comment that the Pharisees have "rejected the purpose of God" (Luke 7:30) "is of programmatic significance."[6] John Darr reaches similar conclusions by studying Lukan characterization from the perspective of reader-response criticism. Like other reader-response critics, Darr discusses how the reader interacts with the text as the story unfolds sequentially. The reader must "build" the characters, guided by the narrator. That is, the reader must fit the bits of information into a consistent pattern to provide an overall understanding of a person or group. The interpreter must respect the "linearity" of the reading process. Failure to do this has led to misinterpretation of the Pharisees in Luke–Acts. Early in Luke they are introduced in strongly negative terms, and this beginning will condition the reader's understanding of the Pharisees through the rest of the story. The "derogatory image of the Pharisees" is "nearly indelible"; therefore, we cannot speak of a positive view of the Pharisees even in Acts.[7] I think Darr poses the issue in a helpful way, namely, as an issue of *reading*.

---

[3] *The Jews in Luke–Acts* (Philadelphia: Fortress, 1987) 97.

[4] *Host, Guest, Enemy and Friend: Portraits of the Pharisees in Luke and Acts,* ESEC 2 (New York: Lang, 1991) 301, 314.

[5] *Conflict in Luke* (Minneapolis: Fortress, 1991) 21–22.

[6] Kingsbury, "The Pharisees in Luke–Acts," in *The Four Gospels 1992: Festschrift Frans Neirynck,* ed. F. Van Segbroeck et al. (Leuven: Leuven University Press, 1992) 1497–512; quotation on p. 1510.

[7] *On Character Building: The Reader and the Rhetoric of Characterization in Luke–Acts,* LCBI (Louisville: Westminster John Knox, 1992) 37–59, 85–126; quotation on p. 125.

Therefore, I will follow his initiative, even though I will modify his conclusions.[8]

We must first admit that there is considerable truth in the negative interpretation of the Pharisees in Luke. They are introduced with great regularity as opponents of Jesus and his teaching. This has a rhetorical function. It is the narrator's way of emphasizing certain issues by presenting them as matters of controversy and a way of contrasting Jesus' position with the position of others, making Jesus' teaching stand out sharply. The contrast not only heightens the reader's awareness of the radical implications of Jesus' words but also suggests that a choice must be made. Thus the Pharisees' role as opponents of Jesus contributes to a rhetoric of decision that is an integral part of the Lukan message. If Jesus had no opponents, his words would have less impact. It is also convenient for the narrator to be able to address dangers in the church by depicting them in the Pharisees.[9] The fact that the Pharisees are regularly given the role of opponents inevitably influences their characterization in Luke. If this role completely dominates their characterization in Luke, they are simply negative stereotypes. Their humanness has been sacrificed for the Gospel's rhetorical purposes.

But that may depend on whether the text requires us to read as Darr reads. Since the reader is so important in Darr's approach, we must understand how he constructs this reader. The reader must be constructed from the text (the text anticipates a particular kind of reader, one for whom this text will be understandable and meaningful) and the extratext (a body of knowledge that constitutes the "cultural literacy" that may be assumed for the time and place of writing). Nevertheless, this reader is always to some extent the modern reader who is trying to read the text through this reconstructed ancient reader.[10] With this I have no quarrel, except that an author, then and now, must anticipate a range of readers who will differ somewhat in opinion and social location. It is a somewhat dangerous simplification to speak of *the* reader. This observation will require

---

[8] Other studies of the Pharisees in Luke–Acts that should be consulted: John T. Carroll, "Luke's Portrayal of the Pharisees," *CBQ* 50 (1988) 604–21; Mark Allan Powell, "The Religious Leaders in Luke: A Literary-Critical Study," *JBL* 109 (1990) 93–110.

[9] Brian Beck provides a good discussion of Luke's use of the Pharisees to warn the church against similar attitudes; see *Christian Character in the Gospel of Luke* (London: Epworth, 1989) 127–44.

[10] Darr, *On Character Building*, 25–29.

us to be more cautious than Darr in stating how the reader will respond to particular developments in the narrative. Since we must think of a range of readers, we must also consider a range of possible responses. The difference in social position among members of first-century churches is one important factor to be considered.[11] Since the reader's social position, as well as unpredictable individual traits, affects the reading experience, we must recognize that the text has limited control over the responses of its readers.

When we consider the reader's appropriation of narrative for her or his own life, we must distinguish narrative from law or doctrine. Narrative tells about another time and place; it does not generalize about all times and places. Its relevance to the present is indirect, suggestive. It is the reader's responsibility to apply the story to the present with appropriate cautions and adjustments. With respect to stereotyped characters, this may require recognizing that stereotypes, while useful in instruction, are not real people. At most they reveal some aspects of real people. Furthermore, even when we ignore questions of relevance and consider only the story as such, we should recognize that there are huge gaps in the Lukan narrative.[12] We are not told the complete life story of anyone, certainly not of the Pharisees. They appear only in a few brief scenes. The relative consistency of their role may give us some sense of persistent character, yet this need not preclude the possibility of change. Indeed, we encounter not just a group but individuals, like Simon the Pharisee in Luke 7:36-50, yet we are told nothing of his life story before and after the one scene in which he appears. Developments before and after might change our attitude toward him, and there is a significant gap within the scene itself that could affect our view of Simon. The Pharisees are without possibilities only if we choose to ignore the gaps that the narrative has left to test our imaginations.

Darr emphasizes that reading is linear; we must follow the narrative in sequence if we are to understand its effect. He chooses to focus on the

---

[11] I have tried to suggest the significance of this for a reading perspective in an article entitled "'Cornelius' and 'Tabitha' Encounter Luke's Jesus," *Int* 48 (1994) 347–56.

[12] Darr is aware that the reader must fill gaps in the narrative in order to make sense of it and illustrates this by the story in Luke 7:36-50 that I will consider later. However, he does not notice the gap in the story that I will discuss below, and this affects his understanding of Simon the Pharisee. See *On Character Building*, 18–20, 32–35.

experience of the first-time reader, who must try to understand the characters in a scene in light of the information given about those characters up to that point in the narrative (not later, for that is not yet part of the reading experience). It is true that reading narrative requires us to combine what we read about characters into some overall pattern of meaning and that our understanding of a character at some point in the narrative will be influenced by what the narrator has told us up to that point.

But we cannot be sure in advance (and sometimes not in retrospect) how the previous narrative should be used to interpret the next scene, for the linearity of reading need not imply that the same characters will always do the same thing. If it did mean that, linearity would be a formula for producing stereotypes in reading. What we have learned previously may serve to set off a development as *new*, contrasting with previous actions of these characters. Or the next scene may be partly similar and partly different, enriching the portrait of the characters. In various ways our previous reading contributes to our experience of the story, but it will be a boring story if the narrator simply repeats what we were told previously about the characters.

These remarks are relevant to the role of the Pharisees in Acts. The narrative in Acts reckons with significant new events: the resurrection of Jesus, its public announcement by the apostles, and the Spirit's coming to the church. It is legitimate, then, for the reader to wonder whether these events open new possibilities for the Pharisees. The logic of the narrative does not require them to act as they did in Luke.[13] And if they are no longer rigid opponents in Acts, they were not as hopeless in Luke as they might have seemed.

A strong statement of a group's opposition can serve to highlight the contrasting behavior of an exceptional individual. In the interrogation of Jesus before the Jewish council in Jerusalem, the opposition to Jesus appears to be unanimous, for "all" ask Jesus whether he is the Son of God, and, hearing his reply, "they said, 'Why do we still have need of testimony?'" Then "their whole assembly brought him to Pilate" (Luke 22:70—23:1). It is a surprise when we later discover that Joseph of Arimathea, a member of the council, did not agree with its decision (23:50-51). Even seemingly

---

[13] This is a response to Kingsbury's argument that Gamaliel in Acts 5:33-39 cannot be open to the possibility that the apostles' mission is from God, for he was part of the Sanhedrin that condemned Jesus. See "The Pharisees in Luke–Acts," 1506.

clear and sweeping statements about opponents may be modified later in the narrative.

Other religious authorities in Luke may not be as favorably described as Joseph of Arimathea (who, the narrator says, was a "good and righteous man"), but, even when suspicious or critical, they sometimes agree with Jesus on important points, and the scene can end without the religious authorities rejecting Jesus' statements. In these scenes the final reaction of the religious authorities is still open; they could react either positively or negatively. Consider the case of the "lawyer" (νομικός) in Luke 10:25-37. "Lawyers" are also mentioned in 11:45, and 11:53 shows that this is another name for the scribes. When the Pharisees are first introduced in 5:17, they are accompanied by "teachers of the law" (νομοδιδάσκαλοι). These, too, are scribes, for the scene continues by referring to "the scribes and the Pharisees" (5:21). These teachers of the law or scribes are repeatedly associated with the Pharisees in their first appearances in Luke (5:17, 21, 30; 6:7), and they show the same opposition to Jesus. They may have a different social role than the Pharisees, but their initial attitude toward Jesus is the same. It is not surprising, then, that the lawyer in 10:25 is suspicious of Jesus and wishes to "test him," nor that he wishes to "justify himself" in 10:29 (compare the Pharisees in 16:14-15). Nevertheless, the scene does not present the lawyer as lacking all religious insight, and Jesus does not respond to him as a hardened opponent for whom there is no hope. Unlike Matthew and Mark, in Luke it is not Jesus but the inquiring religious leader who quotes the double love commandment as summary of the law. Jesus readily agrees with the lawyer. This, of course, leads to the question, "Who is my neighbor?" (10:29), but Jesus and the lawyer begin their discussion in fundamental agreement. Furthermore, after the story of the Good Samaritan, the lawyer correctly answers Jesus' question, showing that he has understood the parable. Therefore, when the scene ends with Jesus' command, "Go and do likewise," it is possible for us to imagine that the lawyer has a new understanding of the command to love neighbor and will begin to treat non-Jews differently.

Commenting on a recent collection of essays on "Characterization in Biblical Literature," Robert Fowler wrote, "Most of these authors want to break away from static or monolithic views of characters. Most want to crack characters open, to give them some wriggle room, to allow for fluidity and multiplicity in characterization."[14] This is a welcome development, I

---

[14] Robert M. Fowler, "Characterizing Character in Biblical Narrative," *Semeia* 63 (1993) 97. Moreover, several scholars have recently argued that characters in ancient literature, contrary to

think. Contributing to these essays, David McCracken emphasized the tendency of biblical narrators to present characters "on a threshold," i.e., "at a potential turning point," so that "their responses are unpredictable and unknowable until the moment when they respond to the words addressed to them."[15] The lawyer who hears the parable of the Good Samaritan is "on a threshold," and the narrator leaves him there. The scene begins with the lawyer's suspicious testing of Jesus; it ends with a new possibility.

If we pay attention to the setting in which Jesus tells the story of the Prodigal Son, we will find the situation to be very similar. "The Pharisees and the scribes were grumbling" because Jesus was welcoming sinners and eating with them (Luke 15:2). In response to this criticism, Jesus tells three parables, with the Prodigal Son as the climactic member of the group. In Luke's narrative setting the sinners whom Jesus welcomed are mirrored by the younger son and the Pharisees and scribes by the elder son, who objects to the father's welcome of his younger brother. In light of this, it is striking that the father shows as much concern for the elder son as for the younger. He leaves the party in order to urge his elder son to share in it. He reassures his angry son by saying, "You are always with me, and all that is mine is yours" (15:31). Then Jesus leaves the elder son on a threshold. The story breaks off at the dramatic moment of decision as we wait to learn the elder son's response to his father's appeal. The Pharisees and scribes are also left on a threshold. Their importance is affirmed in the parable. They have heard the father's earnest appeal, but their response is not indicated.

We see, then, that the Pharisees and other Jewish leaders are regularly presented in conflict with Jesus, but there are also scenes that hold open for them the possibility of insight and change. Such people are more than stereotypical opponents, for growth remains a possibility. This is also true of Simon the Pharisee in Luke 7:36-50, but before discussing him, I want to respect Darr's request that we interpret characters by reading the narrative in sequence. What are we told about the Pharisees in Luke that might

the supposition of some interpreters, are not necessarily simple, static types. See David Gowler, *Host*, 77–176; Fred Burnett, "Characterization and Reader Construction of Characters in the Gospels," *Semeia* 63 (1993) 6–19.

[15] "Character in the Boundary: Bakhtin's Interdividuality in Biblical Narratives," *Semeia* 63 (1993) 32.

influence our understanding of them when we come to the story of Simon the Pharisee?

The Pharisees are introduced at the beginning of a series of controversy stories. There are several significant differences between the Lukan version of these stories and the parallels in Mark. Most remarkable is the fact that the first scene is set in Luke by noting the presence of "Pharisees and teachers of the law who had come from every village of Galilee and Judea and Jerusalem" (5:17). This introduction indicates that the Pharisees show a high degree of interest in Jesus; it also allows Pharisees from every part of the Jewish homeland to witness the healing of the paralyzed man and to ponder its implications. The scene involves conflict, for the scribes and Pharisees object to Jesus' claim to forgive sins. Nevertheless, "Amazement seized all" who witnessed the healing, "and they were glorifying God" (5:26). Presumably the large group of Pharisees and scribes is included. They are not yet hardened opponents.

However, the following scenes reinforce their role as objectors to Jesus' and the disciples' actions. "The Pharisees and their scribes" grumble when Jesus and the disciples eat with tax collectors and sinners (5:30). They also object to Jesus' disciples feasting while others are fasting (5:33). "Some of the Pharisees" accuse the disciples of breaking the Sabbath by plucking grain (6:2), and on another Sabbath "the scribes and the Pharisees" are watching Jesus in order to find a basis for an accusation (6:7). The last statement shows a significant increase in hostility. The Pharisees have learned Jesus' views about the Sabbath. Now they are contemplating action against him. Furthermore, this scene ends with a clear negative reaction to what Jesus has been saying and doing: "They were filled with fury and were discussing with one another what they might do to Jesus" (6:11). Now we seem to have hardened opposition that is willing to take action to remove Jesus.

Yet no action results. We next hear of the Pharisees in 7:30. In contrast to the people and the tax collectors, "The Pharisees and lawyers rejected the purpose of God for themselves, not having been baptized by" John. This is a direct statement about the Pharisees and lawyers by the narrator (not one of the characters in the story), and since most narrative critics believe that the biblical narratives use a "reliable narrator" (not one like Huck Finn, whom we are supposed to recognize as biased and ignorant), this statement would seem to be clear indication of the Lukan view of the Pharisees. Furthermore, Luke–Acts is very concerned with the realization of "the purpose of God," which is salvation for both Jew and Gentile.[16] To reject it is a very serious matter. Yet Meir Sternberg wisely warns us that, in the Hebrew Bible (and I would apply this to Luke–Acts), the narrator tells the truth but not the whole truth. Sternberg explains that the narrator's "statements . . . are rarely complete, falling much short of what his elliptical text suggests between the lines. His *ex cathedra* judgments are valid as far as they go, but then they seldom go far below the surface of the narrative, where they find their qualification and shading."[17] We have already noted that there is some later "qualification and shading" in Luke's presentation of the religious authorities.

After the narrator's remark about the Pharisees in 7:30, Jesus speaks of those who reject him because he is a "glutton and a drunkard, a friend of tax collectors and sinners" (7:34). Does the story of Simon the Pharisee that follows illustrate this reference to rejection of Jesus because he is a friend of sinners? Yes, but it also provides "qualification and shading."

Careful study of this story shows that it is rhetorically shaped to highlight the words of Jesus so that they will make a strong impact on the reader or hearer. As soon as the scene is set, our attention is focused on the woman and her unusual actions. She provokes a response from Simon and then from Jesus. Simon's response is given first so that Jesus can comment upon it. In v. 40 Jesus takes control of the scene in order to defend the woman and set Simon straight. The rhetorical shaping of the scene by the narrator is clear when we notice that it is built upon contrasts. Simon and Jesus make contrasting judgments about the woman. But the woman and Simon also behave in contrasting ways toward Jesus. This contrast is reserved for the climax of Jesus' short speech. We are not told at the beginning of the scene, where we might expect it, how Simon received Jesus. We are only told this by Jesus as he contrasts, point by point, Simon's limited hospitality with the woman's extravagant acts of love (vv. 44-46). The contrast is then summarized in v. 47 as the forgiveness of many sins leading to great love, while little forgiveness yields only little

---

[16] On the importance of God's saving purpose for understanding Luke–Acts as a unified narrative, see Robert C. Tannehill, *The Narrative Unity of Luke–Acts: A Literary Interpretation*, 2 vols. (Philadelphia & Minneapolis: Fortress, 1986, 1990) 1.2–3, 21–22, 40–42.

[17] Meir Sternberg, *The Poetics of Biblical Narrative: Ideological Literature and the Drama of Reading*, ISBL (Bloomington: Indiana University Press, 1985) 51.

love.[18] Finally, Jesus turns to the woman and reassures her in light of the social condemnation she risks in acting as she has.

It is clear that Simon is to some extent a foil who, in making a negative judgment about Jesus and the woman in v. 39, provides the occasion for Jesus to make the opposite case. It is also clear that Jesus is the figure of authority in the scene and that the narrator assumes that Jesus carries the day. Nevertheless, the scene does not reduce Simon to a caricature, a mere collection of negative qualities that invites neither sympathy nor hope. Note the following:

1. The very facts that Jesus' previous encounters with Pharisees in 5:17—6:11 ended with a high degree of conflict and the negative picture of the Pharisees was reinforced in 7:30 make it surprising that a Pharisee would invite Jesus to dinner. Here, it seems, we have a Pharisee who has not yet formed a negative opinion of Jesus.

2. When he does express a negative opinion in v. 39, he says, "If this man were a prophet. . . ." This reflects the crowd's statement about Jesus in 7:16. We can also take it as an indication of Simon's motive in inviting Jesus. That is, one way of filling a gap in this narrative (Why did Simon invite Jesus?) is to assume Simon had heard that some view Jesus as a prophet and wanted to find out for himself. Thus the connection between 7:16 and 39 allows us to view Simon as initially open to recognizing Jesus as a prophet.

3. When the Pharisee cannot square Jesus' contact with the woman with the claim that he is a prophet, Jesus turns to him and addresses him by his name, "Simon." It is unusual for a character who appears in only one scene in the Gospels to be named. Here the scene takes on the intimate quality of direct, one-on-one encounter, and readers are encouraged to view Jesus' dialogue partner not merely in light of group characteristics ("one of the Pharisees") but as an individual. This opens possibilities in the narrative. Will the expectations attached to the group guide events, or will individual characteristics prove to be more important? As we will see, the narrator leaves this question open.

---

[18] There is an ambiguity in the Greek of v. 47. I believe that "because she loved much" in v. 47 expresses the cause of knowing that she has been forgiven rather than the cause of forgiveness. To make acts of love the cause rather than the result of forgiveness conflicts both with the preceding parable and the following statement about little love.

4. Jesus does not simply condemn Simon but helps him to understand. He begins with a parable, which can put a new perspective on the situation by looking at it indirectly through a comparable case. Simon participates in the interpretation of the parable by answering Jesus' question in v. 42, and he answers correctly. By his parable and question Jesus is trying to teach and persuade, not simply condemn. This remains true in vv. 44-47, even though these verses imply criticism of Simon. We might add that Jesus is not Simon's only teacher in vv. 44-47, for, we might say, Jesus is trying to get Simon to accept the woman as his teacher. "Do you see this woman?" he says. She has something to teach you about forgiveness and love.

5. There is a crucial gap at the end of the scene. We are not told how Simon responded to Jesus' persuasive speech. Simon is left "on a threshold," and we can imagine either that he rejects what Jesus has said or that he begins to understand and agree. There are no clear indications of either outcome in vv. 40-50. In v. 49 we do find a reaction from the dinner guests to Jesus' statement to the woman in v. 48. The question "Who is this who even forgives sins?" is an echo of the objection of scribes and Pharisees in 5:21, but it is not as sharply formulated. It could express rejection or just surprise. It is also not clear whether Simon is to be included in those responding in v. 49. The narrator leaves us to ponder how Simon might have responded. Simon's characterization hangs on that response.

The issue of whether Simon is an "open" character or merely a negative stereotype is worth arguing because it affects the story's use in preaching. If he is a negative stereotype, we are simply being asked to reject Simon and what he stands for. If he is an open character, the hearer's relation to Simon may be more complex. Members of first-century churches, and members of churches today, even though they want to identify with Jesus' position, may recognize that they are like Simon. Here the factor of social position, and religion's possible role in social position, must be recognized. Simon is a person of high social standing in his society, and he shuns contact with a woman who is a social outcast. Those who are not social outcasts (the majority of church members today) must recognize that this fact distinguishes them from the woman and places them with Simon in the story. A completely negative picture of Simon will block this salutary recognition, but if Simon is teachable, we can listen with him and learn what he needs to learn. The lesson is not necessarily that we, too, are sinful outcasts (an outcast is defined by *social* position); it concerns our response to outcasts. Jesus says, "Do you see this woman?" Learn from her. You, whose experience of sin is rather mild because it has not meant *social* alienation, can learn from her the depth of God's forgiveness and the resulting power of love. This lesson we must learn if Jesus is to be our guest, for when Jesus comes to our homes, the sinful woman comes, too. It is a package deal. We can't accept Jesus without accepting the outcast whom Jesus forgives, not as a second-class citizen in the church but as one whose experience is vital to our own understanding of God.

Simon is defined by his contrast with the sinful woman and also by his initial conflict with Jesus. These contrasts are important for the story's function; they sharpen the hearer's awareness of a decision that must be made by the hearer. But the story does more than draw sharp distinctions. Simon is a complex character and awakens a complex response. Because Simon resists Jesus and his message, the story encourages Jesus' followers to move away from this resistance, but some of Jesus' followers must also recognize that Simon represents their own social position and religious experience (little forgiveness and little love). Therefore, the way to move away from Simon's resistance is to learn with Simon what Jesus is trying to teach him. It is important that we view Simon as an open character with possibilities for growth, for this helps us recognize our resistance and our possibilities. The story, I believe, could work in a similar way in the setting of the early church.

I began this essay by discussing certain developments in the literary criticism of Luke that have, in some cases, led to strongly negative interpretations of the Pharisees. Negative stereotyping, I have argued, is a reading strategy that is not required by the text of Luke, where there is enough shading and sufficient gaps to produce complex and open characters, if we respond with sympathetic imagination. This discussion has implications for preaching. If the Gospel text presents the Pharisees as negative stereotypes, it is difficult to fault preachers for doing the same. If, however, this is not the necessary effect of the text but the result of ways of reading that do not engage our better selves, then preachers can and should stop treating the Pharisees as merely negative stereotypes, for this robs the Gospel stories of some of their power and value for the church.

Augustine proposed the following hermeneutical principle: We find the true understanding of Scripture and its parts when we discover how it builds the love of God and the love of our neighbor.[19] This principle can easily be misused to deny the difficulties and variety in Scripture. Nevertheless, taking this definition of the center of Scripture as a guide to reading can produce helpful reflection. In much of the biblical narrative it is up to us as readers whether our reading will be guided by the love of neighbor. Our reading of the brief story about Simon the Pharisee and the sinful woman is a case in point. Do we in our reading and interpretation show our love for both Simon and the woman?

---

[19] Augustine, *On Christian Doctrine*, translated by D. W. Robertson, Jr., Library of Liberal Arts 80 (New York: Liberal Arts, 1958) 30.

15

Freedom and Responsibility in Scripture Interpretation

This essay expands on comments in "Should We Love Simon the Pharisee?" with general hermeneutical reflections on indeterminacy in biblical narrative. I present six reasons why narratives like the Gospel of Luke do not and cannot fully control the responses of readers. These observations highlight the freedom of interpreters but also their ethical responsibility, for interpretations can benefit or oppress other persons.

Among other factors, I briefly discuss the influence of varying reconstructions of historical contexts on interpretation. These thoughts are expanded and applied to recent interpretation of First Corinthians in Robert C. Tannehill, "Paul as Liberator and Oppressor: How Should We Evaluate Diverse Views of First Corinthians?" in Charles H. Cosgrove, editor, The Meanings We Choose: Hermeneutical Ethics, Indeterminacy and the Conflict of Interpretations, *JSOTSup (London: T & T Clark, 2004) 122–37.*

The journal *Semeia* has recently devoted two volumes to the issue of textual determinacy or indeterminacy.[1] The leading question, as stated by Robert

---

[1] See *Semeia* 62 (1993) and *Semeia* 71 (1995), edited by Robert C. Culley and Robert B. Robinson.

Culley, is "to what extent and in what manner do texts determine and control their interpretation and to what extent and in what manner is meaning determined by factors lying outside the text in the reading process?"[2] Both the recent emphasis on reading as an active process and an increased willingness to accept multiple readings of the same text lead to this question. There is increasing recognition that, in reading, we are doing something more than absorbing, in pristine fashion, information encoded in the text. In reading we are actively responding to the text's codes, which otherwise remain mute. This recognition need not lead to the extreme view that we can make whatever we want of a text, which would imply that we are communicating only with ourselves. It does imply, however, that we have some freedom, and with it some responsibility, for our interpretive responses to a text. This is true even when we take account of the text's early historical and social context.

The issue becomes important for the conflict between those who approach Scripture with a hermeneutics of suspicion, determined to expose its inadequate ideologies, and those who, in some sense, attribute authority to Scripture in their religious and ethical life. When the first group tells the second group that the real purpose of the text is to promote an oppressive ideology, and makes this point from a position of academic prestige, the pressure of academic authority is being brought to bear on those who read Scripture differently.[3] I do not wish to defend naive readings of Scripture or simple-minded theologies, and I recognize that growth often comes through an appropriate challenge from helpful teachers who share alternative perspectives with their students. I realize that naive readings often ignore valuable parts of the text and neglect important issues. One can also make the valid point that the Bible has been used to oppress people and that some of its content makes that possible. We should not, however, move from this valid point to the implication that some biblical texts are inherently texts of oppression, if their true significance is recognized, without considering the various kinds of indeterminacy in the texts, which offer us some freedom to find good in texts that could be oppressive.

---

[2] Robert C. Culley, "Introduction," *Semeia* 62 (1993) vii.

[3] Daniel Patte has written sensitively about this issue. See *Ethics of Biblical Interpretation: A Reevaluation* (Louisville: Westminster John Knox, 1995) 73–107.

[4] For instance, I would not accept the prohibitions against women speaking in the assemblies or having authority over men that we find in 1 Cor 14:34-35 and 1 Tim 2:11-14.

To be sure, there probably are cases in which we must reject the message of the text if we are to affirm human good for the modern world.[4] I believe it is possible to find biblical warrant for this critical reading of the Bible. When approached in a particular way, the Bible can be self-policing (see the section below on Varying Views of the Center of Scripture). The main argument of this article, however, asserts that the texts grant us more freedom than we commonly recognize, which we can and should use responsibly. In my understanding, to use this freedom responsibly means that we seek to find in sacred texts, whenever possible, a benefit for humanity (including the benefit of promoting harmony with God). In some cases the assumption that the text forces us to a negative conclusion about its significance is the result of insensitivity to the text's possibilities. The problem is not in pointing out that the text may have a negative significance, when used in a particular way, but in implying that this negative reading is the one true way to understand the text.

Gospel Stories as "Works of Art"

Literary studies of the Bible have moved away from aesthetic perspectives. It is useful to return to some of these perspectives for our discussion of freedom and responsibility in interpretation.

When I wrote *The Sword of His Mouth*, I borrowed from Ray L. Hart's discussion of imagination and the work of art.[5] The art object, Hart explains, is something less than the work of art. The art object is a work of imagination with designs on an answering imagination. It is designed to provoke an imaginative response, that is, a response in which the imagination of the viewer, which is often dormant, becomes awake and active. It is only through the answering imagination of the viewer that the art object functions as a work of art. Thus the art object seeks completion in the answering imagination of the viewer. Hart also explains that the imagination is the means by which the self can be transformed and grow. In the imagination new possibilities present themselves, and we become fascinated with them. When the imagination is dormant, we are stuck in

---

[5] *The Sword of His Mouth: Forceful and Imaginative Language in Synoptic Sayings,* Semeia Supplements 1 (Philadelphia: Fortress; Missoula, Mont.: Scholars, 1975) 21–28. See Ray L. Hart, *Unfinished Man and the Imagination* (New York: Herder and Herder, 1968).

our routines. It is doubtful that religious language can be transformative at a deep level unless it engages the imagination.

The component units of the synoptic Gospels are mostly short and simple. Yet the pronouncement stories and aphorisms display an artful sense of literary form, and they are joined as parts of a larger art object, a Gospel. The Gospels and their parts are also rhetorical. While the New Critics wanted to draw a sharp line between literary art and rhetoric, it is not possible to do so. Gospel sayings and stories are designed to provoke commitment and action, but they often make their appeal through forceful and imaginative language designed to jolt the imagination, sacrificing clarity in the process. It is important to note that the command not to be anxious about food and clothing (Luke 12:22-31) uses an elaborate repetitive pattern built around two concrete images (ravens and lilies) and reinforced by strong contrast and strong diction. These observations supply the clue that the purpose of these words is not merely to guide behavior but to transform our imaginative perception of reality so that our behavior may change.[6] The imagination is the door through which a new perception of reality may enter, transforming our commitments, values, and actions.

A sensitive response follows the lines of provocation in the text. The imagination is not being aimlessly stimulated but is being led in a particular direction. The brevity and simplicity of many synoptic scenes contribute to this direction. Much remains unsaid in order to direct attention to what is said. What is said leads the hearer to construct an imaginative scene, and this imaginative scene is able to provoke imaginative thought on a particular issue or situation that is highlighted in the scene. Because the scene is briefly sketched, much is left to the hearer or reader. Jesus' words, as reported in the Gospels, are often aphoristic, metaphorical, and hyperbolic, appealing to the imagination. Thereby his words gain transformative power but renounce precise control. They are powerfully suggestive but ignore important details about application. Furthermore, any message for the hearer or reader is indirect. We are reading a story about other people and another time; Jesus is not talking directly to us. The reader must work out the right response in imaginative thought. Thus the reader has both freedom and responsibility.

---

[6] See Tannehill, *Sword,* 60–67.

Gaps

Any narrator will supply some features of the narrative world but not others. This selective presentation can be understood, in part, as a sign of the narrator's control of the story for rhetorical effect. Directing the hearer's attention toward certain things (and away from other things) gives the story a focus on certain issues and concerns. It would be a distraction, not a contribution to Gospel interpretation, to speculate about Jesus' height. This is an example of a "blank," an omission because it is regarded as irrelevant. But there are also "gaps," omissions that are relevant to interpreting plot and characters.[7] Yet the narrative may withhold the information either temporarily—building suspense toward a future disclosure—or permanently. Biblical narrators are reliable narrators in the sense that their perspectives do not depart from a "truer" perspective, that of the implied author. Nevertheless, the narrator, charged with telling the truth as the implied author sees it, does not necessarily tell the whole truth. Significant ambiguities remain.[8]

The Lukan narrative is reticent about expressing characters' emotions and motivations. The depiction of Jesus weeping over Jerusalem (Luke 19:41) is a striking exception. Emotion and motivation are often relevant to understanding what is going on in a scene, and we may make assumptions about them when we interpret particular scenes, thereby filling some of the gaps. In doing so, we may be cooperating with the narrator, who assumed that the audience would contribute in this way. Yet we are going beyond the text, and it is possible that these gaps might be filled in a different way. We can interpret emotion and motivation in various ways when reading the so-called "cleansing of the temple" scene in Luke 19:45-46.

In evaluating characters, we should remind ourselves how little we are told about them. Even the story of Peter, one of the more prominent Lukan characters, presents only a few incidents from his life story, and many of the characters appear only in one brief scene. We are left to

---

[7] On the distinction between "gaps" and "blanks," see Meir Sternberg, *The Poetics of Biblical Narrative,* ISBL (Bloomington: Indiana University Press, 1985) 236. See also his more extensive discussion of "the relevance of absence" (235–63).

[8] Meir Sternberg's chapter on ambiguity is entitled "Between the Truth and the Whole Truth"; see *Poetics,* 230–63.

wonder about their lives prior to the incident and their lives afterward. In particular, the possible effect of an encounter with Jesus on a person is a relevant gap in the narration of some scenes. In Luke 9:57-62 Jesus addresses three would-be followers with challenging words. How did they respond? We don't know whether to view these persons as hopelessly naive and shallow or whether to assume that their encounter with Jesus changed them to radical disciples. Likewise, the discussion with the lawyer in Luke 10:25-37 ends simply with Jesus' words, "Go and do likewise." Did the lawyer accept Jesus' teaching and try to act like the Samaritan, or not? I think most modern readers are inclined to assume a negative response from the lawyer, but there is a gap at this crucial point. The text is indeterminate.

A gap with broader consequences concerns Jerusalem. The Lukan narrative highlights the rejection of Jesus in Jerusalem and the destruction of the city. In particular, there are four interconnected scenes that emphasize these events (Luke 13:31-35; 19:41-44; 21:20-24; 23:27-31). This emphasis suggests a tragic turn in the narrative after the great expectations in the birth narrative.[9] In discussing the disciples in Mark, I once argued, appealing to Wolfgang Iser, that a negative trajectory in the story line invites the reader to ponder what went wrong and to imagine the better alternative that was missed.[10] The positive alternative need not be fully spelled out; it is the text's function to induce the reader to seek it. The positive possibility that Jerusalem missed when Jesus was rejected is not clearly defined in Luke. There are, to be sure, scriptural promises about the messianic king, which the Lukan narrative applies to Jesus, beginning at Luke 1:31-33. But how these promises were to be realized, if Jerusalem had not rejected its king, is not very clear, and whether and how they could still be realized for the Jewish people are also not very clear. We are left with some hints and considerable ambiguity. It may have been impossible for the author of Luke to fill this gap. The hints and ambiguity are left for the reader to ponder. Since the scriptural promises to the Jewish people are important in Luke, this is an important gap at a theological level.

There is also a gap in application. That is, the Gospels do not tell us how they should be applied to later situations. We need to remember that

---

[9] See Tannehill, "Israel in Luke–Acts: A Tragic Story," *JBL* 104 (1985) 69–85.

[10] See Tannehill, "The Disciples in Mark: The Function of a Narrative Role," *JR* 57 (1977) 395.

the Gospels are stories about other people at another time. Religious believers continue to assert their importance even for later centuries, but a story about the past can refer only indirectly to the present. There must be an interpretive decision that the story of the past applies to the present in a particular way. If we assert that the past applies to the present in some simple and unqualified way, we are the ones who have made that decision. The text does not require it. Even when Jesus uses general language ("Whoever wants to save his life will lose it," Luke 9:24), it may be significant that this language is used in addressing a particular group in a particular situation. The responsibility of appropriate application to other people at other times remains.

Reading Characters as "Open"

Many of the characters in synoptic scenes appear only in a single scene, or they are group characters who tend to play a set role repeatedly. It is possible to regard these as "flat" or "closed" characters—persons with few defining characteristics, no complexity, and with no potentiality for change. This way of reading is especially easy with a group such as the Pharisees, who regularly play the role of Jesus' opponents. Yet we should be wary of assuming that all Pharisees are incapable of sincere listening or positive change. I have argued elsewhere that there is no need to take Simon the Pharisee in Luke 7:36-50 as a closed character.[11] If we do so, it is not because the text requires it but because of the poverty of our imaginations.

Many characters appear in a single Gospel scene. They may be allowed only one characterizing action or situation, sometimes with a bit of dialogue. That does not mean that we must think of them as having only the characteristic revealed in the scene or assume that they always act as described. We are given only a moment in a life history, a moment that poses an issue for reflection. The impression of the moment does not require us to conclude that these persons lack other possibilities or always behave in this way. If we wish, we can understand what is not said about these persons as a thick penumbra of possibilities, making them open characters. Although there has been a tendency to regard biblical characters—at least the minor ones—as flat and static, there is, fortunately,

---

[11] See Tannehill, "Should We Love Simon the Pharisee? Hermeneutical Reflections on the Pharisees in Luke," *CTM* 21 (1994) 424–33.

a willingness to question that conclusion now.[12] Whether characters are viewed as closed or open often tells us more about our reading than about the biblical text.

The freedom that the text gives us to regard many Gospel characters as open or closed carries with it an ethical responsibility. There may not be an exact correspondence between our treatment of characters in an ancient story and our treatment of modern people whom we read about or meet in our daily affairs, but there is likely to be some overlap in our behavior. Reading stories can be imaginative preparation for responding to people. Treating people as closed means refusing to believe in their possibilities. It is an ethical failure, a failure of love. (On the hermeneutical significance of the love commandments, see pp. 283–85 below.)

Statements of Jesus and the outcome of events often imply evaluation of persons in a scene. In the scene of Jesus' visit with Martha and Mary (Luke 10:38-42), Jesus' concluding statement supports Mary against the criticism from her sister. We should, however, be cautious of the conclusions that we draw from such evaluation. The evaluation concerns Mary-at-this-moment and Martha-at-this-moment. The story indicates that when Mary acts as she does in this scene and Martha reacts as she does, Jesus supports Mary. We cannot conclude that Martha is always a complainer nor that Mary is always a silent listener (nor that women should always be silent listeners because Mary was listening at this moment). All of these conclusions read more into the text than is there. This excessive interpretation of Mary's role is part of an interpretation of the passage as an oppressive text, designed to restrict the role of women in the church. This interpretation is supported by reconstructing a particular context for the story in the life of the early church.[13] (One of the ways in which multiple readings become possible is through placing the text in different social contexts; see pp. 281–82 below.) This construction is not necessary

---

[12] Commenting on a recent collection of essays on "Characterization in Biblical Literature," Robert Fowler writes, "Most of these authors want to break away from static or monolithic views of characters. Most want to crack characters open, to give them some wriggle room, to allow for fluidity and multiplicity in characterization." See "Characterizing Character in Biblical Narrative," *Semeia* 63 (1993) 97. See also David Gowler, *Host, Guest, Enemy and Friend: Portraits of the Pharisees in Luke and Acts,* ESEC 2 (New York: Lang, 1991) 77–176.

[13] For this interpretation, see Elisabeth Schüssler Fiorenza, "Theological Criteria and Historical Reconstruction: Martha and Mary, Luke 10:38-42," *Center for Hermeneutical Studies Protocol* 53 (1987) 1–12; and *idem, But She Said: Feminist Practices of Biblical Interpretation* (Boston: Beacon, 1992) 52–76.

to make sense of the text, for the passage makes an excellent point without it (the passage defends the freedom of Mary—and others like her—to devote themselves to Jesus' way even if they neglect the expected social role of women). The proposed construction is not required by the text. To my mind it detracts from a text that could convey an important message. For this and other reasons, I decline to accept it.[14]

Stories affect their audience partly through a complex process of identification between hearers and story characters. Social roles are a factor in this identification process. Thus an ancient woman would have been more likely to see her situation reflected in the stories of women in Luke, while a person of high social standing and wealth would be more likely to recognize himself or herself in stories about such people. If social roles are significant factors in response to the Gospels, reader-response criticism needs to be refined by taking account of the ancient social situation and by recognizing that the ancient audience would probably contain a variety of persons who would respond differently, partly because of their different social positions. Thus we must think of multiple kinds of reading (or hearing) of a Gospel already in its early social context.[15] Furthermore, identification cannot be compelled, and even when it does take place, the hearer may recognize differences as well as similarities. Factors other than social roles may be important. The story allows for differences, because it does not speak directly about the hearers of the story but only about the characters within the story. What the story says about the characters remains a possibility but not a necessity for similar hearers. From this perspective, too, we see that there are multiple options in understanding the significance of a Gospel story.

Drawing Connections

Narrative criticism and reader-response criticism have advocated reading the Gospels as continuous narratives. The stories in Luke (or Luke–Acts)

---

[14] For further discussion, see Tannehill, *Luke,* ANTC (Nashville: Abingdon, 1996) 185–87; and Turid Karlsen Seim, *The Double Message: Patterns of Gender in Luke–Acts* (Nashville: Abingdon, 1994) 97–107, 112–14.

[15] For an experiment in such hearer-response criticism of Luke, see Tannehill, "'Cornelius' and 'Tabitha' Encounter Luke's Jesus," *Int* 48 (1994) 347–56.

can communicate not only as individual scenes but also as parts of a larger whole. Thus we may ask about connections between part and part (one part perhaps reinforcing another, or perhaps supplementing, balancing, or qualifying). We may also ask about connections between the part and the whole. (How does this part contribute to the whole, and how does it take on special meaning in light of the whole?) We may also ask about connections between the text and other texts, such as the Scripture of the early church and Judaism.

Readers seek meaning by drawing connections. An author can assume the reader's tendency to draw connections and seek to guide it, but the author cannot completely control this process. There are literary means of emphasizing certain connections, by comments of the narrator, by interpretive statements from characters to whom the implied author attributes authority, by repetition of themes, etc. Some connections are strongly emphasized in the text, and it will be a fault in reading if the reader misses them. But there are many possibilities of connections. In a lengthy and complex document, the possible connections among parts multiply, and the task of understanding how the parts form a whole becomes complex. When we consider the possible interrelations with the text's social world and important documents within that social world, the number of possibly significant connections becomes enormous. There is broad room for discussion as to which are supported by the text and important in interpretation. Different interpreters will demand different kinds and degrees of evidence in reaching conclusions. Consequently, interpreters will come to different conclusions, resulting in somewhat different readings of the text. The text allows this.

For instance, some interpreters emphasize the similarities between Jesus' dialogue with a lawyer in Luke 10:25-37 and his dialogue with a rich ruler in Luke 18:18-23.[16] The two inquirers ask the same question about what they must do to inherit eternal life. Jesus replies with a counter-question that leads to citation of Scripture, providing a point of mutual agreement between Jesus and the inquirer. Then Jesus adds something that goes beyond the Scripture or its normal interpretation. There is, then,

---

[16] See, e.g., Thomas E. Phillips, "Subtlety as a Literary Technique in Luke's Characterization of Jews and Judaism," in *Literary Studies in Luke–Acts: Essays in Honor of Joseph B. Tyson*, edited by Richard P. Thompson and Thomas E. Phillips (Macon, Ga.: Mercer University Press, 1998) 313–26.

a certain connection between these two episodes. Is it a significant connection? In what sense? Is there a reason why a central Scripture text (the double love commandment and the Decalogue) is cited in each passage? A series of similarities may also highlight remaining differences. Is it significant that there is no indication of a negative response from the lawyer at the end of the first scene, as there is from the ruler at the end of the second (18:23)? Noting such similarities and differences entices us to further thought without providing any firm control of conclusions.

Contexts

Context is important in interpretation, both literary context and social-historical context. Literary studies should not ignore social-historical context, for literature always presupposes language codes and social codes that reflect the shared cultural knowledge of a social world. Knowledge of context can help to specify the significance of a text, to make it more determinate, and much biblical interpretation is an attempt to construct an appropriate context in order to make the significance of the text more specific. In the case of Gospel literature, however, we may question the assumption of a single original context that we may recover in order to specify the text's significance. A Gospel pericope is often useful in a number of possible contexts, and the content of the Gospels is too complex to serve a single purpose or speak to a narrowly defined context.[17] Even if we confine our consideration to the "authorial audience," that is, the audience that the author might have envisioned because it shared the author's time and general location, it is a mistake to think of context as single and limited. A Gospel is suited to nourish faith over a broader time and space. Each Gospel was undoubtedly read many times—to a variety of groups and to the same group over the changing years. It is hard to believe that the author of Luke—which has some literary pretensions—would not have anticipated this, and the other Gospel writers may have as well. In subtle and not-so-subtle ways the context changed even in the early years. Much of the material could accommodate this change because it was not designed for a single context in the first place.

---

[17] Elizabeth Struthers Malbon states the point more strongly. She says, "No text has just one context." See "Text and Contexts: Interpreting the Disciples in Mark," *Semeia* 62 (1993) 86.

The Gospel material passed through a series of contexts before ever becoming part of our Gospels, and it continues to bear the impression of those contexts. The Gospel writers probably did not try to shape the material to a single purpose, and it would have been difficult for them to succeed if they had tried. It is a mistake, then, to overemphasize a particular reconstructed context. We reach a similar conclusion when we consider the early audiences. There would have been a variety of occasions for hearing each of the Gospels, and the hearers on each occasion would vary, each bringing his or her social context to the understanding of the Gospel. We should think, then, of the varied contexts within which the Gospels and their component parts might meaningfully speak, and we should be cautious when we hear claims that a particular reconstructed context is the necessary key to understanding the text.

Consider, for instance, the Lukan story of Jesus' temptations (Luke 4:1-13). This story can be understood in different contexts, with somewhat different effects. It can be viewed only in its story context as a story about the personal struggle of Jesus as he was about to begin his mission. It can be viewed in the context of early christological debates, perhaps as a reply to Jewish skeptics who thought that Jesus was being exalted in place of God. (Note the emphasis on Jesus submitting to the strict theocentric demands of Deuteronomy.)[18] It can also be viewed in the context of the early church's experience of Spirit-power. It then points to Jesus as a model for others who must conquer the temptation to use Spirit-power for the wrong purposes. We need not choose one of these contexts to the exclusion of the others, for it is likely that the story had all three of these functions (and perhaps others as well) within the experience of the early church.

Varying Views of the Center of Scripture

When we consider Scripture as a whole, there is another layer of indeterminacy in interpretation. Scripture is a large library, with parts that are connected in complex ways. There is also tension, for the parts sometimes do not fit neatly together. If individuals and groups are to use this mass of material for inspiration and guidance, they must make judgments about what in Scripture is central or most valuable. These

---

[18] See Tannehill, *Luke,* 89–90.

judgments become guiding principles in interpretation. The material in Scripture that reinforces these judgments takes on special importance. Other passages are interpreted so that they correspond with these judgments, or, if that is impossible, they are reckoned to be unimportant or are openly rejected. This process of deciding what is central may operate in a naive way that ignores the historically conditioned character of biblical writings and their variety. But even sophisticated interpreters must make some judgment as to what is central if they study large portions of Scripture and look to Scripture for guidance.

These judgments vary. The center of Scripture is seen in the election of Israel, in the Mosaic revelation, in justification by faith rather than works, in the christological interpretation of Old and New Testaments, or in particular creeds that become guides for the reading of Scripture. Scripture may provide some foundation for each of these approaches, but there are also difficulties with each of them.

There is another option for understanding what is central in Scripture. In discussing it, I do not wish to imply that this option should eliminate all the others. In fact, I doubt that it can stand by itself. It focuses on biblical commandments, and these commandments, I believe, rest on a perception of a foundational reality that makes them possible and necessary. Nevertheless, I want to suggest that the double love commandment may function as a hermeneutical principle. This approach may help us to deal with some urgent problems in the religious application of Scripture. It may help draw Jews and Christians closer together, since these commands are important to both.[19] And it may help us respond to one of the chief challenges to biblical authority today, the accusation that Scripture conveys an oppressive ideology, particularly through its androcentric perspective.

There is explicit discussion of the center of Jewish Scripture in the Gospel pericope concerning the great commandments (Matt 22:34-40; Mark 12:28-34; Luke 10:25-37). Saint Augustine made the suggestion long ago that the double love commandment should function as a hermeneutical principle in the interpretation of Scripture. This suggestion implies that the authoritative interpretation of Scripture emerges when

---

[19] The agreement in Luke 10:25-28 between Jesus and the lawyer who quotes the double love commandment may indicate a significant area of agreement that is still possible for Jews and Christians today.

we are able to show how it encourages love of God and neighbor.[20] If the commands to love God and neighbor are central to Scripture and central to a faithful life, then we should read Scripture from this perspective and use Scripture in ways that demonstrate such love. As with some of the hermeneutical principles mentioned above, this could be done in a naive way that reduces Scripture to a narrow and monotonous message and ignores all problems. But this need not be the result. How love of God and neighbor are to be shown will still be expressed differently in different parts of Scripture. And the interpreter must face squarely the challenge of those texts that seem not to promote love of God and neighbor—where God appears unlovable and where killing and oppression of neighbors seem acceptable. The interpreter who is committed to the double love commandment as an interpretive principle is then left with at least two options: 1) She or he may seek to show, through careful study of the text, that the passage need not be read in this oppressive way, for there are other options. These options may arise from the elements of indeterminacy discussed earlier in this article. The interpreter need not deny that the text can also be understood in an oppressive way. 2) She or he may decide that the text, because it does not encourage love of God or neighbor, has little or no value for life today, except, perhaps, as a negative example. It may be important for historical studies, but it is not a positive guide for faith and life in the contemporary world. Consistency in following the scriptural principle of love of God and neighbor may require us to say "No" to some passages of Scripture.

It is easy to read the Pharisees in the Gospels as negative stereotypes, characters who are fully defined by negative traits and incapable of positive change. Stereotypes can have a function in teaching, but to regard another as simply a negative stereotype is a failure in love of neighbor. Do the Gospel texts require us to reduce the Pharisees to negative stereotypes, if we are reading accurately? In another article, I asked this question concerning the Pharisees in Luke and recognized that the repeated

---

[20] See Augustine, *On Christian Doctrine*, trans. D. W. Robertson, Jr. (New York: Liberal Arts, 1958) 30–31: "Whoever, therefore, thinks that he understands the divine Scriptures or any part of them so that it does not build the double love of God and of our neighbor does not understand it at all." Augustine then explains that an interpreter who finds this message in a passage where it was not the author's intention has reached the destination appropriate to Scripture even though he or she may be mistaken about the best road.

[21] See Tannehill, "Should We Love Simon the Pharisee?" 424–33.

introduction of Pharisees as opponents of Jesus, the protagonist in the story, easily leads to negative stereotyping. Since there are some exceptions to this negative portrait, however, we need not view Jewish teachers as lacking potential for good. In particular, Simon the Pharisee, who appears in Luke 7:36-50, need not be viewed as a negative stereotype, for the story allows us to understand him as an open character, capable of change, particularly because the scene is open-ended. We do not know how Simon responds to Jesus' teaching.[21] If we are talking only about the potentialities of the text, we can admit that Simon can be read either as a stereotype or as an open character. If we are talking about how a Scripture passage should be used in religious formation, a commitment to love of God and neighbor will lead to the second of these options.

The choice to read Scripture as an invitation to love God and neighbor is a religious and ethical decision, as are other options for deciding what is central in Scripture. Scripture leaves us with some freedom in our decision, and we must take responsibility for the way we use that freedom. Our decision will help determine how we respond to other indeterminacies in the text—to the need for an imaginative response by the reader, to the gaps in the text, to the opportunity to read characters as open, to the various possibilities of drawing connections and reconstructing contexts. The interpreter is a responsible partner in a dialogue with the text and must ask whether and how it is possible to interpret this text so that human benefit flows from it.

16

"Cornelius" and "Tabitha" Encounter Luke's Jesus

In "Should We Love Simon the Pharisee?" I suggested in passing that discussions of "the reader" oversimplify the reading process, even if we try to define that reader through the cultural context of the original readers at the end of the first century CE. There always were multiple readers or hearers and multiple readings, especially if we consider the significance of Luke–Acts for the personal lives of its recipients. One factor about which we have some knowledge is the variation in social location of early Christians. The following essay is an experiment, fragmentary and illustrative, in reckoning with varying social location as a factor in the reading process through imagining how a Gentile centurion like Cornelius and a poor Jewish woman like Tabitha might respond to Luke's unfolding portrait of Jesus.

This article is influenced by two concerns: (1) the desire to recognize the value of reader-response criticism; and (2) the need to integrate literary approaches to the Gospels with traditional historical criticism and the new social-scientific criticism. The guiding question that enables me to bring these concerns together is this: How would two first-century persons, who differ in social location, understand the character Jesus as they follow

286

the public reading of Luke's Gospel?[1] I am studying the characterization of Jesus in Luke's story, while recognizing, as reader-response criticism has done, that the text is only a schema that must be actualized by its audience, and also taking account of the fact, as reader-response criticism has not generally done, that members of an audience with different social locations will to some extent actualize the text differently.

Literary approaches to the Gospels have now established themselves sufficiently that we need not fear losing what we have gained if we endeavor to integrate our work with historical and social-scientific criticism. The need for this is clear even from a literary perspective. As John Darr has argued,[2] the text can only be read with understanding if the reader has access to the "extratext"—a complex body of knowledge consisting of language codes, literary conventions, social codes, some items of general historical knowledge, and some other texts (such as the Septuagint). The text is constructed so as to activate items from the extratext in communicating with the audience. The older historical criticism, the newer social-scientific criticism of ancient Mediterranean society, and studies in literary history can help us understand the extratext.

Darr has laid the foundation for a reader-response approach to characters in Luke–Acts. He argues that readers "build" characters during the reading process. Reader-response critics, in turn, must consciously "build" readers so that the critic can "read" the reader reading the text. Furthermore, "if our interpretive analyses are to be responsible, rigorous, and open to argument, then *we must identify the reader to whom we refer.*"[3] "To some degree," Darr admits, *"the* reader is always *my* reader, a projection of my own experience of reading the text," but the critic should nevertheless attempt to construct a first-century reader with the "cultural literacy" and "cultural scripts" appropriate to the text. This reconstructed reader enables us to imagine the reading process of the original readers.[4] Although Darr is content with a single first-century reader, the original recipients of Luke contained people of different social location (Jew and Gentile, female

---

[1] I am assuming that, in the first-century church, even an educated person would be more likely to encounter Luke's Gospel through an oral presentation to the community than through a private reading.

[2] John A. Darr, *On Character Building: The Reader and the Rhetoric of Characterization in Luke–Acts,* LCBI (Louisville: Westminster John Knox, 1992) 21–22.

[3] Ibid., 23. Italics in original.

[4] Ibid., 25–27. Italics in original.

and male, poor and relatively rich). There would be some significant differences in the way that two persons of different social location would process the presentation of Jesus in Luke. Thus I am attempting to go one step further than Darr in defining the reader, for reader-response critics need to be aware that there were different kinds of readers and multiple readings even in the first century.

For this experiment, I will adopt other features of Darr's method: I will assume that both text and reader must contribute to the actualization of a literary work. I, like Darr, will adopt the viewpoint of the first-time reader or hearer, who will have the full picture of the Lukan Jesus only when the end of the text is reached, but who will repeatedly form and revise pictures of Jesus as the text unrolls. I will try to suggest how expectations are aroused and then revised in the listening process, how the reader might try to build a consistent picture of Jesus from the material in the text and where this would be difficult, and how different hearers might identify with different characters as the reading proceeds.[5] Within the limited space of this article, I can, of course, only begin this task.

Let me introduce my two "readers" or listeners. One I will call Cornelius. He is modeled after, but not identical with, the Cornelius who appears in Acts 10. The other I will call Tabitha. She is modeled after, but not identical with, the Tabitha who appears in Acts 9:36-43. The Gospel of Luke is unique in that it is followed by the story of Acts, which features characters who receive the message about Jesus. In the case of Cornelius, we have a scene in Acts in which Peter retells, in summary, the story of Jesus in its Lukan form (Acts 10:36-43).[6] Taking this scene of Cornelius's receiving Luke's story of Jesus as our clue, we will explore how two persons similar to those presented in Acts might respond to this Lukan story.

I will modify the figures of Cornelius and Tabitha in two ways that reflect judgments about the likely time and place of the writing of Luke–Acts. I will assume that my two listeners encounter the Lukan story some time after AD 70 and that they live outside the Jewish homeland. Tabitha I will move from Joppa to the Jewish quarter of Syrian Antioch. I will locate Cornelius somewhere in the Roman east, but not at Caesarea.

---

[5] Ibid., 30–31.

[6] On the close relation between Acts 10:36-43 and the Lukan form of the story of Jesus, see Tannehill, *The Narrative Unity of Luke–Acts: A Literary Interpretation,* 2 vols.(Philadelphia & Minneapolis: Fortress, 1986, 1990) 2.138–42.

In other respects I would like to retain the basic features of Cornelius and Tabitha. Cornelius is a centurion, either in a Roman legion or in the auxiliary forces. The legionary troops had higher status and pay, but the auxiliary forces also could be commanded by Roman officers. Cornelius is therefore a professional soldier serving Rome and a middle-rank officer. Even though higher officers were usually chosen from the nobility, a centurion, too, had opportunity for advancement because the centurions of a legion were ranked in a hierarchy. The first centurion of a legion held a position of considerable importance and status. Furthermore, a career as a centurion "was financially very advantageous," for "the pay was probably some sixteen times that of the basic legionary salary. In short, a centurion had both considerable military and social status and wealth."[7]

Cornelius has been strongly influenced by diaspora Judaism. Through contact with the local synagogue he learned some of the essentials of Jewish faith. For some time he has been praying to the God of the Jews. He has been a patron of the local Jewish community, contributing generously to the synagogue. Yet he remains a Gentile. More recently, he has joined the community that proclaims Jesus as Messiah.

Tabitha was born of a Jewish family in the Jewish quarter of Antioch. She also has joined the local community that proclaims Jesus as Messiah. She was attracted to this community for two reasons: She experienced healing in the name of Jesus (we will not claim resurrection, as in Acts 9:36-43); and she also lost her husband some years ago and found that the followers of Jesus were offering support for widows in their community. She joined this group of widows and has become one of their leaders in providing clothing for other widows and poor people.

Any real person, of course, will have individual characteristics that cannot be predicted apart from actual acquaintance with this person. Our Cornelius and Tabitha, however, are not real persons. They are constructs that mark socio-historical locations. We will imagine their responses in light of those socio-historical locations, while ignoring the unpredictable features of actual individuals. Nevertheless, we will add this bit of realism to their definition: Although both participate in the local communities that honor Jesus, both have doubts and questions that will affect their hearing of Luke.

---

[7] David Kennedy, "Roman Army," in *ABD* 5.790–91.

Now we will try to imagine how Cornelius and Tabitha might build a consistent picture of Jesus from the data supplied in the story, beginning at the point where Jesus is first mentioned (1:31). Gabriel's words to Mary about Jesus' future role could create problems for both Tabitha and Cornelius because of the heavy emphasis on Jesus' role as Davidic king. For Tabitha, of course, Gabriel is announcing the fulfillment of an ancient promise to her people, which should be a cause of joy, yet recent history does not support the belief that Jesus will restore the throne of David for the Jewish people. Jesus has come and gone. Rome has defeated the Jewish rebellion. Conflict between Jewish followers of Jesus and other Jews discourages the belief that Jesus will be welcomed by Jews as their king.

The problem is even more acute for Cornelius. Although he may admire the Jewish figures in the birth narrative, hearing that Jesus "will reign over the house of Jacob" does not fulfill his hopes, since he is not a member of the house of Jacob. Furthermore, as a professional soldier, sworn to serve the present government, he is likely to be disturbed by the emphasis on Jesus as the promised Jewish king. This emphasis makes it more difficult for Cornelius to reconcile his military profession and his faith. It leaves him open to the charge of disloyalty to Caesar brought against believers in Acts 17:7. ("All these people are acting against the decrees of Caesar, claiming that there is another king, Jesus.") Although Cornelius is attracted to Judaism, he is scarcely comfortable, as an officer in Caesar's army, with the messianic hope in Gabriel's announcement.

Nevertheless, Tabitha and Cornelius are being strongly encouraged to accept the proclamation of Jesus as messianic king. This description of Jesus is given by Gabriel, a messenger who speaks with divine authority. Furthermore, the narrative presents divine promises of wonderful births and then shows them coming to pass, illustrating the scriptural principle that "nothing will be impossible with God" (Luke 1:37; see Gen 18:14). Mary is also praised in the narrative for believing "that there would be a fulfillment of what was spoken to her by the Lord" (Luke 1:45). Hearers of Luke's story are being encouraged to respond in a similar way to the promises in the birth narrative, including the promise that Jesus will sit on the throne of David and reign over the house of Jacob forever.[8]

---

[8] I was alerted to the importance of the theme of belief in God's promises in Luke through a paper presented by David Landry at the 1993 annual meeting of the Society of Biblical Literature.

Tabitha might identify with Mary, not only because she is a Jewish woman but also because Mary speaks in the Magnificat of her humble status. Attraction to Mary would encourage Tabitha to share in Mary's acceptance and then in her joy. It would also encourage her to believe that through Jesus the lowly will be exalted and the hungry fed (1:52-53). Cornelius would be more distant from the characters in the birth narrative. A Jewish priest and two Jewish women provide little opportunity for identification. Furthermore, Mary's Magnificat would create a problem for Cornelius. The message that God, in sending Jesus, "has brought down the powerful from their thrones" (1:52) puts a person of status, who is also a servant of the emperor, in a serious bind. The lowly in Israel can join Mary's song, but her joy is not easily shared by others.

Cornelius's problem becomes more acute with the Benedictus. Here the themes of the annunciation and the Magnificat return, but in sharper expression. Salvation for Israel through the Davidic Messiah is announced (1:69), and it is now defined as "salvation from our enemies and from the hand of all who hate us" (1:71; cf. 1:74). The Roman-Jewish war could not quickly be forgotten by a person like Cornelius, for it would represent his own conflicted loyalties. In this war the Roman army was the enemy of the Jewish people. Yet Jesus the Messiah is being presented as the rescuer of the Jewish people from such enemies. The reference to the "way of peace" at the end of the Benedictus does not solve the problem, if this refers to the peace that comes after the oppressive enemy is overthrown and justice is restored through bringing down "the powerful from their thrones" (1:52). For Tabitha, too, the Benedictus would be disturbing. It would be a reminder that although Jesus came to Israel and was proclaimed Messiah, he did not save Israel from the Roman enemy. Zechariah's words seem to be authoritative, for he speaks while filled with the Holy Spirit (1:67), but for both our hearers there would be a sharp conflict between his prophetic words and the actual course of events.[9]

The announcement to the shepherds does not relieve the difficulty, for the proclamation of the "Messiah Lord" born "in the city of David," who will bring "great joy" to "all the people" of Israel and be their "savior," summarizes the characterization of Jesus to this point without solving the problem created. The announcement of his birth to shepherds and the note that he is "lying in a manger" (2:12) may remind our hearers that he

---

[9] I discuss this conflict further in "Israel in Luke–Acts: A Tragic Story," *JBL* 104 (1985) 69–85.

is coming for the lowly and hungry (1:52-53), but it is still not clear how Jesus can be the Davidic Messiah who frees his people from oppression.

The presentation of the infant Jesus in the temple carries the characterization of Jesus two steps further. (1) In 2:29-32 Simeon's prophetic hymn continues the theme of salvation and develops the theme of light introduced in 1:78-79, but Simeon also connects Jesus with Isaiah's expectation of the servant, who would be a "light of the nations" (Isa 42:6; 49:6). The promised salvation represented by the infant Jesus, then, includes both the Jewish people and the Gentiles. Cornelius's share in the promised salvation is here affirmed for the first time. Yet Jesus remains the "glory of [God's] people Israel." (2) The oracle of Simeon to Mary also adds to the portrait of Jesus. The reference to the fall and rising of many in Israel easily fits the picture of a new king who will put down previous rulers and exalt the oppressed (1:52), but when Jesus is described as a "sign provoking rejection" (2:34), the picture becomes more complex. Hearers can now anticipate that Jesus will encounter rejection. He will not easily mount his throne but must win it against strong opposition. In doing so, he will cause an upheaval in Jewish society.

The narrative, however, does not abandon its theme of salvation for Israel. After Simeon, Anna is introduced, a figure who would be attractive to Tabitha, for she is a devout Jewish woman and, like Tabitha, a widow. Anna speaks about Jesus to "all those awaiting the redemption of Jerusalem" (2:38). The reference to the redemption of Jerusalem is jarring in light of the conquest of the city in AD 70, but the birth narrative does not soften the theme of Israel's salvation from its enemies.

Very strong honor claims have been made for Jesus at his birth. He has been presented as a king whose rule will bless both Israel and the Gentiles—an extreme claim for one born in a manger.[10] Cornelius and Tabitha might expect the narrative to provide further support for this claim, but this support is slow in coming.

The narrative tells that as the child grew, God's "favor" was manifest in his life, especially as precocious wisdom (2:40, 52), which is illustrated

---

[10] Recent discussion of the Mediterranean world as a culture of honor and shame leads me to assume that the first-century audience would be very sensitive to honor claims and initially skeptical of claims that seem unjustified by birth status. See Bruce J. Malina and Jerome H. Neyrey, "Honor and Shame in Luke–Acts," in *The Social World of Luke–Acts,* edited by Jerome H. Neyrey (Peabody, Mass.: Hendrickson, 1991) 25–65.

by the story of the youthful Jesus talking with the teachers in the temple (2:41-51). This story also emphasizes that Jesus has another father than Joseph and that he must act in obedience to that father, even when it causes pain to Mary and Joseph (recall the reference to the sword piercing Mary's soul in 2:35). The portrait of Jesus as the obedient Son of God will be developed further in the temptation story.

"All flesh shall see the salvation of God," according to Luke 3:6, a message that reinforces Simeon's words about light for the Gentiles (for the benefit of Cornelius, among others). The accompanying imagery of bringing down mountains and filling up valleys, when connected with 1:52-53 and 2:34, reminds hearers of the social upheaval required. John's preaching also reminds hearers of the need for repentance. At this point, Tabitha and Cornelius have a chance, if they are alert, to understand how their lives may show repentance and anticipate the new society that Jesus is bringing. In 3:11 John the Baptist instructs those who have two tunics to share one. According to Acts 9:39 Tabitha was doing even better: She was making clothing so that she could share with those in need. Cornelius, too, is given a hint of a way he might participate now in the coming of God's salvation, as John gives instructions to the soldiers (Luke 3:14). Lives must change in anticipation of the "stronger one," who will come as judge and "baptize you in Holy Spirit and fire" (3:16-17). In so far as Cornelius and Tabitha had experienced the power of the Holy Spirit in their religious communities (see Acts 10:44-48) and had seen changes in the followers of Jesus similar to those demanded by John, they would recognize Jesus as the "stronger one." Even though Jesus' kingship was acknowledged by few, his power would be apparent to Tabitha and Cornelius.

The Holy Spirit descends first upon Jesus (3:21-22). It is accompanied by the divine voice that designates Jesus as "my Son." This scene might remind our two listeners that the coming of the Holy Spirit upon Mary was associated with the designation of her child as "Son of God" (1:35). The divine voice also calls Jesus "the beloved," the one in whom God "has taken pleasure." The gift of the Spirit and the statement of the divine voice are strong affirmation of Jesus' special relation to God and chosen role. God is presented as affirming the claims made for Jesus in the birth narrative. The exact meaning of Son of God is still somewhat unclear, however. In 1:32, 35 the title "Son of God" (or "Son of the Most High") both preceded and followed the description of Jesus as the Davidic king, suggesting that Son of God is a synonym for Messiah (cf. 2 Sam 7:14). But the association of Son of God with the Holy Spirit could also suggest that Jesus is God's Son as a Spirit-bearer, a charismatic figure.[11] Our listeners will have to wait for further clarification. The genealogy in 3:23-38 shows that, even as human lineage would be counted, Jesus is a descendant of David and Son of God.

Since Jesus is presented as *growing* in wisdom and God's favor (2:52), his understanding of his role is not complete from the beginning. Therefore, the temptation scene can be understood as a real struggle by Jesus to clarify the meaning of the Spirit's descent and the divine voice. Jesus must reject a false understanding of his role as the Spirit-filled Son of God (proposed by the devil) and discover the true alternative (which he will announce in the Nazareth synagogue). The temptation scene might be of special interest to Tabitha if she is aware of accusations from fellow Jews that Jesus was a rebellious Israelite about whom his followers are making idolatrous claims. The devil addresses Jesus as Son of God and challenges him to exercise his power, but Jesus refuses to remove himself from the discipline and obedience required of all Israel in the wilderness. He is an obedient Son. The second temptation relates to the Messiah's role as ruler, for the devil offers a simple way to achieve world dominion. However, Jesus is unwilling to worship anyone except God. Thus, the question of how Jesus can be the messianic ruler, as promised in the birth narrative, remains open for our listeners. There must be some other way than the devil's.

The Spirit that descended on Jesus following his baptism continues to guide and empower him (4:1, 14). It leads him to a ministry of teaching in synagogues (4:15), which is not the expected role of one who is or will be king. Indeed, through much of his ministry Jesus will appear as a healing prophet, "a prophet mighty in work and word" (24:19), on the model of Elijah and Elisha. Our two listeners have a right to be puzzled at the course of the narrative. The one who was clearly announced as a king by authoritative voices appears through much of the story to be a healing prophet. How can he be the messianic king?[12]

---

[11] See Marcus J. Borg, *Jesus: A New Vision* (San Francisco: Harper & Row, 1987) 41.

[12] However, the return of the theme of Jesus' kingship in 19:11-27, 38-40; 22:28-30; 23:37-38, 42 shows that the birth narrative was not misleading in suggesting that this is an important aspect of Luke's characterization of Jesus.

Jesus' prophetic ministry is defined by the scene in the Nazareth synagogue. After rejecting the devil's false interpretation of his role as the Spirit-inspired Son of God, Jesus announces the true meaning of the descent of the Spirit upon him following his baptism. He uses the words of Isa 61:1-2 to declare that he was anointed with the Spirit for a particular purpose. Although the reference to anointing in this quotation (using the verb χρίω) could suggest his role as the anointed ruler (Χριστός), Jesus states here that he was anointed to proclaim a message. He does not present himself as a ruler.

Both Cornelius and Tabitha should be interested in the content of Jesus' message as announced in Nazareth, but it will affect the two differently. Tabitha, as one of the poor, would understand the importance of Jesus' "good news to the poor." Still, she might question privately whether Jesus' announcement is trustworthy. Is God really acting to rescue the poor from oppression? In her interpretation, the "captives" and the "broken" or "oppressed" might also refer to the poor within Israel or to the situation of the Jewish people after defeat by the Roman army. Cornelius must consider whether good news for the poor is bad news for him. The discomfort that the Magnificat caused would probably return at this point. Cornelius must wait to discover whether Jesus has a place in his community for those with wealth and power.

The way the Nazareth scene continues could create uncertainty for Tabitha, too. The people of Nazareth, initially, are favorably impressed by Jesus (4:22). They also ask, "Is this not Joseph's son?" and this question produces a negative response from Jesus. Those who emphasize that the ancient Mediterranean world was a culture of honor and shame may understand the question as a challenge to what some townspeople regarded as an excessive claim of honor by Jesus. He is not the anointed proclaimer of good news but only Joseph's son.[13] Jesus' response is more appropriate, however, if we bring a different sociological observation to bear on the scene. Strong in-group loyalties, typical of Mediterranean culture,[14] could explain the dialogue in the scene. Then the question "Is this not Joseph's

---

[13] This is the view taken by Richard L. Rohrbaugh in a paper presented at the 1993 annual meeting of the Society of Biblical Literature. His reading of Luke 4:1-30 as an attempt to legitimate Jesus' honor claims is helpful, but I do not think his reading of 4:22b fits the immediate context.
[14] See Bruce J. Malina, *Windows on the World of Jesus* (Louisville: Westminster John Knox, 1993) 47–70.

son?" does not contrast with the preceding praise but indicates that those praising Jesus, quite happily, point out that Jesus is a member of a local family. Since he is part of their in-group, they expect to receive favors from him. Jesus, in response, reacts against the expectation that he owes Nazareth as much or more than Capernaum. Jesus, as a prophet led by the Spirit, is not bound by ordinary group loyalties. As soon as the Nazarenes discover that Jesus will not honor in-group loyalties but, like Elijah and Elisha, will give his benefits to outsiders, Jesus will not even be acceptable in Nazareth (4:24), and this quickly proves to be true.

Tabitha might wonder about the larger implications of this dialogue and conflict. She, as a widow, might be comforted by the reminder in 4:25-26 that Elijah helped a poor widow suffering from famine, but would it be comforting to be reminded that Elijah was sent to a widow in the territory of Sidon and not to the widows of Israel? Pairing the widow with Naaman the Syrian suggests that the contrast in 4:25-26 is not just geographical (land of Israel vs. diaspora) but ethnic (Jew vs. Gentile). If so, Tabitha is being stretched to think beyond personal benefit to consider non-Jewish widows. Cornelius could easily associate himself with Naaman the Syrian, especially if he had sufficient knowledge of Jewish scripture to recognize that Naaman was an army officer. This association may be encouraging, but it does not relieve Cornelius's difficulty with Jesus' good news for the poor.

I must break off my consecutive reading of Luke's story of Jesus at this point owing to limits on space. I would like, however, to add the following remarks.

Since Tabitha has experienced healing through Jesus, the healing and exorcism stories that begin in Luke 4:31 are likely to loom large in her portrait of Jesus. The story in 7:11-17 of Jesus' compassion for a widow might be especially important to her. This story is preceded by a story that would challenge Cornelius. The centurion in 7:1-10 is an outstanding example of faith. The story speaks a soldier's language, for the centurion's faith is demonstrated when he attributes to Jesus an authority similar to that of an officer commanding his troops (7:7-8).

To trace the story of Jesus as Tabitha and Cornelius might have heard it reminds us that different readers of Luke's story will construct the character of Jesus in different ways. Constructing the character of Jesus requires the reader or hearer to assemble many elements of the story into a total picture. Even though different readers receive the same data from the text, they will assemble the elements differently, placing some of them in bright light and allowing some to recede into the background. There is a dialogical process between the reader and the text. On the one hand, the text has rhetorical devices that can influence the reader's work of assembly. Indeed, the rhetorical structure of the text suggests that the implied author anticipated the ways that various readers might respond, offering them various enticements and warnings. On the other hand, the reader's role is important. We should avoid thinking that the text *controls* the reader's responses. A narrative suggests rather than controls. This is clearest when we consider its significance for the reader. The narrative speaks directly about past events but indirectly (if at all) about the reader's present. Readers must decide for themselves what is prescriptive and what is simply descriptive, for a story will contain many elements not meant for duplication. This means that even for first-century recipients like Cornelius and Tabitha there are important interpretive moves that the narrative cannot completely control. Although a religious community may believe that the story has significance for the present, various people must decide *how* this story about the past is significant for the present. If control is exercised in determining that significance, the control may come from forces in the present rather than from the narrative.